THE
ADOLESCENT
PASSAGE

THE ADOLESCENT PASSAGE

Developmental Issues

Peter Blos

INTERNATIONAL UNIVERSITIES PRESS, INC.

New York

Copyright © 1979, Peter Blos

Library of Congress Cataloging in Publication Data

Blos, Peter.
  The adolescent passage.

  Bibliography: p.
  Includes index.
  1. Adolescent psychology. 2. Adolescent psychiatry.
I. Title.
BF724.B498   155.5   78-61245
ISBN 0-8236-0095-5
Second Printing, 1979

Manufactured in the United States of America

To
the Memory of My Father
Physician and Philosopher

Contents

PART ONE
THE MUTUAL INFLUENCE OF THE
ADOLESCENT AND HIS SURROUND

PART TWO
THE NORMATIVE STAGES OF
MALE AND FEMALE ADOLESCENCE

PART SIX
SUMMARY: CONTRIBUTIONS TO THE
PSYCHOANALYTIC THEORY OF ADOLESCENCE

When I was fourteen I was walking down
    the darkened street with a
Boy I had clumsily undressed
The poor child
Like me he was uncomfortable
But he looked it.
I hope, he said
Looking slant-eyed at me
You're not expecting any more of that—
He looked away
And everybody knew

I bled and bled and bled

It was like a black room
And glowing red coals.

I pretend they are all real.

After the summer there was never any place
In the fall I lay among the brittle leaves
At Christmas I went to a new apartment
And a blue flowered bed
And he complained about my age
Like all of them

And I went to the museum
And a lot of doctors

And my mother said the same thing as the
Bad man
But like him
She never really carried me
Crying in her arms.

    — Jessica R., age sixteen

Obtrusion

Embedded in thought
Too mountainous to pick apart
Logical explanations try to make their path
Through a mind of endless obstructions
Intruded by an undying misery
Of gloom, despair and despondency
Of unknown future propositions
Waiting patiently to be set free
From a clutter of befuddled confusion
Only to be denied at the cost of suffering
Mercifully at the foot of god
To be set free in forward motion
Swept away by tides of fortune
Ignored by evil demons ready to
Castrate the magnificence of a second coming.

— Jon B., age sixteen

Acknowledgments

My grateful appreciation goes to the editors and publishers of my writings for granting their permission to include in this volume the papers that first appeared in the following publications:

"The Generation Gap: Fact and Fiction," by Peter Blos, in *Adolescent Psychiatry,* Volume I, edited by Sherman C. Feinstein et al., ⓒ 1971 by Basic Books, Inc., Publishers, New York.

"Reflections on Modern Youth" and "The Overappreciated Child," both published in *Psychosocial Process,* the Journal of the Jewish Board of Guardians (now the Jewish Board of Family and Children's Services).

"Prolonged Male Adolescence," reprinted, with permission from the *American Journal of Orthopsychiatry:* copyright 1954 by the American Orthopsychiatric Association, Inc.

"Psychological Counseling of College Students," reprinted, with permission, from the *American Journal of Orthopsychiatry:* copyright 1946 by the American Orthopsychiatric Association, Inc.

"The Split Parental Imago in Adolescent Social Relations," "The Initial Stage of Male Adolescence," "The Second Individuation Process of Adolescence," "Character Formation in Adolescence," "Preoedipal Factors in the Etiology of Female Delinquency," "The Genealogy of the Ego Ideal," "The Epigenesis of the Adult Neurosis," and "Comments on the Psychological Consequences of Cryptorchism," all published in *The Psychoanalytic Study of the Child.*

"Preadolescent Drive Organization," published in the *Journal of the American Psychoanalytic Association*.

"The Child Analyst Looks at the Young Adolescent," reprinted by permission of *Daedalus,* Journal of the American Academy of Arts and Sciences, Boston, Massachusetts. Fall 1971, *Twelve to Sixteen: Early Adolescence.*

"The Concept of Acting Out in Relation to the Adolescent Process," published in the *Journal of the American Academy of Child Psychiatry,* January, 1963.

"Adolescent Concretization," published in *Currents in Psychoanalysis,* edited by I. M. Marcus. New York: International Universities Press, Inc., 1971.

"When and How Does Adolescence End?" published in *Adolescent Psychiatry,* Volume V, edited by S. C. Feinstein and P. Giovacchini. New York: Jason Aronson, Inc., 1976.

Foreword

The psychology of adolescence aroused my interest early in my professional life, but it was not the field of my first scientific interest, nor the field in which I expected to work.

I started out as a student of biology, and acquired a doctorate in this discipline at the University of Vienna in 1934. My commitment to biology, however, was challenged by my acquaintance with psychoanalysis, which infused the study of the organism, its structure, function, and evolution with the life of human emotions. The practice of psychoanalysis, and in particular child analysis, brought discipline and order to the confluence of the two sciences. I thus made psychoanalysis my profession; adolescent analysis became my major interest and field of research.

Looking back at the beginnings of my psychoanalytic work, I wish to record here the personal influence August Aichhorn exerted on my professional life. This remarkable man had, by the 1920s, acquired international recognition for his work with delinquents. His psychoanalytic insight into delinquent behavior and his technique of rehabilitation and socialization of the asocial adolescent opened up an entirely new field of treatment and theory, based on psychoanalytic psychology. My association with this dynamic innovator and great teacher left an indelible imprint on my mind. The immediate identification with the master determined, slowly but firmly, my interest in adolescence and my commitment to adolescent therapy. Over time, these background influences generated more specific pursuits in my adolescent studies related to and directed by felicitous opportunities which came my way. Personal sensitivities, dispositions, and aptitudes played their decisive role in the topical choice of my research projects. The yield of this research is compiled in this volume. Its thrust, over several decades, has been sustained by my fervor to broaden and deepen the understanding of the adolescent process.

January 1, 1978
Holderness, New Hampshire

PART ONE

The Mutual Influence of the Adolescent and His Surround

This prefatory note is not intended to summarize the content of the five chapters it introduces. It is an attempt, above all else, to reflect basic concepts which I have abstracted from my clinical work and which, over time, have conditioned my way of observing human behavior and contemplating its nature and development. The following remarks should thus be viewed as an attempt to evoke the essential drift of opinion and thought which has given all the clinical issues I have studied a special countenance. I have rendered my increasingly convincing clinical impressions in conceptual terms as the most reliable way to test their theoretical validity and their usefulness in practice.

The human organism emerges from the womb equipped with specific regulatory biological capacities which require a caretaking surround for their proper functioning and growth. Survival depends on the support of biological and human contact needs, both physical and emotional in nature; they are summarized as the mutuality of attachment behavior. An optimal balance is determined by the organism's constitutional variant in adaptability as well as by the empathic presence of the mothering person during the infant's maturational progression. From the beginning of life the human organism is a social animal. With the internalization of the surround, facilitated by the maturation of the sensorium and personalized by the receptive and expressive faculties of an affective, self-aware nature, a decline in the total dependence on the surround follows in time. The advance to the stage of autonomy is predicated on psychic structure formation; this process represents the transformation of experiential influences—discriminately introduced into the child's life by his surround and selectively responded to by the child—into an internal reality with its own lawful order. We refer to this emerging organization of the mind in terms of institutions or systems, comprising id, ego, superego, and ego ideal.

The human organism thus cannot attain or develop a

3

psychic presence without systematic impingements from the outside world. The distinction between an outer and an inner world—as delineated, separate entities—evolves only slowly in the third year of life. It is often argued that the attainment of individuation, internalization, and psychic structure in itself will automatically safeguard the optimal functioning of the psychic organism. We easily take the role of the surround for granted. However, the ever-present impingements issuing from the surround, partially solicited by the child, should be looked at as requisite stimuli to promote growth and sustain psychic life. In their reciprocal activation, these efferent and afferent excitations animate the young child to make choices and exercise avoidances, even though these are neither conscious nor deliberate. The reciprocal process of "fitting in" establishes a pattern of interaction between self and surround which slowly shapes individuality and personal uniqueness. This process of harmonization always lies precariously between the critical alternatives of total object dependency and narcissistic self-sufficiency. We recognize in this fact the intrinsic and precarious relativity and limitation of individual autonomy, often referred to as the human condition.

Experience tells us that the unrelenting impact of environmental influences—social and sensory nutrients, if you will—remains requisite throughout life for the maintenance of optimal organismic—i.e., somatic and psychic—functioning. In speaking of the surround as exerting an essential, perpetual, and, indeed, nutrient impact on the individual, I refer not only to the human, but also to the abstract environment which is operative through social institutions, shared symbolizations, value systems, and social norms. Their content, usage, and complexity, communally and personally, remain in constant flux, regardless of whether we look at them in historical or individual perspective. Psychic autonomy and emotional maturity are achieved through the selective use the child and adolescent make of their particular environmental and constitutional givens which accrue, over time, to distinctive adaptive patterns. Whatever the adaptive pattern may be at any given level, it is actively, although not necessarily consciously and deliberately, chosen and organized by the growing child to protect his psychic integrity, his sense of well-being, his keeping physically intact as well as mentally responsive and alert.

Whenever emotional disturbances preclude the nutrative use of the environment, normal functioning and development are inevitably impaired to a critical degree. The capacity of the psychic organism to use environmental givens in an anabolic, i.e., integrative process points to a biological analog, namely the ingestion of life-sustaining substances and their conversion into living tissue. This process, if working well in all its stages, can be considered the most essential indicator and guarantor of normality and health. This fact is demonstrated impressively during periods of rapid and vigorous development and adaptation, as is the case in early childhood and adolescence. Of course, a modicum of Winnicott's "facilitating environment" or "good-enough mother" is here taken for granted.

Having defined the basic point of view underlying the five chapters to follow, we need to examine its relevancy for adolescence. In the simplest terms we can say that, with the advent of sexual maturation, cognitive leaps to higher levels, and new physical capabilities, a thrust away from infantile family dependencies into the wider social milieu becomes not only feasible but mandatory. The environment of the child, as well as the child himself, gain in complexity with advancing years and with the ever-expanding world of a mutually eliciting, rejecting, and neutralizing interplay of forces. A singularly consequential set of prototypical life experiences can always be discovered within the range of influences that constitute the family matrix from which each individual adolescent emerges. The binding of these influ-

ences into a decisive unitary whole, usually referred to as
identity and character, lies in the degree of integration and
differentiation of which the adolescent ego is capable. The
early childhood milestone of a "me" and a "not me" encompasses at adolescence an infinite range of physical and mental alternatives.

The adolescent is not unprepared for the emotional departure from the family matrix. Earlier developmental disruptions have lead in stages to an increasing independence
from auxiliary egos. Considering the time factor of these
psychic transformations, it appears that the rate of change
is slow or, in other words, that an extended time span is required for their completion. At least this seems to be the
case in the contemporary Western world, in contrast to so-
called primitive societies in which initiation rites deliver
the adolescent with the expulsive swiftness of the birth act
into postadolescence and communal partnership. Whichever
way adolescence proceeds, we can readily observe that the
adolescent's broadened and, indeed, new and unfamiliar
surround inherits functions and meanings that once belonged to the family matrix of childhood. These become subjected during adolescence to modifications by rejection, partial or absolute, transient or permanent—a process to which
I refer here as the idiosyncratic modulation and critical
selectivity of the adolescent. Only via the use of the wider
social surround, in continuation, rejection, or revision of
customary family patterns, does the adolescent acquire stable, durable, ego-syntonic patterns of his own. He becomes
an adult.

The comments made so far have laid the overall conceptual groundwork for the first part of this book. A brief reference to its topical issues follows. The opening chapter of
this section introduces, on a broad scale, a variant of the
age-old theme of generational separateness and polarization. During the fifties and sixties an endemic disarrangement of the normative developmental processes of adoles-

cence occurred within a predominantly white, middle-class sector of America. I was struck in those days by the dividing line youth was drawing between themselves and their elders—those "over thirty"—by demanding that the adult, the parent generation, step aside and admit as well as accept the fact of their uselessness in a new brave world. The insistence by youth that the old generation declare itself obsolete and renounce its privileges as anachronisms shifted the adolescent responsibility for independence to the parent generation as the guarantors of youthful freedom and adult status. This attitude spelled out an unabated and intense family involvement which might best be called a negative dependency. I came to recognize in this malaise a struggle for autonomy by young people who were unable to attain it without the subservient and supportive assistance of the parent generation.

We might recognize in this epochal phenomenon a reflection of a worldwide political and ideational crisis, epitomized by the Vietnam War at its morally worst and by the Civil Rights Movement at its morally best. In this connection we must not overlook the fact that the alienated youth of whom we speak here, white and educated, was, marginally or thoroughly, the product of the superrational child-rearing style of the fifties, which was elaborated and influenced by the mentality of the "affluent society."

This first chapter on adolescent emancipation from family dependencies, through identification with the larger and, indeed, urgent realities of the times, is followed by investigations of narrower problems and their theoretical implications. Each one should be considered a building stone in the construction of a comprehensive theory of adolescence, forming in their totality the developmental lines of normal adolescence and, in the field of adolescent pathology, offering theoretical reference points which might help to narrow down and qualify assessment and prediction. The clinician is always perplexed by uncertainties in the evaluation of

adolescent behavior and emotional states. The dilemma of
either viewing them as normal aspects of the adolescent
process or, in contrast, identifying them as signs of pathology makes differentiating criteria a much desired outcome
of adolescent research. The pursuit of this aim winds like a
red thread through all the investigations reported in this
volume.

The psychic instability and vulnerability of the adolescent are well known. This lability contains the chance for
abnormal development to become permanent as well as the
possibility of overcoming earlier deviant potentials by either
compensating for their debilitating influence or isolating
their distressful interferences. Lately, these kinds of adjustment have been subsumed under the designation "coping mechanisms." The residues of the infantile history of
psychic structure formation remain active throughout all
subsequent stages of development. Indeed, they acquire a
climactive urgency during adolescence when structure alterations lead the way toward adulthood. A clarification of
this process requires a dynamic and genetic description of
the generational dependencies and the severance
movements—emotional, social, ideational—that characterize
the adolescent process.

It has always been known that adolescents are keenly
and passionately involved in their environment at large and
in peer relations in particular. In this respect, the
psychoanalytic theory of adolescence has tended to highlight
the vicissitudes of extrafamilial object finding. Group
psychological issues have remained a tangential subject for
psychoanalytic research proper. I have attempted to broaden
these studies in my chapter on "The Split Parental Imago in
Adolescent Social Relations." What interested me in this
connection was the role of peer relations as a function of the
surround and the unique use the adolescent makes of it. Because I have studied these processes in a psychoanalytic setting, it stands to reason that—due to the methodology

employed—my observations and conclusions are distinctly different from the usual study of group behavior. Both approaches—intrapsychic exploration of the individual and psychological exploration of the individual as part of a group—complement each other well. In terms of my own work, by extrapolation I have made inferences pertaining to certain kinds of group behavior. This reasoning led to the proposition that the sociocentric involvement of the adolescent in peer relations not only contains object libidinal aims, but, in addition, represents an effort to come to terms with the internalized remnants of the preambivalent infantile split into "good" and "bad" objects. The developmental task manifested in these particular adolescent object relations is one of structural change rather than one of libidinal object gratification.

Chapter 1

The Generation Gap

Fact and Fiction

From time to time, new terms make their appearance in our language and, insidiously, acquire a life of their own; they become overextended and overused. In this process they come to serve as convenient labels and ready explanations for whatever appears similar; in short, they become separated from their context of origin. At this point, they say either more or less than was intended when they first sprang from some creative tongue. "Generation gap" is such a term. It is in the process of acquiring the status of eternal truth and reality, similar to a newly discovered star in outer space. The generation gap is an epochal phenomenon that arouses our analytic curiosity. In order to assign to this new term its proper reference, I shall delineate it from a phrase often used as a synonym—"generational conflict."

The formation of a conflict between generations and its subsequent resolution is the normative task of adolescence. Its importance for cultural continuity is evident. Without this conflict no adolescent psychic restructuring would occur. This statement does not contradict the obvious fact that adolescent behavior contrasts, universally and radically,

Distinguished Service Award Lecture presented at the Annual Meeting of the American Society for Adolescent Psychiatry, Miami, Florida, May 4, 1969. First published in *Adolescent Psychiatry*, Vol. I, ed. S. C. Feinstein, P. Giovacchini, and A. A. Miller. New York: Basic Books, 1971, pp. 5-13.

with that of the preceding years of childhood. We must not
forget, for example, that sexual maturation or puberty progresses independently of psychological development. For this
reason, all kinds of infantile drives and needs may find
their expression and gratification in genital activity. We
know from our clinical work that genital sexual behavior is
a most unreliable indicator for the assessment of
psychosexual maturity: no direct correlation exists between
genital activity per se and genitality as a developmental
stage. Present-day emphasis on sexual, that is, genital freedom of action prompts me to emphasize this differentiation
at the outset, because it can be argued on solid clinical
grounds that precocious adultomorphic behavior as such,
and sexual behavior in particular, often impedes rather
than promotes progressive development. In saying this, I
imply that progressive development can only be appraised if
conceptualized in terms of internal changes and internal
cathectic shifts. These internal processes are not necessarily
noticeable, externally, by the casual observer or by the environment; yet, revolutionary dislocations take place intrapsychically, replacing old regimes by new ones. The intensity
of observable signs, the "public noise" if you will, rarely
tells us reliably what kind of psychic accommodation the
adolescent is initiating or consolidating.

Revolutionary psychic changes seldom proceed in the
secret depth of the soul without giving rise to excesses in
action and thought, to turbulent manifestations, to ideational iconoclasm, to special forms of group behavior and social styles. All of these phenomena have been seen as typical of the transition from childhood to adulthood.

At this point I will set down a passage written some
time ago by Aristotle, a keen observer of human nature. In
his *Rhetoric* he had the following to say about adolescence:

> Young men have strong passions, and tend to gratify them in-
> discriminately. Of the bodily desires, it is the sexual by which

they are most swayed and in which they show absence of self-control. They are changeable and fickle in their desires, which are violent while they last, but quickly over . . . bad temper often gets the better of them, for owing to their love of honour they cannot bear being slighted, and are indignant if they imagine themselves unfairly treated. While they love honour, they love victory still more: for youth is eager for superiority over others, and victory is one form of this. Their lives are mainly spent not in memory but in expectation; for expectation refers to the future, memory to the past, and youth has a long future before it and a short past behind it. . . . Their hot tempers and hopeful dispositions make them more courageous than older men are: the hot temper prevents fear, and the hopeful disposition creates confidence: we cannot feel fear so long as we are feeling angry, and any expectation of good makes us confident. . . . They have exalted notions, because they have not yet been humbled by life or learnt its necessary limitations; moreover, their hopeful disposition makes them think themselves equal to great things and that means having exalted notions. They would always rather do noble deeds than useful ones: their lives are regulated more by moral feeling than by reasoning; and whereas reasoning leads us to choose what is useful, moral goodness leads us to choose what is noble. They are fonder of their friends, intimates, and companions than older men are, because they like spending their days in the company of others. All their mistakes are in the direction of doing things excessively and vehemently. They love too much and hate too much, and the same with everything else. They think they know everything, and are always quite sure about it; this, in fact, is why they overdo everything. If they do wrong to others, it is because they mean to insult them, not to do them actual harm. . . . They are fond of fun and therefore witty, wit being well-bred insolence [pp. 323-325].

This description attests to the fixity of developmental stages which are timed and determined by biological processes of maturation; these processes are species-bound. In contrast, the forms by which psychobiological processes are translated into psychosocial expressions have changed widely and endlessly over historical times. Generational conflict is essential for the growth of the self and of civilization.

We can say with confidence that the conflict between generations is as old as generations themselves. This situation could hardly be different, because the child's physical and emotional immaturity determines his dependence on the family (nuclear or extended) and, consequently, lays down the essential models of object relations. The psychic institutions (ego, superego, ego ideal) take their origin from the internalization of object relations and, in fact, demonstrate these origins when adolescent individuation sets in. At this time, the conflicts aroused by regressive and progressive adaptations confront the sexually maturing child with overwhelming challenges and alternatives. Therein lies the conflict between the generations. In essence, it is aroused by an emotional disengagement from the old and by a beckoning of the new that can only be reached via the gradual elaboration of compromise or transformation: psychic structure does not change, but the interactions between the psychic institutions are radically altered. The superego continues to exist and function, but the ego's critical influence and increasing autonomy alter the superego's absolutism and thus change its quality as well as its influence on personality functioning. These developmental achievements stabilize self-esteem in consonance with physical status, cognitive competence, and a value system that transcends the family ethics by seeking a broader base for its realization in society and in humanity.

The generational conflict has been conceptualized around various nodal issues of psychic differentiation: Anna Freud (1958) speaks of the loosening of the infantile object ties and Erikson (1956) of the identity crisis, whereas I have described the same development in terms of the second individuation process of adolescence (see Chapter 8). All these formulations have in common the basic assumption that only through conflict can maturity be attained. We might carry this statement one step further and say that developmental conflict never appears without an affective correlate, such as tension generally, and anxiety and depression more specifically. The tolerance for these painful affects cannot be acquired in adolescence, just as one accomplishes nothing by running to the store to buy a fire extinguisher when the house is aflame. Our genetic way of thinking tells us that the developmental stage for acquiring such tolerance is the latency period. It is at this stage that so much of adolescent trouble is brewed in blissful oblivion.

Before I continue I must define the position from which I look at disaffected youth. The fact that we live in the midst of a social revolution is not the doing of youth at all, even though youth is a carrier of the momentum to effect change. The adult state of mind has to be juxtaposed to that of youthful disaffection. Much of today's adult philosophy reminds me of Voltaire's Doctor Pangloss. As you will remember, Pangloss, the all-knowledgeable tutor of Candide, sends his bright and inquisitive charge off on travels through a world of dubious human excellence. With never-failing sophistry and verbosity (hence his name), Pangloss replies to Candide's intelligent questions about the absurdities of human conduct with the repetitive phrase that the world we live in is—in spite of every appearance to the contrary—"the best of all possible worlds."

It remains a deplorable fact that only through violence are the responsible institutions of society awakened and moved to change. This fact does not, in my mind, grant young people the exalted privilege to employ violence whenever something displeases them or causes them hardship. I fully appreciate a place for violence in the desperate search for a way out of the social morass of our time. I am cognizant that these issues should not be simplified by attaching them to the generation gap. Rather, it is the other way round: the generation-gap-minded youth attaches himself to these broader social issues and thus imbues his

sense of personal separateness and cultural discontinuity
with a viable ideology and an emotional referent.

To pursue my topic, I must now narrow it down to man-
ageable proportions and forgo the dubious courage of advancing into the crossfire of the various disciplines such as
sociology, education, political theory, and history, which all
contribute their share to an understanding of youth today. I
am no Lord Raglan, eager to fight the battle of Balaklava
over again. I rather note my clinical observations as far as
they relate to the generation-gap issue. My presentation
does not pretend to be relevant to the total youth upheaval
of today, but instead focuses on one form of deviant adolescent development familiar to all of us. A few clinical vi-
gnettes will clarify this further.

Recently I had a conversation with a seventeen-year-old
college freshman who had been suspended after his participation in the occupation of a building, a sit-in, and van-
dalism. He explained to me that the university "separated
emotion from action" by substituting "action and thought."
He had expected that college would give him "something
like meaning and relevancy." He did not find it. He then
described to me at great length the endless chain of re-
criminations between "us" and "them." Finally, I interrupted his report by reminding him of our telephone conversation at the time he made an appointment with me. I
had told him then that I knew his mother had suggested
that he talk with me but that I wanted to know why he
wanted to see me. He had answered, "I have a problem of
communication with my father." When I now brought this
telephone conversation to his attention, he told me of a letter he had written to his father from college, asking him to
"just let me be, not argue any more, but understand that I
have to do what I am doing." I said at this point, "I see—
you come from a very close family," whereupon his eyes wa-
tered, and he replied, "Yes, my mother always told me that
I have a very good mind, that I have the germ of a book in

my head." What this boy expected from college was to receive "meaning and relevancy" as a direct continuation of
parental support; in other words, he wished that college
would release him from the bondage of his childhood, just as
he had wished his father could spare him the agony of the
generational conflict. His life had been laid out for him at
home in the friendliest of terms, but it had ceased to be his
own. Being forced to leave college gave him a sense of freedom, independence, and identity which enabled him temporarily to bear his sense of guilt, engendered by his outburst of aggression and wanton destructiveness.

A college girl described her exquisite feeling of elation
while participating in a sit-in. The great disappointment
came when the administration decided not to expel the rebellious students. The girl exclaimed to me, "I wish they
had expelled me. I hate college." My reply—"Can't you
leave college on your own?"—was quickly parried by her
saying, "Oh, no—that would disappoint my mother; I could
never do that."

A nineteen-year-old girl had to leave college on account
of anxiety symptoms. She settled down in a so-called undesirable neighborhood with her boyfriend who had for her
the distinction of being lower class. Coming from a "good"
middle-class family, she felt quite exceptional among her
peers for living with her boyfriend; it afforded her a sense of
maturity, superiority, and independence. Through her boyfriend she found herself in a group of radicals whom she
idealized as the heroic protagonists in the creation of a new
world order, or, rather, in the repudiation, if not destruction, of the old world order in which she grew up. However,
she never could quite trust their sincerity or her own. Being
a radical offered her the opportunity to be pugnacious and
hateful, both of which made her feel "good" and "real." Her
boyfriend's irregular work habits pleased her because he
could thus provide her with constant companionship.
Money, of course, she accepted offhandedly from her pa-

rents. It took arduous analytic work for her to admit that
she was revolted by sexual intercourse. What made her
submit to sex was fear of abandonment and her incapacity
to be alone. This girl had possessed only one friend all
through childhood and adolescence—her mother. A powerful
regressive pull to the preoedipal mother was counteracted
by heterosexual displacement and surrender. The seeming
emancipation concealed the perpetuation of infantile dependency.

All three adolescents came from white, affluent, middle-
class, child-centered homes. Families like these always do
things together, share their feelings freely with one
another, and discuss their problems rationally. The parents
are, often uncannily, attuned to their child's needs way beyond early childhood, indeed all through adolescence. They
do not tolerate their child's anger, anxiety, and guilt well.
Tension, failure, and disappointment, which no child can be
spared, become readily neutralized by a constant flow of
stimulation and encouragement. One might think that such
an abundance of appreciation would last for a lifetime.
Quite the contrary is so often the case. This is due to the
fact that at adolescence an illusory self, nurtured by the parents up through the latency years, is finally rejected in the
effort at a more adequate self-definition.

Actions of revolt or independence, from civil disobedience to sexual freedom, are often the consequences of violent ruptures of dependencies rather than the maturational
signals of conflict elaboration or conflict resolution. The
three adolescents described had rejected their families as
hopelessly out of step with the times, as lacking any insight
into their children's motivations and unable to say anything
relevant to their offspring. These young people keenly felt
the generation gap. The subjective feeling of the gap lies in
its use as a distancing device in which spatial and ideological separations are substituted for inner conflicts and emotional disengagement. The result is an arrest on the adoles-

cent level, owing to *conflict avoidance*; consequently, the maturation arising from *conflict resolution* is forfeited. Not all adolescents who claim there is a generation gap, however, are avoiding conflict. Many must adopt this stance in order to remain part of the group they cherish; they accept the group code only with inner reservations and temporization.

I hinted earlier at the fact that children from such middle-class, usually liberal or progressive, homes are burdened with family ties that are difficult to alter gradually. These affectionate ties find unceasing expression from early childhood till puberty in demonstrative closeness and readily available need gratification. Such upbringing, which is often recommended by the psychological expert or by popularized and misunderstood expert opinion, interferes with normal latency development. The advances of the ego, characteristic for this stage, never become sufficiently detached from object relations and therefore never acquire essential autonomy. In other words, object relations are not given up and replaced by identifications, at least not to the extent that would render the onrush of pubertal drives less devastating or disorganizing. Such children are totally unprepared to deal with the normative adolescent regression because they live in deadly fear of regressive engulfment. They have no other choice but total rupture with the past, spatial self-exile, and oppositional absolutism. Drugs and sexual freedom acquire an important function in this developmental impasse by staving off regressive personality dissolution. The inability to regress prevents the rectification of infantile remnants of maldevelopment and renders the adolescent process incomplete. The sense of a generation gap and of alienation represents the subjective awareness of this impasse as an unbridgeable abyss.

Ironically, this impasse has become a mark of distinction among the young. Erik H. Erikson told me not so long ago of a conversation with a student who stopped him in Harvard Yard. The student led up to the fact that he was in search of his identity. Erikson asked him: "Are you complaining or are you boasting?" We see so many young people today who carry their identity crisis like a badge of honor that should entitle them to diplomatic immunity in the foreign territory of their elders. This comment brings me to another aspect of the generation gap, namely, the contribution of adult society and its institutions to the erosion of generational bonds.

Last summer I walked into the country house of an old friend whose sixteen-year-old generation-gap-minded son greeted me heartily. I waved his greetings aside in mock disgust and said, "I don't talk to anybody under thirty." He was quick with his reply. "Ah," he said, "so you are envious of us!" This little anecdote serves to tell us of the motives that, so the young suspect, govern adults' attitudes toward them. We cannot deny that there is a great deal of truth in it. The American adult's obsession with youthfulness, the commercial exploitation of clothing styles the young have created, the popularization and merchandising of their "thing," all rob the young people of their rightful monopoly.

Adults gaze with fascinated attention at the young, ready to imitate them, marginally, of course, in order to evade getting older. One can observe the reciprocal effect of alienated youth and disquieted adult: the ostentatious performer and the ambivalent spectator. There exists a compelling need in the young to arouse the attention of the adult world, the Establishment, in all its forms. And conversely, there exists a compelling wish of the youth-minded adult to show understanding of the young by acquiescing in the face of the most outrageous demands and "put-downs." The most disconcerting situation presents itself if some young generation-gap rebel is met by a truly fair-minded and dialogue-ready adult. As soon as disagreement enters the dialogue, the totalism of youth asserts itself in the alternative of being "for or against me." The overly sympathetic

adult, by catering to this dichotomy, sidesteps the generational conflict. Whenever he fraternizes with the adolescent,
he blurs the generational, i.e., intrinsic and essential, issues, and compromises himself in the process. The attitude
of the so-called understanding and equalizing adult is perceived by the young as one of surrender, both welcome and
disappointing. At any rate, it relieves young and old of the
agony of conflict and emotional divisiveness. Such détente,
however, deprives the youth of his legitimate terrain,
staked out by mutual and contested claims, the terrain on
which the adolescent must consolidate his divided self on
the road to emotional maturity.

What the adolescent wants from the stereotyped adult is
an admission of his wrongdoing, of his selfishness and his
incompetence. How many times in our consulting rooms
have we not heard the adolescent rage against his parents
and say, "If they only would admit that they are wrong!" Of
course, all this holds true only for those young people who
experience a generation *gap*, which by definition indicates
their incapacity to experience generational conflict. This definition restricts the use of the term "generation gap" because it attaches certain developmental preconditions to it
and therefore gives it psychological meaning.

Much is written today about youth by adults who can
only see the visionary, reformist, and liberating effects of
youth on society. Such an apotheosis or idolatry of youth
remains a highly personal matter, and such enthusiastic
embraces conceal, like most generalizations, the contradictory and heterogeneous elements at work. Looking at the
problem as I do, namely, psychologically, I cannot possibly
be a wholesale apologist for and admirer of all youthful
liberators and iconoclasts. Nor have I attempted to encompass in my exposition the total condition of today's youth;
rather, I have directed my effort toward a definition of
terms and, consequently, toward the delineation of a
psychological type. This type—"the generation-gap

youth"—constitutes, no doubt, a minority; but, then, has not our profession always turned its attention to minorities and to the maladaptive ways of life?

Within the definitions I have presented, it is possible to summarize my thesis. When the generation gap establishes itself as a prolonged distancing device in terms of a wholesale disaffection from the individual's background, then the generational conflict is feeble, without structure and elaboration. On the other hand, if generational conflict asserts itself, working toward individuation and differentiation, then the generation gap as a way of life finds no fertile ground on which to grow and sustain itself. Under these conditions it remains transient and self-liquidating. The extremes of both categories are easily recognizable, whereas the in-between stages, containing ingredients from both quarters, often burden our clinical assessment with doubt and uncertainty. It might be helpful to have the extremes defined in order to recognize the approximations. Only by this laborious process of assessment can we gauge our usefulness to the generation-gap-minded adolescent. Whenever we are able to decipher the message that lies embedded in his action, we can entertain the reasonable hope that he will comprehend what we are saying to him.

Chapter 2

Reflections on Modern Youth

Aggression Reconsidered

The alarming rise of adolescent aggression in all sectors of life, regardless of social class, impels us to reconsider familiar aspects of psychoanalytic theory, in order to determine their particular relevance for our comprehension of this kind of adolescent behavior. Perhaps we shall understand this adolescent phenomenon better if we focus our attention on the vicissitudes of the aggressive drive. The forms in which the unattenuated aggressive drive makes its appearance in adolescence are many and changing; they range from mentation to action or, more precisely, from dream and fantasy to murder and suicide.

The manifest aggression of the adolescent has long attracted the psychoanalyst's interest. Its workings, in terms of endogenous and exogenous determinants, remain a subject of our scientific curiosity. In the relatively short history of psychoanalysis, the early and long-lasting fascination with the vicissitudes of the libido has taken the lead. Investigation of that drive delineated the sexual conflict, which had no doubt acquired a particularly virulent quality in the moral climate of the Victorian era. It was the synchronicity of the age of sexual repression and the existence of a genius

Presidential Address delivered at the meeting of the American Association for Child Psychoanalysis, Hershey, Pennsylvania, April 4, 1970. First published in *Psychosocial Processes: Issues in Child Mental Health*, 2(1): 11-21, 1971.

like Freud that spawned the new science of psychoanalysis.

Be that as it may, the fact remains that preoccupation with the vicissitudes of the libido has only reluctantly and slowly yielded to an ever-deepening concern with the vicissitudes of the aggressive drive. The problem of aggression remains, in many aspects, obscure and beset with riddles at the very time when the clinical manifestations of the aggressive drive are being persistently and increasingly forced upon our attention. Many sexual taboos of the Western world have weakened or seem to have vanished altogether. The adolescent's conscious anguish and guilt feelings in relation to sexuality (autoerotic or heterosexual) have declined remarkably, if we take his behavior and his words at face value. As analysts, however, we soon discover that guilt and anxiety about sexuality have not disappeared; they have simply been removed from consciousness by virtue of the fact that childhood and adolescent sexuality is sanctioned and encouraged by professional expert, parent, and peer.

Not unrelated to the so-called sexual revolution is the impression we gain, from the couch and field observation, that the aggressive drive is pursuing its own independent aims as the result of an insufficient fusion between libido and aggression. At the extremes stand violence, supported by all kinds of ideologies or reasons, and passivity, observable in the "hippie" life style. In either case, aggression turns against the self, the object, or the nonhuman environment, indicating a fateful imbalance or defusion of the two basic drives.

I must confess that in my earlier writings I attributed too large a role in adolescent conflict formation to libidinal strivings, and relegated the aggressive drive to an almost exclusively defensive function. This oversight I have subsequently corrected: my present theoretical model of adolescence rests on the dual instinct theory. Clinical work has convinced me that puberty—namely, sexual maturation—

intensifies the aggressive and the libidinal drives in equal measure. It remains a moot question whether the adolescent drive intensification we so clearly observe might not be due also to drive defusion rather than only to quantitative changes per se. In addition, we must remember that the aggressive drive in its unattenuated or primary form is qualitatively different from aggression employed for defensive purposes. This difference is due to the fact that the aggressive drive, in order to assume a defensive function, has first to be modified by and adapted to the interests of the ego.

Much of present-day ego-syntonic aggression, even if it does appear to be pathognomic in the eyes of many observers, has to be assessed by the psychoanalyst in terms of its function. Aggression is no doubt instrumental in effecting the individual's impingement on the environment in order to shape it so it will adequately safeguard psychic integrity, self-esteem, and social integration. The techniques and politics of alloplastic behavior have to be learned at each stage of development. At adolescence, more than ever before, serviceable models have to be found beyond the boundaries of the family, in the wider ambience of society at large. This formulation highlights the fact that any investigator of adolescent aggression has to enter, marginally but implicitly, the realms of group psychology, sociology, and political science. We must admit that most psychoanalysts do not move knowledgeably or gracefully in these territories.

My deliberations have reached a point where I have to stake out the ground from which I view the issue of adolescent aggression. That ground is limited and specific; it cannot accommodate the totality of adolescent aggressive phenomena. There is no doubt in my mind that present-day adolescent unrest is symptomatic of social and institutional anachronisms or breakdowns: the environment has lost some of its essential function in relation to adolescent development. Youth has always been the most sensitive indicator whenever "Something is rotten in the state of Denmark." The adolescent is telling us, by his maladaptive behavior, about the wanton disarrangement of societal functions, often referred to as anomie. This state of affairs the adolescent expresses, although he is unable to articulate either the real nature of its cause or the measures needed for societal regeneration. Nevertheless, to the young basic causes and final remedies must exist; they are thus construed from fact and fiction with the urgent aim of harmonizing self and surround. What emerges from this process is an amalgam of constructive innovations, often alternating with iconoclastic rages. One or both of these trends either presses for action or does its work in silence without any observable tumultuous manifestations. Here again, the social milieu and the prevalent style of child rearing account for the differences.

It has become apparent lately that peace demonstrations, draft protests, marches, sit-ins, and university riots are only the overt signs of a social revolution that is being shaped by the tragic fact that only violence, destruction, and terror seem to arouse awareness of social attitudes, conditions, and practices that are no longer tolerable. The social phenomenon of youth violence, especially black youth violence, does not belong, exclusively, within the orbit of our professional specialty; it will be affected most constructively and enduringly by the ballot-box and in the courts of law. These comments are meant to convey my awareness of the wider social implications of adolescent unrest and violence, to which the direct contribution of psychoanalysis is limited. In what follows, I shall restrict my deliberations to those aspects of adolescent aggression that can be illuminated by psychoanalytic observation and insight.

In order to develop my thesis I must turn to the problem of adolescent development. It has been an accepted tenet of the psychoanalytic theory of adolescence that the advance to genitality brings to life the instinctual antecedents of childhood and their predominant object relations. Among these, the positive oedipal attachment has played for a long time the key role among the infantile object relations reactivated by sexual maturation. Only gradually and lately have the negative Oedipus complex and preoedipal object relations found their places of singular importance in the theory of adolescence.

We have come to accept the fact that adolescent progressive development always proceeds along regressive pathways; in other words, that genitality can only be reached via the detour of a cathectic connection with pregenital drive positions, including, of course, their respective preoedipal and oedipal object relations. The most fateful danger to the integrity of psychic organization during adolescence lies in this obligatory regression without which emotional maturity cannot be attained. Consequently and importantly, intensification of the sexual drive (pregenital and genital) at puberty does not, in and of itself, represent the exclusive source of psychic dangers, known as oedipal anxiety and sexual guilt. The uniqueness of adolescent development stands out in bold relief when we consider the fact that, in contrast to all other periods before puberty, adolescent progressive development is contingent on and, indeed, determined by regression, its tolerance and use for psychic restructuring.

The far-reaching consequence of this proposition requires elaboration. Somewhat hesitantly, I began with a bold statement, because it will carry us, without delay, *in medias res*. Normally, the progression to genitality is egosyntonic; it is also socially supported by peers and sanctioned by the parental model of sexual partnership and parenthood. Obstacles in the path toward genitality are to be found in drive fixations and superego anxiety. These impediments in the path of development are universal aspects of the human condition; from here issues illness as well as health. Which of these alternatives is to be the permanent legacy of adolescence depends, ultimately, on the reparative

and restorative success of adolescent regression, to which
Anna Freud (1958) has referred as "the second chance."

Regression as an obligatory component of the adolescent
process inevitably constitutes a source of conflict, anxiety,
and guilt. As in any state of psychic emergency, namely,
any critical interference with psychic homeostasis, here too
defensive measures are resorted to. These auto- and alloplastic accommodations to a state of emergency usually appear in a blend of varying combinations. In other words,
they may appear both as internal change and as acting out.
It can be stated, in general terms, that regression to pregenitality and to its respective object relations always bears an
ego-dystonic quality; it tends to lower self-esteem, unless it
reaches the state of infantile megalomania. We have ample
clinical evidence of the regressive movement in the
heightened narcissism of adolescence; such narcissism provides a haven and refuge whenever the adolescent process
has failed disastrously, or else it is visited as a fleeting
resting-place. In either case, adolescent regression represents a danger, which reaches catastrophic dimensions
whenever the regressive pull toward merger with the object
becomes stronger than the reality-bound ego is able to counteract. In that case, annihilation of individual separateness
draws close and the dissolution of psychic structure becomes
imminent; the breakdown of reality testing is always a telling warning. Regression is, by its very nature, unlimited
and bottomless, while progression is assured only by the
ever-increasing delimitation of the self. Regression, in its
ultimate course, gives way to megalomania and primary
narcissism, while progression passes over to an affirmation
of the reality principle and to the acceptance of death. No
wonder adolescents ponder more about death than do those
who are either younger or older.

When I postulated that regression is an obligatory aspect of adolescent development, I had in mind a specific
dynamic function inherent in adolescent regression. It can

best be described by saying that the advanced ego of postlatency competence is brought to bear, through regression, on
infantile conflicts, anxiety, and guilt which the feeble and
limited ego of early years was unable to resolve, neutralize,
or rid of their noxious quality. Those tasks have become the
mandate of the adolescent ego. Conversely, we can say that
only an ego that is commensurate with such tasks has the
qualities of what might be called an adolescent ego.

I have hardly hinted yet at the vicissitudes of aggression
in adolescent regression. Teleologically speaking, adolescent
regression aims at the resolution of infantile dependencies
because they are irreconcilable with adult object relations
and ego autonomy. Most characteristic of infantile object relations is their ambivalence—namely, their intrinsically antithetical affective nature, which affirms object dependency
equally in terms of aggression and libido. A tenuous fusion
is induced by fear of the loss of love and castration anxiety.
Under the influence of adolescent regression this fusion is
partially undone, and primary ambivalence, which includes
both unconditional love (total possessiveness) and irreconcilable hate (total destructiveness) invades the adolescent's
relations to objects, to symbols, to ideas, and to the self.
Anna Freud's (1958) "uncompromising adolescent" uses a
well-known defense which, however, might be looked at as a
derivative of an ambivalence struggle rooted in early object
relations and in the wish for total mastery: the opposing
poles of ambivalence can assume delusional proportions during the adolescent process without being indicators of
psychosis.

We know from studies of childhood that fusion of the instincts in relation to one and the same object can be side-
stepped by dividing the object, or by simply selecting one
part object to love and another to hate, one to possess and
another to destroy. This archaic solution of the ambivalence
conflict in adolescence, except when it is transient, has the
effect of primitivizing object relations permanently. As al-

ways, the level of drive development is deflected onto the ego in terms of ego interests and attitudes; in this case, it appears in the need for objects of love and hate in the outer world. Lasting drive defusion and primary ambivalence render such a behavioral, ideational, and moral stance rigid and uncompromising. Whoever fails to fit this model has to be discarded because no personal need of the object, i.e., no individuality, can be tolerated in "the other."

A continuation of the infant's and toddler's readiness for externalization can be detected in the child's conviction that his parents' aggression is equal to his own—that is, boundless. The child controls his fear of the persecutory parent by repression, by sublimation, and by fusion of the instincts. In similar fashion, the adolescent may expect a persecutory retaliation from the outside world; he fights it off with an extraordinarily impaired sense of reality. A clinical picture such as this demonstrates, in my opinion, that the adolescent ego was not equal to the task of regression. Under these circumstances what we witness is an incomplete or, worse, an abortive adolescence.

It must have become clear by now that regression, as I refer to it in this context, is not defensive in nature, but serves an adaptive function. An adolescent ego is capable of performing the regressive task if it can tolerate the anxiety that ensues from drive and ego regression. This is possible only if the adolescent ego remains sufficiently reality-bound to forestall regression to the undifferentiated stage. An adolescent ego that is not equal to this task will, of necessity, avoid the regressive resolution of infantile conflicts and, concomitantly, fail to accomplish the emotional disengagement from family ties and from infantile fantasies and symbolisms, which will then survive as enclaves within the reality concept. These struggles of disengagement from early object ties are normally played out on the psychic stage between self- and object representations. This staging, of course, is possible only with the use of regression as mediator. Whenever regression has to be avoided, the internal process is played out on the stage of present actualities. In that case, the adolescent externalizes and concretizes what he is unable to experience and tolerate internally as conflict, anxiety, guilt, and depression.

Should the adolescent not be able to reconcile and integrate, through conflict resolution—or simply by "letting go"—the anachronistic needs and wishes of the infantile period, he will tend to affirm his freedom from childhood dependencies by action and imitation. Since he is unable to make regressive contact with his world of the infantile period, he displaces the internal drama onto the public arena. The accompanying defusion of the instinctual drives heightens the intensity of action and emotion; the resolution of conflict remains an external one and can be achieved only through external changes, either forcefully attained or voluntarily offered. This struggle with the environment delays or prevents the restoration of the fusion of instincts. Most importantly, it works against bringing the libidinal and aggressive drives into an alliance—a precondition for the attainment of genitality. On the moral or superego level, unresolved and irreconcilable drive positions—such as infantile and pubertal, dependent and autonomous—appear in the guise of absolutes and opposites, as good versus evil, new versus old, beautiful versus ugly, commitment versus compromise, freedom versus tyranny.

It has become a rather common observation that the middle-class older adolescent, when he encounters the anguish and the depressive moods of normal adolescence, discovers in the socially deprived and the dispossessed a reflection of the disillusionment he is experiencing in relation to his own life and, in particular, to the idealizations of his younger years. Adolescence has always been a state of expatriation and alienation. In the search for a new social matrix of which he can become an integral part, many an adolescent turns to alien militant groups, not realizing that their often legitimate grievances and realistic defiance are for him no more than a screen to keep his internal conflicts out of sight and touch.

It is, of course, the social function of adolescence to embrace an ideology, imbue it with the uniqueness of a particular life history, and transform it into the social and characterological articulations of moral man. Here, however, I am speaking of the shortcuts the adolescent seeks when he attempts to sidestep regression: he then becomes easily seduced by social causes or groups that define for him what is good or evil, and he makes these grievances his own. It is precisely this trend of defensive identification that has prompted the black militant to exclude the white middle-class youth from partnership in his struggle.

If acts of aggression and violence are committed by a member of a group which sanctions the action, this tends to neutralize individual guilt; group vindication easily outweighs superego dictates. I have seen many adolescents use the group as a protective shield against guilt feelings, thus sanctifying aggression in the name of an ultimate good. Parenthetically, this defense is universal; it operates in the Anti-Establishment as well as in the Establishment. No society, in fact, can exist without it. We might refer to it as the social harnessing of aggression by prescribing and ritualizing certain defined and sanctioned modes of aggression, thereby neutralizing individual guilt.

In order to round out my thesis, I must now turn to the adolescent's conceptualization of the environment. The target of adolescent aggression, standing out in bold relief, is the environment. Different adolescents, however, define the environment in different and very special terms.

One ontogenetic fact about the environment should be stated as fundamental—namely, that psychic structure originates in and needs to be supported by the unceasing interaction between the individual and his surround, human as well as nonhuman. In other words, psychic structure is the reflection of environmental influences, after they have been selectively internalized, integrated, and organized into a lasting pattern, which is designated as personality. This interaction—like a metabolic process that sustains and extends life—depends on reciprocity of function; it operates as a feedback system. We assume in this definition that the surround provides those ingredients or nutrients needed by and useful to the human psychic organism for its sound growth and development. To these ingredients also belong the host of external stimuli, quantitatively and qualitatively apportioned by the cultural milieu according to gender, age, place, and time. These stimuli complement maturational readinesses and channel them toward appropriate structure and content, i.e., toward their personal and social functions. Whenever the surround falls below a certain level of complementarity, it acquires a noxious character and the psychic organism, enveloped by it, suffers damage.

Winnicott (1965) has introduced the felicitous concept of the "facilitating environment" to denote the fact that human development can proceed only if external sources of phase-specific experiences are available for the organism to use. This fact is quite obvious when we consider childhood, but it has received less serious consideration from psychoanalysts, educators, and statesmen in relation to youth. This neglect has preserved many outmoded or ineffectual social institutions as lifeless structures.

It is common knowledge that during childhood the particular nature of the surround—especially in terms of object relations and the sense of physical security—is of singular importance. My intention here is to extend this concept into the adolescent period—a time at which the family envelope and the neighborhood both become extended and are carried into the wider realm of society, its institutions and its history, past, present, and future. Should the surround lack the essential conditions that permit the articulation of youthful potentialities and aspirations in relation to something that

really matters—and matters on a scale larger than any individual concern—then the mutually beneficial interactions
between the adolescent and his environment will be critically impaired. Apathy and chaos, rebellion and violence,
alienation and disaffection are the symptomatic consequences of a malfunction in the metabolic social process whose
healthy working is essential for keeping the growing organism and his surround productively conjoined.

The adolescent effort to change the environment is an effort to establish harmony and congruence between psychic
and environmental structures as mutually sustaining each
other. It has been my impression that the present disorganization of social structures and the cynical corruption of
professed communal ideals by public figures act as
psychonoxious agents on the consolidation of late adolescence. Conversely, whatever the defective or obsolete structures of social institutions are, they appear exposed in the
behavior of many adolescents. An existing ego deviancy or
immaturity, hidden and unnoticed within the family structure, will, at adolescence, easily be influenced or swayed by
environmental trends and opportunities, good or evil, productive or wasteful. Every adolescent child is, so to speak,
expectantly waiting to come to terms with the unfinished
business of his childhood when he enters the widened social
stage. It is my contention that adolescent phase-specific regression, should it find no adequate societal support or
reasonable opportunity for sustained developmental progression, will lead the adolescent to adopt a raison d'être by
way of polarization with the world that preceded his own
budding selfhood. For those who come to this stage with
critical ego inadequacies, the peer group becomes the direct
heir to the discarded family envelope without, however,
serving that positive developmental function which youthful
group formations have largely and everywhere sustained.

One last remark on this subject: the positive effect of the
"facilitating environment," which is geared to the norma-

tive requirements of adolescent development, presupposes that the child has internalized, before reaching adolescence, those aspects of the environment that cannot and will never be part of the facilitating environment during the adolescent years. In other words, if the adolescent sets forth age-inadequate expectations or demands, then disruption between organism and environment will once again ensue. Such a stalemate is bound to occur whenever the essential achievements of individuation remained woefully incomplete (see Chapter 8). Fulfillments of all kinds of infantile expectancies are supposed to flow freely and timelessly from the surround if activated by the child's needfulness and desire. Society—or its representative institution—becomes the idealized parent and renders the real parent emotionally obsolete and useless.

In cases of this kind we can usually observe that the oedipal conflict had been weak and its resolution incomplete. This outcome is fostered whenever the parent tries to spare the child the conflictual anxiety of the oedipal phase and soothes the disappointment in his inadequacy and smallness of being a child with lavish assurances of his perfection and promises of his future greatness (see Chapter 14). These narcissistic gratifications usually delay entry into the latency period or render it imitative and deficient.

In the case of the boy, for instance, we observe, retrospectively, that insufficient aggression had been available in relation to the oedipal father. Consequently, the identificatory resolution of the oedipal conflict was lacking in vigor and independence. In other words, the negative Oedipus complex remained the central conflict of his object dependency up to late adolescence. This excessive and unabated aggressive behavior up to late adolescence is in many instances a defense against passive wishes or against homosexuality. This situation does not rule out the possibility that a belated eruption of the ambivalence conflict in relation to the oedipal father may free him—at least partially—from his arrested psychosexual development. In brief, if too great a share of preoedipal caretaking and nurturing dependencies remain attached to the oedipal father, an assertive self fails to emerge and a regression to the passive oedipal constellation follows. An onslaught against some authority, internal or external, will have to be launched in order to reach, belatedly, a firmer hold on the positive oedipal level and, concomitantly, to achieve the consolidation of a—even if infirm—masculine identity.

Adolescents who find themselves enmeshed in this impasse follow, generally, one of two alternative roads: one leads to a retreat into a self-styled "exile" within a narcissistic, often autistic, regression; the other affirms the need for object possession by violent conquest, resisting in that way regressive merger. Aggressive behavior protects this type of adolescent from falling back on infantile dependencies; externalization keeps a life-line to the object world within reach. Of the two alternative roads—given the preconditions and precursors discussed earlier—the one of aggressive interaction with the environment augurs more favorably for an adaptive resolution—after the storm is over. However, too hasty or too pat an answer might ignore the core of the problem, which lies neither in the psychology of the individual nor in the social ills of our times, but is to be found in their mutually anachronistic interactions with and expectations of each other. A truly organismic approach to human behavior has to view individual and surround as a unitary system. There is no period in human life that spells this out more dramatically than adolescence with its aggressive turbulence.

Chapter 3

Prolonged Male Adolescence

The Formulation of a Syndrome and Its Therapeutic Implications

In discussing adolescence a temptation arises which is difficult to resist—namely, to focus on those aspects of personality formation that are significant for the total developmental crisis and are typical for adolescents in general, male or female. The desire to bring unification and order into this maturational phase, which so turbulently brings childhood to its termination, has led to a neglect of the substantive differences between the various modes of adaptation adolescents demonstrate during this period, as well as those differences that set male and female adolescents apart. This comment seems particularly pertinent at the current stage of adolescent research when the dynamic and structural changes of the typical adolescent process have become rather well understood. Apparently the clinical picture of adolescence is far richer than our theoretical formulations have led us to assume. Our various attempts at classification of adolescent adjustment—normal and abnormal—have so far been singularly unfruitful; it is my contention that this disappointing result is due to the meagerness of clinical studies of adolescence which intentionally limit themselves to the elucidation of a specific segment in

First published in *American Journal of Orthopsychiatry*, 24: 733-742, 1954.

the total adolescent process. Such an attempt at classification becomes more useful the more it concentrates on the
substantive differences that clinical observation of the adolescent process permits us to isolate. One focus might be on
the differences between the sexes; the similarities have
been dealt with *in extenso*. With this thought in mind I
have limited myself in this presentation to the problem of
prolonged adolescence in the male.

The term "prolonged adolescence" was introduced by
Siegfried Bernfeld in 1923. The object of his investigation at
that time was prolonged male adolescence as a social
phenomenon observed in European youth movements after
the First World War. Members of these groups presented a
strong predilection for intellectualization and sexual repression, thus delaying the resolution of the adolescent conflict
and, in consequence, the personality consolidation of late
adolescence. The designation "prolonged adolescence" has
acquired over the years a broader connotation with the result that the psychological specificity of the term has been
lost. Prolonged adolescence is a descriptive and collective
term which comprises conditions of heterogeneous dynamic
constellations of which I have selected one for a more detailed study. My observations were made on the American
middle-class young man, roughly between eighteen and
twenty-two, who usually attends college or has, at any rate,
some professional aspirations; this fact, more often than not,
makes him financially dependent on his family during the
years of early adulthood. The clinical picture which I shall
sketch below has been observed with enough frequency to
encourage the presentation of a synoptic summary.[1]

---

[1]In editing this paper for the present volume I could not fail to observe how
radically the phenomenology of prolonged adolescence had changed over the intervening years, from 1954 to 1977. Yet, despite the self-assertion of the college
"drop-out" or the older adolescent's choice of an "alternate life style," and despite
the general acceptance of the "psychosocial maratorium" (Erikson, 1956) in its various behavioral manifestations, the fact remains that the motivations in a large
number of young people are similar, indeed identical, to those described in this
paper. I call the reader's attention to the Postscript which I wrote to "Preoedipal

The term "prolonged adolescence" is used here to refer to a static perseveration in the adolescent position which under normal circumstances is of a time-limited and transitory nature. A developmental phase which is intended to be left behind after it has accomplished its task has become a way of life. Instead of the progressive push, which normally carries the adolescent into adulthood, prolonged adolescence arrests this forward motion with the result that the adolescent process is not abandoned but kept open-ended. In fact, the adolescent crisis is adhered to with persistence, desperation, and anxiousness. An admixture of satisfaction with this state of turmoil is never absent. The observer of such individuals senses quickly the superficial reassurance derived from a condition which keeps the adolescent process inconclusive. The fervent clinging to the unsettledness of all of life's issues renders any progression to adulthood an achievement which is hardly worth the price. This dilemma leads to the contrivance of ingenious ways to combine childhood gratifications with adult prerogatives. The adolescent strives to bypass the finality of choices and options exacted at the close of adolescence.

Living in the twilight of an arrested transition renders the adolescent self-conscious and ashamed. Much of his behavior and mentation aims at the extinction of these dysphoric moods. When he tries to remain in solitude he becomes restless and confused. The inability to be alone forces him to join groups. Company rescues him from daydreaming and autoerotic preoccupation. Friendships with boys are transient and unstable; homosexual involvement is a constant threat. When he becomes attached to a girl, he clings to her with devoted and dependent neediness. He is seemingly capable of intimacy and finds sexual relations (intercourse) satisfying; however, on closer examination these so-

---

Factors in the Etiology of Female Delinquency" (see Chapter 11), bridging the gap of twenty years by comparing the psychological constellations with the epochal changes in the phenomenology of behavior.

called sexual relations appear to be of the forepleasure type. This is to say that the erotogenous zones of pregenitality occupy the leading role in the sexual drive organization, which, due to pubertal maturation, takes the genital focus as its mode of expression. If not always manifest in behavior, this early stage of psychosexual development is identifiable in fantasies, dreams, and preoccupations of a compulsive nature. In heterosexual behavior pregenitality ranges from sheer pleasure in shared nakedness to mutual masturbation to voyeuristic and exhibitionistic practices typical of the "bathroom world," yet it always and eventually finds genital expression. All this is normal enough for the early stages of adolescence and it is equally normal for pregenitality to attain a personal, idiosyncratic quality within the scope of foreplay in adult sexual relations. It acquires a pathognomic character only if the arrest at the preadolescent drive position acquires permanency and ego syntonicity during late adolescence.[2]

Of course, the type of love relationship under discussion here is by no means of a sexual character only; the sharing of interests, of ideas and ideals plays an important part. However, in the intensive, almost addictive, need to share we discern an extreme egocentricity and demandingness which reveals the infantile component of the relationship. The girl chosen is often a fitting challenge to the boy's incestuous attachment; she presents traits of striking difference or similarity to significant family members, be it mother, father, sister, or brother. The girl chosen is usually condemned by the boy's family. It appears that the adolescent, through the choice of his love object, has made a convulsive effort to extricate himself from an infantile involvement. This battle of emancipation fought with his girlfriend as his comrade-in-arms often continues for a long

[2]For a detailed exposition of ego and psychosexual development in preadolescence and its relevancy for the concept of fixation on the preadolescent phase, see Blos (1962, pp. 57-71).

period of time. I have seen such relationships develop into
an early congenial marriage with or without therapy intervening at the impasse in the adolescent struggle of disengagement from the family.

Exalted self-expectations figure dominantly in the lives
of these young men. In one way or another they have as
children shown some promising talent; most of them are
rather gifted and intelligent. Under the influence of parental ambition and narcissistic overevaluation these children
came to expect fabulous achievements from themselves (see
Chapter 14). Fame and greatness, passion and wealth, adventure and excitement figure vividly in their fantasies.
The first failures in a career which supposedly was laid out
in foolproof fashion come down on them with crushing
blows, usually at the juncture between the late high school
and early college years. At no point does the young man
lose the recognition of the fact that failure and possible disaster are staring him in the face. He is annoyed, he is irri-
tated and anxious, but he neither tries to maintain a lifeless phantasmagoria, nor does he regress to childhood positions. He does not seek relief either in asocial acting out or
in retaliatory passivity. The initiative for taking purposeful
action is not lost; in fact, the imminent danger of surrender
mobilizes all existing inner resources to ward off the final
and decisive stage of the struggle. The lives of these adolescents never look quite empty and stale; only upon closer
scrutiny does one realize how lost they are in a void of uncertainty and self-doubt. In order to escape from narcissistic
impoverishment they rally desperately to continued attempts at "making good"; again, upon closer scrutiny these
efforts appear slipshod and of spurious expediency. In all
this turmoil the critical faculty of self-observation is never
entirely lost and is rather easily elicited if the proper cue is
forthcoming in therapy. The well-known schizophrenialike
state of adolescence is not part of this clinical picture.

If we ignore for the moment the many similarities the

above synoptic sketch shares with the picture of adolescence in general, we will see more clearly the essential difference which sets off the cases under consideration from other forms of adolescent turbulence. The difference seems to lie in a remarkable resistivity to the regressive pull in conjunction with a persistent avoidance of any consolidation of the adolescent process.[3] These are the dominant features of the specific condition called prolonged adolescence. Conversely, we might say that prolonged adolescence is the expression of an inner necessity to keep the adolescent crisis open.

The clinical synopsis needs to be complemented at this point by dynamic considerations. From Freud's "Three Essays on the Theory of Sexuality" (1905b) we have learned that with the advent of sexual maturity at puberty a novel distribution of emphasis in sexual experience is introduced which permits the differentiation between fore- and endpleasure, and which, consequently, introduces a rearrangement of instinctual aims. The biological innovation at puberty necessitates a hierarchical rearrangement of the multitudinous childhood positions—modes of gratification and of tension resolution as well as identifications—which, for various reasons, remained indispensable to personality functioning and demanded continued expression. It is a well-known fact that the pregenital drives manifest themselves again as soon as puberty appears. The urgency of a definitive hierarchical organization of drives gains momentum with advancing adolescence and furnishes an incessant maturational forward push.

The need for a hierarchical organization, however, is not restricted to the sexual drives but applies to ego functions as well.[4] This fact might be illustrated by an archaic ego

[3]The adolescent superego is, to a large extent, built on the identification with the idealizing (not the idealized) parent; it supports the self-idealization of the adolescent child to an extent that self-evaluation is critically out of step with actual performance.

[4]I have described elsewhere in greater detail the formation of forepleasure during puberty and its influence on ego restructuring (1962, pp. 174-177).

function such as magical thinking; if magical thinking assumes dominance in adolescence, it disrupts the unity of the ego and consequently disorganizes its capacity of reality testing. Should magical thinking, however, be subordinated to the realm of fantasy or find an outlet in creative work or some kind of "avocation," then the ego can retain its unity. In that case we can say that fantasy-oriented and reality-directed ideation become severed and incompatible. This process of differentiation widens the conflict-free sphere of the ego.

The adolescent process can be considered closed when a hierarchical and relatively inflexible organization of genital and pregenital drives has been attained, and when ego functions have acquired a significant resistivity to regression. Hartmann (1950) has designated this characteristic of the ego—at whichever developmental stage it occurs—as the secondary autonomy of the ego. Obviously, sublimation and defenses play their part in this process. Prolonged adolescence, if it is to be regarded as an indefinite respite on the way to adulthood, results, as any excessive perseveration on a maturational stage, in the deformation of personality attributes. In sharp contrast to the ego-differentiating processes that are typical for adolescent character synthesis, prolonged adolescence reflects the failure to arrive at a stable, indeed inflexible, hierarchical organization of drives and ego functions.[5]

During prolonged adolescence, ego functions—thinking, memory, judgment, concentration, perception, etc.—become impaired from two sources: from an inundation by sexual and aggressive drives belonging to all phases of development and from an ascendancy of archaic ego functions and primitive defenses. The adolescent falls back on the earliest modes of tension management which reveal the fact that latency has effected a meager progress in ego development

---

[5]Characterological issues involved in this hierarchical organization are discussed extensively in Chapter 9.

as well as an inadequate relinquishment of infantile ego positions. In such cases we do not speak of regression, but rather of an activation of never-abandoned stages of early ego development. Let me illustrate this situation with a typical example. Should studying create in the adolescent a tension which he can only alleviate by recourse to autoerotic forms of relief—masturbation, sleep, eating, etc.—or should studying be associated habitually with diverting fantasies, then the tension, indispensable for the comprehension and mastery of a problem, cannot be sustained and any effort at studying is bound to result in failure. In normal adolescence these *modi operandi* are transient and finally relinquished, but in prolonged adolescence this relinquishment is not only not sought, it is avoided and counteracted.[6] The question now arises as to the economic factors that prevent the young men in prolonged adolescence from resorting to any, even an abortive, settlement of the adolescent crisis.

In studying this group of adolescents it became apparent that they shared a typical childhood constellation. They were regarded by both parents, or more emphatically the mother, as destined to do great things in life. For reasons related to their own personality formation, such mothers are prone to bestow on their male child fantasies of inordinate attainments with complete disregard for the child's gender, capacities, and interests. This situation is epitomized by the story of the pregnant woman who proudly replies to a friend who is commenting on her condition: "Yes, I am carrying my son, the doctor." Children who rely on their parents' fantasies about them expect life to unfold according to their mother's or father's promises and expectations. Prolonged adolescence averts the crisis of a crushing realization that the world outside the family fails to recognize the imaginary role which the child had played for almost two decades of his life. Whenever the sources of

[6]The case of an older male adolescent, illustrating in analytic detail the psychic constellation referred to here, is presented in Chapter 16.

identity are overwhelmingly external, the individual will lose his sense of identity if removed from his environment. Wherever he is, he follows the schema of infantile identity maintenance which says: "I am what others believe me to be." When these adolescents attempt the rupture of their childhood dependencies, they soon realize that this move is accompanied by a narcissistic impoverishment for which they are not prepared and which they cannot tolerate. They thus continue to live in the self-image which their mothers, fathers, sisters, or brothers have created for them.

One might say of these young men that their great future lies behind them when they reach the threshold of manhood; nothing that reality has to offer can compete with that easily obtained sense of elation and uniqueness which the little boy experienced when he was showered with parental admiration and confidence. Both parents—for reasons of their own—persistently overlooked the child's early failures, inhibitions, nervous habits, or forms of pathetic self-aggrandizement. The parents' persistent and illusory confidence nullified the significance of failure, and the child came to substitute narcissistic fantasies for reality mastery. Adolescence reveals finally and beyond any doubt that fantasy has never become clearly separated from reality-directed thinking. The sense of time has become affected by the constant substitution of the past for the future and, in addition, by the vague belief that sheer luck in the course of time will accomplish what ordinarily in a man's life takes years to achieve.[7]

If we investigate the early lives of these young men we are not surprised to find startling deviations from the typical process of identification. As children they were always lacking in assertiveness and self-criticism; they placidly accepted the exalted position into which their parents, predominantly their mothers, placed them. Consequently, they

[7]Chapter 14 is devoted to the pathology of this nature in the case of a late adolescent male.

developed a submissive dependency on adulating adults and a narcissistic self-sufficiency, a characteristic which often lends charm and attractiveness to the young boy. As young men these adolescents feel at home in the company of women, but are often ill at ease, fearful, and inhibited in their dealings with men. By identification these young men have internalized the idealized mother and given it structural permanence in the infantile ego ideal, the idealized self. They have early relinquished the competition with the father or the father principle; consequently, passive strivings are always on the verge of breaking through. As adolescents they treat their fathers with affectionate admiration or with pity and contempt, but most often with an ambivalent undulation of affect, borrowing their mother's attitudes. It is not surprising that the adolescent revolt, when it appears, is directed almost exclusively at the mother.

The basic identification with the mother reaches a crisis for the growing boy when puberty confronts him with the problem of sexual identity. This dilemma was aptly expressed by an older male adolescent who said: "There is one thing one should know and be sure of and that is whether one is a man or a woman." When the normal adolescent conflict of bisexuality presses for a final settlement, prolonged adolescence circumvents it by a perseveration in the bisexual position. In fact, this position becomes libidinized and any abandonment of it is resisted rather than sought. The gratifications thus obtainable play into the need for limitless possibilities in life and, simultaneously, assuage castration anxiety by perpetuating the ambiguity of sexual identity. This ambiguity is significantly reflected in the adolescent's vocational or educational floundering, his ineffectualness and eventual failure.

For the narcissistic child there is always an easily accessible escape from conflictual tension at hand; in fact, the child does not experience an internal conflict but rather anger and rage due to narcissistic deflation or deprivation of narcissistic supplies. He circumvents conflict by denial and/or self-aggrandizement. When a child who has used predominantly narcissistic defenses approaches adolescence, it is no surprise that the typical conflicts of this age remain outside of his conscious experience. An adolescent boy of this type becomes apprehensive when he realizes that he falls short of his exaggerated self-expectations; he avidly seeks encouragement from the surround, an endeavor in which he is usually successful since he has become by now a master of exploitative play. He reacts to the inflow of narcissistic supplies with elation and the customary avoidance of conflictual tension. Prolonged adolescence presents the paradoxical picture that there is no conflict to deal with because no conflict is experienced. These adolescents have to be helped to reach the adolescent conflict proper before the consolidation phase of terminal adolescence can be entered.

Adolescence proves for some of these boys a new development full of hope, expectancies, and a subjective state of greater adequacy than they experienced before. Anna Freud (1936) has pointed out that sexual maturation at puberty, as an independent variable, ushers in an ascendancy of masculinity in the passive-feminine boy which temporarily pushes passive strivings into the background; a condition is thus created which is more favorable for a potentially progressive development. The drive toward emotional dissociation from oppressing family ties gains momentarily the upper hand and the adolescent boy feels hopeful as long as the adolescent crisis continues to exist. The incapability to relinquish childhood positions in conjunction with the conscious desire for independence and manly self-assertion outside the confines of the family— both these factors combine to make the prolongation of adolescence the one and only solution within his reach. We have come to understand that the necessity for keeping the adolescent crisis open is a protective measure against two fatal alternatives: regression and rupture with reality (psychotic solution) or repression and symptom formation (neurotic solution). Faced with this dilemma the adolescent ego chooses to avoid either alternative by changing its own nature; thus a way of life is created out of a transitory maturational phase. ". . . it will be possible for the ego to avoid a rupture in any direction by deforming itself, by submitting to encroachments on its own unity and even perhaps by effecting a cleavage or division of itself" (Freud, 1924, pp. 152-153).

Such ego restrictions and ego regression bring the adolescent into disharmony with the demands of society and hamper the executive functions of the ego. The resulting frustrations are neutralized by narcissistic overcompensations, such as inflated optimism and gratifications in fantasy which are akin to illusions. A powerful resource for the maintenance of the narcissistic balance resides in magical thinking which has not been relinquished and has never been firmly superseded by the reality principle. Intentions and potentialities may easily take the place of achievement and mastery. An always present undercurrent of anxiousness is only partly dammed up by the interference of defensive measures. The overflow serves as a stimulant for intensified pseudo actions, which constitute abortive efforts to transpose infantile fantasies into adult activities. To illustrate: A college student who had to prepare for an examination in elementary biology turned passionately to the study of the most erudite articles in the field but neglected to study his textbook or his notes. Paradoxically, he failed because as he explained, "I knew too much."

Conflictual anxiety, which during normal adolescence activates libidinal reorganization and repression, is of negligible motivating power in prolonged adolescence in terms of synthesizing processes. By the ego accommodations described the adolescent crisis is kept open. We can say that the structure of prolonged adolescence is similar to that of a character disorder: in both cases the ego-restricting attitudes are not experienced as ego-alien. However, the rigidity of a character disorder is not present in prolonged adolescence; in fact, the adolescent process is most frequently kept in flux and is accessible to therapeutic mediation. It must, however, not be overlooked that the perseveration in the adolescent position is feasible only within certain limitations of time. Eventually—in the early or middle twenties—prolonged adolescence yields to a more organized and rigid settlement; the narcissistic character disorder describes best the general trend of the pathological development prolonged adolescence will take.

The dynamic and economic conditions of prolonged adolescence are opportune for therapeutic intervention. Personality development is still fluid and still possesses a high degree of plasticity; in addition, the resistive position which the ego maintains on two fronts, namely, against progression and against regression, reveals a considerable strength which can be utilized in the therapeutic process. It is true that young men of this type when they apply for help come with the hope of restoring a narcissistic and relatively tension-free existence, or of facilitating, as by magic, the fulfillment of their contradictory drives, such as self-assertion and submissiveness. What gives them the final push to seek therapy, however, is the narcissistic frustration due to recurrent disappointment or failure in their vocational, educational, and social activities as well as, indeed most poignantly, in their love life. In this picture we discover the prominence of disappointment due to the glaring incompatibility of self-image and reality achievement, of ambition and public recognition. We recognize the anxious urgency to find a hasty way out of the intolerable state of narcissistic despair. But we look in vain for conflictual anxiety as an indicator of an intrapsychic struggle. Owing to this constellation, the solution is still sought as essentially external; therefore, constant demands are made in the early stage of therapy for a sweeping interpretation, an instantaneous revelation of the pathogenic childhood experience, a suggestion or some advice, a formula or a trick, according to the patient's naïve or sophisticated notion of therapy. Whenever such a request is fulfilled, the adolescent feels momentarily better, he is more hopeful and happier. This reaction is in conformity with the accustomed maintenance of self-esteem established in his childhood.

The fact that tension is not structured and organized in terms of psychic conflict points to the direction in which initial therapy has to move, namely, to bring about the experience and tolerance of conflict. In other words, therapy has to help the young man to reach the adolescent conflict proper. Toward this end two therapeutic intentions prevail: (1) to increase tension tolerance, and (2) to expose the narcissistic defenses through critical self-observation and introspection. This therapeutic endeavor makes it imperative for the therapist to abstain from any "deep" or "id" interpretations because they would be only exploited by the narcissistic defense system. The exploitation might be paraphrased by the patient's saying: "Ah—now I know why—so this problem is settled." The euphoric state that follows soon dissipates into disappointment and blaming the therapist because, after all, nothing has happened and nothing has changed. It is therefore imperative that the therapist divest himself of all forms of imputed omniscience and magical powers, which are so reassuring to this kind of adolescent patient. In doing so, the therapist puts himself in direct opposition to the maternal image which was the provider of narcissistic gratification by letting the child share in her greatness. It is most irritating to the adolescent when the therapist replies to his anxious questioning with an "I do not know," but, on the other hand, the patient begins to respect his courage, honesty, and incorruptibility. We must not forget that the adolescent has retained a readiness and needfulness for identification with an adult who possesses those personality attributes in which he desires to share

and which are supportive and useful in terms of developmental progression. The therapist's aim is to replace infantile sharing and merging by identification, to replace the
search for external sources of self-esteem by the discovery of
inner resourcefulness. In fact the exploration and testing,
the validation and differentiation of this resourcefulness as
reflected in the conduct of daily life constitute a large part
of the therapeutic work.

During this initial phase of work it becomes apparent
that the adolescent welcomes the therapist's looking
through the facade of his pretentions and illusions. To illustrate: A man of twenty had attended a lecture and related
all the stupid questions people had asked the lecturer.
When the therapist inquired as to the question he himself
had asked, he replied with complete composure: "None.
What has that to do with it?" When the therapist insisted
on the pertinence of this question in light of his critical attack on his fellow listeners, the patient became flustered
and confessed to his total ignorance and lack of comprehension of the subject matter under discussion, which supposedly was in the field of his special interest. He volun-
teered the fact that his sophisticated and educated conversations were usually based on ideas he had skillfully picked
up from other people without any firsthand knowledge of
the subject. He had not read a book since his first year in
high school, but had cleverly managed to get the reputation
of being one of the well-read students. This comment suf-
fices to illustrate how the narcissistic defense was brought
to the awareness of the patient in one particular instance.
Whether the relinquishment of reading is related to a
childhood conflict does not concern us at this stage of
therapy when the focus is on the disruption of the narcissistic defense system and the exposure of the ego to the experience of tension and conflict.

Whenever stereotyped, archaic ego attitudes are relinquished, new attempts at mastery are tried which are

summarized under the general term of experimentation. This experimentation involves the testing of reality, of the self, and of the interaction between both. In this sense, experimentation and progressive differentiation of the self-image go hand in hand and bring about a more effective functioning. Increasingly adequate mastery becomes a new source—we might say, a legitimate one—of narcissistic gratification. Consequently, the maintenance of the narcissistic balance becomes increasingly determined by self-regulatory processes instead of remaining dependent on external influences. For instance, it is no longer necessary to manipulate the impression other people form about one and then take their opinions as the reflection of one's real self.

During this early phase of therapy we observe that the life of the adolescent becomes enriched by purposeful experimentation; the scope of autonomous ego functions becomes enlarged, while infantile strivings gradually acquire an ego-dystonic quality and become isolated from the executive branch of the ego. Reality achievement and tension tolerance make this progress possible. Concomitantly, the pathogenic determinants become more focused and an organized neurotic disturbance takes shape (see Chapter 16). The patient experiences conflict and anxiety. This development is an indication that psychoanalysis is the next step in therapy. The adolescent's more competent conduct of life, which often comprises economic independence, will make analysis feasible as a long-term undertaking. The change from a therapy in which the transference was used rather actively to a form of therapy in which the transference neurosis is the intrinsic vehicle for personality restructuring often makes a change of therapist desirable but not mandatory. Should, however, the adolescent's integrative capacity, which has been liberated by the treatment of the stalemate of prolonged adolescence, be sufficient to accomplish the final consolidation of late adolescence, then the task of therapy has been completed at this point.

A decision as to the discontinuance of therapy at the end of the first phase described above depends on the balance between the affective mobility gained by the first phase of therapy and the unyielding strength of fixations not affected by it. Should it become evident that the forces which were originally accountable for the condition of prolonged adolescence continue unremittingly to assert themselves, then we have to admit that despite the often impressive improvement in functioning, a progression to emotional maturity remains an illusory expectation; in that case, psychoanalysis must carry the therapeutic work to completion. In other cases, the first phase of therapy effects the relinquishment of the narcissistic defenses of prolonged adolescence, and mobilizes as well as channels the affective resourcefulness of the adolescent to a point from which he can realistically carry forward the adolescent process and bring it unaided to a close.

Chapter 4

Psychological Counseling
of College Students

Our increasing insight into personality disturbances and the increasing recognition of the need for services equipped to deal with these problems have both brought to the fore a new field of therapeutic endeavor which I will call "psychological counseling." In this chapter, an attempt is made to differentiate its scope, function, and technique from other well-established counseling services—vocational, educational, and others.

Psychological counseling deals with individual problem situations which are largely due to irrational factors, where rational solutions (talking it over) or cathartic expression (talking it out) prove inconsequential and of little help. Of this group, only those individuals will gain from psychological counseling who have not yet established a rigid, repetitive, neurotic pattern, but are rather acutely overwhelmed by inner and outer pressures. Unprepared or inadequate to cope with such pressures, the individual resorts to self-protective reactions. Such reactive conditions are most frequent when maturational strains, instinctual as well as environmental, are the rule rather than the exception, namely, during early childhood and puberty. Obviously,

First published in *American Journal of Orthopsychiatry*, 16: 571-580, 1946.

maturational conflicts and crises are crucial periods for the onset of neurotic difficulties.

Among older adolescents, the college student is in a position peculiarly his own. He has postponed, either willingly or under moral or social pressures, the full attainment of adulthood for the sake of educational advantages or social prestige. This protracted adolescence, with its unavoidable effects on the psychic economy of the individual, is still a stepchild of psychiatry and mental hygiene. The problems created by the artificial prolongation of a maturational period affect almost every student at one point of his college career. Most students can cope with this situation, but an appreciable number undergo personality disturbances, some of which are at this time amenable to correction. This group represents a strategic area where preventive psychiatry might well concentrate its efforts.

With such considerations in mind, Brooklyn College organized a psychological counseling service in 1941. It had become evident that its student body—like any student body—presented personality disturbances which often interfered seriously with college work. This situation became a particular concern when a student of promising intellectual ability was unable to function adequately and seemed doomed to academic mediocrity or failure. To become acquainted with the run-of-the-mill student, I devoted part of my time to routine counseling work related to dropping of courses, excessive absences, changes of program, midterm warnings, etc. I came to realize how often such situations are indications of a remote disturbance, and how effective counseling can be if it concentrates on minor symptomatic difficulties as soon as they make their appearance.

Since the psychological counselor is dependent on referrals, it is necessary that others understand his work, his function, and his responsibilities in order to make use of his services. For this purpose I gave seminars to the faculty and to the members of the Department of Student Personnel

over a one-year period. The discussions with the faculty were
rewarding. I found that case presentations best illustrated
which students should be referred and what could reasonably be expected from psychological counseling in terms of
change or improvement. While some students showed improvement within weeks, others required years to show any
signs of growth.

At the time of this writing, psychological counseling is
an established service in the college, and the medical office,
the deans, and the faculty request advice from the
psychological counselor in all cases which lie within his
province. Records are kept confidential; they are not included in the student's folder and are not available to any-
one.

Cases which come to the attention of the psychological
counselor are as diversified as might be expected. Gross
mental disturbances are referred to a clinic or psychiatrist
with the consent and assistance which the student's family
must provide. Neurotic conditions are, if possible, also referred for psychotherapy or psychoanalysis. This leaves us
with a bulk of disturbances which do not fit into any of the
customary classifications of personality disorders. In fact,
when I tried to classify 387 cases, I was appalled to find
that classification would indeed be fitting them into a pro-
crustean bed, for the sake of nosology. I began to realize
that I was dealing with case material which was basically
different from cases seen in a mental hygiene or child guidance clinic; the difference being that no definite symptom
complex had developed in these cases. A dysfunction had
made its appearance in a limited field of the student's life,
which rendered college an unsatisfying or unsatisfactory
experience.

Complaints of this kind rarely come to the attention of
psychiatric or mental hygiene services outside the college,
because the individual is still in the state of seeking solutions by managing the environment or by isolating his con-

flicts in the process of symptom formation. It is precisely at this stage of personality disturbance, when a maturational conflict is acted out rather directly in a displaced form, when the symptom has not yet crystallized into a symptom complex, that psychological counseling is called for. This type of personality disturbance is, in fact, the legitimate field of psychological counseling.

In an attempt to group the problems which have come to my attention over the years, I find none of the customary classifications based on the dynamics of the disturbance useful, but have to resort to the overt complaint or difficulty as presented by the student. The following types of problems are met with regularity: (1) the student who cannot study, who complains of inability to concentrate; (2) the student who is lonely, who cannot make friends; (3) the student who is afraid of examinations, who is unable to speak in class; (4) the student without any purpose or vocational aim; (5) the habitual evader, obstructionist, and complainer; (6) the student in acute conflict with his family; (7) the student with a physical defect; (8) special problems of veterans.[1]

Cases in this state of limited dysfunction can necessarily only receive remedial attention where psychological counseling services are intramural, that is, available within the educational institution. Only then are referrals made early and easily before too many faculty members have tried their latest reading in psychology on the student. Whenever such services are made part of a medical office or a student health service (which is primarily for physical attention), a psychological barrier is erected which tends to eliminate those cases that would profit most from psychological counseling. In addition, it must be recognized that referral to a clinic or psychiatrist is for the college a drastic step, and for the student a frightening one. No one in any educational institution will take the responsibility for it except where

[1] Here I refer to World War II veterans; however, veterans of any war present their unique problems of readjustment to civilian life at a given historical epoch.

the need is obvious. If states of limited dysfunction, of diffuse disturbances of concentration, memory, interpersonal relations, etc., receive remedial attention at the time they become observable and are scrutinized as to their character, the preventive effect of such services will undoubtedly be worth the effort and many times the cost.

An additional advantage of intramural service lies in the ease with which the contact with the counselor can be renewed at any time. In most therapeutic situations we are accustomed to think in terms of time limitations, of termination of contact at a given point of therapeutic achievement. The cumulative process of psychological counseling as described here presents technical problems and therapeutic possibilities which have not yet been fully explored. The fact that the contact with the counselor can be renewed easily at any time has a direct influence on technique. Difficulties can be met progressively: one semester the overt problem might be academic, the next semester sexual, later vocational, etc. Counseling at each time lays the foundation for the progression to the next step of work.

My experience with this type of counseling has impressed me with the fact that the resolution of an acute conflict (e.g., "I can't do my homework because I can never be as good as my father thinks I am") stimulates an integration of the new insight or growth experience which renders the personality capable of moving to a higher level of self-differentiation. This gain in "affective mobility" (*mobilité affective*) as the result of new insight emphasizes and delineates conflicts of which the individual was unaware, and may even lead to resuming counseling. The time an individual needs to integrate therapeutic or growth experiences varies from months to years; often counseling is suspended for that time. The fact that the counseling process as here described never ends but can be resumed at any time seems particularly important for counseling which gravitates around maturational conflicts, as is the case in most of the work with college students. So unorthodox a technique immediately raises the problem of the transference and how it operates in a cumulative counseling process. This problem will be taken up later in detail.

At this point a case illustration will serve to present some typical aspects of psychological counseling. Stanley, an eighteen-year-old sophomore, was referred by his class advisor to the psychological counselor because he complained of feelings of apathy and inability to concentrate. Stanley ranks as a student of superior intelligence. His record is good but uneven; his work has declined of late. He is eager to receive help.

Stanley doubts his intellectual abilities and any decision he makes. He compares himself compulsively with others and asks himself if he is normal. Following the wishes of his family, he started college with the intention of taking over his father's successful business. After he had failed in essential courses prerequisite for the planned career, he decided against it. Now, a year later, Stanley has found a field of his own interest, but feels he cannot be sure that his decision is valid. He wonders whether he should not give up his own desires and follow his father's wishes. Apathy, distraction, absent-mindedness, and apprehensiveness are at the moment dominant. He asks himself: What shall I study? On what shall I concentrate? In what am I talented?

As a child, Stanley was promising, intelligent, and greatly admired by his parents. He stated at first that he was an only child, but admitted after four months that he has an older sister who has been in a mental institution for a number of years. His mother overpowered him with loving possessiveness and inhibited his masculine development. Passive and submissive tendencies were overcompensated by hyperactivity, but he derived no pleasure from it. Of late this hyperactivity has been replaced with a feeling of having no purpose and no future. The desire and fear of taking over his father's business resulted in a state of indecision and apathy. A factor in intensifying this fear is the mental breakdown his sister suffered when she was his present age. At that time she decided, against her parents' wishes, to enter a career of her own choosing. Both Stanley and his sister chose careers in artistic fields. The fear of insanity as a natural consequence of disobeying parental wishes contributed to Stanley's state of indecision. Shortly before he started being counseled, he read books on abnormal psychology until this reading became too disturbing and he "put it all out of [his] mind."

Stanley's disturbance is the result of an inner conflict which has as its conscious and unconscious components the fear of taking over the father's role. The desire to do so represents in its ambivalence the typical recrudescence of the Oedipus conflict on the adolescent level. But we must not overlook the equally strong passive and submissive tendencies. As a defense against these tendencies, Stanley has forced himself into masculine self-assertive behavior which, consequently, is not wholly genuine in its quality. For his weakness in the present struggle Stanley blames his mother because she was not strict enough with him when he was a child. The parents', especially the mother's, boundless trust in him as a child gave him a feeling of omnipotence which helped him in being successful in school without exerting real effort. In his present crisis he has lost this feeling of unquestionable competence, and with it, his self-confidence. His present attitude of ignoring his mother, his apparent indifference to both parents' concern about his future, in brief, his lack of any feeling tone at home, combined with his intense, almost frantic preoccupation with his normality and vocational choice, indicate that he has displaced his conflict with the family into the sphere of academia and college life.

Through the counseling process conscious material which Stanley has carefully kept isolated becomes linked together; for example, the fear of insanity in relation to an autonomous choice and his seeking of reassurance with regard to his normality are brought into awareness. The transference becomes instrumental in loosening up emotional rigidity and provides a new affective experience which has a twofold effect: it helps to strengthen a weak masculine identification and lends support to his inadequate ego in regaining a position of control and objectivity. He can, for example, for the first time in two years, inform his family of his vocational desires. Eventually, he is able to pursue his newly gained interest with less anxiety, becomes freer in making contacts with people, and finally begins to recognize his sexual problems. During the course of counseling, Stanley's difficulties in concentration decrease (he passes the semester with a B average), and he becomes more active and feels less apathetic. The compulsive comparison of himself with others, the doubting of his decisions gradually declines, although it does not disappear altogether.

The process of counseling can be summed up as follows. An emotional stalemate has been broken, even though the basic conflict continues to exist. What has been achieved is the regained capacity to act, to make decisions, to be less morbidly introspective and therefore receptive to new experiences, and to give looser play to inhibited affects. (Stanley was seen thirty-nine times over a period of three semesters.)

A follow-up after ten months shows that Stanley has retained his ability to act, to make contacts with people, to pursue his interest, and that he has maintained a very good academic record. Inadequacy feelings in relation to heterosexual adjustment are still present, but the self-doubt and the indecision in relation to vocational choice, interest, and ambitions are markedly reduced. His activities still bear the stigma of earlier compensatory hyperactivity and still contain compulsive features, but they are better organized, more realistic and stable, and more socially integrated. Among other things, he has founded a club in the field of his creative endeavor.

Why was this case considered suitable for psychological

counseling? In answering this question I will simultaneously clarify some of the theoretical concepts related to
psychological counseling. To start with, we have to remind
ourselves that each personality disturbance has different
layers in terms of which it can be described, evaluated, and
influenced.

In Stanley's case there was at the bottom of his disturbance an emotional conflict which interfered with adequate
ego functioning. When faced with the necessity for emancipation from the family, his ego was too weak to stand up in
the ensuing struggle. Two characteristic ego reactions to a
maturational crisis could be observed: ego restriction and
ego regression. Both these defenses are protective measures:
ego restriction serves to ward off anxiety through inhibition
of function, and ego regression to master anxiety through
archaic ego expressions. Ego restriction was apparent in
Stanley's failure in the courses prerequisite to entering his
father's business. (He failed despite the fact that he had
scored in the tenth decile in this particular field on the
scholastic aptitude test administered at college entrance.)
Ego regression was apparent in Stanley's mistaking similarity for identity (sister's illness) and in his use of will power
and thinking power (magical thinking).

Although reality factors, such as his sister's breakdown
at his age and the father's tireless wooing for his son's submission, were responsible for the reactive state described,
these factors could not be held solely responsible for
Stanley's condition. The recrudescence of infantile conflicts,
clearly the Oedipus complex, determined his reaction to a
disturbing present. In addition, Stanley's condition was affected by maturational conflicts in relation to adolescent
psychosexual development. Although he was able to maintain an outward equilibrium up to late adolescence, the increasing pressure of instinctual and environmental demands
overtaxed the resourcefulness of the ego. Ego inadequacy
was the point on which the counseling effort concentrated,

and not the infantile conflict which was the source of the present predicament.

Psychological counseling does not attempt to resolve unconscious infantile conflicts; in fact, it carefully avoids entering this sphere, which is the realm of psychoanalysis. Psychological counseling deals with the derivatives of these conflicts in terms of ego reactions. In its interpretive aspect it restricts itself to the realm of the ego. In Stanley's case it brought to awareness the relatedness of isolated facts, some of which came only very slowly to the surface. While dissociated conscious material could be related, an insight into ego defenses was gained through the interpretation of omissions, contradictions, denials, forgetfulness, etc. All these efforts would have been fruitless without a purposeful use of the transference. Here the unconscious conflicts which were recognizable during the counseling process found a mode of expression and communication where the direct verbal expression would obviously have been inadequate.

In this connection I should like to mention that every personality disturbance is in some intrinsic way related to unresolved relationship conflicts. It is thus obvious that the relationship in psychological counseling, which can hardly escape from developing into a transference in the proper sense of the term, is a most valuable, if delicate, instrument in dealing with adolescent personality disturbances. Depending on the case, either interpretation or a discriminative, tactful use of the transference, or both, will provide that focal experience which facilitates the regaining of the lost or arrested affective mobility.

In the case here reported, the counselor had to steer away from a repetition of the parental pattern. During the first months, for example, Stanley showed an eagerness to understand himself, an objectivity in looking at the problem, a seemingly mature attitude, which might well have been mistaken as a favorable sign. In its rigidity and detachment, this attitude betrayed its defensive character. It was his way of warding off passive and submissive tendencies in relation to the counselor. Situations, such as the counselor discussing with Stanley rather critically the products of his creative efforts, instead of accepting them indiscriminately as attempts at independence, strengthened his ego by lessening the fear of passivity which loomed dangerously in any situation of unconditional and complete acceptance. The transference experience provided an opportunity for him to express positive and negative emotions without, however, being able to re-experience the family situation due to the counselor's intentionally critical but benign attitude. In this respect, the relationship to the counselor was different from any in his past. It was an extension of the past into the present which, through the mediation of the counselor, exerted a modifying influence on an emotional pattern still in flux.[2]

This use of the transference differs in principle from the use of the transference in psychoanalysis. As is well known, the latter transference serves as a screen on which infantile relationship conflicts are projected. The development of a transference neurosis is in fact the precondition for psychoanalytic therapy. Psychological counseling, in contrast, prevents at all cost a transference neurosis from developing, because it is not prepared to cope with the consequences. It is well to remember that transference phenomena will become manifest during psychological counseling regardless of the counselor's doings. He cannot

[2]Clara Thompson (1945) has expressed a similar idea about the limited use of the transference: "For example, a person who has been dominated by a forbidding father presents without insight a submissive attitude to the therapist, probably based on fear. The fact that the therapist is actually more permissive and tolerant means that the patient finds himself in a more favorable milieu and can develop to a certain point, although nothing is done about his tendency to be dominated. He is still a submissive person, but he has, as it were, put himself under the guidance of a benevolent tyrant, and in his efforts to please the new father he may achieve some worth-while growth for himself. He will probably never become independent, but he will be able to have more freedom under this authority than under the old one" (p. 276).

escape from becoming involved. It is often questioned whether active or passive, directive or nondirective counseling is preferable. In the light of the foregoing, the attitude of the counselor ceases to be a matter of principle, but becomes a variable dependent on the affects in operation and the counseling purpose dominant at the moment. These factors alone determine to what degree and in what manner the counselor participates in the counseling process.

As has been said before, not every personality disturbance that comes to the attention of the psychological counselor is necessarily a case for psychological counseling. There are countraindications which are of particular importance because their recognition will prevent both waste of counselor's time and, even more important, a negative therapeutic experience on the student's part, which might make therapy unacceptable to him for some time. In an appreciable number of cases, therefore, psychological counseling consists solely in making some form of psychotherapy acceptable to the student. The counselor thus avoids participating in the student's maneuvers to depreciate an existing difficulty. (Such maneuvers, which simulate progress and improvement, are often striking. One student, for example, overcame her depression and hysterical conversion symptom as soon as the counselor mentioned psychiatric help.)

Evaluation of a complaint or symptom is necessary before psychological counseling can prognosticate its adequacy. This evaluation must take into account the transitory and permanent elements of the given symptom complex; in other words, it has to assess the maturational (instinctual) and environmental as well as the neurotic or psychotic components of the maladjustment. Where symptoms have assumed neurotic rigidity and repetitiveness, psychological counseling will not bring about any fundamental improvement. Where, however, the conflict has not been fully internalized, and the so-called symptoms are to a large measure due to acutely menacing and aggravating pressures from without (environment) and within (id, superego), there psychological counseling will prove effective. At no point is it overlooked that unconscious conflicts play their part in any personality disturbance, a realization that determines the limited objective with which psychological counseling approaches its task.

The following case will illustrate a situation where psychological counseling was contraindicated. David was referred by the medical office because he impressed the examiner during a routine checkup as tense, nervous, and apprehensive. David talked freely to the psychological counselor; in fact, he enjoyed the interview "more than I had anticipated" and readily arranged a time for his return. David considers himself an introvert who has little contact with people, nor does he desire such contacts. He lives in ideas, feels that he is superior to others, and will not share their "base and primitive interests" like movies, sports, or girls. He has become so used to imaginary company that he can easily dispense with real people. The kindred spirits in whose close company he moves includes Nietzsche, Rimbaud, Baudelaire, Kirkegaard, Proust, and others. He argues that "they all lived in a shell." His only complaint is that he feels "totally unproductive." He is not concerned about his social isolation, his disinterest in and remoteness from people. He feels misunderstood at home. "I am an anomaly in my family."

David is an only child. Overprotected by his mother, he was never allowed to play unsupervised with other children until the age of eight. He can still recall standing behind the front gate of the family house, with clean hands and creased knee pants, looking at the outside world and the free children. Although David liked to talk to the counselor, his attitude remained the same through several interviews: distant, colorless, friendly but slightly condescending, verbose, and repetitious. He had to convince the counselor that he, David, was like one of those many "misunderstood and neurotic geniuses." "I am like them" was his stereotypic explanation. His isolation was his distinction and proof of superiority. Academically he succeeded extremely well.

This case was considered unfit for psychological counseling because the conflict was totally internalized and fantasy constructions had replaced any interpersonal relationship. The student's history and present symptoms indicated a serious neurotic disturbance (obsessive-compulsive neurosis), possibly with schizoid trends. Through periodic follow-up interviews the counselor kept an eye on the student, waiting until he would express the need for psychiatric help, which was explained to him on several occasions.

The line of demarcation separating the field of psychological counseling from bordering therapeutic disciplines is not as neat and clear-cut as one would desire. In the first place, the field is new and still undefined; in addition, it should be remembered that adolescents present symptom complexes which would be considered far more serious if they appeared at another age. Adolescents show reactions to maturational stress which are often difficult to differentiate at first sight from neurotic or psychotic conditions. Sylvan Keiser (1944) has stated clearly what experience has taught the clinician who works with adolescents: "We believe that many benign psychopathological reactions of the adolescent period are incorrectly diagnosed as schizophrenic. A good number represent reactive states dependent on the recrudescence of infantile conflicts occurring during adolescence" (p. 24). However, information about the student's life, the duration of the overt conflict or the symptom, the degree of alloplastic ego activity in conjunction with transference phenomena will aid in an evaluation of the acute problem for which the student seeks help and will determine whether or not psychological counseling is indicated. This decision can usually not be reached before a number of exploratory interviews have taken place.

Psychological counseling as presented here is based on the application of psychoanalytic psychology. With its special technique, it must be based on a coherent psychological system or theory which provides the counselor with the conceptual tools for the understanding of the dynamic and economic problems involved in each case. The fact that the counselor must differentiate between those clients who belong in his domain of competence, and those who need other types of help and therefore are better off without any psychological counseling, raises many questions with regard to training and supervision. Besides the technical training in psychology, I believe that the psychological counselor should have undergone psychoanalysis as a professional prerequisite for this type of work. Extensive supervision on the job is another essential aspect of the training in this field. Such a cursory statement requires elaboration, but the purpose of this chapter lies in another direction and, therefore, the problem of training is only mentioned in passing.

In summarizing, it might be said that the protracted adolescence of college youth tends to precipitate personality disturbances of the reactive type, which interfere seriously with the successful life, academically and socially, of the student. Such maturational disturbances are detected at an early stage only where psychological counseling services are intramural and a simple but effective referral system is set up.

Chapter 5

The Split Parental Imago in Adolescent Social Relations

An Inquiry into Group Psychology

A Basic Assumption

To become human is predicated on human contact and interaction. While the morphology of the human species is the result of an evolutionary process, the psychological development of each individual is essentially determined and stabilized by a social process, by a system that welds organism and surround together. The contraposition of individual and environment tends either to overstate the individual's independence from his social matrix or to understate the dependence of the individual on the social envelope, be this the family or the wider social ambience. This fact has become eminently clear from infant research which has taught us to conceive of the mother-infant unit as a bonding of infant and surround or, in other words, as a system (Sander et al., 1975). Epigrammatically, Winnicott has expressed this thought by saying: "There is no such thing as a baby" (James, 1970, p. 81).

Abraham A. Brill Memorial Lecture, presented at the New York Academy of Medicine, New York City, 1975. First published in *The Psychoanalytic Study of the Child*, 31: 7-33. New Haven: Yale University Press, 1976.

Individual and Social Psychology

The perceptual discreteness of subject and object, of observer and the observed, of individual and group, easily obscures the intrinsic points of their indivisibility. The student of human behavior could not fail to notice the idiosyncratic perceptions of various individuals within an apparently homogeneous surround. The ensuing dualistic point of view is reflected in separate conceptual frameworks, each with its own descriptive as well as explanatory model. As a result, individual and social psychology have pursued their separate investigations. This dichotomy is conspicuous in the field of psychoanalysis. Yet, the importance of the social and physical environment for the development of man's mind has always found full acknowledgment in psychoanalytic theory. This recognition cannot be stated more clearly than in Freud's own words: "We have repeatedly had to insist on the fact that the ego owes its origin as well as the most important of its acquired characteristics to its relation to the real external world" (1940, p. 201).

If we contemplate the awesome fatefulness social behavior—in its destructive and creative forms—plays in human affairs, we may wish that psychoanalysis, as a general psychology, had contributed more to the understanding of group behavior. As early as 1944, Heinz Hartmann expressed the belief that sociological problems could be studied through individual analysis and deplored the paucity of such explorations by practicing psychoanalysts.

The first systematic exploration of the social and physical environment in relation to psychic development was carried out in the study of infants. The detailed observations of the normative sequences from primitive to differentiated object relations and their influence on the formation of the self helped the analyst to understand more fully the regressive movements in children, adolescents, and adults. The contemporary, extreme forms of adolescent social behavior force the inquiring mind of every adult toward a fuller comprehension of these social phenomena. Analytic contributions to the study of adolescent social psychology have been scanty and sketchy; they have never merged smoothly or lastingly with the main body of psychoanalytic knowledge, despite brilliant beginnings made here and there.

One eminent obstacle in the pursuit of adolescent social and group psychology is to be found in the psychoanalytic recapitulation theory of adolescence. This theory states in essence that oedipal object relations are relived in adolescence; in the process, infantile libidinal and aggressive dependencies are given up and replaced by extrafamilial object involvements with age-mates and by new identifications within the wider world of personalities, values, ideas, ambitions, or, generally speaking, by mature ego-ideal formation. The recapitulation theory postulates that the Oedipus complex is resolved, for better or for worse, at the end of early childhood and reappears, essentially unchanged, at adolescence. A renewed resolution is now sought in consonance with the sexual maturation of puberty. It has been my impression that the resolution of the Oedipus complex at the end of the phallic phase is normally only a partial one. In other words, there is merely a suspension of some oedipal issues, a détente which characterizes the latency period. It is therefore a continuation and not only a recapitulation of the oedipal conflict that we observe at adolescence (Blos, 1962). The social locus for the actualization of both recapitulation and continuation shifts with increasing but relentless crescendo away from the family and into the group life of sexual maturants, usually referred to as peers.

It is, of course, no accident that much of what has been written by psychoanalysts on group psychology is related to adolescence. This age represents, par excellence, the stage in life when exclusive group relations among peers assume,

conspicuously and dramatically, a preoccupation and al-
legiance that brush all other concerns aside with passionate
single-mindedness. Such global characteristics of behavior
do not lend themselves to psychoanalytic investigations. In
turning to group-psychological issues of adolescence, I follow
a time-honored analytic principle that seeks to reduce
global behavioral phenomena to their discrete components
for detailed study. We know that one adolescent behavioral
item, such as rebelliousness, can serve a multitude of functions (Waelder, 1930). This ever-changing function of one
single facet of social behavior and its unpredictable alternation in valence render adolescent social behavior fickle and
capricious.

It is far from my intention to submit a comprehensive
psychoanalytic group psychology. I intend to report observations and ideas from adolescent analyses that have a bearing on group-psychological issues. I emphasize this fact because group-psychological data and their theoretical formulations are usually based on the findings of a participant
observer who is engaged in group interaction, be this a
street gang or a sophisticated therapy group. My own
group-psychological investigation, in contrast, lies embedded in the analytic treatment situation and therefore represents one particular aspect, equal in importance to all
others, of the patient's mental life as it unfolds during
psychoanalytic work.

The Beginnings of a Psychoanalytic Social Psychology

A word about Freud's "Group Psychology and the Analysis
of the Ego" (1921) is called for at this point. When Freud
entered the field of social psychology with the publication of
"Totem and Taboo" (1913b), he was struck by the fact that
he had ventured into a new bridge-building venture and
into the most far-reaching speculative thought. The discreteness of the two disciplines—individual and social

psychology—was for Freud clearly evident, yet their essential complementarity was equally apparent to him. He expressed the disquieting recognition of their separateness and fusion in a letter to Ferenczi written in 1911 (November 30), at the time he formulated his concepts of social psychology in "Totem and Taboo." He wrote, "With all that I feel as if I had intended only to start a little liaison and then discovered that at my time of life I have to marry a new wife" (Jones, 1955, p. 352). This apprehension about conceptual monogamy is still with us. It was of little consequence that Freud affirmed the homologous foundations on which individual and social psychology rest by saying, "In the individual's mental life someone else is invariably involved, as a model, as an object, as a helper, as an opponent; and so from the very first individual psychology, in this extended but entirely justifiable sense of the words, is at the same time social psychology as well" (1921, p. 69).

Freud's broadening of psychoanalytic psychology was a step of singular significance. Of course, Freud attempted at the time to apply the libido theory to group psychology by defining the group within the dynamic context of leader and group members. He arrived at the following formulation: "*A primary group of this kind is a number of individuals who have put one and the same object in the place of their ego ideal and have consequently identified themselves with one another in their ego*" (1921, p. 116). We should remember that at the time of this formulation, ego ideal and superego were used interchangeably. What, in 1921, was conveyed by the term "ego ideal" we would, in present-day terminology, attribute to both the superego and the infantile ego ideal (see Chapter 15). The latter would account for the regressive nature of group behavior, a characteristic which Le Bon (1895) and McDougall (1920) have described in detail and to which Freud has added the dimension of intrapsychic cathectic shifts. The representative groups Freud chose to exemplify his thesis were church and army. This limited focus necessarily excluded innumerable types of groups. Redl (1942) has contributed greatly to the structural differentiation of groups, many of which have no leader and lie outside of Freud's model. It is conceivable that Freud's conceptual restriction to one type of group formation accounts for the fact that his social psychology became a landmark monument rather than a launching platform for studies in this field.

As so often happens, contemporary social perplexities force our attention onto old issues. More recently, large-scale social dislocations, in conjunction with endemic, irrational behavior among the young, have posed the question of a deleterious influence which social institutions, mores, and morals might exert on the personality of the adolescent. The workings of these social phenomena are by no means clear to us; however, there are indications that they cannot be relegated solely to ontogenetic history and its reductivist logic. The ensuing questions—broad, urgent, and disquieting—beseech us; I shall return to them later.

The Split Parental Imago[1]

It is a common observation that adolescents have the tendency to see people and the world in "black or white." Whatever the opposites are, they remain, for the time being, irreconcilable, segmented, and absolute. Modulation or compromise is taken as a sign of weakness or insincerity. The image of the self is not exempt from this radical way of ordering the outside world, regardless of the violence it does to perception and reason. The adolescent is intermittently

---

[1]The word "imago" is infrequently used at the present time in the psychoanalytic literature. Its usefulness, however, is not exhausted. Since the clarity of this term and what it signifies is essential for the understanding of this chapter, a definition is in order at this point: "Unconscious prototypical figure which orientates the subject's way of apprehending others; it is built up on the basis of the first real and phantasied relationships within the family environment" (Laplanche and Pontalis, 1973, p. 211).

cognizant of the fact that the radical division into opposites is somewhat unreal and not fully supportable, yet he finds himself unable to heed such advice. With all his might he tries to contradict Heraclitus' epigram: "You can never step twice into the same river." It appears as if the adolescent were saying, "I know that the world is not actually run that way, but for the time being, it has to be as I say; I have to start from the beginning and put together a new order, my own order in my own world." In this state of mind the adolescent attributes antithetical qualities to objects in a primitive way as, for example, the "good" or the "bad."

We know that originally the "good" and "bad" mother is not the identical object in the mind of the child. Each is separate and discrete, a reification of sensations along the pleasure-pain spectrum. The voices of memory and discriminatory cognition are not yet audible. Only with the formation of object and self-constancy is the synthesis of part objects feasible; the whole object can then emerge. However, the potentiality that this process may become reversed under stress is never totally extinguished during life; it must be considered part of the human condition. Mahler, Pine, and Bergman (1975) have commented along these lines; they state that the struggles of splitting point to "many uniquely human problems and dilemmas—problems that sometimes are never completely resolved during the entire life cycle" (p. 100).

In adolescent analysis we often attribute to a conflict of ambivalence what turns out to be of preambivalent origin. The transient adolescent dialectic of "either-or" reaches back to preverbal signals of "no" and "yes." The cephalogyric motion and gesture of "no," described by Spitz (1957), makes its debut around the fifteenth month of life. Another, even earlier, root of basic polarities lies in the symbiotic stage of infancy, when the child not only derives a sense of omnipotence by sharing with the mother her all-powerful state, but is concomitantly in constant danger of losing this vital source of well-being. The elevated position of the mother is maintained first by splitting and later by idealization. The reality distortions, inherent in both, reappear at adolescence in the transient idealization of self and object. Eventually, this idealization, when tempered by reason and judgment, becomes deflected from self and object, finding its permanent abode in the mature ego ideal (see Chapter 15).

The highest order of absolutes and opposites in the antithetical world image of adolescence is to be found in the polarity of male and female, active and passive, inside and outside, me and you, good and bad. These basic emblematics attach themselves to the representational world. Thus, for example, a certain female adolescent may conceive of a scientific book or simply of any big volume as male, while novels or art books carry a female designation; similarly, daydreaming or off-time nibbling of food may be seen as female, while intellectual activity and physical exertion are considered male. The experience of the self within such global antitheses tends to promote extreme mood swings. The adolescent's tendency to polarization or intolerance of gradation and compromise is reflected in semantic characteristics of this age. For example, everybody (the self included) is either brilliant or stupid, exciting or boring, friendly or hostile, sexual or asexual, active or passive, good or bad, giving or greedy, attractive or ugly, creative or ordinary, turned inward or outward. There is never an "unfriendly" or "not so friendly" person or self. The qualifying prefix "un," which indicates gradations of meaning, is rarely, if ever, part of adolescent speech, unless savoir faire graciously conceals in public the raw extremes of emotion and thought.

In a general way, we are used to this kind of polarization from adolescent behavior. Anna Freud (1958) has referred to the "uncompromising adolescent," while I have used the term "adolescent totalism" in my writings (Blos, 1962).

These terms refer to a defensive process, such as oppositionalism and withdrawal, both of which constitute
normal characteristics of object relations during the second
individuation process of adolescence (Chapter 8). What we
observe here is part of a normative conflictual condition.
The polarization to which I refer in this presentation is genetically different because its roots lie in the preambivalent
stage of infancy when the split-object experience constitutes
a normative, preconflictual sensation of the immature
somatic and psychic organism.

Preamble to a Clinical Study

Before introducing a clinical illustration I must make a
general comment about the analysis of my late adolescent
patients. I have noticed that the stubborn perseverance of
the split parental imago becomes clearly evident and manifest only toward the terminal phase of analysis. By that
time the conflicts of ambivalence, oedipal and preoedipal,
the conflicts of sexual identity, and the reverberation of infantile trauma have been analyzed and worked through.
However, there remains a residue of inner disharmony that
surfaces periodically, precluding the final reconciliation of
opposites and in no way diminishing the exaggerated use of
absolutes in conceiving reality, object, and self in moments
of stress. It seems conceivable that these pockets of primitive modes of thought and reality testing are not amenable
to change or resolution in the same psychic realm of interpretive work where analysis has attained good therapeutic results. Evidently, the residual clinical phenomenon belongs to a genetic category that differs essentially from the
neurotic conflict with which it has to be linked up. The remaining pockets of primitive perception and thought can be
looked at as the rock-bottom residue of the early split-object
experience, a normative and not a defensive one, which has
been filtered out over the years of analysis from the neurot-

ic organization that precipitated the illness. Here I make a
distinction between a developmental and a conflictual component in personality dysfunction.

   The principle of causality implicit in genetic reasoning
does not apply equally in the realms of conflictual problems
and developmental vicissitudes. In fact, the classical
psychoanalytic intervention proves inadequate to the task
whenever a critical developmental incompleteness or dys-
chronicity within the forward movement toward earliest
psychic differentiation has established itself. A developmental lag is not necessarily, or primarily, due to an internal
conflict, but it can secondarily give rise to a conflict when
the growing child, or later the adolescent, can no longer ignore the consequences of the developmental encumbrance.
The child may turn to restorative devices in fantasy or action in order to maintain a tolerable narcissistic balance.
Minor or major distortions of reality are frequently apparent. The analyst's interpretive approach of helping the still
immature ego to become aware of defense and what is defended against proves ineffectual within these particular
areas of developmental immaturity, because no unconscious
conflictual determinant exists that would render the
maladaptive functioning a psychic stabilizer, nor does this
kind of stalemate support a secondary gain, as is the case in
neurotic symptom formation. Anna Freud (1974) has
clarified the distinction between developmental and conflictual pathology by saying, "so far as the developmental progress itself is defective or unbalanced due to either innate or
environmental conditions, we cannot expect interpretation
to undo the damage, even if it clarifies the past and may
help the child towards better ways of facing and coping with
its consequences" (p. 16).

   The demarcation between conflictual and developmental
pathology is usually not as clear-cut as the above description might imply, especially in patients whose analysis
coincides with exigent developmental tasks, as is the case in

adolescence. We know that conflictual psychopathology can throw developmental progression into disarray and confusion. The loosening of fixations through the analytic process will set development in motion again, even at a delayed schedule. This developmental activation requires environmental facilitation and support, in relation to which age-appropriate strivings, freed by therapeutic work, can exercise and practice their potential. We should be mindful of Piaget's (1954) words: "Maturation alone causes nothing; it merely determines the range of possibilities for any given level." Such environmental assistance is of greater import the younger the child and recedes into relative insignificance in the analysis of the older child and adolescent, when the higher levels of cognition, abstraction, and symbolic expression transpose the arena of action, actuality, and experience onto the mental stage and onto the therapeutic situation.

In late adolescent analysis we come across particular obstacles that must be accounted for by specific problems of development which have left a lasting imprint on mental life. What appears as a developmental deficit is quite often an aspect of normal development that has been adhered to beyond its timing; thus, anachronistic modes of functioning continue to exist alongside of normal phase-appropriate conflicts and their normal or abnormal resolutions. The developmental defects to which I allude in this context belong to the preoedipal period; their roots extend into the preverbal stage. One might ask the question, in view of the typical and normal adolescent phenomenology, whether such incompletenesses, gross or minute, in earliest structure formation do not universally make their reappearance at this age. I shall adduce below some linguistic characteristics of adolescence to support this view. The adolescent tendency to idealize or to condemn harks back—at least partially—to the early splitting mechanism which reaches a workable synthesis in the adolescent consolidation process. The task of deidealization is central to the adolescent process; in fact, adult personality formation is contingent on the completion of this task of psychic differentiation. What I have referred to as a typical developmental obstacle in late adolescent analysis represents, simultaneously, a phase-adequate regressive phenomenon. It represents the universal dilemma of adolescence. As we well know from experience, the word "reality" becomes a "dirty" word for adolescents in this state of regression. A similarity to the borderline patient is apparent, but this seems to me rather an analogous than a homologous likeness; long ago, Siegfried Bernfeld (1923) and, later Anna Freud (1936), alluded to one aspect of normal adolescence as resembling the state of an incipient psychosis.

Clinical Illustration

Various adaptations of analytic technique to the developmental stage of adolescence are practiced whether acknowledged or not. The validity of such digressions from the standard technique during childhood and its terminal stage, adolescence, is gauged by the maturational level of the ego and the degree of its dependency on the environment. These adaptations of technique should not be confused with parameters, which are dictated by the nature of the psychopathology or by extraordinary exigencies in the life of the adult patient. My personal style in adolescent analysis—and increasingly fewer cases lend themselves to this form of therapy—is one of adherence to the classical model. Within this setting it may happen that the analyst spontaneously makes a comment which evokes an extraordinary reaction in the patient, an event that often leads to a new and surprising insight for analyst and patient. What might look like a gratuitous benefit may well be due to an intuitive and unconsciously correct timing of an intervention.

A reaction of this nature was evoked by my comment to

a young woman, a late adolescent patient, when she entered the office wearing a strikingly colorful poncho. It touched my aesthetic sense as singularly beautiful and I said so. The patient, always articulate, reacted to this comment with a surprisingly long silence; finally, she explained that my comment had made her extremely anxious. She was taken totally by surprise—I had suddenly become "real" to her, frighteningly real like the monsters of her childhood nights. The sanctuary quality of the office was dispelled. Had my comment, like a surprise attack, aroused oedipal panic and flight? She knew that she had kept a segment of her inner reality apart from the analysis, thus keeping me uncontaminated by any of her ugly, selfish, mean, and voracious urges. She had always kept her boundless rages against me under reasonable control and speedily made amends by compliance. On this occasion, she spoke of an imaginary, but essential oneness with a "good" mother, in this instance the analyst. The perfection of the object could thus restore life and self to a harmonious and safe state in moments of need. She said to me, "I tried so hard to keep you a woman." The obvious oedipal implications of this incident represented, at this stage of her analysis, a defensive effort against the regression to the frightful world of the "good" and "bad" mother and, pari passu, the "good" and "bad" self. Her intercepted forward flight onto the oedipal level, the vagaries of which had been extensively analyzed, left her literally speechless. At the same time her mind became inundated by imagery—the form of preverbal mentation. She conjured up monsters, witches, and fairy godmothers; a powerful urge seized her to curl up on the couch and go to sleep. When the patient was struck by the fact that the "fairy-godmother" analyst and the "witch-monster" analyst had no either-or reality, but were, in various admixtures, the essence of personal existence and completeness, a new focus and movement invigorated the analytic work.

It is a most painful realization that the object world will

not shape itself in response to and in consonance with subjective needs whenever they arise. In fact, this realization is
ignored as long as is possible without precipitating a break
in the sense of reality. Michael Balint (1955) has described
this stage of treatment: "When finally settled in this second
phase, these patients feel as if they were wrapped up in
some cosy, warm, structureless darkness which envelops
them and protects them from the unsympathetic and unfriendly external world, represented quite often by the
analyst. To open their eyes in this stage means to destroy
the friendly darkness and to expose themselves to the unsympathetic, indifferent or possibly hostile external world of
separate objects" (p. 237).

Incidents occasioned by the patient herself, but similar
to the one mentioned above, interfered repeatedly with her
need to experience the analyst on the level of early splitting, to secure oneness with the good object. The partial developmental failure in the progression to "whole-object" representations had thrown a shadow on all subsequent developmental stages, which nevertheless remained open and
responsive to analytic work. In fact, only after the analytic
work had provided the patient with a firm foothold on the
oedipal level could the regression to earlier stages be ventured without panic of re-engulfment and loss of self. Then
it could be observed how the infantile splitting mechanism
gradually yielded in the transference to the stage of ambivalence and to the integration of antithetical emotional
states into whole-object relations; this advance facilitated
the tolerance for the imperfections in the object world. A
unification of the split self—the evil and the perfect—
followed in time. The changing relations between superego
and ego that occur alongside this synthesizing process speak
of the influence the residues of the early splitting
mechanism exert on superego functioning.

In my patient it was the resolution of the early
dichotomy that opened the way to the revisitation and reor-

ganization of the oedipal and pubertal conflicts which had so pathologically impeded her ego development. This phase in adolescent analysis often requires a transient, judicious interaction in preverbal communication through personalized gesture and speech. Later one can revert to that rigorous analytic work which originally facilitated the profound regression. At this point the door opens to a "reworking through"—if this paradoxical term is permissible—of those awarenesses, syntheses, and conflict resolutions which antedate, in the analysis, the regression to the stage of the split parental imagos. Once the patient is on this path of reworking through, the analytic objective of establishing ego continuity appears within reach. The present is relieved of the burden to repeat the past, and, simultaneously, the future is fundamentally altered. "The novelty of every future demands a novel past" (Mead, 1932).

The Concept of the Autoplastic Milieu

The dyadic unit of infant and caretaking adult and, later, the expanding environment on which the young child articulates the separation-individuation process, each leaves a narrow margin of choice. Not only does infantile dependency keep the world of possibilities restricted, but constitutional givens determine, to a large extent, the infant's capacity to elicit actively from the environment those responses that promote his physical and psychological growth. When the adolescent process revives the early stage of the split parental imago with its characteristic ambitendency (Mahler, Pine, and Bergman, 1975), this primitive stage has—by that age—become intertwined with oedipal passions and anxieties, with ego and ego-ideal intentionalities, with superego revisions, and with the mastery of a broadened object world. They seek, in unison as it were, expression and articulation in the wider social environment. The inordinate importance of group life is synonymous with

adolescence itself. Whatever adolescents do, they do in extremes; often episodically, often without letup. We have
come to look at acting out as a phase-specific form of adolescent behavior (see Chapter 12). This phenomenon might
well be due to the fact—at least partially—that the adolescent has regressively revived that stage of expressive motility that belongs to the preverbal and early verbal stages of
life. The concrete and the symbol, the act and the meaning
therefore lose their distinctiveness, either for brief moments
or for longer periods of confusion. It is characteristic that
adolescent group life is of an exclusive nature, being
restricted to peers or, roughly speaking, to those equal in
age. We are well acquainted with the role peer relations
play in the emotional disengagement from the family.

Beyond this familiar aspect, I wish to turn attention to
the split parental imago of the preoedipal period as a universal, regressive way station in adolescent personality consolidation. I presented the fragment from the analysis of a
late adolescent girl in order to give a clinical account of this
way station's nature and of the course by which it was
reached. How the ambitendency of early childhood filters
into the interaction system of adolescent peer relations is
the topic of social psychology, which I shall now elaborate
more fully.

Conceptualizing my observations, I pose the thesis that
adolescents externalize the remnants of the infantile, preverbal ambitendency within the peer group. They use, so to
speak, a self-created social milieu in order to modulate and
synthesize the often only tenuously integrated split parental
imagos, thereby attempting to overcome the sense of inner
divisiveness, disharmony, and uncertainty, as far as it
stems from this particular source. The social relations
within the adolescent peer group contain an identifiable aspect to which I refer as the *autoplastic milieu*—the adolescent's capacity to initiate and promote a social milieu for
the sole purpose of integrating and harmonizing the re-

sidues of split-object dichotomies. In reviving the split imagos by proxy in the autoplastic milieu, the adolescent institutes, autonomously, a transactional social system with the purpose of changing himself, but not his environment. Should others change in this process by a gratuitous complementation—and this very likely always happens— this does not constitute an intrinsic function of the autoplastic milieu. The successful use of the autoplastic milieu implies, temporarily at least, a considerable, yet circumscribed, decline of reality testing. This segmented ego regression, however, does not prevent other kinds of adaptation from forging ahead.

In the present context I shall focus on the quasi relationships of the autoplastic milieu in which the adolescent makes use of his peers for the sake of attaining a basic inner unity. This particular species of peer relations is not a genuine one. Relations of this nature vanish like ghosts without any sense of loss, or clear remembrance. It must not be overlooked that many other species of relationships—genuine, imitative, exploratory, and so forth—run their course concomitantly at this stage. In fact, such paradoxical parallelisms are truly adolescent modes of personality functioning.

The incapacity to use the environment for self-development is considered pathognomic for the young child, as it is for the adolescent. The adolescent's use of the peer environment for this particular purpose represents a special normative aspect of adolescent social relations. What we witness is the modulation and synthesis of experiential givens, such as early pleasure-pain accommodations. One of these reaches backward to the early splitting mechanism. Of course, subsequent normal development has lifted the internalized infantile object relations onto a symbolic level, thus promoting the usefulness of symbolic processes, such as language and thought, for the advancement of the maturational process. It always remains a delicate task for the

clinical observer of adolescence to draw the line between
what is repetition and what is a new creation, between
what is merely the re-edition of an old text and what are
newly added lines which render it a partially new book.

Two Case Illustrations

A seventeen-year-old boy was brought to my attention
on account of his rebelliousness, unruliness, opposition to
the conventionality of education and academic learning,
emotional aloofness and self-centeredness, arrogant haugh-
tiness, and inaccessibility to reason, persuasion, or punishment. Episodically, all these traits changed to compliance
and excessive conformity and back again to irresponsibility
and indifference. The unpredictability of this engaging and
bright boy exasperated and confounded his parents and
teachers who nevertheless granted him a perpetual benefit
of the doubt.

This adolescent boy was caught in the storm center of
his emotional disengagement from his parents. His behavior
was governed by opposing trends—dominance versus submission, emotional closeness versus distance, self-
disparagement versus object idealization, self-idealization
versus object disparagement. Consciously, the boy had his
dialectics worked out well: he rejected and disparaged his
mother as a shallow, self-centered, exhibitionistic, status-
minded, illogical, and unreasonable woman. He was sure
that any achievements he might attain would be used by
her to show off to her friends; in other words, she would
steal them from him. The father, in contrast, was seen in a
more favorable light; even though he was unassertive and
reserved at home, avoiding disagreements with his wife and
failing to stand up for his son, the boy thought of him as a
realistic, rational, considerate, and competent man. The boy
perceived his conflict in crude polarities. Fortified by his
dialectics, he managed his life with adults in a repetitive
cycle between conformity and contrariness.

The discussion of his peer relations revealed some of the crucial dynamics of this boy's maladaptive behavior. He could report his social interaction pattern with remarkable articulateness. In the first place, as he himself pointed out, he belonged to several incompatible groups, while emotionally he belonged nowhere. He moved in and out of these groups, being aware of his moving toward and away from his peers, from almost relating to cutting himself off abruptly. He was also aware of his cynical aloofness and the contrived image he projected for effect. In one kind of group he came on strong; he spoke with authority and conviction, but removed himself from the group before he got engaged in any personal and meaningful way. In another kind of group, he was withdrawn and quiet, projecting the image of the thinker who has much on his mind, is self-sufficient and philosophical. He sensed the unrealness of this social stance. He said, "I have so many masks to wear; one for each group; I change them so easily."

One might be misled by attributing the role-playing to identificatory ambivalence in relation to mother and father imagos. This view is of course partially correct, but the polar positions simultaneously reflect the split parental imagos which the boy had tried and failed to synthesize. This failure became manifest in his repetitive maladaptive behavior. The ensuing social promiscuity left him unsatisfied and lonely. He had no use for the "contemptible and mindless" group, but was unfailingly ensnared by it. From the "congenial and brilliant" group, which he respected, he withdrew again and again, being afraid of its potential power over him. Wandering from one group to the other left him with no social habitation where he had a sense of belonging.

The two polar groups represent the social reification of the "good" and "bad" mother imagos, experienced as a dichotomy in the self. The boy was struck by my comment that he seemed to display in one group the traits which he despised, but secretly envied, in his mother. Her omnipotence gave her power over others, obviously over the father and, in the past, over the little boy. The basic polarity, experienced as envy and fear, if adhered to beyond its timing, is bound to contaminate the formation of the Oedipus complex. In that instance, the "good" and "bad" mother imagos are overlaid on the triad of the oedipal configuration with the consequence that the oedipal figures partake in the premordial paradigm of the early infantile period. This kind of fixation appears as the "all-good father" and the "all-good mother" at the oedipal stage. Of course, we are familiar with the normally shifting positive and negative valence within the oedipal triad; however, what I intend to emphasize here is the quality of part-object relations that are decidedly characteristic of the early infantile stage of object relations. A consequence of a quasi-oedipal stage, as described above, can be observed in the deviant or incomplete structuring of the superego at the end of the phallic phase. The case of the boy reported here offers a clinical illustration of my theoretical propositions. I might add that the patient's relentless effort to advance to an uncontaminated oedipal stage was again and again defeated by preoedipal residues. He finally initiated a renewed and determined effort in the same direction during his adolescence via the use of the autoplastic milieu within the social matrix of peer relations.

In the social interaction at adolescence the depreciated and the idealized parental imagos are revived vis-à-vis their respective and contrived double in the peer environment, with the aim of their unification. In the social arena of peer relations, the boy acted out the "good" and "bad" parental imagos, actively and passively. He contrived in peer cliques those representative "group objects" that corresponded by spurious analogy to the primitive parental dichotomies of the past. These analogies are usually founded on abstract characteristics, such as values, standards, interests, sophistications, and morals. The quasi relatedness is an obvious feature of the peer behavior through which this boy lived out a parody of his residual split-object and split-self dichotomies.

This emotional struggle bears striking similarities to the rapprochement subphase described by Mahler, Pine, and Bergman (1975). They are recognizable in the particular use the adolescent makes of the peer group by eliciting those kinds of response that facilitate internal change, especially within the representational system of self and object. The ego autonomy that has accrued during the in-between years is bound to give a novel cast to the earlier resolutions of inner divisiveness. The social ingenuity and inventiveness of the adolescent are in this process as essential as the "facilitating environment" (Winnicott, 1965), on which the autoplastic milieu is articulated.

Another example of group participation in terms of the autoplastic milieu is given by a late adolescent patient who was a member of a woman's group. The split self- and object representations were articulated within the timely issues of the Women's Liberation Movement. The unconscious issue of liberation pertained in my patient to the liberation from the preoedipal mother. This fact did not deprive the social issue, women's liberation, of its objective validity. The dichotomy in my patient was one of dominating others or being dominated by them. Letting herself be dominated was, for my patient, being good by repudiating her mean, rapacious, and aggressive impulses. She had to keep up an unrelenting vigilance to prevent any antagonistic urges from being acted upon and thus becoming known to others. She could think of herself only as being all good or all bad; others were fitted into the same mold. (Superego issues related to this constellation are not under consideration here.) When the patient dared at one meeting to express her aggressive thoughts and affects, hurling them at a particularly obnoxious member of the group, she sensed an oppression lifting from her mind. After this incident, the group gradually lost its raison d'être for her. The process of disengagement was accompanied by a heightened social differ-

entiation with the result that she formed a friendship with
one woman, while other group members became relegated
to various levels of social relatedness. The analysis of her
group membership revealed the overriding aim to come to
terms with early dichotomies in object relations. Her tan-
trum in the group brought the issue of the split parental
imagos into the analytic work with magnified clarity.

The decisive point was reached by my patient when she
said, "I feel about my women's group like one global person;
the only fitting name I can give to it is 'mother.'" An imputed homology of the group and the mother imago constituted the patient's autoplastic milieu in which she struggled
to transcend her infantile dichotomies. It might therefore be
stated that the group of the autoplastic milieu is an organized composite of part-object (mental) representations,
experienced as quasi individuals in the outer world. The patient's forward step toward synthesis and reconciliation elevated her object relations to a higher level of differentiation. She had by now become aware of the overpowering regressive pull to the preoedipal mother.

Whenever this pull becomes inordinately strong at puberty, it gives rise—in the female—to homosexual yearnings
and antagonistic affects toward the male. In manifest behavior we usually observe the reverse. For my patient, at
the juncture between infantile ambitendency and mature
ambivalence, only the reanalysis of the Oedipus complex
could resolve the enmity between male and female, active
and passive, dependence and independence, good and bad.
In short, only the tolerance of the coexistence of antithetical
qualities in subject and object can temper the cruel world of
the either-or, of perfection versus nothingness.

An Excursion into Linguistics

Earlier I referred to language and linguistic style as indicators of the regressive and the integrative processes of

adolescence. We are familiar with the fact that the symbolic function of language assists the young child in the mastery of reality by the gradual transition from emotional to propositional language. The operation of intelligence is based on the acquisition of language or of a symbol system. The lawfulness of grammar itself assists the child's mind in bringing order into the world around him. Ernst Cassirer (1944) has observed that "Physical reality seems to recede in proportion as man's symbolic activity advances" (p. 43). The acquisition of a word for a familiar thing not only establishes a symbolic code, but also defines a new social cohesiveness among individuals who use the identical symbols. What I have in mind here are the generational changes of language and the creative role which adolescence plays in this process. With the creation of a new word or the use of a familiar one with a new reference, a new identity between name and thing is established, a new meaning has emerged. The ever-changing vocabulary of adolescent slang illustrates well the linguistic originality of each generation.

The idiomatic language of the adolescent offers a striking example of linguistic inventiveness. New words and new syntax become imperceptibly part of the spoken, if not the written, language. In contrast to former times, when adolescent jargon remained restricted to the realm of the young, the adult in contemporary America tends to adopt the innovations of youth, such as clothing, grooming, or idiomatic speech. When the Vietnam War came to an end and the prisoners of war who had been living for years in isolation from their families returned to their homeland, the United States Air Force issued a glossary of idiomatic adolescent speech in order to enable the returning soldier to converse with his adolescent children and the teenage community at large (*New York Times*, March 8, 1973). It is impressive to look at the extensive idiomatic or slang vocabulary that had accumulated during the war years.

Adolescent linguistic inventiveness pertains to words as

well as to syntax. Much of it is borrowed, especially by
American middle-class youth, from the established speech of
other, lower-class, ethnic groups. The idiomatic speech confirms a new social cohesion between sexual maturants, who
discard some of the speech they were taught as children.
This situation is particularly true for the educated adolescent for whom the use of slang establishes a linguistic distancing from the world of childhood. At one point baby and
toddler talk gave way to correct speech. But in the beginning, "elementary human utterances do not refer to physical things . . . they are involuntary expressions of human
feelings, interjections and ejaculations" (Cassirer, 1944, pp.
148-149).

Idiomatic adolescent language recaptures some of the
emotional quality which baby words possessed and, in fact,
have never lost. The novel characteristic of adolescent
idiomatic language, often referred to by young people as
"gut" or "soul" talk, lies in the communal age-bond it establishes. Should this kind of speech be adopted by the adult
(especially the middle- and upper-class parent), the adolescent will listen to it—if he listens at all—with amused for-
bearance or disdain. The *pars pro toto* rejection of traditional language diminishes with age, and so does the need
to conform with the obligatory adolescent argot. It acquires
facultative usage and remains reserved for special social occasions; part of it becomes incorporated into current speech.

Individual and Environment

The realization of the autoplastic milieu brings about its
own destruction. It is, in other words, self-liquidating
through the process of late adolescent consolidation. The
outcome of this process is, however, not entirely predicated
on the individual's life history, but remains, to some intrinsic extent, codetermined by external circumstances, such as
prevalent opportunities, mores, and expectations emanating

from the social environment. There is no doubt that internalized standards immunize the child against antisocial and self-destructive behavior, but experience teaches us that the threshold of seductibility and contagion can be lowered perilously by social influences.

The dynamics of "contagion" in the behavior of children and adolescents have been extensively described by Redl (1956). Le Bon (1895) had already used this term in his study of crowd behavior. There is no argument, at least not in principle, that children need protection against influences that are injurious to their development. It remains a disputed question how far into adolescence this personal and institutional guardianship (by school, church, court, etc.) is to be kept operative. Two questions arise: one refers to the timing and measure of parental or institutional relinquishment of its protective and regulatory presence, and the other concerns itself with the choice of child-rearing practices that best assure the autonomous conservation of personal integrity in times of stress.

During the recent past we have seen with an impressive number of adolescents how often the arduous process of adolescent individuation is bypassed by substituting action and concrete thinking for internal, i.e., psychic change. We can recognize in this substitution a grotesque reflection of prevailing characteristics of the so-called older generation, which has afforded competitive superiority and material success a supreme honor on which the sense of self-worth so critically depends. The generational variance of these ideals can be observed in their periodic reversal as to content and valence. Thus, the adolescent antihero was born. He is by no means of the same breed as the antihero of Sartre, Beckett, or Pinter. The heroic act of the adolescent antihero is the vilification of tradition and the debunking of absolute values. The attention traditionally given to grooming, beautification, cleanliness, academic learning, sexual fidelity, to mention only a few, is reversed into a preoccupation

with their opposites and adhered to with a rigorous conformism that cements various youth groups into antihero or
counterculture conclaves. Under the influence of value reversal, to be a dropout from college, to engage in sexual activity as a wanton, sensuous experience, briefly, to "do your
thing," has become for many young people the status symbol of maturity. Helene Deutsch (1967) has devoted a
monograph to this topic; she explores the social influence
and pressure of the peer culture on the sexual behavior of
women college students. She emphasizes the danger of emotional infantilization which this kind of compliance to the
moral code of the group engenders. The tentative and episodic
abandonment of the individual value system for the sake of
gaining group acceptance is paid for by a sense of alienation
and identity diffusion (Erikson, 1956).

The picture of the new morality would be incomplete
without reference to its positive achievements. Much constructive social, political, and moral criticism has been articulated with the help of the changing social mores of
youth. I have only to mention the moral fortitude of the
Vietnam War resisters or the fact that it was the young
who heard Rachel Carson's (1962) cry in the wilderness of
the "silent spring" and started a crusade against ecological
devastation. At the time of this writing, environmental protection has become a respectable public issue. Unfortunately, many participants in these fights turn out to be ideological freeloaders, trapped in the self-serving cause of laying
to rest the ghosts of their private past. Having lost contact
with the broader issues they profess to serve, they proclaim
their floundering a virtue and characteristically lend direction to those whose chronic indecisiveness has brought them
to an impasse at the crossroads of late adolescence.

In simple words the question could be asked whether
what is called "bad company" can derail individual development onto regressive tracks or, generally speaking,
into deviate forms of adaptation. We like to believe that the

individual's response to the environment is solely determined by the complementarity of "inside" and "outside," of
the individual and the social, or, in other words, by the protective and regulatory presence of ego and superego. The
degree to which these psychic structures are in constant
need of environmental, personal as well as institutional,
complementarity or support is still an open question. At any
rate, individual psychology alone will not render intelligible
the totality of this social phenomenon. We might have to
consider some determinants of man's behavior which are of
a different order from those we customarily turn to for
causal and explanatory references.

Zeitgeist As Environment

Here I want to turn to the ideas of Michael Polanyi (1974),
the physical chemist and historian of science, who has
explored man's changing view of the physical world, how it
has affected the state of the modern mind, and, consequently, the behavior of modern man. His inquiry lies, so
to speak, beyond economics and swaddling. About these two
disciplines we are fairly well informed. To direct our
thoughts toward Polanyi's focus of interest, we might recall
the Copernican revolution and the subsequent altered relation of man to the physical universe. The impact which the
changing view of the physical world, as the consequence of
scientific discoveries, has on the contemporary mind contributes significantly to the shaping of the *Zeitgeist*—that elusive and penetrating temper of an era, intellectual and
mental, by which we are surrounded as by a climate.

The increasing reliance on the laws of physics and
chemistry, for example, moved the tangible and the
measurable into the foreground of man's awareness as the
most reliable and controllable agents to insure the betterment of individual and society. The limitless potentiality of
the machine and the infinite assemblage of new substances

offered hope and assurance of having found the trustworthy means by which man was to be delivered from the imperfections of the human condition. With the employment of more and more research in the physical sciences, the betterment of the human condition and the moral perfection of man seemed assured. Polanyi reasons that the reliance on and the use of the natural laws, not governed by moral principle, brought man into the dichotomy of positivistic skepticism and moral perfectionism. The pursuit of knowledge as an aim in itself gradually replaced moral values or, at least, cultivated them in isolation from knowledge and action. In consequence, the amoral act could exist in conflictless harmony with the claim of the highest moral principles.[2] This dichotomy of mental attitudes was foreshadowed in modern literature. I allude here to the gratuitous crime of Dostoevsky's Raskolnikov, of Gide's Lafcadio, of Camus's Mersault (*The Stranger*), and many more. Polanyi refers to their attitudes as "moral nihilism charged with moral fury." The trust in the principle of the machine and in scientific discoveries and inventions as the guardians of man's outer and inner security have thus exerted a pervasive influence on the individual mind.

Complete skepticism deprives life of its meaning, and only a meaningless act, devoid of any moral motive, restores in man the sense of authenticity. I have heard adolescents speak of such motiveless acts of violence or depravity with a sense of pride; they use phrases such as, "I did it for kicks," "It's just an experience," "It means nothing." Quite apart from family history, the *Zeitgeist* represents a societal matrix in which adolescents have to find their bearings, often with an intemperate affirmation of their moral integrity. One does not have to be literate to be affected by this prevailing temper of an era, neither does one have to be personally concerned with the issues or trends embodied in it; its influence reaches—as by osmosis—everyone within its

[2]The Nixon era offers a convincing demonstration of this state of mind.

orbit through the mass media whose echo surrounds us and through the social institutions in which we dwell. *Zeitgeist* and individual are conceived here as a functional unit, a dialectic process, a system.

Closing Remarks

A psychoanalytic social psychology of adolescence must one day clarify what is a "good-enough" environment for the adolescent period or, at least, delineate the categories under which this issue can be described and studied. Comparable to infant and early childhood research, where the subject and its surround are conceived as a system and not merely as discrete entities of subject and object, so also at the stage of adolescence, the mutual use of individual and environment should be studied in relation to the specific developmental tasks that have to be dealt with at this stage of sexual maturation. I have addressed myself, specifically, to one of the many uses the peer-group object and the individual adolescent make of each other. This issue, I have tried to demonstrate, is a clinically identifiable component of adolescent group psychology.

Should the contraposition of individual and social psychology yield to their integration with time, this will very likely contribute little, probably nothing, to the treatment of the neuroses, as their existence is confined to the secluded arena of internal conflicts, where insight alone can disrupt the perpetuity of infantile maladaptive patterns. On the other hand, the influence of a psychoanalytic social psychology on the field of prevention might be considerable, and its usefulness will certainly declare itself in the treatment of that multitude of disorders which remain unaffected by psychoanalysis proper. Here, I have particularly in mind the disordered and disoriented adolescents whose contagious influence on their peers has been growing by the sheer weight of their numbers. Is this social phenomenon perhaps due to the anachronism of dysfunctional social institutions or, generally, to critical deficiencies in an environment that fails to provide some of the social nutrients essential for the process of adaptation during adolescence? In all probability, these are the critical factors at work.

Epilogue

In the twenties Freud was told about a "multidimensional system of characterology" on which some younger colleagues had embarked. As told to us by Robert Waelder (1958), Freud opened the meeting—held, as usual, in his waiting room—by saying that he felt "like a skipper of a barge who had always hugged the coast and who now learned that others, more adventurous, had set out for the open sea. He wished them well but he could no longer participate in their endeavour." Freud closed his comment with the following words, "But I am an old hand in the coastal run and I will remain faithful to my blue inlets" (p. 243).

I feel that I have ventured here far out into the open sea, navigating a vessel that perhaps is not quite seaworthy. The voyage, however, was undertaken with precautionary installations that kept me in touch—via Telstar—with the steady coastal traffic that moves in tested and secure channels of navigation. So far, the high swells of the open sea have caused me no panic, because the contact with some of the trusted skippers in the home waters has kept up remarkably well.

PART TWO

The Normative Stages
of Male and Female
Adolescence

The word "adolescence" is commonly used as if a set of unitary characteristics would define an age span which roughly encompasses the second decade of life; yet everybody knows that this is not the case. The emphasis remains too often on what is broadly typical of the adolescent boy and girl, while the vastly contrasting developmental stages and the gender-specific and sex-determined differences are taken for granted. The onsets of puberty in girl and boy are not synchronous, their respective maturation and development do not proceed at an equal rate nor are they of a wholly comparable nature. Whatever the psychosexual and ego position on which the adolescent boy or girl temporarily dwells—be this, for example, the early adolescent tomboy or the juvenile misogynist—it is always part of a prelude to the ultimate formation of ego and sexual identity. Whatever the social accommodations the adolescent boy or girl pursues temporarily, they always represent the prelude to the formation of a social identity. Both ultimately determine the adult sense of self.

The contribution that psychoanalysis, with its special methodology of inquiry, has made to this issue is the tracing of developmental and normative stages, thus establishing an epigenetic pattern of an orderly progression from infancy through adolescence to adulthood. By studying samenesses and differences in male and female adolescent development I have endeavored in my work to render this schema more inclusive and complete. The genetic and the developmental points of view, as leading concepts, have governed and directed my investigations of origins, integrations, and transformations throughout the adolescent process. My study of developmental sequences was finally organized by the delineation and definition of phases (preadolescence, early adolescence, adolescence proper, late adolescence, postadolescence) and their developmental characteristics. The usefulness of these differentiations became most evident in adolescent pathology, because they helped

101

to clarify not only etiology and dynamics but also to locate the points along the adolescent process where a critical "developmental derailment" had occurred in a particular case. In this connection I have spoken of adolescent fixation points.

Most profitable in the construction of developmental sequences has been the study of adolescent regression. In some form or other, regression always occurs during adolescent development. The function of regression in adolescence as a nondefensive phenomenon has afforded this seemingly infantilizing process the position of a normative occurrence. Adolescent regression brings the advanced faculties of the ego to bear on those childhood vicissitudes that could only be dealt with inadequately and incompletely during the early years of life. This typical aspect of adolescence permits me to say that the developmental progress of adolescence is predicated on the capacity to regress. I have called this normative, nondefensive form of regression at adolescence: regression in the service of development. This perilous developmental step—seemingly backward—can only be taken successfully when supportive influences and facilitations are available in the environment. Facilitations referred to in this context comprise not only tension-reducing or gratificatory supports and easings of dysphoric states, they comprise, equally, the exposure to age-specific conflicts and frustrations, to anxiety and guilt as challenges to adaptive accommodations and resolutions. Adolescence, like any other developmental stage, is marked by typical conflicts, external and internal, which, by their very nature, promote progressive development. It is therefore not in the best interest of development to sidestep the conflict between the generations or between the adolescent and his environment. It remains a challenge to the parent generation and the social planner how best to keep the ensuing stress constellations within the boundaries of adolescent tolerance and adaptability.

Adolescent regression is the central theme of my study "The Second Individuation Process of Adolescence." The potential dangers of this obligatory regression render adolescents most prone to the outbreak of emotional illness. The two extremes—the one of regression avoidance (flight into adultomorphic roles) and the other of perseverance on the regressed level (psychosis)—both represent well-known pathological states of adolescence. In both instances, the function of adolescent-specific regression has miscarried.

The successful disengagement from infantile internalized objects depends on the completion of psychic restructuring through regression. I have summarized these findings by saying that postadolescent personality formation is predicated on a regressive detour to adulthood. The always incomplete—even if workable—psychic transformations from childhood to adulthood find a buttressing structure in characterological stabilizations. In the discussion of character I have advanced the opinion that character formation receives its decisive thrust and enduring fixity during the adolescent period.

Chapter 6

Preadolescent Drive Organization

It has always been a basic tenet of psychoanalysis to comprehend human behavior at any stage in relation to preceding, current, and anticipated events, or to view it as an instant in a continuum of mental experience. This developmental concept has thrown light on those complex processes of adolescence which, in the not too distant past, were linked solely to the advent of sexual maturation. The genetic approach to adolescent research has made adolescent behavior tell something of its nature by revealing something of its history.

The "Three Essays" (Freud, 1905b) established the sequential patterns of psychosexual development; furthermore, it brought into focus the biphasic nature of sexual development as a characteristic of man. The early phases of drive development and zonal organization have been explored in detail and have lately become more precisely coordinated with the formation of psychic structure. It is noteworthy that although the second broad stage in psychosexual development—puberty—has been explored in its larger aspects, it still awaits a comprehensive theory and the elaboration of its sequential patterns. I shall attempt in the following to integrate observation and theory in a small sector of adolescent psychology, namely, preadolescence.

The familiar dictum that adolescence is a "second edi-

First published in *Journal of the American Psychoanalytic Association*, 6: 47-56, 1958.

tion" or a "recapitulation" of early childhood has meaning only as far as it emphasizes the fact that adolescence contains elements of preceding phases of development in much the same way as any other and earlier phase of psychosexual development is significantly influenced by preceding drive and ego development. The prerequisite for entering the adolescent phase of drive and ego organization lies in the consolidation of the latency period; otherwise the pubescent child experiences a simple intensification of prelatency characteristics, exhibiting infantile behavior of an arrested rather than a regressive nature. It would be of interest to delineate those essential attainments of latency that are the preconditions for a successful advance to adolescence. In our analytic work with adolescents—mainly young adolescents—we indeed pay particular attention to those latency deficits that preclude adolescent-specific conflicts. Whenever latency has not been satisfactorily established, and the patient shows substantial developmental lags, we supplement or preface analysis with educational efforts to bring about some essential latency attainments. This practice, in fact, occurs more frequently than is usually made explicit; the large number of child patients with retarded or deviant ego development has, over the years, given legitimacy to "the widening scope of psychoanalysis" as applied to the analytic work with children and adolescents.

Example

In the case of a well-developed ten-year-old boy who showed learning difficulties, social inadequacy, and bizarre thinking, there appeared abruptly at the age of ten an expressed desire to sleep in his mother's bed and keep his father away from her. Demands for embraces and kisses alternated with the wish to be picked up by the mother like a younger child or to be allowed to sit on her lap. The mother tended to yield to the child's wishes. It seemed essential that the mother at the very beginning of the child's analysis develop a resistance to her son's sexual advances and learn to frustrate him while offering substitute gratifications commensurate with his age. The fact that it was the mother and not the father who restrained him actively from the realization of his oedipal wishes influenced the child's reaction in a decisive way.

The boy reacted to the mother's prohibitions with repression of his oedipal wishes and with a show of sad resignation. He became compulsively preoccupied with schoolwork; he would fill workbook after workbook with his answers, checking them incessantly. This compulsive behavior served as a defense against anal retaliatory fantasies directed at the frustrating mother; the fantasies were acted out in relation to the mothers of his schoolmates. Only after this regression and displacement was worked through did oedipal material appear in the analysis; castration anxiety became prominent by denial, projection, and confused thinking. The boy's interest turned to castration themes derived mainly from the Bible: the killing of a male lamb at Passover, the Lord who "will smite all the first-born in the land of Egypt," Herod's slaying of the little children of Bethlehem, fear of a wild bull near his house in the country. I believe that without the accessory use of educational interference (the mother's refusal to gratify his infantile sexual wishes), the analysis of this boy would not have been feasible.

Developmental Differences in the Preadolescent Boy and Girl

Let us now turn to the state of preadolescence in its typical appearance, signaling the termination of the latency period. It is a well-known fact that in early puberty[1] we observe a

[1]The term "puberty" is used here to denote the physical manifestation of sexual maturation, e.g., prepuberty refers to the period just preceding the development of primary and secondary sex characteristics. The term "adolescence" is used to denote the psychological processes of adaptation to the condition of pubescence, e.g., the state of preadolescence can continue overly long and remain unaffected by the progression of physical maturation.

quite different psychological development in boy and girl. The dissimilarities between the sexes is striking; descriptive psychology has paid extensive attention to this period and has accumulated a wealth of relevant observational data. What strikes us in the boy is his circuitous route via pregenital drive cathexis toward a genital orientation; the girl turns far more readily and forcefully toward the other sex. Only with reference to the boy is it correct to say that the quantitative increase of the instinctual drive during preadolescence leads to an indiscriminate cathexis of pregenitality. The resurgence of pregenitality marks, in fact, the termination of the latency period in the male. In the girl we usually observe a far more modulated resurgence of pregenitality, a fact that reveals, by its very diversionary tactics, that this developmental juncture represents a more complex crisis for the girl than for the boy.

At this particular stage of male adolescence we observe an increase in diffuse motility (restlessness, fidgetiness), as well as in oral greediness, sadistic activities, anal activities expressed in coprophilic pleasures, and "dirty" language. There is a disregard of cleanliness, a fascination with odors, and skillful production of onomatopoetic noises. A fourteen-year-old boy, who started analysis at ten, put it aptly when he said retrospectively: "At eleven my mind was on filth, now [age fourteen] it is on sex; it is very different."

We have hinted already that the preadolescent girl does not show the same features as the boy; she is either a tomboy or a little woman. The preadolescent boy will shy away from this young Diana, who seductively displays her charm while roaming the wilderness with a pack of hounds. The mythological reference is used to point to the defensive aspect of the boy's pregenital drive cathexis, namely, his avoidance of the castrating woman, the archaic mother. From fantasies, play activities, dreams, and symptomatic behavior of preadolescent boys, I have come to the conclusion that castration anxiety in relation to the phallic woman is not only a universal occurrence of male preadolescence but can be considered to be its central theme. Is this recurrent observation possibly due to the fact that we see in analysis so many young adolescent boys with passive strivings who come from families with strong mothers, determined to shape their sons in accordance with their lifelong fantasies? Such possibilities deserve our careful consideration.

Example

In several dreams of an obese, submissive, inhibited, compulsive eleven-year-old boy, there repeatedly appeared a naked woman. Her lower body parts were not well remembered and were vaguely seen; the breast replaced the penis, either as an erectile or excretory organ. This boy's dreams were always prompted by experiences in a coeducational school where the competition between boys and girls offered him endless proof of the female's malice, her foul play and her predatory viciousness. The compulsive reassurance by masturbatory activity, when interpreted in the above-mentioned context, led to a sleep disturbance with the prevalent idea that his mother might kill him during the night.

Castration anxiety, which had brought the oedipal phase of this boy to its decline, raised its ugly head again with the onset of puberty. In the preadolescent phase of male puberty we can ascertain that castration anxiety is related to the phallic mother, but experienced toward the female in general. Passive strivings are overcompensated and the defense against passivity generally receives a powerful support from sexual maturation itself (A. Freud, 1936). Before a successful turn toward masculinity is effected, however, the employment of the homosexual defense against castration anxiety is characteristic. It is precisely this particular and transient conflict resolution that we witness in the young adolescent boy. Descriptive psychology has labeled this typical group behavior the "gang stage," and dynamic psychology refers to it as the "homosexual stage" of preadolescence.

Nothing similar or equal appears in the life of the girl. The dissimilarity in male and female preadolescent behavior is foreshadowed by the massive repression of pregenitality which the girl has to effect before she can move into the oedipal phase; in fact, this repression is a prerequisite for normal development of femininity. The girl, in turning away from the mother due to narcissistic disappointment in herself and the castrated woman, represses the instinctual drives intimately related to her maternal care and bodily ministrations, i.e., the total scope of pregenitality. Ruth Mack Brunswick (1940), in her classic paper on "The Preoedipal Phase of Libido Development," states: "One of the greatest differences between the sexes is the enormous extent to which infantile sexuality is repressed in the girl. Except in profound neurotic states, no man resorts to any similar repression of his infantile sexuality" (p. 246).

The girl who cannot maintain the repression of her pregenitality will encounter difficulties in her progressive development. Consequently, the young adolescent girl normally exaggerates her heterosexual desires and attaches herself to boys, often in frantic succession. Helene Deutsch (1944) remarks, "In the prepuberty of girls, attachment to the mother represents a greater danger than attachment to the father. The mother is a greater obstacle to the girl's desire to grow up, and we know that the condition of 'psychic infantilism' found in many adult women represents the outcome of an unresolved attachment to the mother during prepuberty" (p. 8).

In considering the dissimilarities between male and female preadolescence it is necessary to remember that the oedipal conflict in the girl is not brought to such an abrupt and fateful termination as is the case in the boy. Freud (1933) states: "Girls remain in it [the oedipal situation] for an indeterminate length of time; they demolish it late and, even so, incompletely" (p. 129). Consequently, the girl struggles with castration anxiety (fear and wish) in relacence; in fact, the prolonged and painful severance actions from the mother constitute the major task of this period.

As has been pointed out, the boy in preadolescence struggles with castration anxiety Zfear and wish) in relation to the archaic mother and consequently turns away from the opposite sex; the girl, in contrast, defends herself against the regressive pull to the preoedipal mother by a forceful and decisive turn toward heterosexuality. In this role the preadolescent girl cannot be called "feminine" because she so obviously is the aggressor and the seducer in the game of pseudo love; indeed, the phallic quality of her sexuality is prominent at this stage and affords her for a brief period an unusual sense of adequacy and completeness. The fact that the average girl between the ages of eleven to thirteen is taller than the average boy of the same age only accentuates this situation. Benedek (1956) refers to endocrine findings: "Before the procreative function matures, before ovulation sets in with relative regularity, the estrogen phase is dominant, as if to facilitate the developmental tasks of adolescence, namely, to establish emotional relations with the male sex" (p. 411). Helene Deutsch (1944) has referred to "prepuberty" of the girl as "the period of greatest freedom from infantile sexuality." This condition is normally accompanied by a forceful "turn to reality" (Deutsch) which, so it seems to me, counteracts the resurgence of the infantile drive organization.

The phase-specific conflict of female preadolescence reveals its defensive nature particularly well in those cases in which a progressive development has not been sustained.

Female delinquency, for example, offers an instructive opportunity for the study of the preadolescent drive organization in the girl. I have already cited Deutsch's (1944) remark that in the "prepuberty of girls, the attachment to the
mother represents a greater danger than the attachment to
the father." In female delinquency, which broadly speaking
represents sexual acting-out behavior, the fixation on the
preoedipal mother plays a most decisive role (see Chapter
11). In fact, female delinquency is often precipitated by the
strong regressive pull to the preoedipal mother and the
panic such surrender implies. It is my opinion that the girl's
turn to heterosexual acting out, which at first sight seems
to represent the recrudescence of oedipal wishes, proves on
careful scrutiny to be related to earlier fixation points lying
in the pregenital phases of libidinal development; excessive
frustration or overstimulation or both were experienced. The
pseudo heterosexuality of the delinquent girl serves as a defense against the regressive pull to the preoedipal mother.
This pull is so frantically resisted because—if given into—it
would bring about a fatal rupture in the development of
femininity by falling back on a homosexual object choice. A
fourteen-year-old girl, when asked why she needed ten boyfriends at once, answered with righteous indignation: "I
have to do this; if I didn't have so many boyfriends they
would say I am a lesbian." The "they" in this sentence comprises the projection of those instinctual urges the girl endeavors to contradict so vehemently by her demonstrative
and provocative behavior. A rupture in the girl's progressive emotional development brought about by the advent of
puberty constitutes a more serious threat to personality integration than is the case in the boy. The following case
abstract illustrates a typical delinquent breakdown of the
female preadolescent drive organization, and lays bare the
crucial emotional task the girl normally has to accomplish
at this stage before she can advance to adolescence proper.

PREADOLESCENT DRIVE ORGANIZATION

Example

Nancy, age thirteen, was a "sex delinquent."[2] She had indiscriminate sexual relations with teenage boys, and tormented her mother with the tales of her exploits. She blamed her mother for her unhappiness; she had experienced feelings of loneliness since childhood. Nancy believed that her mother never wanted her and made incessant and unreasonable demands on her. Nancy was obsessed by the wish for a baby; all her sexual fantasies pointed to the "mother-baby" theme and basically, to an overwhelming oral greed. She had a dream in which she had sexual relations with several teenage boys; in the dream she had 365 babies, one a day for a year from one boy, whom she shot after this was achieved.

The sexual acting out ceased completely as soon as Nancy developed a friendship with a young, married, promiscuous, pregnant woman of twenty who had three children. In the friendship with this girlfriend-mother Nancy found the gratification of her oral and maternal needs while she was protected against homosexual surrender. She played mother to the children, took devoted care of them while their mother walked the streets. From this friendship Nancy emerged at fifteen as a narcissistic, rather prudish person, interested in acting and attending an acting school. She failed to progress to heterosexual object finding.

In normal female development the phase of preadolescent drive organization is dominated by the defense against the preoedipal mother; it is reflected in the many conflicts which arise between mother and daughter during this period. A progression to adolescence proper is marked by the emergence of oedipal strivings which are first displaced and finally extinguished by an "irreversible process of dis-

[2]Her case is reported at greater length in Chapter 11.

placement," aptly designated by Anny Katan (1951) as "object removal." This phase of adolescent development lies outside the scope of the present communication.

The Case of Dora[3]

Having defined the preadolescent drive organization in terms of preoedipal positions, I want now to relate my remarks to the first analysis of an adolescent girl, that of Dora (Freud, 1905a). Dora was sixteen when she first visited Freud and eighteen when she started treatment. At the end of "The Clinical Picture" Freud introduces an element which he confesses "can only serve to obscure and efface the outlines of the fine poetic conflict which we have been able to ascribe to Dora. . . . For behind Dora's supervalent train of thought which was concerned with her father's relations to Frau K. there lay concealed a feeling of jealousy which had that lady as its *object*—a feeling, that is, which could only be based upon an affection on Dora's part for one of her own sex" (pp. 59-60). We could paraphrase the last part of this sentence by saying: which could only be based upon an affection on the girl's part for her mother. It is with great fascination that we read Freud's account of Dora's relationship to her governess, to her girl cousin, and to Frau K. Freud noted that Dora's relationship to Frau K. had a "greater pathogenic effect" than the oedipal situation which "she tried to use as a screen" for the deeper trauma of having been sacrificed by her intimate friend, Frau K., "without a moment's hesitation so that her [Frau K.'s] relations with her father might not be disturbed" (p. 62). Freud continues in his last conclusion to point out "that Dora's supervalent train of thought, which was concerned with her father's relations with Frau K., was designed not only for the purpose of suppressing her love for Herr K., which had

[3]A more extensive discussion of the Dora case is to be found in Chapter 19.

once been conscious, but also to conceal her love for Frau K., which was in a deeper sense unconscious" (p. 62).

The observation is familiar that oedipal strivings are more conspicuous and loud in adolescence than the preoedipal fixations which indeed are so often of more profound pathogenic import. In the case of Dora, the analysis had come to an end "before it could throw any light on this side of her mental life." The adolescent conveys to us again and again that he desperately needs a foothold on the oedipal level—a sex-appropriate orientation—before earlier fixations can become accessible to analytic investigation. In this connection a reference to a young, passive adolescent boy seems relevant. During three years of analysis (age eleven to thirteen) he stubbornly maintained an image of his "milk-toast" father as the strong and important man in the family. The powerful father, an illusory figure of his imagination, served this boy as a defense against preoedipal castration anxiety. This boy never permitted himself to criticize, doubt, or question the analyst: the analyst always had to be right. He would not allow himself to look at the clock for fear of insulting the analyst. Finally, the analysis of the transference brought to light the boy's fear of the analyst; his fear of retaliation and injury. The analysis of oedipal castration anxiety eventually opened the way to the far more disturbing anxieties in relation to the preoedipal mother. The working through of these earlier fixations resulted in a realistic, if disappointing evaluation of the father. The maintenance of an "illusory oedipal" situation seems to mask a strong preoedipal fixation.

Conclusion

I have concentrated in this brief communication on the preadolescent drive organization. From here the road leads to shifts in drive organization which are progressively and more firmly rooted in the biological innovations of puberty, namely, the establishment of orgastic pleasure. This biological innovation necessitates a hierarchical arrangement of the multitudinous residual childhood positions which, for individual reasons, have remained cathected and press for continued expression and gratification. This arrangement results finally in a highly personal pattern of forepleasure. The concurrent ego development takes, as always, its cue from the existing drive organization and its interaction with the environment. Consequently, we can observe in adolescence the tendency toward a hierarchical arrangement in ego organization as well; in fact, whenever this fails to occur, a general aimlessness and shiftlessness will follow which in many cases precludes a stable engagement in and adjustment to work. It has been my experience that in these cases the pathology of drive organization deserves careful scrutiny, which may require a long period of clinical investigation and analytic work.

I shall leave this thought before it carries me beyond the boundaries of this chapter. If I focused on one small aspect of the total problem of adolescent psychology, it was done in the belief that, in turn, the larger issues and trends of adolescence would become better understood. Since the days of the "Three Essays" (Freud, 1905b) psychoanalytic insight into adolescence has grown steadily. However, Freud's words from "The Transformations of Puberty" (1905b) are still worth repeating: "The starting-point and the final aim of the process . . . are clearly visible. The intermediate steps are still in many ways obscure to us. We shall have to leave more than one of them as an unsolved riddle" (p. 208). Today, as urgently as then, it is the problem of the "intermediate steps" that clamors for our attention.

Chapter 7

The Initial Stage of
Male Adolescence

Before taking up the subject matter of this chapter I shall stake out the conceptual dimensions within which my observations will be formulated. This introduction seems desirable because it relieves me of the constant reference to modulating notions of the issues I shall discuss and places them once and for all into the context of a broad point of view. It should be made explicit at the outset that I conceive of "individual" and "environment" as complementary operational abstractions whose mutual influence on each other is a continuous process (see Chapter 5). Usually one side or the other of the total process, i.e., either "social man" or "instinctual man," is described at crucial points of intersection. The total process is best studied in terms of interaction systems or in terms of projective-introjective processes which find a documentation, as it were, within the ego or, to be specific, within the ego's object- and self-representational world.

I view adolescence in its broadest terms as the second individuation process (see Chapter 8), the first one having been completed toward the end of the third year of life with the attainment of object constancy. What Mahler (1963) describes as the psychological "hatching" process in infancy

---

First published in *The Psychoanalytic Study of the Child*, 20: 145-164. New York: International Universities Press, 1965.

becomes in adolescence the emergence from the family into the adult world, society at large. Not until the close of adolescence do self- and object representations acquire firm boundaries. At this point they become resistive to cathectic shifts, with the result that constancy of self-esteem and inner regulatory controls for its maintenance or recovery are successfully established (Jacobson, 1964). Adolescent individuation can also be described as a progressive disengagement from primary love objects, i.e., from the infantile parental figures or their substitutes (A. Freud, 1958). Adolescent individuation leads the way to adult object relations. This advance, however, remains a pyrrhic victory if it is not complemented by the emergence of a distinct social role, a sense of purpose and of fitting in, which jointly secure a solid anchorage in the human community.

The finding of new identifications, loyalties, and intimacies outside the accustomed family dependencies permeates adolescent progressive development all along, but is most urgent at the closing stage of adolescence, which, indeed, is defined by these very achievements. What we witness is an extraordinary spectrum of idiosyncratic accommodations within the realms of maturation, structuralization, and adaptation. The cross-cultural approach to the study of adolescence as well as research into the historical morphology of adolescence have taught us a lesson in the enormous plasticity of adolescent drive and ego organizations in conjunction with the formation and buttressing influence of social roles and social institutions.

As a closing remark to this introduction, I want to point to the fact that adolescence is composed of distinct developmental phases which are not as narrowly time-fixed as those of early childhood; yet, both periods of development have in common a sequential pattern of distinct phases. Each adolescent phase can be described along three lines: in terms of (1) typical drive and ego modifications, (2) an integral conflict to be resolved, and (3) a developmental task to be fulfilled (Blos, 1962; Deutsch, 1944). In other words, each phase must make its singular contribution to personality development; if it does not, a miscarriage of the adolescent process ensues. The deviate course of development thus initiated can be understood in terms of adolescent fixation points.

The bisexual orientation, tolerated within certain limits during childhood, comes to an end with the advent of pubescence, i.e., with sexual maturation. More accurately, one should say that it is the task of adolescence to render bisexual propensities innocuous through drive and ego accommodations, which attain their definitive form during the consolidation period or the terminal phase of adolescence, namely, late adolescence. The adolescent progressive development of the boy and that of the girl are neither identical nor parallel, but both involve the poignant differentiation of qualities which in our minds are associated with being a man or a woman. While certain social roles contribute to the sense of self and transcend the gender condition, every analysis reveals that the basis of the sense of identity is to be found in the clarity with which sexual identity is reflected in the self. A major contribution to this formation—in fact, the final and decisive one—is made during adolescence (Blos, 1962; Greenacre, 1958).

One anticipatory hint remains to be given before I present the substantive material on male adolescence. Although the manifestation of aggression constitutes one of the most formidable and dramatic aspects of male adolescent behavior, it has not been satisfactorily traced within the adolescent process or in relation to psychic restructuring. The study of the initial phase of male adolescence throws light on the vicissitudes of the aggressive drive by elucidating one particular component of it. This component—phallic aggression and phallic sadism—stands out in great clarity at the phase of preadolescence when the genital phase asserts itself anew after a temporary decline

during the interposing period of latency. This decline is
more apparent than real because it is due to the ascendency
of ego expansion which renders id influences relatively less
dominant and prominent at this age.

Male Preadolescence

Let us start at the beginning of adolescence and turn our
attention to the phase of male preadolescence. The most
remarkable observation about the preadolescent boy is his
decisive turning away from the opposite sex as soon as the
first strivings of puberty increase drive pressure and upset
the balance between ego and id as it prevailed during the
latency period. Object-libidinal gratifications appear blocked
and are, indeed, often violently resisted. The aggressive
drive becomes pervasively dominant and finds expression
either in fantasy, play activity, acting out, or delinquent
behavior.

   You will recognize this kind of boy if I remind you of the
many therapy hours you spent with him while he was playing with, drawing, or impersonating battleships and bomber
planes and accompanying their attacks with a gunfire of
onomatopoetic noises in endless repetition. He loves gadgets
and mechanical devices. He is motorically restless and
jumpy, and is usually eager to complain about the unfairness of his teacher, assuring us that the lady is out to kill
him. In his behavior, language, and fantasies, the resurgence of pregenitality is easily recognized. An eleven-
year-old boy who had started analysis at ten illustrated this
development aptly by saying: "My favorite word now is
'crap.' The older I get the dirtier I become."

   The behavior described above conceals only thinly the
ever-present fear of passivity. The object of this fear is the
archaic mother, the preoedipal, active (domesticating)
mother who is the prototype of the witch in folklore. The
fear revolves around surrender to the archaic mother, and

the wildly aggressive impulses are directed toward the overwhelming and ominous woman giant. On the genital level of prepuberty this constellation is experienced as castration fear in relation to the woman, the preoedipal mother. The erect penis cathected with aggressive impulses evokes at this stage the fear of reaching uncontrollable destructive intensity. The counterphobic role of physical daring and accidents is often clearly recognizable as an effort to assuage castration fear: "Nothing will happen to me—I will come through unscathed." It is surprising to see how little of this fear is related at this phase to the father; in fact, the boy's relationship with him is often surprisingly good and positive. Even if it is not personally close or congenial, it is usually neither fearful, nor competitive, nor hostile.

In 1963, in a child psychiatric clinic in Sweden I was told in strictly descriptive, i.e., statistical and by no means dynamic terms, that boys of eleven to thirteen show predominantly problems of aggression against their mothers, while among boys of fourteen to seventeen the aggression shifts toward the father. This observation fits well into my theoretical formulations, which are based on a comparatively small sample of adolescent boys. The preadolescent boy perceives the often aggrandized father, or other men for that matter, as an ally rather than a rival. The discrepancy between a weak father and his son's perception of him is often quite startling. Only after the defensive idealization of the father has crumbled do we come to realize that the boy drew enormous reassurance, in face of his castration anxiety, from an apparently strong father who had not been weakened, degraded or dominated, i.e., had not been castrated, by the mother "witch."

The preadolescent boy has no use for female sentimentalities; in fact, he would rather die than surrender his feelings and consequently his bodily self to the tricks and traps of female affection, endearment, and amorousness. He remains a man among men. A delightful account of this stage in a boy's life is given by Lincoln Steffens (1931):

> One of the wrongs suffered by boys is that of being loved be-
> fore loving. They receive so early and so freely the affection
> and devotion of their mothers, sisters, and teachers that they
> do not learn to love; and so, when they grow up and become
> lovers and husbands, they avenge themselves upon their
> wives and sweethearts. Never having had to love, they cannot;
> they don't know how. I, for example, was born in an atmos-
> phere of love; my parents loved me. Of course. But they had
> been loving me so long when I awoke to consciousness, that
> my baby love had no chance. It began, but it never caught up.
> Then came my sisters, one by one. They too were loved from
> birth, and they might have stayed behind as I did, but girls
> are different, my sisters seem to have been born loving as well
> as loved. Anyhow, my first sister, though younger than I,
> loved me long before I can remember even noticing her, and I
> cannot forget the shock of astonishment and humiliation at
> my discovery of her feeling for me. She had gone to Stockton
> to visit Colonel Carter's family, and in a week was so
> homesick for me that my father and mother took me with
> them to fetch her. That was their purpose. Mine was to see
> the great leader of my father's wagon train across the plains
> and talk livestock with him. You can imagine how I felt
> when, as we walked up to the house, the front door opened
> and my little sister rushed out ahead, threw her arms around
> me and cried—actually cried—with tears running down her
> cheeks, "My Len, my Len."
>   I had to suffer it, but what would Colonel Carter think,
> and his sons? [p. 77].

The many sadistic fantasies and actions of preadolescence are telling reverberations of the infantile sadomasochistic struggles in which mother and child are normally
engaged during the pregenital phases of learning body controls. When the boy enters preadolescence we normally witness a regression to pregenitality and to the actualization of
its modalities on the genital level. By virtue of this fact delinquency threatens to become virulent at this phase.
Whether this will be a transient or permanent deviancy depends first and foremost on the proclivity toward acting out.

The precondition for acting out is not to be found in adolescence; it is anchored in an incomplete separation between child and need-satisfying object, the latter being later replaced in delinquency by the always available environment as a tension-relieving part object.

The girl appears to the preadolescent boy—consciously or unconsciously—as the incarnation of evil; in his eyes she is catty, bitchy, double-crossing, possessive, or downright murderous in her very nature. When we listen to the tales of boys at this age, we detect the theme of the mean and dangerous female woven with such realism into the recounting of daily events that fact and fiction are often difficult to sort out.[1] The preadolescent boy's tendency to give credence to his inner experience by laminating it to his perception cannot simply be relegated to the defense of projection. Of course, there is no doubt that the often almost delusional quality of his perception attests to this mechanism. At the same time one must acknowledge an adaptive effort to come to terms with infantile anxieties or fantasies by keeping them reality-bound so they may be tested and mastered. This very fact presents an obstacle in treatment because it works against the accessibility of fantasies as well as against the awareness of affects, especially if they are of an infantile, dependent, or passive nature. This condition has led many therapists to assume a direct and active role in the treatment situation and to deviate by dire necessity from the psychoanalytic therapeutic model. We have come to accept the fact that modifications of treatment technique during adolescence are based on the "working conditions at

[1]The preadolescent boy who rushes into heterosexual activity offers no refutation of this formulation. In fact, the analysis of the preadolescent boy, but more often the reconstruction of this phase in cases of older male adolescents, reveals the counterphobic aspect of these precocious heterosexual relations as well as an overcompensation of passive tendencies. (This note was added in the middle seventies when the mores of the times had encouraged early sexual relations and when it occurred to many observers that a revolutionary shift in the schedule of adolescent psychosexual development had been established.)

hand," which are dictated by the dynamic constellation of this developmental stage.

One well-protected fantasy, preserved from the age of about five years and used again at the age of eleven to arouse genital stimulation, was revealed in installments by a boy in analysis. He did not reveal the accompanying sexual arousal until two years later, when he spontaneously corrected his earlier denial. The fantasy was this: "I always thought girls were wound up with a key which was stuck into the side of their thighs. When they were wound up they were very tall; boys in proportion were only one inch high. These tiny boys climbed up the legs of these tall girls, got under their skirts and into their underwear. In there hammocks were hanging down from nowhere. The boys climbed into the hammocks. I always called this to myself 'riding the girl.' " We recognize in this fantasy the overpowering largeness of the female, the phallic mother, who has robbed the boy of his masculinity: the boy had no key to make him tall. Furthermore, we recognize the passive, reclining, blissful state of being an appendix to her. A fixation on this level will render the boy's later object relations to the female passive, immature, and frustrating.

The above fantasy contains typical elements which I have often come to recognize in the analysis of older adolescents as a fixation on the preadolescent phase. In a case of this kind a male college student related two alternating fantasies which he had entertained since early puberty: (1) to be stroked on the genital by an older woman who is dressed while he is naked and who sits beside him while he is lying down; (2) to be loved, admired, and aggrandized by a very beautiful and highly intelligent girl who possesses firm and protruding breasts. The thought of finding himself in the company of such a goddess (the archaic mother) made him feel weak and small ("a nothing"); it made him literally tremble with fear. By sharing in the grandeur of an unattainable girl the patient expected to restore the sense of infantile completeness, power, and safety he once possessed when he was a part of the mother. In such cases castration fear in relation to the archaic mother becomes absorbing to such a degree that any resolution of the Oedipus complex is precluded.[2] The outcome of this impasse, which I designate a preadolescent fixation, is apparent in a homosexual orientation (latent or manifest) which at the terminal stage of adolescence has usually entrenched itself and become more or less conscious. The drive pathology slowly permeates ego functions and a condition of failure or dissatisfaction prevails. This result brings many such cases to our attention. As a warning against sweeping generalizations, however, we should keep in mind the sobering fact that psychoanalytic therapy attracts a preponderance of boys with passive trends. The aggressive drive in these cases is usually inhibited, relegated to fantasy, or bound in symptom formation.

As always in maturational crises, when dangers alert the ego to take extraordinary measures to secure the continued integrity of the psychic organism, the ego in turn advances in its mastery of anxiety and gains greater independence from primitive helplessness. Therefore, after a lengthy account of the regressive drive organization of male preadolescence, I must emphasize that the ego normally emerges strengthened from the struggle with the archaic mother. Ego growth is particularly evident in the realm of social competence, in physical prowess in team-oriented combat, in aim-inhibited competition among boys, in an awareness of tested body skills which allow freedom in action, inventiveness, and playful adventure, in short, in the emancipation of the body from parental, especially maternal, control, care, and protection. From these various sources accrues a sense of total ownership of his body,

[2]Despite the important and persistent role of the preoedipal stage a progression to the oedipal phase will nevertheless take its course. We never fail to observe how significantly the infantile dyadic relationship is woven into the oedipal constellation, rendering the Oedipus complex weak and without conflictual vigor.

which the boy has never before experienced to this
degree—except, perhaps, as a toddler.

In order to approach an elusive aspect of preadolescence
I shall now embark on a tour de force. It is not necessary to
belabor the point that delinquency during puberty commonly shows an arrest of emotional development or a fixation on the preadolescent level. This is equally true for boys
and girls. I now want to call attention to a clinical fact
which is familiar to everyone working with adolescents,
namely, the observation that male delinquency is manifested primarily in an aggressive struggle with the object
world and its representative authority figures, while female
delinquency usually encompasses sexual acting out (see
Chapter 11).[3] The universality of this clinical fact is impressive; on the study trip in 1963, I found it confirmed by every
observer in the field of delinquency from Oslo across the
continent to Jerusalem. The most commonly heard explanation of this clinical fact states simply that it is the result of
the double standard or that it is due to the absence of any
legal protection of male virginity; both these arguments beg
the question. Similar reasoning can certainly not be ad-
duced to render a related clinical fact more intelligible, i.e.,
the relatively frequent occurrence of father-daughter incest
as contrasted to the almost nonexistent mother-son incest
during the adolescent years.

Observation forces us to conclude that the delinquent
boy possesses a greater capacity for the psychological elaboration of his sexual drive than does the delinquent girl.
Consequently, in the case of the boy we witness symbolic
actions replacing direct genital expression as tension-
regulatory behavior. I attribute this far more diversified re-

---

[3]The changes in sexual behavior, customs, and morality over the last twenty-
five years have given a totally different diagnostic and prognostic valence to adolescent sexual behavior. I have dealt with this issue in my Postscript (1976) to
Chapter 11.

pertoire of delinquent behavior to the easier availability or regressive cathexis of pregenitality in the male. The girl, in contrast to the boy, resists with far greater determination the regressive pull to the preoedipal mother. She takes flight from a surrender to primal passivity into heterosexual acting out, which at this stage might more appropriately be called "cuddling." It seems that, in the case of the boy, regression to pregenitality is neither as dangerous to his sex-appropriate development nor as violently resisted as in the case of the girl. While the preadolescent boy's regressive behavior is there for the world to see, the girl's, in contrast, is shrouded in secrecy (such as shoplifting) and kept behind closed doors.

Sexual excitation in the pubertal boy manifests itself in genital arousal, erection, and orgasm with ejaculation. Orgasm at this stage contains the threat of an uncontrolled and uncontrollable state of psychomotor excitation and confronts the ego with the danger that primitive aggressive impulses will break through. There are indications which point to a defusion of instincts at this phase. Be this as it may, we observe that the boy seeks, with ingenuity and persistence, discharge channels for his aggressive drive by displacement or substitution. A similar situation does not exist for the girl delinquent, who never experiences orgasm in her regressed sexual relations, i.e., her "cuddling." She finds ample outlets for her aggressive impulses in the provocative, seductive, fickle, and demanding behavior which characterizes her general conduct and, in particular, her relationship to her partner.

For the boy there exists no passive modality of somatic drive discharge that remains in consonance with his sex-adequate masculine functioning. The phallus serves at the dawn of adolescence as a nonspecific discharge organ for tension from any source and is cathected, in this phase, with aggressive energy reflected in wildly aggressive, sadis-

tic fantasies. Genital sensations and sexual excitation, including orgasm, can derive at this early pubertal stage from
any affective state (fear, shock, anger, etc.) or fierce motor
activity (wrestling, chasing, rope climbing, etc.); often it is a
combination of both. The aggressive or, rather, the sadistic
drive associated with the phallus can inhibit its heterosexual employment through the rise of retaliatory anxiety. It
must be remembered that at this stage of adolescent development the male genital has not yet become the bearer
of specific sensations that are part of postambivalent interpersonal emotions. Only through the gradual involvement
in an affectionate-erotic relationship, real or imagined, will
the aggressive admixture of the sexual drive be tamed and
domesticated. Only then will the libidinal aim, the preservation and protection of the love object, restrain the aggressive drive from pursuing directly its primitive aim; a mutuality of gratification is thus obtained. Before this stage is
reached, however, the boy normally elaborates symbolic
representations of his sexual drive which indeed involve active as well as passive expressions of instinct gratification.
The overwhelming role sadism plays at this age needs no
elaboration; it is well known from the behavior of the preadolescent boy and, for that matter, of the male delinquent.

The emotional proximity of libidinal and aggressive impulses and their rapid change from one to the other are constantly displayed in the treatment sessions of young adolescent boys. A typical incident in therapy will briefly illustrate the abrupt shift from sexual preoccupation to the
arousal of aggressive-destructive fantasies. Chris, a boy of
thirteen, in psychotherapy for exhibitionistic behavior and
social immaturity, was talking with his therapist about
"wet dreams" and about his infantile sex theories, which
had survived behind a facade of factual enlightenment.
While discussing intercourse in terms of "the man urinating
into the vagina," he ventured to ask whether women actu-

ally have testicles and a penis. At this point his mounting excitement became suddenly shrouded in silence, until it burst forth in his vivid description of a new gun "which would not disintegrate a person, but would set fire to a person's clothing, his body, and even blind a person." Restraining his aggressive fantasies, he abruptly shifted to the suggestion that scientific efforts should be directed toward peaceful goals, such as the invention of an X-ray machine that could tell immediately after conception whether the baby would be a boy or a girl.

The violence of the sadistic phallic impulses of this phase can best be investigated in their unmitigated nature in older male adolescents who are fixated on the preadolescent level and continue to be engaged in the relentless struggle with the preoedipal (archaic) mother. We commonly discover in such cases fantasies of rage elaborating the destructive and mutilative aggression against the body of the woman whose protection is desired and whose domination is feared. It remains, at this point, a diagnostically important matter for the clinician to determine to what extent these affects, fantasies, and attitudes are derivatives of the infantile split maternal imagos, the "good" and "bad" mother, and therefore belong to the preambivalent stage of object relations. On the other hand, it needs to be ascertained to what extent the rage is genetically a remnant of oral and anal sadism, which at the genital phase of preadolescence and under the impact of sexual maturation appears in the modality of phallic sadism. As a positive aspect, we recognize in phallic sadism an effort which is familiar to us from earlier stages and which often has been only partially completed—the effort to establish autonomy over the erogenous zone that has risen to dominance at a particular stage of psychosexual development. The conflicts, drive propensities, and ego efforts of preadolescence are only dimly apparent when this phase is traversed smoothly, but they represent phase-specific sources of anxiety which we recognize whenever a developmental failure occurs at the initial stage of male adolescence.

The Case of Ralph

Before I continue to trace the next phase of adolescent development, it might prove useful to illustrate the conceptualization of preadolescence with clinical data. Besides illustrating theory, the case material also serves as a convenient bridge leading to the phase that comes after preadolescence but is still part of the early stage of male adolescence.

Ralph is a twelve-year-old boy with a chronic chip on his shoulder. He says of himself: "Trouble follows me like a shadow." He feels victimized: the world is unfair to him, everybody abuses his kindness and gets him into trouble by accusing him unjustly for misdeeds he has never committed. He is a sensitive boy who cannot tolerate the slightest criticism. He bullies his peers and controls his parents with a histrionic show of his moods. He has an unsatiable hunger for recognition and power over people. Over the years he has perfected two social roles: the teaser and the trickster. He uses both activities compulsively and indiscriminately to control others and to attract the limelight of attention. In school he is a serious behavior problem, totally indifferent to punishment or kindness. His tricks arouse the wrath of his peers when they become flagrantly sadistic. On one occasion he felt ignored by a boy who sat next to him on a public bus; Ralph thereupon put a match to the newspaper his schoolmate was reading and thus forced attention on himself. On the other hand, the tricks he plays on the teachers usually find the acclaim of his peers as, for example, when he introduced a topic in which he knew the teacher was personally interested and by this ruse managed to waste class time and to avert a scheduled test.

Ralph is fascinated by fire, by firecrackers, and by gory traffic accidents which usually involve a victim being ripped apart or maimed. He would never, he protests, go for tricks such as "putting firecrackers into the mouths of frogs or burning cats' tails." The sadism in Ralph's teasing and playing tricks is obvious, as is his fear of attack, or bodily injury, of being overpowered and controlled. These fears are particularly intense in relation to his mother and to his women teachers. His fantasies of retaliation on women are made up of sadistic, bloody tortures such as scalping them or drawing blood by punching their hands. In fighting off the castrating archaic mother through substitute figures in his present life, Ralph has made his father an ally in the struggle by insisting that he is a strong and clever man, which, indeed, he is not and certainly not in the eyes of his wife. Ralph justifies his father's shady deals, such as buying and selling stolen goods, as remarkable feats of shrewdness and courage. Identification with him has made Ralph a delinquent who, for example, forged with extraordinary skill a bus pass to which he was not entitled. This boy was unable to see his father realistically or critically until the conflict with the preoedipal mother became resolved; then and only then did Ralph's delinquency become dispensable and fade away.

The therapeutic approach to this problem centered around Ralph's complaints about his body intactness. Castration anxiety and ambivalence toward the mother had become organized around an early childhood trauma. Ralph introduced the trauma of body damage by referring to a big scar on his lower abdomen and thighs which was the result of a third-degree burn he had sustained when left on a radiator at the age of fifteen months. This account proved to be factually correct, even though the details of the event were not remembered by the mother. Ralph concluded his story by saying that he had a "hole in his leg" which was caused by the burn, and he assured the therapist that his "skin was left sizzling on the hot radiator." He would now constantly cut his fingers accidentally, tear the scabs of healing wounds and make them bleed again. "Where was my mother when I burned?" he asked the therapist in helpless rage. When he finally revealed the fact that his mother forbade him during his childhood to eat sugar so he would not become a diabetic, the scene was set for acquainting Ralph with the fact that his mother had bizarre ideas, that these ideas had become his reality, and that he defended himself against her domineering influence, her distortions of reality, and her morbid fears. He came to see his mother as strange and mentally ill, which, indeed, she was. The unmasking of the witch-mother facilitated the investigation of the boy's own distortions of reality as well as of the catastrophic dangers by which he felt surrounded in a hostile world, namely, the world of an unprotective, destructive mother imago.

Two changes became apparent in therapy after the fear of the woman (castration fear and wish) was traced to its central core: he became critical of his delinquent father and he became an accomplished magician. He even had a business card printed and performed as a pro at social occasions for a fee. The teaser and trickster had become socialized. The use of his hands was conspicuous also in his new interest in jewelry making, in which he became skillful—to the scorn of his father who wanted him to "work with his brain and not with his hands." He defeated his father's dictum, which amounted in his unconscious to a masturbation prohibition, but he could neither succeed in his craft nor gain real satisfaction from his accomplishments. Ralph condemned his father's moral corruption and shoddy values by angrily opposing him in thought and action. Ralph felt utterly defeated when his father remained unwilling to reform and live up to his son's ideal. For this reason Ralph became repeatedly depressed, experiencing the father's rejection of his wishes as a deliberate hurt, which left him with a sense of being neglected, ignored, and not loved by him.

After four years of therapy, it became evident that a delinquent and perverse career had been averted, that a sense of body intactness had been restored, that the fear of the female had been appreciably reduced, and that progressive adolescent development had been kept in motion. The disappointment in the father, however, remained a source of dysphoria and discouragement; the son's attempt at converting the father to his way of life remained a futile but never-relinquished wish, giving the prospect of achieving emotional maturity a limited if not doomed probability.

Early Adolescence

A review of this case in terms of the sequence of clinical manifestations and their changes leaves little doubt that the cathexis of the "good father" imago—the aggrandizement of the father and the accompanying ebb of conflictual strife with him—represents a typical defensive operation of male preadolescence. The aggrandizement of the father attenuates the boy's castration fear in relation to the archaic mother and therefore bears hardly any resemblance to the positive Oedipus complex. In this context we can speak of an oedipal defense or, if you will, of a pseudo-oedipal formation. The oedipal defense of the boy is clinically observable in two ways. One is marked by the obstinate perseverance of the negative oedipal position which, by its nature, entails an exaggerated idealization of the father and a pervasive passive-feminine attitude. The other appears in the adolescent boy as an overstated preoccupation with maleness, with an affectionate or sexual possessiveness of the mother or females in general, which is too glibly verbalized and clung to in defense against the regression to pregenitality and to the archaic, castrating mother imago. I have come to realize, however, that an oedipal constellation is not the substantive content of this conflict, despite its resemblance

to that clinical picture. The confusion stems from the manifest behavior, namely, the boy's admiration and envy of his
father while he seemingly wards off his possessive love for
the oedipal mother. Whenever therapy misjudges the essence of this conflict it finds itself in a stalemate. We have
seen in the case of Ralph that, with the resolution of the
conflict in relation to the archaic mother, a progression to
the oedipal father became apparent. This progression in
psychosexual development is marked by the abandonment
of the phallic mother and the ascendancy of the female
mother. Envy of her and identification with her is typical
for a transitional stage at the termination of preadolescence. It is quite probable that this aspect of preadolescent
development precipitates at this phase the conflictual elaboration of the negative Oedipus complex. This passive drive
constellation leads in its course to the central conflict of the
phase of male early adolescence. We shall now turn our attention to the vicissitudes of drive and ego typical of this
phase.

   At the turning point toward early adolescence Ralph's
progressive development came to an impasse because he
was unable to sustain the discord with and estrangement
from the father on the level of an ideational, moral, attitud-
inal, and vocational approach to life and action. He was unable to form an ego ideal that could exist and function independent of a love object in the outer world. Ralph endeavored to shape his father into his ideal partner in real life.
To put it differently: Ralph failed to detach sufficient narcissistic object libido from the oedipal father which, in turn,
could sustain an impersonal ego ideal. Consequently, the
ego ideal never became consolidated as a psychic institution
(see Chapter 15). Reflections of this failure were clearly visible throughout his efforts at psychic restructuring. A fixation in early adolescence is responsible for the specific aspect of psychopathology which in the case of Ralph remained unsolved.

The therapeutic progress described above is often all that therapy can accomplish at this stage of adolescence. We might ask whether it is our knowledge of theory and technique that confronts us with the same limitations child analysis has demonstrated or whether these limitations are not an integral aspect of treatment whenever it is carried out during a phase of ongoing development. Experience tells us that a large proportion of children terminate analysis when considerable gains have been achieved, only to continue it at a later age, usually in late adolescence or post-adolescence when a new wave of insurmountable emotional difficulties again threatens to engulf their lives. In cases of prolonged adolescence, therapy itself easily becomes a holding action because it represents a promise that the fulfillment of narcissistic fantasies can indeed become a reality through the magic of treatment, that is, through benign parent volition (see Chapter 3). The stalemate in Ralph's adolescent development will no doubt require treatment to be resumed. It seems to me that the time for the resumption of therapy will arrive when the failures of his relationship to both sexes, as well as the aimlessness and frustrations in his vocational and social life, have mobilized a crisis of more than usual severity in late adolescence or soon thereafter. Due to therapy in the initial stage of Ralph's adolescence he will no longer be able to fall back on acting out; in addition, a condition for internalization has been established which—so to speak—has laid a promising foundation for the continuation of therapeutic work in the future.

We are now well prepared to turn to the phase of early adolescence, which is initiated on the drive level by certain characteristic changes (Blos, 1962). One of these changes concerns the shift from a merely quantitative drive increase (preadolescence) to the emergence of a distinctly new drive quality. A retreat from the preadolescent regressive position becomes apparent. Pregenitality loses increasingly, often slowly and only gradually, the role of a satiatory function.

By becoming relegated to a subordinate or initiatory role—mentally and physically—it gives rise to a new drive modality, to forepleasure. This shift in drive organization eventually elevates genitality to a place of dominance. The hierarchical organization of the drives and its definitive and irreversible character both represent an innovation which decisively influences ego development. The ego, so to speak, takes its cue from the shifts in the instinctual organization and elaborates in its own structure a hierarchical organization of ego functions and of defensive patterns. I shall return to this point later.

Early adolescence initiates the protracted attempt at loosening early object ties. It is no surprise, then, to see the rise of a series of predicaments over object relations and, in fact, an ever-narrowing concentration on these transactions. We expect this development to follow the ontogenetic lines of object relations we encountered previously in preadolescence, when the boy's ambivalence to the preoedipal mother became the source of anxiety and the focal conflict to be mastered.

Pubertal maturation normally forces the boy out of his preadolescent defensive self-sufficiency and pregenital drive cathexis. We come to realize that the forward movement of object libido leads in its initial form to an object choice made according to the narcissistic model. The individual history of object relations immediately calls to mind that aspect of the oedipal constellation which falls under the most powerful repression in the male child, namely, his passive attachment to the father, the negative Oedipus complex. The oedipal position of the little boy, which can be paraphrased as "I love whom I like to be," is only gradually, and seldom completely, replaced by the alternative of "I will become whom I envy and admire." This latter step leads to the resolution of the positive Oedipus complex and consolidates the superego precursors in the formation of the superego as a psychic institution. With this structure completed or, at least, on its way, the child enters the latency period, only to face again the preoedipal and oedipal themes at the various phases of adolescence. Only then and in a sequential order of psychic restructuring is the Oedipus complex brought to a definitive resolution.

It has been my experience that the drive development of early adolescence reflects an effort on the part of the boy to come to terms with the father as his oedipal love object. In my analytic work with adolescent boys I find this theme an ever-present source of conflict requiring the most laborious effort to make it accessible to the therapeutic process. I am inclined to say that the unfolding of object libido in male adolescence meets its first and often fatal impasse when the recrudescence of the passive attachment to the oedipal father dominates the emotional scene. Of course, we immediately recognize in the excessive exacerbation of this predicament the incomplete resolution of the preadolescent phase which culminates in the resistance against regression to primal passivity. Should the regressive trend be followed, it will aggravate profoundly the conflicts and impediments that are the normal developmental aspects of early adolescence.

The study of adolescence demonstrates with abundant clarity that the mastery or resolution of the positive and negative Oedipus complex is not totally accomplished in early childhood but is the task of adolescence, i.e., the genital phase. The intervening latency period plays an important economic role which is decisive for the outcome. The enormous gains in ego expansion and autonomy which accrue from the latency period furnish the structural resources that are essential for the encounter with puberty. An abortive latency period precludes the unfolding of adolescence and results in an unmitigated reactivation of infantile sexuality (perversions). It is obvious that these early drive modalities manifest themselves on the level of pubertal maturation and seek gratification under the aegis of those ego resources that have accrued in the course of the intervening years of development.

To summarize: After the regressive position of male preadolescence the forward movement of object libido leads in its first step to a narcissistic object choice. That this choice remains within the confines of the same sex should be no surprise. The phase of early adolescence is the time of friendships with unmistakably erotic overtones, either attenuated or more or less consciously experienced. Mutual masturbation, transient homosexual practices, mutually granted scoptophilic gratifications, shared transgressions or crimes, idealizations, feelings of bliss and elation in the presence of the friend—these are experiences in which the narcissistic object choice is manifested. Furthermore, these experiences often bring about the sudden termination of friendships whenever the intensity of the instinctual drive arouses homosexual panic or, to be specific, mobilizes passive wishes. A fixation at this phase is familiar to us from the analysis of older male adolescents whose object relations are disturbed and who will "fall in love" (often only in a fleeting fantasy) with every male peer or male adult whose mental or physical faculties are momentarily envied. What is of interest here is the course this development follows, namely, the accommodations of drive and ego which either facilitate or preclude progressive development.

It is my contention that the phase of narcissistic object choice is brought to a settlement by a process of internalization, giving rise to a new institution within the ego—the ego ideal. The ego ideal, as discussed here, is the heir of the negative Oedipus complex. Transient identifications of the adolescent period play a major part in giving the ego ideal additional content and specific direction. Of course, the ego ideal can be recognized in prestages reaching back into early childhood. However, its first determined move toward consolidation as a psychic institution coincides with early adolescence or, to be more specific, with the termination of this phase. With the decline of this phase, narcissistic and homosexual object libido becomes absorbed and bound (neutralized) in the formation of the ego ideal. From this source it derives its inexhaustible vitality and strength. Submission to or, rather, affirmation of the ego ideal makes any suffering, even voluntary death, a matter of uncompromising choice. The establishment of the ego ideal attenuates the dominance of the superego by the reliance on an implicitly ego-syntonic guiding principle without which life loses inner direction, continuity, and meaning. Violations of the two institutions are followed by either guilt (superego) or shame (ego ideal). Any discrepancy between the ego ideal and the self-representation is felt as a lowering of self-esteem or as shame, which is warded off by "paranoid" defenses, typical of adolescents at this stage (Jacobson, 1964). The fact that the ego ideal embodies not only an individual but also a social component, as Freud (1914b) indicated, makes the ego ideal a controlling agency particularly well suited for the adolescent process of disengagement from family dependencies.

In my study of ego-ideal formation during the phase of male early adolescence and, especially, of ego-ideal pathology I have come to realize that Freud's (1914b) formulation of the ego ideal is of particular relevance for an understanding of adolescence. The passages I have in mind read as follows: "In this way large amounts of libido of an essentially homosexual kind are drawn into the formation of the narcissistic ego ideal and find outlet and satisfaction in maintaining it" (p. 96). "Where no such ideal has been formed, the sexual trend in question makes its appearance unchanged in the personality in the form of a perversion" (p. 100). In other words, the forward movement of object libido to heterosexual object finding is precluded by a perseverance of the early adolescent position. In that case the next phase, adolescence proper, is never reached; however, by imitation of social forms of behavior a more mature position can—at least for a while—be simulated.

Ego-ideal pathology—foreshadowed by antecedent conditions, to be sure—reaches a stage of dynamic specificity at the phase of early adolescence. The case of Ralph afforded us a glimpse into the pathology of this phase. The specific aspect that is due to the failure of ego-ideal consolidation does not always become readily apparent within the total clinical picture. In fact, it is my experience that it is often blurred and pushed out of sight by a pseudo-oedipal maneuver, by a defensive preoccupation with heterosexuality, by a professed impatience to grow up and do important things in life. Put to the test, such aspirations often collapse like a house of cards, as the case of Ralph has demonstrated. The adolescent caught in this impasse searches desperately for a meaning in life, or he at least tries intellectually or through acting out to keep the outcome of this impasse within the bounds of his own powers, his own decision, and his own choice. My experience with cases of prolonged adolescence has taught me that the crisis which we witness so frequently in the late adolescent male is rooted in arrests and incomplete resolutions of those developmental tasks that belong to the initial stage of adolescence.

This brings me to the end of my effort to delineate within the initial stage of adolescence the phase-specific conflicts, tasks, as well as failures in terms of drive and ego organizations. If we view these failures and their catastrophic impact on development as fixation points, their reflections can be recognized in the psychopathology of many late adolescent boys or young men who were not able to bring the adolescent process to a close. We recognize in most cases the ongoing struggle within the initial stage of adolescence and come to realize that this stage contained obstacles which proved to be insurmountable and constituted, consequently, a permanent barrier to progressive development. The study of this stage, then, makes its contribution to an understanding of developmental failures in the young adolescent boy; furthermore, it throws light on a larger problem that pertains to the vicissitudes of the aggressive drive which commonly play a prominent role in the clinical picture of the male adolescent.

Chapter 8

The Second Individuation Process of Adolescence

The biological processes of growth and differentiation during puberty effect changes in the structure and in the functioning of the organism. These changes occur in a typical and sequential order, called maturation. The psychological changes of adolescence also follow a developmental pattern but of a different order, since these changes draw content, stimulation, aim, and direction from a complex interplay of inner and outer impingements. What we eventually observe are new stabilizing processes and alterations of psychic structures, both of which are the result of adolescent accommodations.

At the points where both the pubertal maturation and the adolescent accommodation intersect in order to become integrated, there we find the critical stations of adolescent development. I have described these stations, clinically and theoretically, in terms of adolescent phases (Blos, 1962). They are the milestones of progressive development, each marked by a phase-specific conflict, a maturational task, and a resolution that is preconditional for the advance to higher levels of differentiation. Beyond these typical aspects of the adolescent phases, we can recognize a thread in

---

First published in *The Psychoanalytic Study of the Child*, 22: 162-186. New York: International Universities Press, 1967.

psychic restructuring that winds through the entire fabric
of adolescence. This unrelenting component is manifest with
equal pertinacity in preadolescence and late adolescence. It
is conceptualized here as the second individuation process of
adolescence. In my previous studies of adolescence I have
repeatedly emphasized the heterogeneity of phases in terms
of the positions and movements of drive and ego. My attention turns now to a process of a more pervasive order whose
sameness in direction and in aim extends without letup
through the entire period of adolescence.

I propose to view adolescence in its totality as the second
individuation process, the first one having been completed
toward the end of the third year of life with the attainment
of self- and object constancy.[1] Both periods of individuation
have in common a heightened vulnerability of the personality organization. Both periods share the urgency for changes
in psychic structure in consonance with the maturational
surge forward. Last but not least, both periods—should they
miscarry—are followed by a specific deviant development
(psychopathology) that embodies the respective failures of
individuation. What is in infancy a "hatching from the
symbiotic membrane to become an individuated toddler"
(Mahler, 1963) becomes in adolescence the shedding of family dependencies, the loosening of infantile object ties in
order to become a member of society at large or, simply, of
the adult world. In metapsychological terms, we would say
that not until the termination of adolescence do self- and object representations acquire stability and firm boundaries,
i.e., they become resistant to cathectic shifts. The oedipal
superego—in contrast to the archaic superego—loses in the

[1]In speaking of the second individuation process of adolescence it is understood
that the separation phase of infancy (in Margaret Mahler's sense) is not involved
in this higher-level process of psychic differentiation. The primal experience of "I
and not-I," of self and object has no comparable resonance in normal adolescent
development. A regression to this latter stage is typical for the psychotic adolescent; it is seen in merger symptomatology and transient depersonalization
phenomena of adolescence.

process some of its rigidity and power, while the narcissistic institution of the ego ideal acquires a more pervasive prominence and influence. The maintenance of the narcissistic balance is thus further internalized. These structural changes render the constancy of self-esteem and of mood increasingly independent from external sources or, at best, dependent on external sources of one's own choosing.

The disengagement from internalized objects—love and hate objects—opens the way in adolescence to the finding of external and extrafamilial love and hate objects. The reverse was true in early childhood during the separation-individuation phase, when the child gained psychological separateness from a concrete object, the mother. This was achieved through the process of internalization that gradually facilitated the child's growing independence from the mother's presence, her ministrations, and her emotional supplies as the chief, if not the sole, regulators of psychophysiological homeostasis. The progress from the symbiotic oneness of child and mother to that of separateness from her is marked by the formation of internal regulatory faculties which are assisted and promoted by maturational—especially motor, perceptual, verbal, and cognitive—advances. The process is at best a pendular one, as we observe again in the second individuation process of adolescence. Regressive and progressive movements alternate in shorter or longer intervals, easily giving the casual observer of the child a lopsided maturational impression. Only observation over a period of time enables us to judge the behavior of the average toddler or of the average adolescent as to its normal or deviant nature.

Adolescent individuation is the reflection of those structural changes that accompany the emotional disengagement from internalized infantile objects. The complexity of this process has been, for some time, in the center of analytic attention. In fact, it is by now axiomatic that without a successful disengagement from infantile internalized objects, the finding of new, extrafamilial love objects in the outside world is either precluded, hindered, or remains restricted to simple replication and substitution. The ego is intrinsically involved in this process. Up to adolescence, the parental ego has been selectively available to the child as a legitimate ego extension. This condition is an integral aspect of childhood dependency in the service of anxiety control and self-esteem regulation. With the disengagement from infantile libidinal dependencies in adolescence, the accustomed ego dependencies of the latency period are repudiated as well. Therefore, at adolescence we observe relative ego weakness due to the intensification of the drives, as well as absolute ego weakness due to the adolescent rejection of parental ego support. Both kinds of ego weakness are enmeshed in our clinical observations. The recognition of these disparate elements of adolescent ego weakness is not only of theoretical interest but also of practical usefulness in our analytic work. A case illustration will clarify this point.

A young adolescent boy, tormented by castration anxiety, had borrowed his mother's magical defense: "Nothing bad will ever happen as long as you don't think about it." The boy's use of thought control in the service of anxiety management revealed two components, inextricably linked together. The drive component resided in the boy's masochistic submission to his mother's will and advice, while the ego component became recognizable in his borrowing the mother's magic in order to assuage his anxiety. The child's ego had identified with the mother's anxiety-control system. With the advent of puberty the renewed and, indeed, frantic employment of the mother's magic only increased his dependency on her, thus indicating the only course his sexual drive could take, namely, toward infantile sadomasochistic submissiveness. In using his mother's magic device, he made himself the victim of her omnipotence by sharing her falsification of reality. The libidinization of submission obstructed progressive development. The magic device could become ego-alien only after the ego had gained in critical self-observation and in reality testing. To put it differently: only after the castration anxiety in relation to the archaic mother was recognized, could the phallic modality assert itself and counteract the passive-submissive trend. A growing capacity of reality testing paralleled the repudiation of infantile ego positions, thus enlarging the scope of the autonomous ego.

The disengagement from the infantile object is always paralleled by ego maturation. The reverse is equally true, that is, adolescent inadequacy or impairment of ego functions is symptomatic of drive fixations and infantile object dependencies. The cumulative ego alterations that parallel drive progression in each adolescent phase accrue in a structural innovation that is the ultimate result of the second individuation.

Without doubt, during adolescence unique and new ego capacities or faculties appear, such as, for instance, the spectacular advances in the cognitive sphere (Inhelder and Piaget, 1958). However, observation has left us wondering about their primary autonomy and, furthermore, their independence from drive maturation. Experience teaches us that, whenever drive development lags critically behind adolescent ego differentiation, the newly acquired ego functions are, without fail, drawn into defensive employment and lose their autonomous character. Conversely, an advance in drive maturation affects ego differentiation and functioning favorably. The interacting stimulation between drive and ego proceeds most vigorously and effectively if both operate and progress within an optional proximity of each other. The loosening of the infantile object ties not only makes way for more mature or age-adequate relationships, but simultaneously the ego becomes increasingly antagonistic to the re-establishment of outmoded and partly abandoned ego states and drive gratifications of childhood.

Psychoanalysts who work with adolescents have always

been impressed by this central concern with relationships. The intensity and extent of object-directed drive manifestations or inhibitions should, however, not obscure the radical alterations in ego structure that take place during this time. The sum total of these structural changes survives adolescence as enduring personality attributes.

What I endeavor to convey is the particular character of psychic restructuring in adolescence when shifts in object libido bring about ego alterations which, in turn, give the process of object losing and object finding ("pushing away" and "holding on") not only a greater urgency but also a broader adaptive scope. This circular response has normally diminished by the close of adolescence with the result that the ego has acquired a distinct and definitive organization. Within this organization there remains a wide scope for elaborations during adult life. The ego ideal affects these elaborations decisively.

We shall now turn to the course individuation follows during adolescence. In studying this process we have learned much from those adolescents who sidestep the transformation of psychic structure and replace the disengagement from internal objects by a polarization of them; in such cases social role and behavior, values, and morality are determined by being demonstratively different or, in fact, simply the opposite of the internalized imago. Ego disturbances, apparent in acting out, learning disorders, lack of purpose, procrastination, moodiness and negativism, are frequently the symptomatic signs of crisis or failure in the disengagement from infantile objects and, consequently, they represent a derailment of the individuation process itself. As clinicians we recognize in the adolescent's wholesale rejection of his family and of his own past the frantic circumvention of the painful disengagement process. Such avoidances are usually transient and the delays are self-liquidating. They may, however, assume ominous forms. We are familiar with the adolescent who runs away, drives off in a stolen car, leaves school, "bums" his way to nowhere, takes to promiscuity and to drugs. In all these cases the concreteness of action stands for the achievement of a developmental task as, for example, when geographical removal from home substitutes for psychological distancing from childhood dependencies. In one way or another, these adolescents have usually removed themselves, emphatically and with finality, from their families, convinced that no useful communication is possible between the generations. In the assessment of such cases one often arrives at the conclusion that the adolescent is "doing the wrong things for the right reasons." One cannot fail to recognize in the emergency measures of a violent rupture with childhood and family continuities the escape from an overwhelming regressive pull to infantile dependencies, grandiosities, safeties, and gratifications. The effort itself to separate from infantile dependencies is in consonance with the adolescent task but the means employed often abort the maturational momentum.

For many adolescents this violent rupture constitutes a respite, a holding position, until progressive development is rekindled. For many, however, it becomes a way of life which sooner or later leads back to what, at the outset, was to be avoided, namely, regression. By forcing a physical, geographic, moral, and ideological distance from the family or the locale of childhood, this type of adolescent renders an internal separation dispensable. In his actual separateness and independence he experiences an intoxicating sense of triumph over his past and slowly becomes addicted to his state of apparent liberation. The countercathectic energy employed in upholding this stage of life accounts for the often striking inefficacy, emotional shallowness, procrastination, and expectant waiting which characterize the various forms of individuation avoidance. True enough, physical separateness from the parent or polarization of the past through change in social role, style of dress and grooming,

special interests, and moral choices often represents the
only means by which the adolescent can maintain his
psychological integrity during some critical stage of the individuation process. The degree of maturity ultimately attained, however, will depend on how far the individuation
process advances or where it comes to an impasse and is left
incomplete. It follows from the above that the second individuation is a relative concept: on the one hand, it depends
on drive maturation and, on the other hand, it depends on
the acquired durability in ego structure. The second individuation therefore connotes those ego changes that are the
accompaniment and the consequence of the adolescent disengagement from infantile objects.

Individuation implies that the growing person takes increasing responsibility for what he does and what he is,
rather than depositing this responsibility on the shoulders
of those under whose influence and tutelage he has grown
up. In our times it has become a pervasive attitude of the
more sophisticated adolescent to blame his parents or society ("the culture") for the shortcomings and disappointments of his youth or, on a transcendental scale, to see in
the uncontrollable powers of nature, instinct, fate, and similar generalities the ultimate and absolute forces governing
life. It appears senseless to the adolescent who has taken
such a position to rise against these forces; rather, he declares that an attitude of resigned purposelessness is the
true hallmark of maturity. He adopts the nonchalant stance
of Mersault in Camus's *The Stranger*. The incapacity to
separate from internal objects except by detachment, rejection, and debasement is subjectively experienced as a sense
of alienation. We recognize in it the endemic mood of a considerable segment of present-day adolescents, promising and
gifted sons and daughters who have grown up in ambitious,
yet indulgent, usually middle-class, often progressive and
liberal, families.

In studying the morphology of adolescent individuation

in historical perspective we come to realize that each epoch evolves predominant roles and styles through which this adolescent task is implemented and socialized. Such epiphenomena of the individuation process always stand in opposition to the established order in one way or another.[2] It remains a crucial difference whether this new way of life becomes the displaced battleground of liberation from childhood dependencies, thus leading to individuation, or whether the new forms become permanent substitutions of childhood states, thus precluding progressive development. The pathognomic valence of a physical separation like "running away," "leaving school," or rushing into adultomorphic, especially sexual, styles of life can be determined only if viewed in relation to the contemporary ethos (*Zeitgeist*), to the total milieu and its traditional sanctions of behavioral forms that give expression to pubertal needs. Pubertal drive intensification reactivates primary object relations within the context of certain preferential, pregenital drive modalities. Libido and aggression, however, do not simply shift in an about-face move from primary love objects to nonincestuous ones during adolescence. All along, the ego is intrinsically involved in these cathectic shifts, and it acquires in the process the structure by which the postadolescent personality can be defined. Adolescent individuation, then, reflects a process and an achievement, both of which constitute integral components of the total adolescent process.

I shall now leave the description of familiar adolescent accommodations and turn to a discussion of their theoretical

[2]As an example, one might think of the ostentatiously simple and comfortable clothes, introduced by a fraction of educated German male youth during the second half of the eighteenth century as a reaction to the French refinement and daintiness of men's clothing. Tearing off the delicate laces from their shirtfronts was complemented by an open display of exuberant emotionality between male youths (tears, embraces). Similarly, the wig was replaced by free-flowing natural hair. The influence of Rousseau and a reaction to the "phoniness of the Establishment" were combined in these youths who created their own unconventional and natural style and, beyond that, added their share to the political ferment of the times.

implications. The process of disengagement from infantile objects, so essential for progressive development, renews the ego's contact with infantile drive and infantile ego positions. The postlatency ego is, so to speak, prepared for this regressive encounter and capable of different, more durable and age-adequate solutions of infantile predilections. The reinstatement of infantile drive and ego positions is an essential component of the adolescent disengagement process. Relatively stable ego functions, for example, memory or motor control, and furthermore, relatively stable psychic institutions, for example, superego or body image, will undergo remarkable fluctuations and changes in their executive functions. The trained observer can recognize in the transient breakdown and in the final reconstitution of these functions and institutions their ontogenetic history. One is tempted to speak, mechanistically, of an adolescent reassemblage of psychic components within the framework of a fixed psychic apparatus.

The superego, once considered an inflexible postoedipal institution, undergoes considerable reorganization during adolescence (A. Freud, 1952a). The analytic observation of superego changes during adolescence has been most instructive for studying the mutability of protoadolescent psychic structures. We shall now take a closer look at the changeability of this postoedipal institution. The regressive personification of the superego appears in great clarity during the analysis of adolescents. This permits us to glance at its origin in object relations. The unraveling of the process that led to superego formation is like a film played backward. Excerpts from the analysis of two adolescents will illustrate this. Both of them were unable to conform with any routine requirements of daily life; both of them were failures in work of any kind and, also, in love of any kind.

An older adolescent boy became puzzled by the fact that he was equally neglectful of what he liked to do and of what he disliked to do. The latter he could easily understand, but the former made no sense to him. He became aware of a preconscious thought that accompanied his activity or the choice of it. He asked himself: "Would my mother consider what I do a good thing; would she want me to do it?" The affirmative thought automatically spoiled the activity, even if it was one of a pleasurable nature. At this impasse he became totally inactive, trying to ignore the mother's constant mental presence and her influence on his life of choice and action. He continued the recounting of his dilemma by saying: "When I know that my mother wants me to do what I want to do—namely, if we both want the same—then I get embarrassed and I stop whatever I am doing."

An older adolescent girl, who all through childhood had guided her actions to win the praise and admiration of those close to her, embarked in her late adolescence on a way of life that stood in stark opposition to family standards and style. She had stopped being what she thought others wanted her to be. To her distress, her self-chosen independence afforded her no sense of self-determination because, at every turn, the thought of her parents' approval or disapproval intervened. Her decisions, she felt, were not her own, because they were guided by doing the obverse of what would please her parents. A total stalemate of action and decision making resulted. She drifted hither and yon in the fickle breeze of circumstances. All she could do was to delegate parental guidance to her friends of both sexes, living vicariously through their expectancies and gratifications, while being tormented by the constant fear of succumbing to their influence or, on a deeper level, of merging and losing her sense of self.

In both cases the enmeshment of the superego with infantile object relations resulted in a developmental impasse. What normally is accomplished during latency, namely, a reduction of infantile object dependency through identification and through the organization of the superego, had failed to succeed in both cases. Instead, primitive identifications, laid down in the archaic superego and in precursory stages of the superego, had left their powerful imprint on these two adolescents. Uniqueness fantasies and grandiose self-expectations, once realized through identification with the omnipotent mother, made all goal-directed action painfully insignificant and disappointing. The adolescent task of superego reorganization threw these two adolescents back onto the archaic level of primitive identifications (A. Reich, 1954). The origin of the superego in oedipal and in preoedipal object relations renders this psychic institution the subject for a radical revision in adolescence. It is no wonder that superego disturbances constitute a uniquely adolescent deviancy. Whenever the secondary autonomy of ego functions has only tenuously been achieved in childhood, object libido continues to gain gratification in their exercise. This heritage will throw superego functions into a disastrous disarray with the advance of pubertal maturation. Should adolescent behavior be dictated, massively and lastingly, by a defense against infantile object gratification, then the adolescent reorganization of the superego is precluded; in other words, adolescent individuation remains incomplete.

Analytic work with adolescents demonstrates, almost monotonously, the reinvolvement of ego and superego functions with infantile object relations. The study of this subject has convinced me that the danger to ego integrity does not derive solely from the strength of the pubertal drives, but comes, in equal measure, from the strength of the regressive pull. Discounting the assumption of a fundamental enmity between ego and id, I have come to the conclusion that the task of psychic restructuring by regression represents the most formidable psychic work of adolescence. Just as Hamlet longs for the comforts of sleep but fears the dreams that sleep might bring, so the adolescent longs for the comforts of drive and ego gratification but fears the reinvolvements in infantile object relations. Paradoxically, only through drive and ego regression can the adolescent task be fulfilled. Only through regression at adolescence can the residues of infantile trauma, conflict, and fixation be modified by bringing to bear on them the ego's extended resources that draw, at this age, support from the developmental momentum of growth and maturation. This forward movement is made feasible through the ego differentiation or ego maturation that is the normal heritage of the latency period. The reality-bound and self-observing part of the ego is normally kept, at least marginally, intact during the regressive movements of adolescence. Thus the dangers of regression are reduced or regulated, averting the catastrophic danger of the regressive loss of self, of a return to the undifferentiated stage, or of merger.

Geleerd (1961) has suggested that "in adolescence a partial regression to the undifferentiated phase of object relationship occurs." In a later paper, based on her earlier study, Geleerd (1964) broadens her view and states that "the growing individual passes through many regressive stages in which all three structures participate." This last-mentioned formulation has been affirmed by clinical work and is by now an integral part of the psychoanalytic theory of adolescence. Hartmann (1939) laid the foundation for these developmental considerations in his formulation of "regressive adaptation." This adaptive modality plays a role throughout life in all kinds of critical situations.

What I emphasize here is the fact that adolescence is the only period in human life during which ego and drive regression constitute obligatory components of normal development. Adolescent normative regression operates in the service of development. Regression as a defense mechanism operates alongside regression in the service of development. The differentiation of these two forms of regression in clinical work is no easy task; in fact, it is often not feasible and remains moot, at least for a stretch of time. In a narrow sense, the subject of my investigation is the mutual influence of, or the interaction between, ego and drive regression

THE ADOLESCENT PASSAGE

as they effect changes in psychic structure. The process and the achievement of structural change are conceptualized here as adolescent individuation, and the prominent role of the decathexis of infantile object representations in adolescent psychic restructuring is emphasized. The phase-specific regression initiates transient, maladaptive hazards and maintains a state of high psychic volatility in youth (see Chapter 12). This condition accounts for much of the perplexing behavior and unique emotional turbulence of this age.

In order to expound further the function of adolescent regression, it might be useful to compare it with the regressive movements of early childhood. States of stress that overtax the child's adaptive capacity are in early childhood normally responded to by drive and ego regression. Regressions of this nature do not, however, constitute developmental steps that are preconditional to ego and drive maturation. In contrast, adolescent regression, which is not defensive in nature, constitutes an integral part of development at puberty. This regression nevertheless induces anxiety more often than not. Should this anxiety become unmanageable, then, secondarily, defensive measures become mobilized. Regression in adolescence is not, in and by itself, a defense, but it constitutes an essential psychic process that, despite the anxiety it engenders, must take its course. Only then can the task be fulfilled that is implicit in adolescent development. It cannot be emphasized enough that what, initially, in this process serves a defensive or restitutive function turns, normally, into an adaptive one and contributes decisively to the uniqueness of a given personality.

In the process of adolescent psychic restructuring we observe not only drive regression but also ego regression. Ego regression connotes the re-experiencing of abandoned or partly abandoned ego states which either were citadels of safety and security, or once constituted special ways of coping with stress. Ego regression is always in evidence in the adolescent process, but only as far as it operates purely defensively does it work against the evolvement of the second individuation. We cannot but recognize, retrospectively, in many an adolescent's vagary, that a strategic retreat was the surest road to victory. *Reculer pour mieux sauter.* Only when drive and ego regression reach the immobility of an adolescent fixation does progressive development come to a standstill.

Ego regression is, for example, to be found in the re-experiencing of traumatic states, of which no childhood was ever wanting. In self-contrived confrontations with miniature editions or proxy representations of the original trauma in real life situations, the ego gradually acquires mastery over prototypical danger situations. Adolescent play-acting and experimentation as well as much of delinquent pathology (see Chapter 13) belong to this, often maladaptive, ego activity. Normally, however, a broadened ego autonomy ensues from the struggle against and with the remnants of childhood trauma. From this point of view, adolescence can be contemplated as offering a second chance for coming to terms with overwhelming danger situations (in relation to id, superego, and reality) that have survived the periods of infancy and childhood.

Adolescent ego states of a regressed nature can also be recognized in a return to "action language" as distinguished from verbal, symbolic communication, and furthermore, in a return to "body language," to somatization of affects, conflicts, and drives. The latter phenomenon is responsible for the many typical physical complaints and conditions of adolescence, epitomized by anorexia nervosa and psychogenic obesity. Such somatization is particularly evident in girls, in contrast to boys; it is part of that libidinal diffusion that in the female normally effects the erotization of the body, especially its surface. Object libido deflected on body parts or organ systems facilitates the formation of "hypochondriacal sensations and feelings of body changes that are well known clinically from initial stages of psychotic illness" (A. Freud, 1958, p. 272). During adolescence we may encounter these same phenomena but without psychotic sequelae.

Contemplating the "action language" of adolescent behavior, one cannot fail but recognize in it the problem of active versus passive. This antithesis constitutes the earliest one in individual life. It is not surprising that with the onset of puberty, with the bewildering crescendo of instinctual tension and physical growth, the adolescent falls back on old and familiar modes of tension reduction. Drive regression, in search of one of these modes, leads ultimately to primal passivity, which stands in fatal opposition to the maturing body, to its emerging physical competencies as well as to newly unfolding mental capabilities. Progressive development points to an increasing degree of self-reliance, to an ever greater mastery of the environment, indeed, to its volitional transformation, thus bringing the realization of desires and aspirations within closer reach.

Regressed ego states are also identifiable in the well-known adolescent idolization and adoration of famous men and women. In our contemporary world these figures are chosen predominantly from show business and sports. They are the collective great ones. We are reminded of the idealized parents of the child's younger years. Their glorified images constituted an indispensable regulator of the child's narcissistic balance. It should not surprise us that the bedroom walls, plastered with posters of collective idols, become bare as soon as object libido becomes engaged in genuine relationships. Then, the pictorial flock of transient gods and goddesses is rendered dispensable almost overnight.

Infantile ego states are, furthermore, recognizable in emotional states akin to merger. Such states are frequently experienced in relation to abstractions such as Truth, Nature, Beauty or in the involvement with ideas or ideals of a political, philosophical, aesthetic, or religious nature. These ego states of quasi merger in the realm of symbolic representations are sought as temporary respite and serve as safeguards against total merger with the infantile, internalized objects. Religious conversions or merger states induced by drugs belong to this realm of ego regression.

Limited ego regression, typical as well as obligatory in adolescence, can occur only within a relatively intact ego. Normally, the ego aspect to which we refer as the critical and observing ego continues to exercise its function, even if conspicuously diminished, and thus prevents ego regression from deteriorating into an infantile state of merger. There is no doubt that adolescent ego regression puts the ego to a severe test. It has been pointed out earlier that, up to adolescence, the parental ego makes itself available to the child and lends structure and organization to its ego as a functional entity. Adolescence disrupts this alliance, and ego regression lays bare the intactness or defectiveness of early ego organization, which derived decisive positive and negative qualities from the passage through the first separation-individuation phase in the second and third year of life. Adolescent ego regression within a defective ego structure engulfs the regressed ego in its early abnormal condition. The distinction between normal and pathognomic ego regression lies precisely in the alternative whether ego regression to the undifferentiated stage is approximated or consummated. This distinction is comparable to that between a dream and a hallucination. Regression to a seriously defective ego of early childhood will turn a developmental impasse, so typical of adolescence, into a temporary or permanent psychotic illness. The degree of early ego inadequacy often does not become apparent until adolescence, when regression fails to serve progressive development, precludes the second individuation, and closes the door to drive and ego maturation.

In following the development of schizophrenic children

whom I had treated successfully in early and middle childhood, I became aware of the fact that they encountered a
more or less serious recurrence of their early pathology in
late adolescence. This relapse usually occurred at the time
of their leaving home to go to college, after they had made
in the intervening years remarkable strides in their
psychological development (e.g., learning and communicat-
ing) as well as in social adaptation. The developmental
function of adolescent ego regression came to naught when
early ego states, from which the second individuation process must draw its strength, were reactivated and proved
critically defective. The nuclear pathology flared up once
more. The failure of the emotional disengagement from the
family during adolescence demonstrated how extensively
these children had lived on borrowed ego strength in the intervening years. Therapy had enabled them to derive emotional nurture from the environment. This capacity stood
them in good stead during their second acute illness; indeed, it carried them through and made their recovery possible. When the psychological navel cord has to be cut in
adolescence, children with early ego damage fall back on a
defective psychic structure that is totally inadequate to the
task of the adolescent individuation process. While these
cases throw light on the structural problems of a certain
adolescent psychopathology, they also hint at a treatment
continuum of childhood psychosis or childhood schizophrenia, reaching into or having to be resumed again in the
adolescent, usually the late adolescent, years.

A characteristic of adolescence that cannot escape our
notice lies in the frantic effort to keep reality-bound, i.e., to
be active, to move about, and to keep doing things. Furthermore, it appears in the need for group experiences or
individual relationships of vivid and acute involvement and
affectivity. The frequent and often abrupt change of these
relationships with either sex highlights their ungenuine
character. What is sought is not the personal bond but the

sharpness of affect and the emotional agitation evoked by it. Into this realm belongs the pressing need to do things "for kicks," thus escaping affective loneliness, dullness, and boredom. This picture would be incomplete without mention of the adolescent who seeks solitude and splendid isolation where he conjures up in his mind affective states of extraordinary intensity. These propensities are best designated as affect and object hunger. What all these adolescents have in common is the need for sharp, intense affective states, be they marked by exuberance and elation or pain and anguish. We can look at this affective condition as a restitutive phenomenon that follows in the wake of internal object loss and concomitant ego impoverishment.[3]

The subjective experience of the adolescent—expressed in the quandary of "Who am I?"—contains multitudinous perplexities. It reflects what is conceptualized as ego loss and ego impoverishment. Ego loss remains throughout adolescence a constant threat to psychological integrity and gives rise to forms of behavior that appear deviant but need to be assessed as efforts to keep the adolescent process in motion by a frantic—even if maladaptive—turn to reality. The clinical picture of many a delinquent, if viewed within this perspective, often reveals more of a healthy component than he is usually credited with (see Chapter 12 for clinical examples).

At this point I wish to reconsider adolescent object hunger and ego impoverishment. Both these developmental transient conditions find compensatory relief in the group,

[3]It seems at first sight a contradiction to speak of "ego impoverishment" when object libido is deflected on the self. However, a healthy ego cannot tolerate well and for long being cut off from object relations. The flooding of the self with narcissistic libido becomes ego-syntonic only in the psychotic adolescent; for him, the real world is dull and colorless. The "normal" adolescent experiences a sense of frightening unreality in mounting narcissistic isolation from the object world. Masturbation, therefore, can never offer a permanent form of gratification because, eventually, it lowers self-esteem. While masturbation fantasies may arouse guilt feelings through superego interdiction, we cannot ignore the fact that the lowering of self-esteem derives in large measure from the weakening of the bond with the object world or, in other words, from a critical narcissistic imbalance.

the gang, the coterie, contemporaries generally. The peer group is a substitute, often literally, of the adolescent's family (see Chapter 5). Within the society of the adolescent's contemporaries lies stimulation, belongingness, loyalty, devotion, empathy, and resonance. I am reminded here of the healthy toddler in Mahler's study (1963) who shows during the separation-individuation crisis an amazing capacity to "extract contact supplies and participation from the mother." In adolescence these contact supplies are obtained from the peer group. The toddler requires the help of the mother to reach autonomy; the adolescent turns to the contemporary horde, of whatever type, to extract those contact supplies without which the second individuation cannot be realized. The group permits identifications as role tryouts without demanding any permanent commitment. It also allows for interactional experimentation as a severance action from childhood dependencies, rather than as a prelude to any new and lasting, personal and intimate relationship. Furthermore, the group shares and thus alleviates individual guilt feelings that accompany the emancipation from childhood dependencies, prohibitions, and loyalties. We can summarize and say that, by and large, the contemporaries ease the way to membership in the new generation within which the adolescent has to establish his social, personal, and sexual identity as an adult. Whenever peer relationship simply replaces childhood dependencies, then the group has miscarried its function. In such cases, the adolescent process has been short-circuited with the result that unresolved emotional dependencies become permanent personality attributes. Under these circumstances life within the new generation unfolds strangely like a shadow play of the individual's past: What was to be avoided most repeats itself with fateful accuracy.

An older adolescent girl, stalemated in a rigid anticonformity position that served as a protection against an unusually strong regressive pull, put so well into words what I have endeavored to say that I shall let her speak. In contemplating an instance of nonconformity, she said: "If you act in opposition to what is expected, you bump right and left into regulations and rules. Today, when I ignored school—just didn't go—it made me feel very good. It gave me a sense of being a person, not just an automaton. If you continue to rebel and bump into the world around you often enough, then an outline of yourself gets drawn in your mind. You need that. Maybe, when you know who you are, you don't have to be different from those who know, or think they know, who you should be." A statement like this asserts the fact that a firm social structure is a necessary condition for adolescent personality formation to evolve.

I shall now turn to the broader consequences of the fact that regression in adolescence is the precondition for progressive development. I inferred from clinical observation that the adolescent has to come into emotional contact with the passions of his infancy and early childhood in order for them to surrender their original cathexes; only then can the past fade into conscious and unconscious memories, and only then will the forward movement of the libido give youth that unique emotional intensity and power of purpose.

The profoundest and most unique quality of adolescence lies in the capacity to move between regressive and progressive consciousness with ease that has no equal at any other period in human life. This fluidity might account for the remarkable creative achievements—and disappointed expectations—of this particular age. The adolescent experimentation with self and reality, with feeling and thought will, if all goes well, give a lasting and precise content and form to individuation in terms of its actualization on the environment. The choice of a vocation, for example, represents one such crucial form of actualization.

In the process of disengagement from primary love and hate objects, a quality of early object relations appears in the form of ambivalence. The clinical picture of adolescence demonstrates the defusion of instinctual drives. Acts and fantasies of raw aggression are typical of adolescence in general and of male adolescence in particular. I do not mean that all adolescents are manifestly aggressive, but rather that the adolescent aggressive drive affects the drive balance as it existed before adolescence and calls for new adaptive measures. The form these measures take, be this displacement, sublimation, repression, or reversal, is not the issue at this point of my inquiry. The analysis of manifest aggression leads ultimately to elements of infantile rage and sadism, in essence, to infantile ambivalence. Infantile object relations, when revived at adolescence, are bound to appear in their original form, that is to say, in an ambivalent state. Indeed, it remains the ultimate task of adolescence to strengthen postambivalent object relations. The emotional instability of relationships and, above and beyond that, the inundation of autonomous ego functions by ambivalence generally creates in the adolescent a state of precarious lability and incomprehensible contradictions in affect, drive, thought, and behavior. The emotional fluctuation between the extremes of love and hate, activity and passivity, fascination and disinterest, is such a well-known characteristic of adolescence that it requires no elaboration. However, this phenomenon is worth exploring in relation to the subject of this investigation, namely, individuation. A state of ambivalence confronts the ego with a condition that—due to the ego's relatively mature state—is felt as intolerable, yet it remains, temporarily at least, beyond the ego's synthesizing capacity to deal with this condition constructively. Much that appears to be a defensive operation, such as negativism, oppositionalism, or indifference, is but a manifestation of an ambivalent state that has pervaded the total personality.

Before pursuing these thoughts any further, I shall illustrate them with an excerpt from the analysis of a seventeen-year-old boy. I shall concentrate in what follows on those aspects of the analytic material that reflect the disengagement from the archaic mother and that have a direct bearing on the topic of ambivalence and individuation. The boy, able and intelligent, related to people on an intellectualizing level, better to adults than to peers. A passive-aggressive attitude pervaded all his relationships, especially within the family. One became aware of a tumultuous inner life that had found no expression in affective behavior. The boy was given to moodiness, secretiveness, uneven work performance in school, periodic stubbornness, and negativism coupled with a cold demandingness at home. Within this fluctuating picture one could discern an all-pervasive, haughty, impenetrable superciliousness that bordered on arrogance. This abnormal state was well fortified by compulsive-obsessive defenses. The choice of this defense in and of itself hints at the dominant role of ambivalence in the pathogenesis of this case.

Not until the boy's fantasies became accessible was it possible to appreciate his need for a rigid and unassailable defense organization. His every act and thought was accompanied by a, heretofore unconscious, involvement with the mother and her fantasied complicity, good or bad, in his daily life. He possessed an insatiable need for closeness to his mother, who had left him from early life on in the care of a well-meaning relative. The boy had always admired, envied, and praised his mother. The analysis helped him experience his hate, contempt, and fear in relation to her whenever his intense wishes for her material generosity were thwarted. It became clear that his actions and moods were determined by the ebb and flow of love and hate that he felt toward his mother or that he imagined his mother felt toward him. In consequence, for example, he would not do his homework when the thought prevailed that his academic achievement would please his mother. At other times it was the reverse. When he received an award at school, he kept it a secret from his mother so she could not use his achievement as a "feather in her own cap" or, in other words, take it away from him. When he went for a walk he did so in secret, because his mother preferred an outdoor boy and, to put her in the wrong, he would then let her scold him for not getting any fresh air. Should he enjoy a show or invite a friend to his house, it ruined the pleasure of the event when his mother showed delight and approval. In retaliation, he practiced the piano, as his mother wanted, but played everything fortissimo, knowing well that the loud sound would get on his mother's nerves. Playing loud substituted for shouting at her. The realization of his aggression made him anxious.

At this point, the analysis of the boy's ambivalence became blocked by a narcissistic defense. He experienced himself as being an outsider to the drama of life, as being uninvolved in the events of the day, and as seeing his surroundings in blurred and fuzzy outlines. The usual compulsive-obsessive defense (cataloguing, filing, repairing) failed in coping with this emergency. He found this state of depersonalization quite unpleasant and disconcerting. The analytic work began to flow again when he became aware of the sadistic aspect of his ambivalence. Then, the strange ego state left him. He felt and verbalized his impulse toward violence, to strike out and hurt his mother physically whenever she frustrated him. The sense of frustration was not dependent on her objective actions but rather on the ebb and flow of his needs. The replication of infantile ambivalence was apparent. He was now able to differentiate between the mother of the infantile period and the mother of the present situation. This advance made it possible to trace the involvement of ego functions in his adolescent ambivalence conflict and bring about the restoration of their autonomy.

It was interesting to observe how in the resolution of the ambivalence conflict certain selected attributes of the mother's personality became attributes of the boy's ego, such as her capacity to work, her use of intelligence, and her able sociability, all of which had been the objects of the son's envy. On the other hand, some of her values, standards, and character traits were rejected by him as undesirable or repugnant. They were no longer perceived as the mother's arbitrary unwillingness to be whatever would please and comfort her child. A secondary object constancy in relation to the mother of the adolescent period became established. The omnipotent mother of the infantile period was superseded by the son's realization of her fallibilities and virtues. In short, she became human. Only through regression was it possible for the boy to re-experience the maternal image and institute those corrections and differentiations that effected a neutralization of his preoedipal ambivalent object relation. The psychic reorganization described here was subjectively experienced by the boy as a sharp realization of a sense of self, of that awareness, and conviction, best summarized in the phrase "this is me." This state of consciousness and the subjective feeling reflect the emerging differentiation within the ego that is here conceptualized as the second individuation process.

The first exhilaration that comes with the independence from the internalized parent or, more precisely, from the parental object representation is complemented by a depressed affect that accompanies and follows the loss of the internal object. The affect accompanying this object loss has been likened to the state and work of mourning. Normally, a continuity in the relationship to the actual parent remains after the infantile character of the relationship is given up. The work of the adolescent individuation is related to both parental object representations, infantile and contemporary. These two aspects are derived from the same person but at different stages of development. This constellation tends to confuse the relationship of the adolescent to his parent who is experienced partly or wholly as the one of

the infantile period. This confusion is worsened whenever
the parent participates in the shifting positions of the adolescent and proves unable to maintain the fixed position as
an adult vis-à-vis the maturing child.

The adolescent disengagement from infantile objects
necessitates first their decathexis before libido can again be
turned outward in the search of phase-specific object gratifications in the wider social ambience. We observe in adolescence that object libido—in varying degrees, to be sure—is
withdrawn from outer and inner objects and is converted
into narcissistic libido by being deflected onto the self. This
shift from object to self results in the proverbial self-
centeredness and self-absorption of the adolescent who fan-
cies himself to be independent from the love and hate objects of his childhood. The flooding of the self with narcissistic libido has the effect of self-aggrandizement and an overestimation of the powers of body and mind. This condition
affects reality testing adversely. To cite a familiar consequence of this state, I remind you of the frequent automobile
accidents of adolescents which occur despite their expert
skill and technical knowledge. Should the process of individuation stop at this stage, then we encounter all sorts of
narcissistic pathology of which the withdrawal from the object world, the psychotic disorder, represents the gravest
impasse.

The internal changes accompanying individuation can be
described from the side of the ego as a psychic restructuring
during which the decathexis of the parental object representation in the ego brings about a general instability, a sense
of insufficiency and of estrangement. In the effort to protect
the integrity of the ego organization, a familiar variety of
defensive, restitutive, adaptive, and maladaptive maneuvers
are set into motion before a new psychic equilibrium is established. We recognize its attainment in a personal and
autonomous life style.

At the time when the adolescent process of individuation

is in its most vigorous season, deviant, i.e., irrational, erratic, turbulent behavior is most prominent. Such extreme measures are employed by the adolescent to safeguard psychic structure against regressive dissolution. The adolescent in this state presents the clinician with a most delicate task of discrimination as to the transient or permanent or, simply, as to the pathognomic or normal nature of the respective regressive phenomena. The perplexing ambiguity that clinical assessment has to cope with derives from the fact that a resistance against regression can be as much a sign of normal as of abnormal development. It is a sign of abnormal development if resistance against regression precludes the modicum of regression essential for the disengagement from early object relations and infantile ego states or, in short, preconditional for the reorganization of psychic structure. The problem of regression, both ego and drive regression, reverberates throughout adolescence in an either noisy or quiet way; the phenomenology is multiform, the process is the same. These regressive movements make the attainment of adulthood possible and they have to be understood in these terms. They also represent the nuclei or adolescent fixation points around which the failures of the adolescent process become organized. Adolescent disturbances have drawn our attention, almost exclusively, to the regressive symptomatology within the context of drive gratification or to the defensive operations and their sequelae. I submit that resistance against regression is, in equal measure, a cause for concern, as it may present a persistent and insurmountable roadblock in the course of progressive development.

Resistance against regression can take many forms. One is exemplified in the adolescent's forceful turn toward the outside world, to action and bodily motion. Paradoxically, independence and self-determination in action and in thought tend to become most violent and reckless whenever the regressive pull possesses an inordinate strength. I have observed that children who were extremely clinging and dependent during childhood resort in adolescence to the reverse attitude, namely, detached distance from the parent or the parental code of conduct at any cost. In doing so they achieve an apparent but illusory victory. In such cases, action and thought are simply determined by the fact that they represent the obverse of the expectations, wishes, and opinions of the parents or of their substitutes and representatives in society such as teachers, policemen, and adults generally or, more abstractly, law, tradition, convention, and order anywhere, in any form, and regardless of social purpose and meaning. Here again, transient disturbances in the interaction between the adolescent and his environment are qualitatively different from those that acquire premature permanency by molding, in a definitive fashion, the ego's relation to the outside world, thus bringing the adolescent process to a premature standstill rather than to a normative termination.

Based on our experience with the neurotic child and adult we have grown accustomed to concentrating on defenses as the major obstacles in the path of normal development. Furthermore, we tend to think of regression as a psychic process that stands in opposition to progressive development, to drive maturation, and to ego differentiation. Adolescence can teach us that these connotations are both limited and limiting. It is true that we are ill prepared to say what, in a regressed state during adolescence, is simply the static resuscitation of the past and what heralds psychic restructuring. It is reasonable to assume that the adolescent who surrounds himself in his room with posters of idolized persons not only repeats a childhood pattern that once gratified narcissistic needs, but simultaneously takes part in a collective experience that makes him an empathic member of his peer group. Sharing the same idols is tantamount to being part of the same family; however, a crucial difference cannot escape us, namely, that the new social matrix at this stage of life promotes the adolescent process through participation in a symbolic, stylized, exclusive, tribal ritual. Regression under these auspices seeks not simply to re-establish the past but to reach the new, the future, via the detour along familiar pathways. A sentence by John Dewey comes to mind here. "The present," he says, "is not just something which comes after the past. . . . It is what life is in leaving the past behind."

The thoughts assembled here have drifted toward a converging goal because they share the common objective of elucidating the changes in ego organization brought about by drive maturation. It has become convincingly clear from clinical investigations of the adolescent process that both the task of disengagement from primary objects and the abandonment of infantile ego states necessitate a return to early phases of development. Only through the reanimation of the infantile emotional involvements and of the concomitant ego positions (fantasies, coping patterns, defensive organization) can the disengagement from internal objects be achieved. This achievement, then, hinges on drive and ego regression, both ushering in, along their course, a multitude of, pragmatically speaking, maladaptive measures. In a paradoxical fashion one might say that progressive development is precluded if regression does not take its proper course at the proper time within the sequential pattern of the adolescent process.

In defining the individuation process as the ego aspect of the regressive task in adolescence, it becomes apparent that the adolescent process constitutes, in essence, a dialectic tension between primitivization and differentiation, between regressive and progressive positions, each drawing its impetus from the other, as well as each rendering the other workable and feasible. The ensuing tension, implicit in this dialectic process, puts an inordinate strain on both ego and drive organization or, rather, on their interaction. This strain is responsible for the many and varied distortions and

failures in individuation—clinical and subclinical—that we
encounter at this age. Much of what appears, at first glance,
as defensive in adolescence might, more correctly, be identified as a precondition for progressive development to get
under way and to be kept in flux.

Chapter 9

Character Formation in Adolescence

The problem of character formation is of such vast scope that almost any aspect of psychoanalytic theory is related to it. This fact tells us at the outset that we deal with a concept of enormous complexity or with integrative processes of the highest order. It is a sobering and welcome limitation to concentrate on the adolescent period and investigate, in this circumscribed domain, whether this particular stage of development affords us insight into the formative process of character and, consequently, throws light on the concept of character in general. It would not be the first time in the history of psychoanalysis that the nature of a psychic phenomenon is illuminated by the study of its formation.

Whoever has studied adolescence, regardless of his theoretical background, has been aware of changes in the maturing personality that are generally identified with character formation. Even the untutored observer of youth, or the adult who retrospectively contemplates his own adolescence, cannot fail to notice that, with the termination of adolescence, a new mode of dealing with the exigencies of life is in evidence. Behavior, attitudes, interests, and relationships appear more predictable, show a relatively greater stability, and tend to become irreversible, even under stress.

The psychoanalytic observer of adolescence can attest to these findings. However, he asks himself which psychic

First published in *The Psychoanalytic Study of the Child*, 23: 245-263. New York: International Universities Press, 1968.

171

mechanisms or which developmental processes are at work
in character formation. The process of formation, indeed,
raises the questions: "What takes form?" and "What gives
form?" Furthermore, what are the preconditions for the
formation of character, and why and to what extent does it
occur at the stage of adolescence? Precursors of character
can be discerned abundantly in childhood. We would not,
however, attribute to these rather habitual ways in which
the ego deals with id, superego, and reality the designation
of character because the integrated, rather fixed pattern of
its disparate components is still lacking. Due to the adolescent step forward in the organization of character traits,
Gitelson (1948) has referred to "character synthesis" as the
essential therapeutic task during the adolescent period.
Empirically, we all have come to similar conclusions and
look at the formation of character in adolescence as the outcome of psychic restructuring; in other words, it is the
manifest sign of a completed, although not necessarily complete, passage through adolescence. We all have had occasion to observe how the analysis of an adolescent, especially
an older adolescent, moves toward its termination by the silent emergence of character. What, however, do we mean by
this obvious "something" that emerges? This question forces
us to consider some pertinent aspects of psychoanalytic
characterology.

Character Traits and Character

The etymological root of the word "character" in the Greek
verb "to furrow and to engrave" has always remained part
of the concept of character in regard to the permanency and
fixity of pattern or design. These permanencies are represented, in terms of personality, by distinctive traits or
qualities and by typical or idiosyncratic ways of conducting
oneself. Even the style of life and temperamental attitudes
have been here and there brought into the broad scope of
character.

In the psychoanalytic literature on character we encounter an imprecise and inconsistent use of terms. The interchangeable use of "character," "character type," and "character trait" has been particularly confusing. We can, roughly, distinguish four approaches to classical psychoanalytic characterology. In the first approach (Freud, 1908; Abraham, 1921, 1924a, 1924b; Jones, 1918; Glover, 1924), the character trait is traced to a specific level of drive development or drive fixation (e.g., oral character traits); in the second (W. Reich, 1928, 1930), the defensive aspect of the ego represents the decisive factor (e.g., the reactive character, character armor); in the third (Freud, 1939), it is the fate of the object libido that determines the character (e.g., the narcissistic or anaclitic character); and in the fourth (Erikson, 1946), it is the influence of environment, culture, and history that engraves a patterned and preferential style of life on people (the psychosocial definition of character). Of course, these four determinants of character traits and of character are not mutually exclusive; on the contrary, they appear in various admixtures and combinations. The salient feature of each characterological formation is the implicit ego syntonicity and absence of conflict, in distinction to neurotic symptoms and, furthermore, the patterned fixity of the characterological organization.

Two widely accepted definitions of character read as follows:

> ...the typical mode of reaction of the ego towards the id and the outer world [W. Reich, 1929, p. 125].

> ... the habitual mode of bringing into harmony the tasks presented by internal demands and by the external world, is necessarily a function of . . . the ego [Fenichel, 1945, p. 467].

Character originates in conflict, but, by its very nature, it prevents the arousal of signal anxiety through the codification of conflict solutions. The automatization of dealing with idiosyncratic danger situations represents a considerable step forward in personality integration and functioning.

Indeed, character formation can be conceptualized from an adaptive point of view, and clinical evidence in support of such a thesis is easily obtainable. The economic gain inherent in character formation lies in the release of psychic energy for the expansion of adaptive inventiveness and the actualization of human potentialities. The economic gain in character formation was stated clearly by Freud (1913a): "repression either does not come into action [in character formation] or smoothly achieves its aim of replacing the repressed by reaction-formations and sublimations" (p. 323). Having observed these substitutions in the analysis of adolescents, I wonder whether the countercathexis of the reactive (defensive) character does not restrict rather than expand the adaptive scope of self-realization. I shall return to this question later.

The transformation of drive fixations into character traits is so universal and so well documented that it requires little comment. It might, however, not be superfluous to mention that instinctual predilections in combination with special sensitivities constitute inherent aspects of human development. When drive fixations are transformed into character traits, the qualitative and quantitative factors due to endowment bestow on each character a highly individualistic countenance.

We are familiar with the host of character traits that take their origin, separately or mixed, in the various levels of psychosexual development. Secondarily, the ego makes use of such proclivities by drawing them into its own realm and employing them for its own purposes. We then speak of the sublimation type of character. If the instinctual predilection gives rise to conflict, then the automatization of defenses marks the character in some decisive fashion, as is exemplified in the reactive character. We can see that the fixed ego attitude of dealing with danger (e.g., "avoidance") has a broader, more inclusive scope than a character trait derived from drive transformations (e.g., "obstinacy"). Such circumscribed, enduring, and fixed ego reactions, however, cannot be discerned in children because the child's ego remains partly and significantly interlocked with parental and environmental object dependencies up to the age of puberty. Although we certainly can discern distinct character traits in the child, what appears as character in childhood is mainly a pattern of ego attitudes, stabilized by identifications, which, as we know, can undergo a most radical revision during adolescence. Here lies one further reason for stating that character formation and adolescence are synonymous. Precocious character consolidation occurring before puberty should be looked at as an abnormal development, because it precludes that essential elasticity and flexibility of psychic structure without which the adolescent process cannot take its normal course.

The distinction between character traits and character corresponds with the developmental line of demarcation drawn by adolescence. Character traits, then, are not identical with character per se, nor is character simply the sum total of character traits. Of course, we can trace in each individual oral, anal, urethral, and phallic-genital characteristics or character traits, but none of these explains a person's character, nor can it do justice to a person's character as a monolithic structure. If we recognize in a person a degree of orderliness, stubbornness, and frugality, we no doubt are confronted with anal character traits. We hesitate, however, to call that person an anal character unless we know more about the economic, structural, and dynamic factors, indeed, the degree to which these traits are still cathected with anal eroticism and the extent to which these traits have become emancipated from infantile bondage and in time acquired functions far removed from their genetic source.

We are reminded here of Hartmann's (1952) statement that defensive ego functions can lose their defensive nature in time and become valuable and integral ego assets serving

a far wider function than the original defensive one. Similarly, it can be said that "reactive character formation,
originating in defense against the drives, may gradually
take over a host of other functions in the framework of the
ego" (Hartmann, 1952, p. 25); that is, it may remain a part
of the personality despite the fact that its original raison
d'être has vanished. Hartmann's point of view opens up two
avenues of thought: either the defensive nature of the character trait is altered because it is emptied of its countercathexis, or the id component is afforded a nonconflictual
gratification in the exercise and maintenance of character.
Could it be that the attainment of the genital level of drive
maturation during adolescence facilitates one or the other of
these outcomes? Furthermore, could it be assumed that
these transitions or modifications of character traits into
character formation are the cardinal achievement of adolescence? We certainly ascertain in character formation integrative processes, structurings and patternings that belong to
a different order than the mere bundling together of traits,
attitudes, habits, and idiosyncrasies. Lampl-de Groot (1963),
following a similar line of thought, has modified the definitions of character given earlier (W. Reich, 1929; Fenichel,
1945) by saying that character is the habitual way in which
integration is achieved.

The Function of Character

My remarks, up to this point, about character formation
have carried an implicit assumption that should now be
stated directly and affirmatively. It should, however, be
borne in mind that these propositions are laid down here
only to pave the road to the central theme of this investigation, namely, the relationship between the adolescent process and character formation.

It is assumed that character, as a definitive component
of adult psychic structure, performs an essential function in
the mature psychic organism. This function is manifested in

the maintenance of psychosomatic homeostasis, in patterned self-esteem regulation (A. Reich, 1958), in the stabilization of ego identity (Erikson, 1956), and in the automatization of threshold and barrier levels, both shifting in accordance with the intensity of internal or external stimuli. This regulatory function encompasses the containment of affective fluctuations (including depression) within a tolerable range as a major determinant in character formation (Zetzel, 1964).

The more complex a psychic formation, the more elusive the total configuration or organization becomes to the observer. The concept of character is a case in point. We have to content ourselves with the study of components or, more precisely, with a description of the whole in terms of the function of its constituent parts. The whole can then be assembled as a psychic entity from these fractional comprehensions (Lichtenstein, 1965). Two investigative approaches are thus open to us: (1) to study observable functions in order to impute structure (dynamic, economic principle), and (2) to trace the growth of a psychic formation and see how it comes into its own (genetic principle). These approaches are not the result of an arbitrary choice, but are forced upon us by the nature of our subject. Character formation is, generally speaking, an integrative process and as such aims at the elimination of conflict and anxiety arousal. We are reminded of Anna Freud's (1936) statement that the ego cannot be studied when it is in harmony with id, superego, and the outer world; it reveals its nature only when disharmony between the psychic institutions prevails. We are faced with a similar dilemma in studying character. Here, too, we can clearly describe pathological character formation, while the typical process of character formation remains elusive. In the analysis of adolescents we cannot fail to notice how character takes shape silently, how it consolidates proportionate to the severance from and dissolution of infantile ties, like the phoenix rising from its ashes.

Let us return to the question of why the formation of

character occurs at the stage of adolescence or, rather, at
the termination of adolescence. Generally, we recognize developmental progression by the appearance of new psychic
formations as the consequence of differentiating processes.
Drive and ego maturation always leads to a new and more
complex personality organization. Adolescent drive progression to the adult genital level presupposes a hierarchical arrangement of the drives, as is reflected in the organization
of forepleasure. Ego maturation, distinctly influenced but
not wholly determined by drive progression, is reflected in
qualitative cognitive advances, as described by Inhelder and
Piaget (1958). Looking at development and maturation in
terms of differentiating and integrative processes, we can
now ask: Which of these processes in adolescence are preconditional for character formation?

I shall approach this problem by investigating some aspects of typical adolescent drive and ego progressions that
make character formation not only possible but mandatory
for the stabilization of the newly attained personality organization of adulthood. If it were possible to describe character in terms of observable functions, and character formation in terms of preconditions or of epigenetic sequences or
abandoned developmental stages, then the aim of this exploration would be more within our reach. Zetzel (1964) has
emphasized the developmental aspect of character formation
and speaks of a developmental task which, I think, belongs
to the phase of late adolescence. Zetzel's expansion of the
definition of character formation is noteworthy; she states:
"Character formation . . . includes the whole range of solutions, adaptive or maladaptive, to recognized developmental
challenges" (p. 153).

The Adolescent Process and Character Formation

I have chosen four adolescent developmental challenges
which I have found to be closely related to character formation. In fact, character formation remains stunted or as-

sumes an abnormal slant if these challenges are not met with reasonable competence. It should be evident that I look at character formation from a developmental point of view and see in it a normative formation that reflects the result of progressive ego and drive development at adolescence. One might compare it to the emergence of the latency period as a result of the oedipal resolution. Whenever the oedipal stage is prolonged beyond its proper timing, latency development remains incomplete or defective. We are accustomed to consider the decline of the Oedipus complex as a precondition for latency to come into its own. In a comparable and similar perspective I introduce here four developmental preconditions without which adolescent character formation cannot take its proper course; the attainment of adulthood will thus remain stunted.

The Second Individuation

The first precondition I shall discuss encompasses what has been called the "loosening of the infantile object ties" (A. Freud, 1958), a process which, in its wider scope, I have conceptualized as the second individuation process of adolescence (see Chapter 8). The developmental task of this process lies in the disengagement of libidinal and aggressive cathexes from the internalized infantile love and hate objects. We know how closely infantile object relations are interwoven with psychic structure formation, as demonstrated, for example, by the transformation of object love into identification. I do not have to remind you that object relations activate and form ego nuclei around which subsequent experiences coalesce, and that they induce and sharpen idiosyncratic sensitizations, inclusive of preferences and avoidances. The most dramatic and fateful formation derived from object relations is the superego. Conflicts of the infantile period and of childhood give rise to the many character traits and attitudes which can, at those times, be easily observed *in statu nascendi*.

We recognize in the disengagement from infantile object ties the psychological counterpart to the attainment of somatic maturity, brought about by the biological process of puberty. The psychic formations that not only were derived from object relations, but, more or less, still maintain close instinctual ties to infantile object representations are affected, often catastrophically, by the second individuation of adolescence. Again, the superego demonstrates, by the degree of its disorganization or disintegration at adolescence, the affective affinity of this structure to infantile object ties. I can only hint here at the fact that many controls and adaptational functions pass over from the superego to the ego ideal, namely, to a narcissistic formation. The love of the infant's parents is, partially at least, replaced by the love of the self or its potential perfection.[1]

The psychic restructuring, implicit in what I have described above, cannot be accomplished without regression. The relentless striving toward increasing autonomy through regression forces us to view this kind of regression in adolescence as regression in the service of development, rather than in the service of defense. In fact, adolescent analysis demonstrates convincingly not only the adolescent's defense against phase-specific regression, but also the task of the analysis to facilitate regression.

Adolescent regression not only is unavoidable, it is obligatory, that is, phase-specific. Adolescent regression in the service of development brings the more advanced ego of adolescence into contact with infantile drive positions, with old conflictual constellations and their solutions, with early object relations and narcissistic formations. We might say that the personality functioning which was adequate for the protoadolescent child undergoes a selective overhaul. The ego's advanced resourcefulness is brought to bear on this task.

[1] The interconnections between infantile object relations, superego, and ego ideal are dealt with in Chapter 15.

In the course of adolescent psychic restructuring the ego draws drive propensities and superego influences into its own realm, integrating these disparate elements into an adaptive pattern. The process of the second individuation proceeds via regressive recathexis of pregenital and preoedipal positions. They are, so to say, revisited, lived through again, but with the difference that the adolescent ego, being in a vastly more mature state vis-à-vis infantile drives and conflicts, is able to bring about shifts in the balance between ego and id. New identifications ("the friend," "the group," etc.) take over superego functions, episodically or lastingly. The adolescent's emotional and physical withdrawal from, or opposition to, his world of childhood dependencies and security measures makes him, for some time, seek a protective cover in passionate, but usually transient, peer associations. We then observe shifting identifications with imitative and restitutive connotations as expressed in posture, gait, gesture, attire, speech, opinions, value systems, etc. Their shifting and experimental nature is a sign that character has not yet been formed, but it also indicates that social adaptation has transcended the confines of the family, its milieu and tradition. These social way stations, significant as they are, have outlasted their usefulness with the unfolding and implementation of a life plan, with the capacity for adult object relations, and with a realistic projection of the self into the future. Then we know that a consolidation of the personality has come about, that a new forward step in internalization has been taken, that inner consistencies and uniformities have become stabilized, that behavior and attitudes have acquired an almost predictable countenance, reliance, and harmony.

Residual Trauma

I shall now turn to the second precondition for adolescent character formation, which will throw light on the function of character. I hope to show that character takes over homeostatic functions from other regulatory agencies of childhood. In this connection we have to consider the effect of trauma on adolescent character formation (see Blos, 1962, pp. 132-140). The use of the term "trauma" in this paper corresponds with Greenacre's (1967) definition. She writes: "In my own work I have not limited my conception of trauma to sexual (genital) traumatic events, or circumscribed episodes, but have included *traumatic conditions*, i.e., *any conditions which seem definitely unfavorable, noxious, or drastically injurious to the development of the young individual*" (p. 277).

My clinical observations over the years have given rise to the theoretical formulation that follows. The analysis of older adolescents has demonstrated to me that the resolution of the neurotic conflict, the weaning from infantile fantasies, will bring the analytic work to a good end, without, however, having eliminated all residues of the pathogenic foundation on which the illness rested. These residues remain recognizable in special sensitivities to certain stimuli, external or internal, as well as in affinities to, or avoidances of, experiences and fantasies, or in somatic proclivities, despite the fact that all these aspects have been dealt with exhaustively in the analysis. By the end of the analysis, these residues had lost their noxious valence due to ego and drive maturation. In spite of this, they continue to require constant containment; that is, they are still factors to be reckoned with in the maintenance of psychic homeostasis. It is my contention that the automatization of this containment process is identical with the function or, more precisely, with a part function of character. Such permanent sensitizations to special danger situations of a traumatic valence are to be found, for example, in the experience of object loss, passive dependency, loss of control, decline of self-esteem, and other structurally and affectively injurious conditions.

It is assumed here that trauma is a universal human condition during infancy and early childhood, leaving, even under the most favorable circumstances, a permanent residue. The adolescent process, unable to overcome the disequilibrizing effect of this residue, assimilates it through characterological stabilization, namely, by rendering it ego-syntonic. I draw here on Freud's (1939) distinction between a positive and a negative effect of trauma. The negative reaction aims at the removal of any memory or repetition of the trauma, a reaction that leads to the reactive character formation, via avoidances, phobias, compulsions, and inhibitions. The positive effects "are attempts to bring the trauma into operation once again—that is, to remember the forgotten experience . . . to make it real, to experience a repetition of it. . . . [The effects] may be taken up into what passes as a normal ego and, as permanent trends in it, may lend it unalterable character-traits" (Freud, 1939, p. 75).

The high noon of this integrative achievement lies in the terminal period of adolescence when the enormous instability of psychic and somatic functions gradually gives way to an organized and integrated mode of operation. The residual trauma ceases to alert the ego repetitiously via signal anxiety once it has become an integral part of the ego. The residual trauma has become an organizer in the process of character formation. A state of helplessness and vigilance has been counteracted by character formation. Character, then, is identical with patterned responses to prototypical danger situations or signal anxiety; in other words, character is identical with the conquest of residual trauma: not with its disappearance, nor with its avoidance, but with its continuance within an adaptive formation. In the character disorder this process has miscarried: the characterological stabilization has become maladaptive.

From residual trauma emanates, so to speak, a persistent and relentless push toward actualization of that formation within the personality which we designate as character. Due to its origin character always contains a compulsive quality; it lies beyond choice and contemplation, is self-evident and compelling. The psychic energy required for character to take form is derived, in part, from the cathexis the residual trauma contains. Those adolescents who sidestep the transformation of residual trauma into character formation project the danger situation into the outside world and thus avoid the internal confrontation with it. By having failed to internalize the danger situation, the chance for coming to terms with it is forfeited; projecting it at adolescence onto the outside world results in a state of apprehension over victimization; indecision and bewilderment ensue. Erikson (1956) has described this impasse as the adolescent psychosocial moratorium. Experience tells us that it either leads to a belated character formation or to a pathological outcome. We gain the impression that the formation of character encompasses more than superego influences, identifications, and defenses. We are now ready to state that in character formation there is an integrative principle at work which bends the various contributing and confluent components to a broadening of the ego's secondary autonomy. Erikson's concept of ego identity (1956) belongs in this realm of clinical impressions.

In the analysis of older adolescents we can observe the luxuriant fantasy life of adolescence shriveling up with the consolidation of character. Greenacre (1967) comments on the fact that whenever a traumatic experience was associated with an underlying fantasy, the fixation on the trauma is more persistent than in cases where the trauma was bland and incidental. Is it possible that in adolescent character formation not only the experiential side of the residual trauma, but also the pre-existent fantasy associated with it, are absorbed in the ego organization? The thought has often been expressed that instinctual drives find expression in the exercise of a so-called healthy character. At any rate, we are now willing to say that the characterological stabilization of residual trauma advances the independence of man from his environment, from which the traumatic injury originally emanated at a time when pain was identical with the outside of the self or with the nonself.

Ego Continuity

I now come to the third precondition for adolescent character formation. Again, clinical observation has shown the direction and cleared the path to a conceptual formulation. I have described certain cases of adolescent acting out in which the maladaptive behavior represents an effort via action language to contradict a distortion of the family history that was coercively forced on the child. I have designated such a distortion as "family myth" (see Chapter 12). It differs from the classical family romance in that the distortion is forced on the child from the outside, calling in question the validity of the child's own perception. The study of a considerable number of such cases has convinced me that adolescent development can be carried forward only if the adolescent ego succeeds in establishing a historical continuity within its realm. We can see this effort at work in the ubiquitous critical re-evaluation of the parents or, by displacement, of their societal representations. We know well that much of what the child perceives has been determined by what he is supposed to perceive. The corrective measure at adolescence restores the integrity of the senses, at least to some degree. Whenever this effort falters, a partial foreclosure of adolescent development follows; the psychic restructuring of adolescence remains incomplete. Besides delinquency, much of the quandary and adventurousness of youth as well as their creative, especially literary, productions can be studied from this point of view.

The establishment of historical ego continuity appears, of course, in every analysis, but in adolescent analysis it has an integrative and growth-stimulating effect that lies beyond conflict resolution. One adolescent spoke for many in saying that one cannot have a future without having a past. Again, we observe a tendency toward internalization or, conversely, toward a disengagement (on the ego level) from the adult caretaking environment which has acted as the trustee and guardian of the immature ego of the child. It seems that ego maturation, along the lines I have just described, gives rise to the subjective sense of wholeness and inviolability during the adolescent years, when the envelope of the family has outlived its former usefulness. Of course, the sense of wholeness and inviolability has much in common with the psychological qualities that we ascribe to the reflection of character on subjective feeling states.

Sexual Identity

In order to complete the set of preconditions that promote adolescent character formation, a fourth one has to be mentioned, namely, the emergence of sexual identity. While gender identity is established at an early age, it has been my contention that sexual identity with definitive, i.e., irreversible boundaries appears only belatedly as the collateral of sexual maturation at puberty. Before physical sexual maturity is attained, the boundaries of sexual identity remain fluid. Indeed, a shifting or ambiguous sexual identity, within limits, is the rule rather than the exception. This is more apparent in the girl than in the boy. I have only to remind you of the acceptability, socially and personally, of the tomboy stage in the girl and of the deep repression of breast envy in the preadolescent boy. At any rate, puberty represents the demarcation line beyond which bisexual admixtures to gender identity become incompatible with progressive development. Clinically, this can easily be observed in the adolescent's growing capacity for heterosexual object finding and in the decline of masturbation, both of which advance parallel with the formation of sexual identity.

It is not my purpose here to trace the origin or the resolution of bisexuality. But it needs to be stated that, as long as the ambiguity or, indeed, the ambivalence of sexual identification lasts, the ego cannot escape being affected by the ambiguity of the drives. The maturational exigencies of puberty normally stimulate integrative processes of increasing complexity, but they will lose momentum, direction, and focus as long as sexual ambiguity prevails; that is, maturational processes will be defeated all along the line. Subjectively, this is experienced by the adolescent as identity crisis or identity diffusion, to use Erikson's (1956) terms. In the pursuit of our subject we conclude that the formation of character presupposes that sexual identity formation has advanced along a narrowing path, leading to masculine or feminine identity.

At this juncture, in late adolescence and postadolescence, we can observe how persistently remnants of the bisexual orientation have been debarred from genital expression and absorbed in character formation. The role of the ego ideal, the heir of the negative Oedipus complex, so important and decisive at this turning point of late adolescence, can only be hinted at here (for a more complete presentation, see Chapter 15).

The Genealogy of Character

The four preconditions which I have outlined rest on antecedents reaching back into the earliest history of individual life. We have good reason to assume that, beyond the experiential aspects, there are also embedded in the character structure components that hark back to biological givens. It follows from this view that adolescent character formation is affected, adversely or beneficially, by constitutional conditions as well as by infantile antecedents and their lifelong effect on psychic structure and conflict.

The characterological stabilization of drive and ego vicissitudes is not, however, identical with character. The four preconditions must be transcended in some fashion before the homeostatic function of this new formation that we then call character is regulated. The credentials of character are to be found in the postadolescent developmental level which, if attained, renders character formation possible; in other words, character formation reflects the structural accommodations that have brought the adolescent process to a close. The extent to which the four preconditions have been fulfilled, or the extent to which the four developmental challenges have been met, will determine the autonomous or defensive nature of the character that ensues. With the termination of childhood during the pubertal period, adult somatic structure and functioning are reached; this attainment has its psychological counterpart in the consolidation of the personality or in the formation of character.

It must have become clear during this presentation that in talking about character, one is constantly tempted to speak of healthy or pathological character formation. I have not offered in my schema any explicit accommodation of the so-called character disturbances, character disorders, or the vast spectrum of the pathological character. Proceeding from clinical observation of adolescents and on the basis of analytic data, I have arrived at the conclusions and formulations I have submitted. These have to be brought into harmony with observations of similar substance but derived from other characterological phenomena and from other periods of life. This task lies beyond the scope of my present investigation.

The Evolutionary Aspect of Character

I realize with apprehension that I have not heeded my initial admonition too well and have burdened this presentation with a vast array of theoretical concerns. This is the risk one runs in discussing character formation. There remains, however, still one further comment on this subject to which I shall now turn.

I have approached character formation as a corollary to drive and ego maturation at the stage of puberty. In doing so I have lifted it out of its ontogenetic matrix and assigned to it a function commensurate with the concurrent biological, i.e., sexual, maturation and the morphological attainment of adult status. Each stage of maturation increases the complexity of the psychic organization. Character reflects on the level of personality development the attainment of the highest form of psychic structure formation and functioning.

In the analytic literature references, explicit or implicit, to the complex structure and function of character can be found in various designations that attribute to character a holistic, integrative principle: the synthesizing function of the ego, fitting together (Hartmann), identity formation, organizing principle, consolidation process, the self, the whole person, etc. All these terms connote the subjective experience that one's character is identical with one's self. Psychic life cannot be conceived without it, just as physical life is inconceivable without one's body. One feels at home in one's character, or *mutatis mutandis* one's character is one's home and is, indeed, a dependable and reliable protector of the self. One accepts a shortcoming of one's character the way one accepts a physical imperfection. One does not like it, but there it is. When Lawrence Durrell (1961) was asked whether he was aware of any specific weakness as a writer, he gave the following answer: "My great weaknesses come from my character, not from lack of talent; I am hasty, rash, impulsive at moments when I should be timid, reserved and objective, and vice versa. My prose and poetry clearly show this weakness." We cannot fail to detect in this statement a note of pride for possessing the courage to accept one's weakness. A comment by Lichtenstein (1965) is pertinent to this observation: "Insofar as we are perceiving such an invariant as a characteristic of our own inner world (Hartmann), we tend to refer to it as the *experience* (Erlebnis) of our Self" (p. 119). Character formation establishes new invariants in the psychic life, and thus heightens and stabilizes the experience of the self. This, essentially identical, experience was derived in childhood from the invariants—reliability and sameness—of the environment.

Character structure renders the psychic organism less vulnerable than it has ever been before, and the maintenance of this structure is secured against any interference from any quarter, internal or external. If must be, one dies for it before letting it die. The overvaluation of one's own character makes it apparent that character formation is cathected with narcissistic libido and that narcissistic gratification is a legitimate gain derived from the exercise of character.

I am aware that I have spoken above in anthropomorphic metaphor instead of psychological concepts. This digression I shall correct by pointing out that the four preconditions are essentially a forward step in internalization and consequently in a furtherance of independence from the environment. A higher level of integration is thereby reached which contains new homeostatic possibilities. In this sense we can say, applying the genetic point of view, that the utter dependence of the human infant on environmental, protective stability has achieved in character formation its contraposition, namely, the internalization of a stable, protective environment. While content and pattern of character are socially determined, only internalization renders the psychic organism greatly independent from those forces that brought it into existence. While character structure is of a most durable and irreversible nature, only a degree of openness and flexibility assures its enrichment and modulation during adult life.

The evolutionary aspect of character formation lies in the internalization of dependencies and the formation of a progressively complex psychic structure. The function of character lies in the maintenance of this psychic structure, which is self-regulatory, namely, automatized, and thus reduces the infliction of psychic injury to a minimum. It goes without saying that the level of psychic organization thus achieved facilitates the unfolding of man's boundless potentialities.

In character formation we observe, on the ontogenetic level of personality development, an evolutionary principle that has its parallel, on the phylogenetic level, in advancing independence of the organism from the conditions of its environment. This evolution has reached its apex in man. Claude Bernard (1865) has expressed this principle by saying that "The constancy of the internal milieu is the condition of the free life."[2] In this sense, we can view character formation in an evolutionary perspective and contemplate it is as a closed system that, through its operation, maintains its adaptive function and facilitates the creative use of the human potentiality. The processes of internalization and automatization in character formation establish and stabilize the psychic internal milieu, thus enabling man to shape his environment, singly and collectively, by impressing on it those conditions that correspond most favorably with the inviolability and integrity of his personality.

[2]Although Claude Bernard worked in the fields of physiology and biochemistry, the organismic principle he formulated is equally applicable to the psychological exterior and interior milieu.

Chapter 10

The Child Analyst Looks at the Young Adolescent

The literature on adolescence has shown of late a distinctly new trend: an increasing, even if only trickling number of papers and books have begun to deal with the early years of adolescence. This trend is noteworthy because not so long ago most studies in adolescence had been devoted exclusively to the older age group. The singular attention paid for such a long time to the older adolescent, the spectacular and tumultuous youth, appears in retrospect a myopic vision. Should it not have been obvious to bring light first to the dawn of the adolescent process, instead of studying it in isolation at high noon?

Two factors account for the rising interest in the young adolescent. In the first place, the life style of the young adolescent is becoming increasingly similar to that of the older boy and girl; everything that is typical for middle adolescence is happening at a younger and younger age. This shift occurred quite dramatically in the sixties. During this decade the young adolescent appropriated, more and more aggressively, the position of the middle adolescent. He thus cut himself loose increasingly earlier from latency behavior and social role. The dislocation of traditional expectations rapidly altered the social presence of the young adolescent

First published in *Daedalus*, Fall 1971, pp. 961-978.

in family and school, on playground and street. The new balance between behavior and age not only alerted the expert in the field, but public concern urged him to throw light on this phenomenon.

Second, we must remember that research in adolescence, especially in the field of psychoanalytic psychology, has introduced a developmental differentiation of the adolescent process as a whole. This research has afforded the opening stage of adolescence (preadolescence) the exclusiveness of a developmental phase. My own work has aimed at the developmental delineation of five adolescent phases, each one defined in terms of drive and ego positions, somatic maturation and the surround, as well as phase-specific conflicts and their resolutions. For some time I have emphasized the fact that the initial stage of adolescence presents a most crucial period of the adolescent process as a whole.[1] Whatever follows later as, for example, identity formation, personality consolidation, character formation, or second individuation is augured favorably or unfavorably by the resolution of those particular developmental challenges that precede the unleashing of the adolescent turbulence of later years.

From our acquaintance with early child development we are used to thinking of a rather fixed proximity between age, maturation, and development. This close parallelism does not hold true for adolescence. Menarche and first ejaculation do not occur at a chronological age as narrow as smiling, sitting up, or teething. This difference becomes understandable if we acknowledge the fact that life during the first decade has brought about an increasing mutual disengagement from the caretaking person and progressively diminished any simple correlation between

[1] I have described preadolescence in Chapter 6. The five adolescent phases are discussed in *On Adolescence: A Psychoanalytic Interpretation* (Blos, 1962). In my book *The Young Adolescent: Clinical Studies* (Blos, 1970), I have illustrated the preadolescent phase with two treatment cases, a boy and a girl.

the somatic and the psychic systems of the organism. For example, performance expectancies, emanating from the social environment, rival more and more those triggered off by physical maturation alone. While pubertal maturation remains the biological initiator of adolescence, the advanced state of personality formation allows all kinds of transformatory influences to be brought to bear on the sexual drive. The monolithic cohesiveness between drive and behavior, so characteristic for the early years of life, is no longer as clearly in evidence at puberty. With this reservation in mind, we can nevertheless say that adolescence is the sum total of accommodations to the condition of puberty. The form these accommodations take depends to a large extent on extrinsic, normative impingements from the surround.

As stated above, the study of adolescence as a whole involves several maturational and developmental stages. While there is, obviously, an orderly sequence of stages, their timing is diverse as to onset and duration. As a child analyst I shall concern myself with psychological development or, in other words, with that process of psychic restructuring we call adolescence. The phenomenology of this process is dictated by the epochal characteristics of a given historical time and environmental trend and style. Consequently, it can take on a myriad of different forms, constantly changing in appearance. Yet, we assume that the attainment of sexual maturation and full body stature is given psychological form and content by prevalent social exigencies: social expectancies and taboos impose on the pubertal boy and girl, any time and everywhere, similar if not identical requirements for psychological modifications and reorganizations.

Preparation for Adolescence

It can be readily observed that the child, around the age of ten to twelve, loses some responsiveness to controls by adults, by the clock, by the routine of tasks, by the dictates of conscience. We witness the waning of the alliance between child and adult which, during middle childhood (latency period), had neutralized, by way of identification, the conflicts of earlier years. Emotional containment breaks out of its relatively narrow latitude with the first physiological signs of puberty (hormonal changes) and brings, in its wake, a growing intensity, unpredictability, and uncontrollability of affective responses. Environmental influences, communally and individually, turn these liabilities into either rebelliousness or inhibition, depending on the prevailing mores and pervasive ethos. Delays and restraints are, by no means, intrinsic impediments to the successful completion of the adolescent process. Any socially elicited retardation or acceleration of adolescence, however, is bound to reach a critical point, beyond which structural damage and maldevelopment are induced. Damage derives equally from a "too much," as from a "too little," from a "too early" as from a "too late."

Another source of developmental derailing stems from an essential incompleteness of the stage that precedes adolescence. We are therefore well advised to foster latency development to the fullest as the precondition for a competent entry into adolescence. The psychological mastery of pubescent drive intensification—libidinal or aggressive—is determined by the level of ego differentiation and ego autonomy, both attained, in large measure, during the latency period. Among these attainments, the most significant one is probably the ego's distancing from the id. This forward move in ego autonomy during the latency period results in the expansion and firm reliability of such ego functions as cognition, memory, anticipation, tension tolerance, self-awareness, and the ability to distinguish between reality and fantasy, or between action and thought. Whenever these facilities remain critically underdeveloped, we speak of an incomplete or abortive latency. Many disturbances of

early adolescence are due to such developmental deficiencies. We search in vain for the signs of a transition into
adolescence: what we find is an intensified revival of infantile drive expression and drive management. This is not a
regression, because no forward position has yet been
reached.

The transition into adolescence can be effected only if
pubertal drive tensions lead to phase-specific conflict formation and conflict resolution. This step presupposes a capacity for internalization, as opposed to unmodulated drive discharge or prolonged dependency on environmental responsiveness to the needs of the child. In the latter case the conflict remains an external one, raging between child and environment, with the child expecting, even demanding, that
the environment change; no other measure is in the child's
reach by which he can control his discomfort and anxiety,
both arising from a sense of helplessness, due to a dearth of
phase-appropriate coping skills.

The crisis of the latency period has been well pinpointed
by Erik Erikson's polarity of "industry versus inferiority,"
as these are the antagonistic foci around which middle
childhood consolidates. The mastery of the world, concretely, symbolically, and conceptually, begins to serve as a
self-regulatory source of self-esteem (instead of the earlier
dependence on object love) and, beyond that, lifts the
idiosyncratic childhood experiences onto the level of com-
municable and communal forms of expression. In saying
this, we have already set foot onto the bridge that leads into
the world of the young adolescent.

The Initial Stage of Adolescence: The Young Adolescent

It is common knowledge that instinctual tensions rise in the
wake of pubertal maturation. The initial reaction of the
young adolescent is a puzzling one, because infantile modalities of drive and ego positions are reactivated. He seems
to be going backward instead of forward.

It has often been observed that the boy's latency achievements, the domestication and transformation of infantile drives, fall into shambles with the onset of puberty. What we witness is a regression in the service of development, manifested in oral greed; rapaciousness; smuttiness; oblivion to unkemptness, dirtiness, and body odors; motoric restlessness; and experimentation in every direction of action and sensation (especially food and daring). Well-established ego functions suffer within this regressive turmoil, as is evidenced by the decline in concentration and neatness which boys display in school. The girl seems to possess a greater sublimatory capacity, or else she is given credit for virtuous achievements simply because she can conceal with such ease her less virtuous features. Many a boy of this age takes this seeming ability as proof of her superiority. Hence he ridicules and derides her mercilessly and defensively.

Adolescent development progresses via the detour of regression. By coming into renewed contact with infantile positions, the older child is given a chance to overhaul, as it were, the defects, infirmities, and irrationalities of infancy by confronting these very conditions with an ego of advanced competency. This "work" is of the utmost importance and determines the entire course adolescence will take. It requires time and facilitation to accomplish this developmental task. In general terms it can be said that the intensity of the regressive pull is proportional to the intensity with which "independence and freedom" are sought or, conversely, to the severity of the inhibition and submissiveness that are warded off.

We have reached the point in our description where the similarity between male and female adolescence comes to an end. The boy's preadolescent regression is more massive than the girl's; it is action-oriented and concretistic. In the first onrush of pubescence the boy turns away, with derision and contempt, from the opposite sex. The girl, by contrast, pushes romantic (heterosexual) or plainly sexual thoughts or fantasies into the foreground, while regressive trends assert themselves peripherally and more secretively.

It is a striking fact that the boy upon approaching puberty—and for some years to follow—entertains a rather unconflicted and, indeed, congenial relationship with his father. There is no evidence of the awesome Oedipus complex. Quite to the contrary, the boy at this stage has little, only conditional, or no use at all for mother and sisters, indeed, for the female sex in general. We must remember that pubertal drive intensification, in conjunction with strangely new and untested bodily sensations and affective states, invokes regulations along the body-mind continuum which hark back to the child's infantile training period. Here lies the first and momentous beginning of acquiring the ownership of one's body and the ecstasy of a "self." A similar ecstasy, yet far more complex, is re-experienced by the young adolescent when he enters the second individuation process at the dawn of puberty. The fateful struggle of early body regulation remains permanently associated with the mother of early childhood. Her renewed assertion of power in taking over the guardianship of his growing body becomes anathema to the young adolescent boy. He resists the mother of his infancy to such a degree that he—easily and irrationally—attributes to her "witchlike" powers, which soon are imputed to the entire world of the female.

It remains the psychological task of the boy at this stage to abandon the gratifications and avoidances of early childhood. By so doing the boy prepares himself for the ultimate potency of a man. The sidestepping of this phase-specific task invites all kinds and degrees of sexual maldevelopment. With the rise of the boy's self-control and emotional emancipation, his irrational fear of the female declines proportionally, thus promoting his entry into the phase of adolescence proper. Before this can take its course, however, the boy's relationship to his father undergoes a change. The emotional closeness to him fades away while the ego ideal gains in ascendancy, acquiring qualities that are distinctly different from those of the ego ideal of early childhood (see Chapter 15).

The ego ideal constitutes a prerequisite for the choice and pursuit of a vocational goal and ideational stability. Whenever the formation of the ego ideal is critically impaired, a sense of uncertainty, floundering, indecisiveness, restlessness, and lowered self-esteem ensues. Under these conditions, whatever door flies open and promises a departure from this impasse gives the adolescent a short-lived sense of direction and purpose.

It follows from what has been said that the boy's emotional conflict during early adolescence centers primarily on the mother. The "mother" in this context is the internalized mother of infancy (the preoedipal mother), not the actual mother of the present. This fact is responsible for much of the irrationality and misunderstandings between mother and adolescent child. To overcome this irrationality remains the challenge of this age. The emotional vulnerability of the young adolescent boy is twofold; both aspects can be termed adolescent fixations. One aspect consists in the boy's incomplete disengagement from the preoedipal mother with the consequence of marked ambivalence in later relationships and of an inordinate need for nurturing (preadolescent fixation). The other aspect lies in the perseverance of his emotional attachment to the father (early adolescent fixation) with the consequence of a divided loyalty to the sexes and persistent doubts about his masculinity.

A similar constellation holds for the girl, yet with a different resolution. Regressively, the girl seeks emotional closeness to the nurturing, protective mother of early childhood. A very special relationship often develops in which the mother becomes the confidante of the girl ("I couldn't wait to get home and tell my mother") and an advisor in the bewildering emotional turmoil of this age. This partnership has a decisively positive influence on the girl's emerg-

ing femininity and, in addition, protects her against precocious emotional independence and sexual involvement. A
widespread misconception interprets the young adolescent
girl's emotional needs as an oedipal involvement with the
father. Indeed, the father often feels obliged to flirt with his
daughter in order to enhance the girl's confidence in her
femininity. The oedipal constellation, however, belongs to a
later stage. The misconception finds apparent support in the
fact that, whenever the regressive pull to the mother of
early childhood becomes too intense, feelings of oppositionalism, aversion, or estrangement take over, rendering the relationship to the mother highly ambivalent; in defensive flight the girl turns to the father or she becomes
"boy-crazy." Should a proclivity to acting out already exist,
it is not uncommon that the girl will take flight to the opposite sex as a countermeasure against the unduly severe
regressive pull ("female sexual delinquency").[2] Here it
seems important to note that, normally, the young adolescent of both sexes seems, for short stretches of time, to be
comparatively unfettered by the dependency on, the search
for, and the revival of infantile relationships. The subjective
sense of freedom from childhood dependencies is, however,
constantly disrupted by passionate and ambivalent struggles with parents, siblings, and teachers in which closeness
and distance are sought at the same time.

From the beginning of her adolescence, the girl is far
more preoccupied with the vicissitudes of object relations
than is the boy; his energies are directed outward toward
control of and dominance over the physical world. The girl,
in contrast, turns—either in fact or fantasy—with deep-felt
emotionality, mixed with romantic tenderness, possessiveness, and envy, to the boy. While the boy sets out to master
the physical world, the girl endeavors to deal with relationships. Some girls unite in competitive coteries, sharing se-

[2]The defensive heterosexuality of the girl is discussed from a clinical point of
view in Chapter 11.

crets and observations (such as who in the class has menstruated or what new eyeshadow or hairdo the teacher wears and on account of whom), never tiring of carrying on love affairs from afar. Other girls negate or postpone the acceptance of their femaleness through living the life of the tomboy or of the studious pupil. The strategy of delay the girl employs at this age is supportive of normal female development. The girl's regressive escapades always remain counterbalanced by her turn to the other sex. She rarely loses herself as completely and persistently in regressive behavior as the boy. In fact, girls at this age are known to be better students than boys and their capacity for introspection is superior. Of course, what the girl at this stage has acquired is not genuine femininity; a more discerning look convinces us that it is aggression and possessiveness that dominate her relationship to the other sex. These infantile modes of object relation barely hide the narcissistic aspect of her yearnings—namely, the need to find a sense of completeness through object possession.

I have found that the emotional vulnerability of the young adolescent girl is twofold. Both aspects are due to the perseverance ("getting stuck") in a normally transient position of development. One aspect consists of her incapacity to resist and overcome the regressive pull to the preoedipal mother (preadolescence), thereby reinstituting, perhaps permanently, the primitive ambivalence of early object relations in the intimate affiliations of her life. The other aspect is to be found in her incapacity to relinquish the typical bisexual identity of early adolescence. If the tomboy position becomes a lasting one, instead of being transient, the girl's progression to femininity will be seriously imperiled. It should be evident that the developmental challenge for the girl at this phase consists in the successful resistance to the regressive pull to the preoedipal mother, in the renunciation of pregenital drive gratifications, of infantile dependency needs, or of physical contact hunger in one form or another, and, last but not least, in the acceptance of her femaleness. Much of the maladaptive behavior which breaks out during adolescence proper and late adolescence shows clearly the insufficient relinquishment and, a partial or total failure to resolve the tasks and challenges described above.

Under normal circumstances the young adolescent girl deals with the vicissitudes of emotional disengagement from the mother intrapsychically and takes her time to harmonize her emotional and physical needs. She cannot accomplish this task, however, without the mother's help and protection. Not that the girl, necessarily, likes such interferences or consciously wishes for them, but it remains the mother's prerogative and duty to have her opinions and judgments heard on issues of developmental import.

I have dwelled rather expansively on the opening stage of the adolescent process. This I did intentionally, because the importance of this stage is generally not appreciated sufficiently nor is its complexity defined succinctly enough in the literature. After the decline of the opening stage of adolescence there unfolds a wholly new and distinct stage, adolescence proper, which represents proverbial adolescence. The resuscitation of oedipal conflicts dominates this stage in terms of drive progression; the ego, concomitantly, elaborates this forward movement in terms of higher levels of differentiation. The process of the second individuation (see Chapter 8) is vigorously pushed ahead with the result that character formation (see Chapter 9) lends enduring and irreversible structures to the adolescent personality. I must confine the description of this stage to these few and general comments, because a detailed exposition of its course would exceed the format of this essay. Instead, I shall turn to a consideration of some broad concerns which have a bearing on adolescent development from the ages of about twelve to sixteen.

Current Factors in Adolescent Development

The Earlier Onset of Puberty

We are in a position to say—after about fifty years of observation—that pubescence starts about four months earlier every ten years.[3] This changing schedule has been cited as being responsible for the earlier display of adolescent behavior, such as the clamor for independence and the turn to genital sexuality. Since biology cannot be argued with, the simplistic conclusion has been drawn that, for example, family and school must accommodate themselves to the earlier arousal of pubertal needs.

I intend to follow a different line of reasoning by pointing out, first of all, that the sexual drive constitutes a most extraordinarily malleable and transformable "instinct" as to object and aim. At the time when sexual functioning arrives (about age thirteen), the personality has acquired a complexity which can well accommodate delay, repression, or transformation (sublimation) without endangering, and in fact aiding and solidifying, the adolescent process. We must not forget that adolescence is a culturally determined transition from childhood to adulthood; although it takes its cue from bodily changes (puberty), it puts the ensuing rise of drive tension to its own societal purpose.

In today's society the time required to prepare the pubertal child for adult functioning (vocation, citizenship, parenthood, and so forth) has been obtained by the prolongation of adolescence. The ability to devote energy, dedication, and perseverance to this process derives from a partial inhibition of the drives (sublimation) or, at least, from their delayed gratification and uncommitted state. In order for society and adolescence to fit together, the biological schedule has been radically interfered with for the benefit of both. In this sense, we speak of prolonged adolescence as

[3]It stands to reason to expect the biological trend to level off in time, even if we do not know exactly where this level is.

a necessary condition in an industrial society. And even more, an open, democratic society must, for its own survival, support educational upward mobility. It must therefore accept the risks inherent in such accommodations and the unavoidable psychological tensions in a culturally protracted adolescence. In this connection we must acknowledge the fact that without a high level of psychological differentiation, the adolescent is neither able nor fit to cope with the differential learning required of him. An ever-increasing demand for advanced cognitive mastery is made on all those who desire to enter the complex vocations of an industrial or technetronic society.

We have ample evidence that an acceptance of the young adolescent as a self-directing, sexually active "young person" interferes severely with the preparatory functions of this stage. We can say that ego building at this time augurs more promisingly for the attainment of maturity than the early adolescent striving for a full sex life. To extend adolescence downward would deprive adolescents of the psychic properties that enable them to endure that complex process of adaptation and prolonged dependency (schooling and financial support of some sort) which present-day society demands from an increasingly larger segment of youth. I submit that a prolongation, rather than an abbreviation of childhood is desirable if not, indeed, imperative. The young adolescent of thirteen—regardless of his primary and secondary sex characteristics—is still, psychologically, a child. This fact should be acknowledged by family, by school, and by society at large. These institutions must continue to extend their containing and protective roles, rather than push the young adolescent ahead under the misleading banner of "the earlier and the faster, the bigger and the better."

What I am proposing, then, is the prolongation of childhood status, rather than the institutionalization of a downward extension of adolescence by blindly following a biological trend. In connection with this thesis I submit, furthermore, that the separation of the sexes in school during these early adolescent years (not during the entire adolescent period) is, psychologically and biologically, well advised. It is not necessary to recount here the well-known intellectual, physical, social, and psychological discrepancies that make boy and girl of this age ill-fitting companions in work and play. We do not, by such a separation, deprive the sexes of their normal development—quite the contrary. The boy who shows a precocious preference for girl playmates is the one whose maleness proves in later years (late adolescence or early adulthood) shakily established, while the young boy who keeps company with boys as a young adolescent tends to settle, later on, more firmly and lastingly in his masculine identity.

The Young Adolescent in Relation to Social Class and Educational Philosophy

The general schema of psychic restructuring during initial adolescence, as outlined above, can be demonstrated in the most heterogeneous phenomenology of adolescence. Process and content need to be delineated, each in its own right, before both can be brought into a functional relationship to the social context in which they find expression. That social class is a factor in adolescence is not a new concept. European working-class adolescents were studied in the thirties and the "social locus" (ghetto, urban middle class, rural or regional environment, migrant worker, and so forth) is taken today for granted as an influence that molds decisively the course of adolescence. Unfortunately, we still lack sufficient data to evaluate accurately the various forms and schedules of adolescence in relation to the attainment of social and emotional maturity.

Experience has impressed on me the fact that prolonged adolescence, especially prolonged early adolescence, enhances the capacity for complex cognitive functions (Piaget's

"stage of formal operations"). The prolongation of childhood
(Piaget's "stage of concrete operations") allows additional
time for the acquisition of that large body of factual knowledge (be this science, mathematics, language, geography, or
history) which is later put to integrative use, when mean-
ingfulness and relevancy of knowledge and learning move
into the forefront of the educational experience.

It is axiomatic that the prevailing educational
philosophy exerts a decisive influence on the form maturation will take. Educational philosophies reflect values and
ideologies held by the parent generation and projected on
the young. The educated classes are most prone to be influenced by the treatises of the sophisticated experts whose
expostulations and theories have given rise to all kinds of
misunderstandings. One of them might be paraphrased as
follows: since sexual maldevelopment is implicit in every
neurosis and considered (popularly) as "proof of parental failure," it follows that emotional health is assured by not only
accepting, but by actually fostering, heterosexual expression
in early adolescence. Furthermore, I have observed a widespread fear which takes possession of many a mother at the
time her son arrives at early adolescence. She notices his
typical prepubertal pudginess around the hips in conjunction with his disinterest in girls and his preference for male
companionship; all this seems to foreshadow homosexuality.
By shortcircuiting a developmental detour of utmost importance, the boy is forcefully yanked away from his normal
course. This example should convince the expert (myself included) how much he has to remedy by way of public
enlightenment—which brings me to my next point.

Mass Media, Commercialism, and the Generation Gap

With the gradual, but radical, obsolescence of tradition
in family life, as reflected in child rearing, nutrition, man-
ners, and moral stringencies, parent and child tend to rely

more and more on the plethora of public advice the mass media deliver into the home. Tradition has been replaced by the expert who offers answers to all of life's problems. The family has thus become, gradually, a laboratory for the application of all kinds of counsel which either fuse, contradict, or replace traditional patterns. Parents who reluctantly or eagerly put the bewildering jumble of advice into practice soon abdicate their personal responsibility in favor of choices made by the expert; they thus surrender their own convictions rather than pass judgment on what has been offered them. This submission to the expert has drained ever larger sections of parental actions or attitudes of consistency, integration, and integrity. In the face of such synthetic guidance, a child becomes unresponsive and confused. The "scientific" upbringing of children has turned out to be far more problematical than it seemed at first; indeed, many glorious expectations have come to dismal disappointments.

Of course, we must accept the fact that the mass media are with us for good and will continue to shape the minds of parents and children. Commercialism makes goods desirable to children through advertising and children, in turn, badger their parents to provide these goods. A particularly unsavory huckstery arises when the spontaneous innovations (especially in clothing) by the young become commercially exploited, that is, stylized and glamorized for mass consumption. This synthetic image, full of expectations and promises, has its special impact on the young adolescent. It is the age when opposition to family values and patterns starts to assert itself and parents, especially in urban areas, are hard pressed whenever they practice their parental privilege by setting limits and by affirming their personal values. Quickly, the exercise of parental authority is condemned by the young as authoritarianism and old-fashioned narrow-mindedness.

Opposition to parental guidance, silent or vocal, belongs

to the stage of initial adolescence. What is new is the self-doubt of the adult—whether to grant the adolescent child his wishes and his request for freedom, thus speeding up his "mature" independence, while ignoring that tension and antagonism represent essential conflicts of this period. Developmental progression is more hampered than assisted by removing conflict on principle. Parents who are unable to tolerate this tension either leave the child to his own devices, or they support, explicitly and expectantly, his clamor for grown-upness. In both instances the phase-specific task (outlined above) is aborted. The sequelae will become apparent at a time when the normative influences of parent or school have lost their impact and stringency. A misordered sense of developmental timing has, in such instances, dealt with the budding conflict between the generations by pushing adolescence precociously ahead. As a consequence, the syndrome of the generation gap will emerge later as a self-protective rupture by which unresolved family dependencies and animosities are removed in wholesale fashion and fixed in the polarities of young versus old, of under versus over thirty, or us versus them. It is my opinion that the subjective experience of the so-called generation gap is an indication of a developmental deficit, i.e., a defensive avoidance of the painful and tortuous generational conflict.[4]

This particular aspect of modern youth applies, almost exclusively, to middle-class families. There we see, upon close inspection, that the family unit of parent and child has prolonged an unusually close emotional involvement which neither one is able or ready to relinquish when puberty arrives. In order not to mislead the reader I must add that this closeness is not necessarily an idyllic and blissful bond; it is, more often than not, a tie racked with open or silent struggles. Be this as it may, such a predicament is

[4]The generation gap experience of youth belongs to the normal course of disengagement from the past. I refer above to a specific type of the generation-gap experience which I have explored as an epochal phenomenon of the sixties in Chapter 1.

aggravated by a habituation to incessant sensory stimulation (TV, radio, hi-fi, and drugs). The incessant neediness
for outside stimulation reduces the faculty to be alone with
oneself, or, in psychological terms, to attend to inner
promptings and workings or, generally, to an autochthonous
fantasy world. The process of internalization renders the
demarcation between the inner and the outer world sharp
and keen, with the result that acting out in later adolescence becomes dispensable as a means to problem solving.

The phenomenon of "acting older" often turns out to be a
mimetic adaptation which has its onset in early adolescence, whenever the environment has become insensitive to
the developmental needs of the young. These needs lie
equally in stimulation and in restraint. Despite the fact
that the young adolescent has acquired sexual maturity, he
still remains a child or, rather, he stands on the threshold
of slowly leaving childhood behind for good. Not until the
end of adolescence is this step completed. Physical stature
and procreative capacity are the most unreliable indicators,
at least in our society, of emotional maturity, that is, independence from the parent generation.

The trend of the young adolescent to reach beyond his
age, to be older by acting older, is complemented by the desire of the adult to be younger than his age. The fear of getting old has turned many an adult into a nostalgic expat-
riate from youth, who shuns neither ingenuity nor expense
to stem the tides of aging. The young adolescent's violent
rejection of his partial childhood status finds its complement
in the adult's terror of leaving his youth behind. In this
sense the adolescent is right when he says that adults want
to appropriate "his thing."

Psychic Structure and Social Structure

Adolescence never occurs in a social vacuum. Society always bestows on the adolescent generation a unique and decisive impression which, so it seems, can obliterate many

formative influences of the family. The collective integration by the young of the epochal impact of society (be this conformity or oppositionalism) is subsumed under the concept of "youth culture," "peer culture," or "adolescent subculture." This social phenomenon can best be understood if we contemplate the adolescent developmental task as a psychological disengagement from the family and a simultaneous engagement in the wider context of society. The personal and intimate ties of love and hate, which were the heartbeat of the child's social matrix, become slowly replaced by the immersion into the anonymity of society, represented by its social institutions. Personal intimacy and emotional bonds become a matter of choice and private concern, thus complementing the impersonal, yet meaningful and essential, affiliations and identifications, disaffiliations and counteridentifications, with social institutions and their executive functions.

During adolescence the child passes, gradually but persistently, from the highly personal family envelope to the eminently impersonal societal envelope. In this transition we witness the steady arousal of affective responses to social, moral, and ideological issues. Should this response remain a direct displacement from childhood idealizations or grievances, then, and only then, can we speak of a miscarriage of adolescent psychic restructuring. Then we can say that the shadow of renewed childhood rage and blame has fallen on the environment.

On the basis of these observations and principles, I endeavor to make the point that no adolescent, at any station of his journey, can develop optimally without societal structures standing ready to receive him, offering him that authentic credibility with which he can identify or polarize. Whenever society lacks, to a critical degree, the quality of a reasonably stable and integrated structure, then the maturing child turns exclusively to his contemporaries, his peers, in order to create by and for himself that social extrafamilial structure without which he cannot maintain his psychic integrity. As in most self-styled emergency and rescue actions of the child, the adolescent, too, protects himself against noxious environmental influences at the price of some measure of self-limitation. The extremism ("totalism") of adolescent attitudes and actions, however, is by no means determined exclusively by the life history of the individual. The contemporary condition of society—whatever its character—is a decisive, contributing factor. According to the nature of infantile trauma, the fateful juxtaposition of adolescent developmental urgencies and societal resourcefulness and facilitations will become the organizing experience from which the universal childhood complexes (what the kids call "hang ups") take their final form and expression.[5]

Observation and study of youth permits us to say that the psychic structure of the individual is critically affected, for better or worse, by the structure of society. This idea is not novel by any means. What I am emphasizing here is the fact that the successful course of adolescence depends intrinsically on the degree of intactness and cohesion of societal institutions. It is not necessary to belabor here the fragmented, disoriented, antiquated, cynical, and corrupt state of many social institutions at the time of this writing. Let me conclude by saying that the clever little boy in "The Emperor's New Clothes" can be found today almost everywhere and that his small voice has grown to a mighty chorus.

The increase of maladaptive behavior among the young cannot be related, solely, to their upbringing, to the laxity, severity, or neglect of family, school, community, or church. Anomie is a decisive determinant. To call the "unconforming" adolescent "sick" is a meaningless attribution; the hope to stem this teeming tide through individual or group coun-

[5]The function of trauma in the late adolescent consolidation process is discussed elsewhere (Blos, 1962, pp. 132-140).

seling, through confrontation sessions or psychotherapy, must remain—in the light of what has been said—another labor of Sisyphus. Of course, there always have been and still are adolescents who require therapeutic interventions of various kinds. But I speak here in terms of an epidemic "cop-out" and of an alarming rise in breakdown (psychosis). The strategy for normalization lies, to a large extent, outside individual rehabilitation. It is to be found, rather, in the restructuring of the environment—for example, the school and the juvenile court—and, above and beyond that, in the reform of the legislative and executive functions of government on all levels. This would constructively affect the attitude of the young toward the adult world.

Summary

In discussing the young adolescent I have described his psychological development in terms of psychic reorganization. I have traced the accommodations of the drives to the state of puberty and indicated the emergence of ego capacities that parallel physical maturation and changing social status. The conclusion was drawn that the beginning stage of adolescence decides critically the subsequent course of adolescence. Reasons for a prolongation, rather than an abbreviation, of early adolescence were set forth, despite the fact that physical maturation has been occurring at an earlier age. Societal structures in relation to individual psychic structures were afforded an eminent role in the transition from family dependencies to societal partnership.

My intention throughout has been the explication of developmental principles and the localization of those critical conditions that either promote or impede the adolescent process. These considerations demanded that I pay explicit attention to the stage from which the young adolescent emerges as well as the one to which he is tending. The adolescent in mid-passage, the proverbial adolescent of about fourteen to sixteen (adolescence proper), was not given equal treatment. I elected to concentrate on pre- and early adolescence because these stages are the most crucial and least understood of all the stages that comprise the adolescent process. What I was aiming at, in essence, was the exposition of a developmental point of view which might offer reference points for the coordination of normative adolescent progression and environmental supportive influences and standards.

PART THREE

Acting Out
and Delinquency

Turning to the problem of delinquency we confront one of the adolescent developmental impasse situations which tell us that the adolescent process has failed or is about to fail. Delinquent behavior can be a sign of distress, or a particular adaptive style—maladaptive in the eye of the observer—for which the externalization of conflict is symptomatic.

In previous sections of this book—especially in Part One—I have dealt with the adolescent and his surround; I pointed out the way in which both shape each other in a circular activation. I endeavored to establish the fact that both these orbits have reciprocal influences and are inextricably intertwined; in the case of the preoedipal child I described these orbits as individual autonomy on the one hand and as the societal matrix on the other. Any reference to these coexisting orbits as quasi-isolated entities remains a conceptual contrivance. With this reservation in mind, the separate study of individual and sociocultural processes is justifiable and, indeed, useful for the sake of their discussion and clarification.

The exploration of delinquency poses questions quite different from those that gave rise to the preceding inquiries. We shall now become concerned with very special kinds of uses the individual makes of his surround. In this connection, it is the action system, its meaning and function within the adolescent process that attracts our attention. Transient delinquent behavior in adolescence points to a psychological crisis but not, in and of itself, to a pathognomic event. A differential evaluation of a particular delinquency is always of essence. We shall discover that some of the maladaptive uses the adolescent makes of his environment represent frantic efforts to overcome obstacles that interfere with maturation, socialization, or, in essence, with the second individuation process. The frantic efforts to overcome these obstacles become manifest in maladaptive behavior generally and in alloplastic symptom formation in

217

particular. Delinquent behavior fosters a developmental arrest; even if only transient, it may seriously impede or, indeed, abort the adolescent process and acquire the inflexibility of a symptom.

The extremes of adolescent maladaptive development are well known to every observer of adolescence, professional and layman alike. They are most clearly demonstrated in their polar manifestations. On the one hand, we recognize the adolescent's lack of emotional responsiveness and his stagnant disengagement from the world around him; in contrast, we witness the adolescent's irrepressible, indiscriminate, exploitative, and egocentric involvement in the world of things and people. The former is the state of emotional withdrawal and the latter is the state of acting out. It is the problem of acting out that concerns us at the moment.

Two components of the normal adolescent process play into pre-existing asocial tendencies: the defusion of the basic drives, libido and aggression, and furthermore, the maturational intensification of the action system. In the light of the defusion of the basic drives in adolescence, we come to realize that the fusion of the drives in early childhood represents one of the most remarkable and decisive steps toward humanization and socialization. We observe, for example, in male preadolescence—usually the onset time of delinquency—that certain typical manifestations of the aggressive drive break forth. I have referred to these as phallic sadism and conceptualized their appearance as the result of regression and drive defusion. Only the "refusion" of the drives will reintegrate these primitive, preambivalent affects into mature object relations. In spite of the regressive primitivizations, we must not lose sight of the fact that the intensification of the action system supports the forward movement toward autonomy and toward the affective distancing of the self from dependency objects.

Unfortunately, the term "acting out" carries, by innuendo, all kinds of derogatory connotations. Consequently, its potentially positive aspect is often ignored. This narrow point of view is rooted in the history of the concept of acting out. Therefore, I have traced and brought up to date the history of the concept. From my own clinical work emerged a more complex conceptualization of the term, which accommodates acting-out phenomena that are essentially different from the standard formulation. Traditionally, acting out is viewed as an impulse discharge due to a faulty superego structure and a defective system of impulse control. What seemed to me relevant within the total picture of acting out were the different ways in which the intensification of the action system manifests itself in male and female delinquency. An effort is made here to conceptualize these differences, observed clinically and documented with case material.

In order to broaden and amend the standard concept of acting out, some of the subsequent studies focus on acting-out behavior as a highly organized form of communication via the action system. It will be shown that, in those cases under consideration, the symbolic system of language and thought has become partially lost to the adolescent as an expressive instrumentality for thought and feeling; consequently, he employs a particular modality of coded communication through action. Certain cases of delinquency and of maladaptive addiction to action in general are subjected to a detailed investigation of "acting out in the service of development." Cases will be discussed where the so-called delinquency or acting out—some of it without running afoul of the law—appears as a resolute and purposeful effort to resist regression and stem an imminent loss of identity (ego disintegration). I shall indicate how the deciphering of the action language succeeded in lifting the maladaptive, self- and object-destructive behavior to a higher level of mental functioning, thus making it gradually dispensable. We are here reminded of Hippocrates' enigmatic words about which the healing practitioners have

pondered for ages: "The illness is the cure." Certain forms of
acting out which I shall describe in detail give these words
a new relevance. In these cases of delinquency, the
therapist lends his ear (and his imagination) to the language of action in order to resolve the paradox—should it
apply to the case at hand—of doing the wrong thing for the
right reason.

Chapter 11

Preoedipal Factors in the Etiology of Female Delinquency

In the study of delinquency we can distinguish two fronts of inquiry. I speak of the sociological determinants on the one hand, and the individual psychological process on the other. These two fronts of inquiry are essentially different; yet by the very fact that they study the same phenomena, they become readily confused, to the detriment of clarity and research. Both aspects are intrinsically and essentially interwoven in each case. However, our understanding of a case will be incomplete as long as we fail to distinguish between the "early unconscious predisposing factors (so-called endopsychic factors)" and the "constitutional and precipitating factors" (Glover, 1956). This differentiation has led us to speak of latent and manifest delinquency. In this chapter I shall restrict myself to a discussion of some predisposing psychodynamic factors as they can be reconstructed from the overt delinquent behavior and supported by the historical data in the case.

Delinquency, by definition, refers to a personality disturbance which manifests itself in open conflict with society. This fact alone has pushed the social aspect of the problem into the forefront and has stimulated sociological research which in turn has thrown light on those environ-

First published in *The Psychoanalytic Study of the Child*, 12: 229-249. New York: International Universities Press, 1957.

mental conditions significantly related to delinquent behavior. My focus here is on the individual process; I hope
this will not be construed as an expression of my disregard
for the contribution sociological research has made in this
field. The study of delinquency has by necessity always
been multidisciplinary and it should not be claimed by any
one discipline as its exclusive domain.

Delinquency statistics tell us that antisocial behavior
has been on the rise for some time; this goes hand in hand
with a general rise in breakdowns of adaptive behavior in
the population as a whole. Thus, the rise in delinquency
cannot be considered as an isolated phenomenon but must
be seen as part of a general trend. This view becomes even
more convincing if we accept the opinion, supported by
Healy, Aichhorn, Alexander, Friedlander, and others, "that
the differences in the psychological make-up of the delinquent and the non-delinquent are of a quantitative rather
than of a qualitative kind" (Friedlander, 1947).

Recently, we have also seen a change of symptom picture in the field of the neuroses; the classical conversion
hysteria is less prevalent nowadays and has given way to
other forms of personality disturbances, best summarized as
ego pathologies. Anxious parental "gratification-readiness"
and even gratification-anticipation of children's instinctual
needs, way beyond the stage of infancy, seem to account for
many cases of low frustration tolerance and dependency
which we observe in children. Contributing to this confusion
is the parents' surrender of their own intuitive know-how to
advertisements and pronouncements by the expert. Under
such conditions the child's ego is exposed to insufficient and
inconsistent stimulation (positive and negative) with the result that more or less permanent ego defects ensue; they become most apparent in the malformation of delaying and
inhibiting functions. The strong drive toward immediate
discharge of tension is typical of the delinquent, and the age
of the rise of instinctual tension is puberty. At this time the
individual normally re-enacts his personal drama on the

wider stage of society, and it is of course at this juncture of maturational stress that the inadequacy of the ego becomes apparent.

If I compare the cases of delinquency that come to our clinics today with those cases I remember from my work with Aichhorn in Vienna in the twenties, I am struck by the difference, i.e., the predominance of poor ego integration and impulse disorders which we see today. Aichhorn's classic remark (1925), that the delinquent has to be turned into a neurotic in order to make him accessible to treatment, seems applicable today to only a small portion of the delinquent population.

The study of the psychodynamics of delinquency has always been prone to become ensnarled in general and overall formulations. Prevalent ideas in the field of human behavior and motivation have a tendency to provide the master plan for its solution. In fact, etiological determinants change with prevalent psychoanalytic research; the instinct-gratification theory as well as the theory of the missing superego have been left way behind; considerations of ego pathology have moved into the foreground. I do not question Kaufman's and Makkay's (1956) opinion that an "infantile type of depression" due to "actual or emotional desertion" is found to be a "predisposing and necessary element in delinquency," but it is equally correct to say that depressive elements are to be found in all types of emotional disturbances of children. What puzzles us most in the delinquent is his incapacity to internalize conflict, or rather his ingenious circumvention of symptom formation by experiencing an endopsychic tension as a conflict with the outside world. The exclusive use of alloplastic, antisocial solutions is a feature of delinquency that sets it apart from other forms of adaptive failures. It stands in clear contrast to the psychoneurotic or the psychotic solution, the former representing an autoplastic and the latter an autistic adaptation.

Up to a certain point all cases of delinquency have

psychodynamic similarities, but it seems to me more profitable to study their differences. Only by this method shall
we penetrate into the more obscure aspects of the problem.
In expressing a warning of this kind, Glover (1956) speaks
of "etiological clichés" such as the "broken home" or "separation anxiety." He continues: "It requires no great mental
effort to assume that traumatic separation in early infantile
years must have a traumatic effect; but to convert this into
a *direct* determining environmental factor in delinquency is
to neglect the central proposition of psycho-analysis that
these predisposing elements acquire their pathological force
and form in accordance with the effect of their passage
through the varying phases of the unconscious Oedipus
situation" (pp. 315-316). My clinical and theoretical remarks proceed from this point, especially as far as preoedipal fixations preclude the oedipal stage from consolidating
and thereby preventing emotional maturation.

Some Theoretical Considerations in Female Delinquency

It has always been my opinion that male and female delinquency follow separate paths, indeed are essentially different. We are familiar with the different manifestations of
both, but we would like to be better informed about the origin of the divergencies. Our thoughts immediately turn to
the divergent psychosexual development of the boy and girl
during early childhood. And, furthermore, it seems relevant
to recall in this connection that the structure of the ego depends to a significant extent on the existing drive organization, which is subject to different vicissitudes in the male
and female. The study of identifications and the self-
representations to which they lead in boy and girl explains
some of the dissimilarities in ego development in the two
sexes.

  If we review the cases of male and female delinquency of
which we have intimate knowledge, we gain the impression

that female delinquency stands in close proximity to the perversions; the same cannot be said with regard to the boy. The girl's delinquency repertoire is far more limited in scope and variety than the boy's; furthermore, it lacks significantly in destructive aggressive acts against persons and property, and also concedes to the boy the rich field of imposterlike adventure. The girl's wayward behavior is restricted to stealing of the kleptomanic type, to vagrancy, to provocative, impudent behavior in public, and to frank sexual waywardness. Of course, these offenses are shared by the boy offender; they constitute, however, only a fraction of his transgressions. In the girl, it seems, delinquency is an overt sexual act or, to be more correct, a sexual acting out.[1]

Let us look at the way this disparity comes about. In female delinquency the infantile drive organization, which has never been abandoned, breaks through with the onset of puberty and finds a bodily outlet in genital activity. The pregenital instinctual aims, which dominate the delinquent behavior of the girl, relate her delinquency to the perversion. An adolescent boy who, let us say, is caught in an ambivalence conflict with his father may defend himself against both castration fear and castration wish by getting drunk, by destroying property, or by stealing a car and wrecking it; his actions often are, even if abortive, nevertheless an attempt to sustain progressive development (Neavles and Winokur, 1957). The boy's typical delinquent activities contain elements of a keen interest in reality; moreover, we recognize his fascination with the struggle waged between himself and people, social institutions, and the world of nature. In contrast to this, an adolescent girl who possesses an equal propensity to acting out will, let us say, take revenge on her mother, by whom she feels rejected, by seeking sexual relations. Girls of this type have

---

[1]The general validity of this statement has been challenged by the changes in adolescent sexual behavior since this study was made. For a re-evaluation see my Postscript (pp. 246-253).

told me of persistent fantasies during sex play or coitus, such as: "if mother knew, it would kill her" or "you see [mother], I have somebody too." Aichhorn, in a paper on sexually delinquent girls (1949), considers the predisposing condition to outweigh any environmental factor. With reference to the rampant juvenile prostitution in Vienna after World War II he states that his observations led him to believe that "a specific instinctual constellation must be one of the determinant factors, but that environment and constitution can only be concomitant factors" (p. 440). Perhaps cases of delinquent girls who have been classified as psychopaths might be viewed as cases of perversion.

More recently, Schmideberg (1956) pursues similar trends of thought. She contrasts the neurotic and the perverse reaction or symptom, emphasizing the fact that the former represents an autoplastic and the latter an alloplastic adaptation. She continues: "In a certain sense the neurotic symptom is of a more social kind, while the perverse is more anti-social. Thus there is a rather close connection between the sexual perversions and delinquent behavior, which is by definition anti-social" (p. 423). The impulsivity which is equally strong in acting-out behavior and in the perversions is well known. I hesitate to generalize as Schmideberg does, but would stress the point that the identity of delinquency and perversion outstandingly corresponds with the clinical picture of female delinquency, while it constitutes only one special variant in the diverse and far more heterogeneous etiology of male delinquency.

It is a justifiable request at this point to ask for the reasons for the view that male and female delinquency are differently structured. For this purpose it is necessary to turn our attention to the differences that distinguish the psychosexual development of the male and the female child. I do not intend to retell a well-known set of facts, but instead I shall highlight some relevant points of difference between the sexes by focusing on selective stations in the developmental schedule of early childhood. The developmental foci in what follows also represent potential points of fixation which lead the adolescent boy or girl into essentially different crisis situations.

1. All infants perceive the mother in early life as the "active mother." The characteristic antithesis at this period of life is "active" and "passive" (Brunswick, 1940). The archaic mother is always active; the child is passive and receptive in relation to her. Normally, an identification with the active mother brings the early phase of primal passivity to an end. It should be noted here that a bifurcation in the psychosexual development of boy and girl is already foreshadowed at this juncture. The girl turns gradually toward passivity, while the boy's first turn toward activity becomes absorbed later in the identification the boy normally forms with his father. It should not be concluded from this remark that femininity and passivity or masculinity and activity are synonymous. The emphasis is of a tendentious kind; therefore, it is not of an absolute dualistic order but of a qualitative and potential one, inherent in and characteristic of both sexes.

The early identification with the active mother leads the girl via the phallic phase into an initial active (negative) oedipal position as a typical step in her development. When the girl turns her love needs to the father, the danger always exists that her passive strivings toward him will reawaken early oral dependency; a return to this primal passivity will preclude the successful advancement to femininity. Whenever an unduly strong father attachment marks the girl's oedipal situation, we can always suspect behind it an unduly deep and lasting attachment to the preoedipal mother. Only when the girl succeeds in abandoning her passive tie to the mother and advances to a passive (positive) oedipal position can she be spared the adolescent regression to the preoedipal mother.

2. The first love object of every child is the mother. The

girl abandons at one point this first love object, and seeks
her sense of completeness as well as of fulfillment in her
femininity by turning toward the father; this turn always
follows a disappointment in the mother. Due to the fact that
for the boy the sex of his love object never changes, his development is more direct and less complicated than that of
the girl.

In contradistinction to the boy, the girl's oedipal situation is never brought to an abrupt decline. The following
words of Freud (1933) are relevant: "Girls remain in it [the
Oedipal situation] for an indeterminate length of time; they
demolish it late, and even so, incompletely" (p. 129). The
oedipal constellation of the girl continues to be part of her
emotional life throughout the latency period. At any rate,
we observe in female adolescence a regressive pull which
exerts its influence in the direction of a return to the
preoedipal mother. This regressive pull, determined in its
strength by the existent fixation, is often reacted against by
the exercise of excessive independence, hyperactivity, and a
forceful turn toward the other sex. This impasse is dramatically displayed at adolescence in the girl's frantic attachment to boys in the attempt to resist regression. Adolescent regression in boy and girl alike appears as passive
dependency with an irrational overvaluation of the mother
or, manifestly, a mother representative.

3. The question has often been asked why preadolescence in the boy and the girl is so markedly different.[2] The
boy approaches heterosexuality, when it is ushered in by
puberty, via a prolonged perseverance in preadolescence,
with an uninhibited, public display or often elaborate recapitulation of pregenital drive modalities, apparent in such
traits as smuttiness, neglect of body care, gluttony, and
motor excitability. Nothing of comparable scope can be ob-

[2]There is no doubt that social milieu has an accelerating or retarding influence
on adolescent development. Consequently, a meaningful comparison of developmental patterns can only be made between boys and girls from a similar milieu.

served in the preadolescent girl or, to be more correct, her pregenital revival remains more secreted from her observing environment.

The fact that the girl approaches heterosexuality more directly and speedily than the boy is significantly determined by the girl's fear of regression. Preadolescence as a phase is marked by heterogeneous libidinal aims in boy and girl and gives rise to marked tension in children of this age.

The difference in preadolescent behavior is foreshadowed by the massive repression of pregenitality which the girl established before she moved into the oedipal phase; as I have stated before, this repression is a prerequisite for the normal development of femininity. The girl turns away from the mother or, to be more precise, withdraws from her the narcissistic libido which was the basis for the comforting overvaluation of her and transfers this overvaluation to the father. All this is well known. I therefore hasten to make the point that the girl, in turning away from the mother, represses those instinctual drives that were intimately related to her mother's care and bodily ministrations, that is, the total scope of pregenitality. The return to these modes of gratification at puberty constitutes the basis for correlating female delinquency and perversion; regression and fixation appear as necessary and complementary conditions.

It seems, then, that the girl who in her adolescence cannot maintain the repression of her pregenitality will encounter difficulties in her progressive development. A fixation on the preoedipal mother and a return to the gratifications of this period often result in acting-out behavior which has as the central theme "baby and mother" and the re-creation of a union in which mother and child are confused. Adolescent unmarried mothers and their attitudes toward their babies offer ample opportunity to study this problem. A seventeen-year-old girl told me after an abortion that she was doing strange things when she was all alone at home. She walked around the house saying in an anxious, tiny

baby voice: "Mummy." She added: "I must be crazy." Needless to say, an agitated conflict with the mother dominated
the girl's emotional life.

In contrast to the condition that prevails in the girl I
want to point briefly to the different situation of the boy.
Since he preserves the same love object throughout his
childhood, he is not confronted with a necessity to repress
pregenitality equal in summary sweep to the girl. Ruth
Mack Brunswick (1940), in her classic paper on the "Preoedipal Phase of Libido Development," says: "One of the
greatest differences between the sexes is the enormous extent to which infantile sexuality is repressed in the girl.
Except in profound neurotic states, no man resorts to any
similar repression of his infantile sexuality" (p. 246).

The adolescent boy who returns to pregenital drive
gratifications during transient regressive episodes finds
himself still in relative consonance with his progressive
sex-appropriate development; he is certainly not in any
fatal opposition to it. Behavior disturbances due to these regressive movements are not necessarily as injurious to his
emotional development as I consider them to be in the case
of the girl. "Paradoxically, the girl's mother relation is more
persistent, and often more intense and dangerous, than the
boy's. The inhibition she encounters when she turns toward
reality brings her back to her mother for a period marked
by heightened and more infantile love demands" (Deutsch,
1944).

4. It follows that there are basically two types of female
delinquents: one has regressed to the preoedipal mother,
and the other clings desperately to a foothold on the oedipal
stage. The central relationship problem of both is the
mother. These two types of adolescent delinquents will
commit offenses which look alike and are equal before the
law, but are essentially different in dynamics and structure.
In one case we have a regressive solution, while in the
other an oedipal struggle prevails, which, it is true, has

never reached any degree of internalization or resolution.

Theoretical considerations tend to support the thesis that female delinquency is often precipitated by the strong regressive pull to the preoedipal mother and the panic surrender implies. As we can readily see, two solutions are available to the girl who is faced with an oedipal failure or disappointment which she is unable to surmount. She either regresses in her object relation to the mother or she maintains an illusory oedipal situation with the sole aim of resisting regression. This defensive struggle is manifested in the compulsive need to create in reality a relationship in which she is needed and wanted by a sexual partner. These constellations represent the paradigmatic preconditions for female delinquency.

5. A few words about the latter type first. It is my impression that this type of delinquent girl not only experienced an oedipal defeat at the hands of a—literally or figuratively—distant, cruel, or absent father, but also has witnessed her mother's contemptuous dissatisfaction with her husband; both mother and daughter share their disappointment. A strong and highly ambivalent bond continues to exist between them. Under these circumstances no satisfactory identification with the mother can be achieved; instead, a hostile or negative identification forges a destructive and indestructible relationship between mother and daughter. Young adolescent girls of this type quite consciously fantasy that if only they could be in their mother's place the father would show his true self, that is, he would be transfigured by their love into the man of their oedipal idealization. In real life such delinquent girls promiscuously choose sexual partners who possess glaring personality defects which these girls deny or tolerate with masochistic submissiveness.

In more general terms we might say that the delinquent behavior is motivated by the girl's need for the constant possession of a partner who allows her to surmount in fantasy an oedipal impasse—but more important than this, to take revenge on the mother who hated, rejected, or ridiculed the father. Furthermore, we observe the delinquent girl's desire to be sexually needed, wanted, and used. Spiteful and revengeful fantasies with reference to the mother abound; in fact, the sex act itself is dominated by such fantasies with the result that no sexual pleasure is ever obtained. In these girls we look in vain for a wish to have a baby; if pregnancy occurs, it is an act of revenge or competition which is reflected in the attitude to the infant: "It might just as well be given away."

6. In the case of female delinquency based on regression to the preoedipal mother we witness an entirely different dynamic picture. Helene Deutsch (1944) has called our attention to the girl's dissolution of passive dependency on the mother as a precondition for the normal development of femininity; these "severance actions" are typical for early adolescence. Deutsch continues: "A prepubertal attempt at liberation from the mother that has failed or was too weak can inhibit future psychologic growth and leave a definitely infantile imprint on the woman's entire personality" (p. 21).

The delinquent girl who has failed in her liberation from the mother protects herself against regression by a wild display of pseudo heterosexuality. She has no relationship to or interest in her sexual partner, in fact her hostility to the male is often severe (see Nancy's dream of 365 babies below). The male serves to gratify the girl's insatiable oral needs. She may be consciously obsessed by the wish for a baby. This wish, in its make-believe childishness, is reminiscent of the little girl's wish for or play with a doll.

Thus behavior, which at first sight seems to represent the recrudescence of oedipal wishes, proves on careful scrutiny to be related to earlier fixation points lying in the pregenital phases of libidinal development. At that time severe deprivation or overstimulation or both were experienced.

The pseudo heterosexuality of these girls serves as a defense against the regressive pull to the preoedipal mother and, therefore, to homosexuality. As noted in Chapter 6, one fourteen-year-old girl, when asked why she needed ten boyfriends at once, answered with righteous indignation: "I have to do this; if I didn't have so many boyfriends they would say I am a lesbian." This same girl was preoccupied with the idea of getting married. She related these fantasies to her female therapist in order to elicit her protective care. When the therapist showed indifference to her marriage plans, the girl burst into tears, accusing her with these words: "You push me! I don't want to get married!" Here we can see clearly how the heterosexual acting out receives its urgency or its decisive "push" from the frustrated need to be loved by the mother. This girl's preoccupation with marriage masked her longing for the preoedipal mother and found a substitute gratification in the guise of heterosexual pseudo love.

It is a well-known fact that an acute disappointment in the mother is frequently the decisive precipitating factor in illegitimacy. By proxy the mother-child unit becomes reestablished, but under the most foreboding circumstances for the proxy child. Such mothers can find satisfaction in motherhood only as long as the infant is dependent on them; they turn against the child as soon as independent strivings assert themselves. Infantilization of the child is the well-known result.

7. One more possibility is open to the girl who is fixated on the preoedipal mother—identification with the father. This resolution of the oedipal conflict is often due to a painful rejection by the father. The girl who thus assumes the masculine role watches jealously over her mother and defies any man who aims at possessing her. We usually refer to this constellation as penis envy; in the etiology of female delinquency this factor does not deserve the overwhelming importance which was once awarded to it. Of course, its role

in kleptomania cannot be denied and the preponderance of this symptom in women testifies to its etiological significance. The dynamic factor of penis envy, however, cannot be separated from the underlying accusation that the mother's seemingly willful withholding of expected gratification has prevented the child from overcoming oral greed.

Case Illustration

The theoretical considerations which have occupied our attention up to this point need now to be brought back to the individual case where they were studied originally. The case abstract which follows concerns Nancy, a young adolescent girl.[3] The treatment aspect of the case is not made part of the record here; it is the language of behavior to which we shall lend our ear.

When Nancy was thirteen years old she presented the family, the school authorities, and the court with a problem of sexual delinquency; her stealing was only known to her mother. At home Nancy was uncontrollable and loud-mouthed; she used obscene language, cursed her parents, and had her own way, disregarding any adult interference. "The names Nancy calls me are so sexy," the mother repeatedly complained. Despite her seeming independence, Nancy never failed to report her sexual exploits to her mother, or at least hinted at them sufficiently to arouse her mother's curiosity, anger, guilt, and solicitude. With glee she showed her mother stories she had written consisting mostly of obscene language. Nancy was an avid reader of "dirty sex books"; she stole money from her mother for their purchase. Nancy's mother was willing to give her the money, but Nancy explained to the therapist, "I wanted to *take* the money and not have it *given* to me."

Nancy blamed her mother angrily for not having been firm with her when she was a little girl: "Mother should

[3]Nancy's female therapist was supervised by me.

have known that I acted up in order to get her attention and to have adults fuss over me." She, Nancy, would never marry a husband who says only "dearie, dearie"; she preferred a man who slaps you when you are wrong. The criticism implied in this remark was obviously directed against her weak father. She did not blame him for being a man of no education, who earned a modest income, but for his indifference and his ineffectual role in the family.

Nancy grew up in a small apartment located in a crowded city neighborhood. Nancy's family wanted the "finer things in life" for her and found ways and means to pay for them; thus Nancy had received lessons in acrobatics, ballet, and elocution. With puberty came the end of all these refinements.

Nancy was preoccupied with sex to the exclusion of almost everything else. This interest reached abnormal proportions soon after menarche at age eleven. She boasted of her many boyfriends and her sexual relations. She asked her peers at school to join her "sex club." Nancy only liked "bad boys" who stole, lied, and had a criminal record, boys who "know how to get around a girl." She herself wanted to steal and smoke, but she did not accompany the boys on their delinquent excursions because she "might get caught." Nancy was puzzled by the fact that she could always get a fellow if another girl was after him but not otherwise. She had established a position of respect among the girls because she would challenge them quickly to a fist fight: "I have to show them that I am not afraid of them."

Nancy admitted to the therapist that she desired sexual relations but denied having ever given in to her desire; she said that she used her body only to attract boys and get their attention. She was, however, observed being intimate with several boys on a roof top and was found there "dazed, disheveled, and wet." It was at this time that the case was taken to court; Nancy was put on probation under the condition that she receive treatment. In light of the evidence,

Nancy no longer denied to the therapist that she had sexual relations. She experienced neither genital sensation nor sexual pleasure. She expressed her hope to have a baby and explained that she engaged in sexual relations to take revenge on her mother. She, Nancy, would keep the baby and marry the boy. Her mother, she was convinced, did not want her and, in fact, had never wanted her. At this time Nancy had a dream in which she had sexual relations with teenage boys. In the dream she had 365 babies, one a day for a year from one boy, whom she shot after this was accomplished.

Nancy daydreamed a great deal; her fantasies concerned marriage and she was consumed by the wish for a baby. She was afraid of not being attractive to boys and never getting married. Physically, Nancy was well developed for her age, but she was dissatisfied with her own body, especially her skin, hair, height, eyes (glasses), and ears (the lobes were attached to the sides of her head). At home she was extremely modest and never allowed her mother to see her in the nude. Nancy could think of only one reason for all her troubles, disappointments and anxieties—her mother; she was to be "blamed for everything that made her unhappy." She accused the mother of taking her friends—boys and girls—away from her, of begrudging her the happiness she found in having friends, of putting a lock on the phone to cut her off from the world. Nancy said she needed girlfriends, close friends, who would become her blood sisters; she and Sally scratched their initials into each other's arms with a razor blade as proof of their eternal friendship. The mother scolded Nancy when she showed her the scars; this to the daughter was another demonstration of her mother's not wanting her to have any close girlfriends. In disappointment she had tried to run away from home, but the tie to her mother always proved to be too strong; before long she returned.

Despite her vehement rejection of her mother, Nancy

needed her presence at every turn. She would, for instance, insist that her mother accompany her on her visits to the therapist. Being at a loss about a summer job, Nancy thought that her mother should take a job as a camp counselor and she would assist her as junior counselor. Nancy was totally unaware of her mother's unfitness for such a job, nor was she able to assess reasonably her own abilities.

If mother, Nancy continued her accusations, had only had more babies, not just one child and a girl at that, Nancy was sure that her life would have taken a different turn. During the first interview with the therapist, who inquired sympathetically about Nancy's purpose in seeing her, Nancy maintained a long, sullen silence and then suddenly began to cry. In her first words she expressed her overwhelming need to be loved: "As an only child I have always been so lonesome." She always wanted a baby brother or sister and begged her mother to get one. She had a dream in which she was taking care of babies; they were really her girlfriend's babies (see below) and Nancy's mother remarked in the dream: "It is a shame that such cute children have no proper mother to take care of them; let's adopt them." In the dream Nancy was overjoyed and ran to her therapist to tell her that they were adopting babies. The therapist replied that it would cost a lot of money, and Nancy answered, "But don't you know we are loaded?" Waking up from the dream Nancy asked her mother to take in a foster child. "The child," Nancy said, "will have to be a boy as I only know how to diaper boys." She fancied herself having a summer job taking care of children in a family, way out in the country. When she was a little older, age fourteen, she actually took a summer job with children as a helper in the nursery school of a community center. There she was a child among children, an older sister who helped the little ones with their play. Nancy always liked to baby-sit; she loved to hold a baby in her arms, especially if the baby was very young. When her cousin became pregnant, Nancy looked forward to taking care of the baby, but added, "I will baby-sit free for three months, that's fun, but later I shall get paid."

Nancy attached herself during these years of sexual preoccupation to a young pregnant woman of twenty who had married at the age of sixteen, had three children, and lived an erratic and promiscuous life (her husband was absent). Nancy vicariously shared this woman's sex life and motherhood; she took care of the children during their mother's absence from her home. This necessitated staying overnight when the young woman did not return for a day or two; consequently, Nancy became a truant. Once she brought the three children to her own home to take care of them while her friend was engaged in her sexual escapades and was not heard from for three days. Nancy emphatically sided with her woman friend against the husband with whom, Nancy said, she was once in love. She also protested violently her mother's accusations against her friend, commenting to the therapist: "My mother has a mind like a sewer." Nancy knew that she understood her friend; she knew that her friend was unhappy because her father had died early in her life and she never loved her mother. "It's no use," Nancy said, "arguing with Mother." She summed it up by saying: "My mother and I just don't understand each other." After such fights Nancy suddenly became afraid that the aggravation she had caused her mother might kill her since she suffered from high blood pressure.

Nancy had found a temporary haven, indeed a dangerous one, in the home of her married girlfriend. She felt safe in the close friendship with this pregnant mother who knew how to attract men and get many babies. Nancy also relished the jealous anger of her own mother who disapproved of this friendship. Now, Nancy felt, she possessed a girlfriend-mother with whom she could share everything. During this time Nancy withdrew from girls of her own age, feeling that they no longer had anything in common. An embarrassing testimony of the fact that she had outgrown her peers was her response to a group of girls discussing clothes; to the question, "What kind of clothes do you like best?" Nancy blurted out, "Maternity clothes." Such incidents drew Nancy more deeply into the make-believe family life with her girlfriend. Nancy loved this woman and, as she said to the therapist, "I can't get her out of my mind."

In her relationship to the therapist Nancy fluctuated between closeness and distance; this instability is well expressed by her own words: "When I think of coming to the office, I don't want to come; but when I am here, I am glad, and I feel like talking." She finally admitted that she would like to be confidential with the therapist but gave her a warning by confessing that she really was a "compulsive liar." She made the suggestion to the therapist that they both should reveal to each other the secrets of their lives; then they could learn from each other. The need for intimacy which exerted its emotional pull toward the therapist was conversely responsible for her repeated running away from her.

Nancy finally came to repudiate the "crude, rough stuff of the teenagers" and her fancy moved into the direction of professional acting. Here she drew on interests and playful activities belonging to her latency years. Wild and childish daydreams of meeting movie actors, fainting in front of them, and being discovered as the new star, eventually gave way to a more sober approach to the study of acting. From acting Nancy expected to "become a lady"; by this she meant: to be gentle, to speak gently, to act gently; then, she was sure, people would like her. Nancy had been given the following explanation by her mother when she started to menstruate: "Now you are a lady."

Nancy clung to her acting all through her adolescence; in fact, she achieved at the age of sixteen a modest degree of recognition in a summer stock production. The stage had become the legitimate territory where her impulsivity was

allowed expression in many directions and where her
exhibitionistic needs became slowly tamed by the aesthetic
code of acting itself. By this time Nancy had become somewhat of a prude; she was a good mixer with her peers but
only to promote her self-interest in dramatic productions.
As good a manipulator as her mother, Nancy now became
narcissistically related to her environment and learned how
to exploit others. The interest in acting had become Nancy's
identity around which her personality integration took
shape. The core of this identity hails back to the "finer
things in life" which Nancy's mother had always wanted for
her daughter. In adolescence Nancy reverted to these aspirations which were instilled in her by lessons in the performing arts during her latency years. It was precisely this
artistic endeavor that served in adolescence as an avenue
for sublimation of the unresolved fixation to the mother.
The vocational identity rescued Nancy from regression and
delinquency, but it also prevented a progression to mature
object relations; it was, after all, still mother whose desire
she continued to gratify by her artistic activity. When reminded once at the age of sixteen of her wish for babies, she
snapped back with disgust, "Babies is kid's stuff."

It seems hardly necessary to point out those aspects of
the case that illustrate the etiological importance of the
preoedipal mother fixation in Nancy's delinquent behavior.
Her pseudo heterosexuality appears clearly as a defense
against the return to the preoedipal mother and against
homosexuality. The only safe relationship Nancy found was
a *folie à deux* with a pregnant mother-girlfriend; this attachment and transitory identification rendered the sexual
acting out temporarily expendable. However, an advance in
her emotional development was precluded until a turn to a
sublimated endeavor, namely, becoming an actress, had
firmly taken possession. This ego ideal—adolescent and
probably transitory—resulted in a relatively more stable
self-representation and opened the way to adolescent ex-

perimentation and to ego-integrative processes.

Nancy's delinquent behavior can only be understood in conjunction with the personality disturbance of her mother. Upon closer inspection of the family pathology we recognize—quoting Johnson and Szurek (1952)—"the unwitting employment of the child to act out for the parent his own poorly integrated and forbidden impulses." The diagnosis and treatment of this type of antisocial acting out has become a familiar one for those clinicians whose wits have been sharpened by the research Johnson and Szurek have conducted over the last fifteen years. The "collaborative treatment" in Nancy's case followed the outline drawn by them.

My curiosity is aroused by another set of facts. From the analysis of certain adult parents we know of their delinquent, perverse, and deviant unconscious fantasies, and we also know how often the parent is identified with the child and his or her instinctual life at a particular age. However, many children of such parents show no tendency toward acting out the delinquent, perverse, and deviant unconscious strivings of their parents; in fact, many demonstrate in this respect a resistivity which in the case of Nancy was totally lacking. Children normally seek in their environment compensatory experiences which will to some degree make up for the deficiencies in the emotional life of the family. This phenomenon is especially true for children in the latency period, but also for younger children who establish meaningful relationships with older siblings, neighbors, relatives, family friends, teachers, and others. In contrast, children like Nancy are totally unable to supplement their emotional experiences in their broader environment, and continue to live their impoverished social life in the narrow confines of the family.

It seems, then, that a special kind of interaction between parent and child must be at work to prevent the child from establishing progressively a more or less independent life.

This special quality of the parent-child relationship lies in a sadomasochistic pattern which has not only permeated the child's instinctual life but has adversely affected ego development as well. Primal ambivalence rooted in the biting stage of oral organization constitutes a nucleus from which a lasting pattern of interaction between mother and child emerges; this pattern is carried like a *leitmotif* through all the stages of psychosexual development. The polarities of love-hate, giving-taking, submission-domination continue to exist in an ambivalent, reciprocal dependency of mother and child. The sadomasochistic modality gradually inundates all interaction between child and environment; it eventually influences ego development via the introjection of an ambivalent object. As a consequence, inhibitory functions are poorly developed and tension tolerance is low. The stimulus hunger of these children represents the lasting expression of their oral greed. Does perhaps the impulsivity which we observe in Nancy's acting-out behavior constitute an essential quality of an all-pervasive sadomasochistic drive organization? We should remember here, as Szurek (1954) pointed out, that the "two factors, the libidinous fixations and the internalization of the parents' attitudes, determine which impulses of the child became ego-syntonic and which are repressed. To the extent that these factors interfere with the child's satisfactory experience in any developmental phase, the internalized attitudes are revengefully (i.e., sadistically) caricatured and the libidinous impulses are masochistically distorted, i.e., the libidinous energy of both id and the superego is fused with the rage and anxiety consequent to the repeated thwarting" (p. 377).

The case of Nancy is of interest in the light of these considerations. Therefore, we shall now turn to her early life in search for those experiences which played a primary and predisposing role in terms of the sadomasochistic fixation on the preoedipal mother and the eventual adaptive failure at puberty. The transactional meaning of the delinquent behavior is not without consequence for therapeutic technique; however, this problem cannot be elaborated here.

Nancy was an only child, born two years after marriage. She was wanted by her mother, who desired to have many children. The husband had intended to wait ten years; his wife, unable to bear this delay, had applied for a foster child, but her request was turned down. Soon after she became pregnant.

Nancy was breast-fed for six months; at four months the infant started to bite the nipple, causing the mother considerable pain. Despite the mother's protestations, the doctor insisted that the mother continue to nurse; two months later, when nursing had become an ordeal, she was permitted to take the baby off the breast. Thus for two months mother and child were engaged in a battle over sucking and biting, over offering and withholding the nipple. A lasting effect of this period can be recognized in Nancy's persistent refusal to drink milk. Thumb sucking started at the age of three months; it was forcibly suppressed by the use of gloves. We can assume that the infant obtained sufficient stimulation and gratification from nursing at an early age. Nancy started to talk at about one year and walked well at sixteen months.

Some events in the life of this child are of special interest. When Nancy entered kindergarten she vomited daily before school; this symptom disappeared after several weeks of enforced attendance. The teacher then noticed that Nancy ignored her presence in a way that suggested defective hearing. Tests, however, proved this assumption to be incorrect. When Nancy started the first grade she had temper tantrums in school and would try to run away. Her mother waylaid her and returned her forcibly to the classroom; after a few weeks her running away ceased for good. From this time on her conduct in school was a constant cause for complaints. All through her latency years Nancy was "stubborn, quick-tempered, a grumbler and a complainer."

Nancy slept in the parental bedroom until the age of
eight. At that time she was given a room of her own. She
then started to have nightmares and would come to her parents' bedroom. No disciplinary action kept her from disturbing her parents' sleep. Finally, when Nancy refused to
return to her room one night, the mother made her sit for
the rest of the night in a chair in her parents' bedroom.
After this ordeal the child surrendered, stayed in her own
room, and no longer complained about having nightmares.

Nancy knew very few children and played with them
rarely; she preferred to stay in the company of her mother.
She had "imaginary companions" all through her early
childhood and very likely during her latency years; in her
early adolescence she still used to talk to herself in bed and
forbade her mother to listen in. The mother was just as
curious about her daughter's private life as Nancy was
about hers. With reference to Nancy's lack of friends the
mother remarked, "Nancy wants too much love."

Two complementary factors in the early mother-child interaction seem to have predisposed Nancy and her mother
to a lasting ambivalent attachment. The mother expected to
have babies in order to gratify her own infantile needs,
while Nancy—perhaps endowed with an unusually strong
oral drive—made demands on the mother she in turn was
not capable of fulfilling. This battle over self-interests
which were not reciprocally tolerated was destined to continue without letup and without settlement up to Nancy's
puberty. Her submissiveness to the mother's cruel discipline, her surrender of oral needs in exchange for masochistic gratification reveals the progressive integration of a
sadomasochistic object relationship which precluded the development of any successful individuation; to the contrary,
it resulted in the child's close, symbiotic entanglement with
the archaic mother.

Nancy's attempts at separation in early childhood and
puberty are apparent in her creation of "imaginary com-

panions" and in her attachment to the mother-girlfriend at the age of thirteen. These attempts at liberation were unsuccessful; pseudo heterosexuality was the only avenue open to this impulse-driven girl to gratify her oral greed, to take revenge on the "selfish" mother, and to protect herself against homosexuality. Having traced Nancy's delinquent behavior back to the predisposing antecedents residing in the second (sadistic) oral phase, the circle seems to be closed.

A typical personality configuration leading to delinquency in puberty was the subject of this genetic inquiry. The preceding theoretical discussion alluded to other configurations which, however, were not illustrated by clinical material. The case of Nancy should be considered representative of only one type of female delinquency.

Postscript
1976

It is always a sobering exercise to re-examine a paper that one has written a score of years ago and scrutinize it in the light of present-day reality. Such a second look is particularly worthwhile when the original paper proposed theoretical formulations concerning a certain type of female asocial behavior and did so with the explicit purpose of giving the therapy of these adolescent girls a meaningful, i.e., clinically effective, focus. A reassessment of ideas related to female sexual delinquency seems especially urgent at the present time when the social scene of adolescence has undergone such radical changes in terms of mores, values, and their behavioral expressions, generally referred to as life styles.

Delinquency always contains a social reference, and consequently, is contingent on the deviance from social norms or prevalent expectancies of behavior. The individual motivational system, or the dynamic configuration, of delinquency is always influenced by social tradition and social change. This consideration only repeats the opening sentence of my original paper, namely, that in delinquent behavior we have to consider predisposing and psychodynamic factors in correspondence with social norms of the intrinsic milieu.

It is obvious that what we called sexual "acting out" in the 1950s cannot apply equally to the sexual behavior of the adolescent in 1976. Sexual (genital) activity of the young in the seventies has become the legitimate form of youthful behavior through the entire adolescent period, from the preadolescent to the late adolescent phase. We have witnessed over the years the almost total disappearance of privacy or secrecy in sexual matters. Indeed, it impresses the observer of adolescents that the openness of their heterosexual relations has the ring of a declaratory insistence that the parental generation be involved, positively or negatively, in the sexual behavior of the young. We can furthermore observe that the traditional ritualization of gender behavior has to a large extent faded away or has been progressively wiped out with a programmatic zeal by the girl. As a result, the openly seductive aggressiveness of the girl—especially the young adolescent girl—often exceeds the boy's proverbial sexual aggressiveness of old. The designation "sexual acting out" has lost much of its meaning when this kind of behavior has largely ceased to be in "open conflict with society." Whenever a so-called deviant form of behavior acquires widespread acceptance within a significant segment of the population, the stigma of deviancy fades away and the behavioral expression—in this case, the genital activity of the young girl—becomes an increasingly fallible indication of abnormal development.

The question has often been asked in which way and to what extent the sexual behavior of the adolescent girl has been influenced by the pill and the Women's Liberation Movement. It is my opinion that these two innovations—one technological and one ideological—are far more consequential among older adolescent girls, especially within the college population, but have an insignificant bearing on young adolescent girls of—roughly speaking—junior high school age. To be sexually active and to let it be known among peers as well as adults has become a symbol of status along the maturity scale. In the extreme—and this extreme has acquired the characteristics of a movement—sexuality has become equated with mere action and experience. It has ceased, therefore, to be contingent on a personal and emotionally significant—i.e., intimate—relationship which transcends the sexual act and the gratificatory dependency. The ease and seemingly conflictless freedom with which the young girl consummates the sexual act proclaims that to her the disapproving voice of the parents—most often the mother's voice—is but a reflection of their old-fashioned, total ignorance of the importance of the sexual experience.

Enlightened middle-class mothers, realizing their helplessness vis-à-vis the sexual revolution, turn their attention to the prevention of pregnancy and suggest to the girl that she take the pill or practice some form of contraception. Thus, the pill has displaced old-fashioned "morality"; easy, safe contraceptive preparedness has made "judgment and inhibition" dispensable in matters of sexual intercourse. Sexual experimentation without personal or romantic involvement has carried away young adolescents since time immemorial. What we observe today is the practice of sexual experimentation as an aim in itself and an extension of this stage of sexual behavior into late adolescence under the security of the pill. Might we not extrapolate at this point from developmental studies generally and remind ourselves of the fact that the perseverance on any developmental stage beyond its normative timing invites the potential of a deviant or lopsided developmental progression? We shall return to this issue.

One particular feature of the pill is entirely psychological; it permits a temporary dissociation between swallowing a pill and the sexual act itself. All other contraceptive devices involve genital manipulation, whereas the pill is as innocuous as a vitamin capsule. The fact that the pill is orally administered has subtly influenced not only the parental but also the public attitude toward the sexual behavior of the adolescent girl.

With the availability of the pill, boy and girl have become equals in the unencumbered and safe attainment of the sexual experience and the particular pleasure related to it. What has been said in the not-too-distant past about masturbation in adolescence—that it represents (especially for the boy) a nonspecific voluntary regulator of tension generally—can be applied widely to the function of adolescent intercourse. The subject of sex, promoted by advertisement, screen, and the printed page, has become a kind of panacea and its exercise per se the equivalent of emotional maturity. The peer group has come to endorse as mature the sexually active boy and girl. In other words, the peer group with its characteristic fostering of conformity has come to equate adolescent heterosexual behavior with independence, individualism, and adulthood. This behavioral mandate has replaced almost totally the initiation rites of old and is now imposed by adolescents themselves or by the so-called peer culture without adult participation or traditional ritualization. As in all standardized behavior it is not only a personal wish or desire that activates choice and form of emotional or sexual expression; the social persuasion of the significant milieu is an equally salient determinant of behavior.

Under the impact of pubescent urges, the mass media, and peer-code pressures, many an adolescent girl goes "through the paces" of "making love" in accordance with social expectations, but without being emotionally involved. The use of the sexual act as a means to attain a sense of fulfillment and of group belongingness leads many girls to frustration and disappointment in their desperate search for happiness via promiscuous behavior. We might refer to this state as psychophysical dichotomization of the sexual act. This posture is normal enough as a temporary and experimental transition, but, if practiced as a "life style" during the entire adolescent period, it throws a shadow on the future sex life of the adult. This becomes apparent in a persistent difficulty or failure to integrate the physical sexual act with mature emotional responses. The short-circuiting of adolescent emotional development by dependence and reliance on genital activity or, to put it differently, the side-stepping of psychic restructuring by habitually using sexual satisfaction as a substitute for internal conflict resolution, leaves its mark on psychosexual development. Frigidity and emotional infantilism, both adumbrated earlier in life, often reach a definitive fixity in adolescent psychophysical dichotomization. Perhaps it is the incompleteness of the sexual experience that has afforded the "techniques of love making" such an influential and prominent place in present-day adolescent and adult sexual behavior.

It follows from all this that contemporary trends in adolescent sexual behavior have made it meaningless to speak of "sexual delinquency." It has become extremely difficult for the clinician to assess the "normality" of the girl's heterosexual behavior when sexual intercourse has become "de rigueur" among an ever-growing segment of the female adolescent population, from early to late adolescence. Under these circumstances we have to reorient ourselves within a changed and ever-changing context of biological technology (contraceptive devices), adolescent mores, personal choices, developmental stages, and maturational givens.

In setting aside the outworn terms of "female sexual delinquency" and "sexual acting out," I propose using the following distinctions in the evaluation of phase-appropriateness in relation to the sexual behavior of the present-day adolescent girl. I shall describe three categories or types, which in actuality blend in various measures, but which provide a framework for the purpose of assessment.

1. Sexual intercourse is predominantly the expression of an adolescent severance conflict in relation to childhood dependencies. One can detect in the adolescent an awareness, vague or poignant, of the ego-alien quality of the sexual behavior. In these cases the impulsive sexual expression via intercourse usually declines or is spontaneously given up. Through the process of internalization, which constitutes an intrinsic aspect of the second individuation process of

adolescence, a psychic resolution of the severance conflict is gradually achieved. The girl must have some capacity for tolerating frustration or tension for these internal changes to take their course. In psychoanalytic parlance, these psychic mechanisms are referred to as repression, displacement, and sublimation. Girls who attempt this kind of resolution have to strike a balance between personal autonomy and the fierce social pressures of peer persuasion and dogmatism. Caught in this predicament, many girls resort to role-playing and pretend publicly to have an active sexual life until they have gained the inner strength to declare their personal choice of intimacy and their individualistic style of sexual conduct, independent of peer censorship.

2. Sexual intercourse is practiced in conformity with the social influence of the peer group and the mass media. As a collective severance ritual it ought to establish the boundaries between the generations and lead to the relinquishment of adolescent sexual conformism. However, this form of (often promiscuous) sexual behavior loses, in the typical case, its developmental raison d'être and acquires the permanence of a life style. As such it extends throughout adolescence into early adulthood, essentially unchanged.

3. The girl practices sexual intercourse (often starting in early puberty): (a) as a defense against regression to the preoedipal mother; (b) as a gratification of infantile contact hunger ("cuddling") with genital anesthesia; (c) as an active caring for her partner by yielding to his physical needs in identification with the idealized mother of her preoedipal past. The emotional involvement is equivalent to the little girl's doll play, which has usually been perfunctory or nonexistent in her early life.

The adolescent representatives of these three categories show the same manifest sexual behavior. It remains the clinician's task to sort out the etiological and the dynamic factors in the girl's sexual behavior. To assess the manifest sexual behavior has become complicated by the normalization and increasing acceptance by society of intercourse from early puberty onward. Differentiations in adolescent sexual behavior, however, are of importance if we consider the consequences of adolescent psychosexual development for the sexual life of the adult woman and her competence as a future mother.

It seems to me that the girl whose sexual behavior is determined, principally, by the influences described in the first two categories has not abandoned her progressive psychosexual and psychosocial development, even though, for many a girl, induced or imposed forms of sexual behavior may endanger her advance to emotional maturity. The third category clearly represents a catastrophic arrest in emotional development. I have encountered in my clinical work of late the same constellation I described in my paper of 1957. Due to the public tolerance of early intercourse, the pathological aspect of the sexual behavior of some of these girls often remains obscured. There are, however, indices in the overall clinical picture that point to the abnormal character of the young adolescent girl's sexual activity. I have in mind signs of depression, so-called borderline features, extreme moodiness, and a florid, infantile fantasy life.

Only a careful assessment singles out this girl from the other two categories. We ascertain in her sexual behavior an attempt to maintain her fixation on the tie to the preoedipal mother by using the environment as an infantile emotional "holding-on" position. It is common knowledge that with the advent of sexual maturation, the genital expression of libidinal and aggressive drives gains ascendancy and becomes—for a stretch of time—the focal avenue for the actualization of pregenitality as well. Should a developmental arrest, exacerbated by regressive trends, consolidate into a permanent condition, we encounter the type of girl who is sharply set off from the two other categories, regardless of the fact that they all share a sameness of sexual behavior.

It is utterly senseless to call all of them "sexual delinquents"; yet we have to single out the regressed, immature girl as one in need of help and protection. She is a seriously endangered adolescent child, despite the universal clamor for sexual freedom as the unfailing road to emotional maturity.

We have to realize that intercourse for the emotionally arrested adolescent girl is not directly associated with genital pleasure, strictly speaking. The pleasure she seeks and experiences is of an infantile nature along the continuum of visceral satiation and contact-comfort; it is therefore dissociated from the biological reality of sexual functions, one being conception. In this respect, the pill has altered little or nothing in her sexual behavior or in her comprehension of the sexual act. If she wants a baby, this seemingly maternal wish is the expression of an infantile desire to reestablish the child-mother unity (merger), or she simply seeks the comforts of body contact without any genital sensation or arousal. In the context of these infantile associations or this immature emotional and physical neediness, it is no surprise that contraception in any form remains an extraneous and dissociated set of irrelevant and useless knowledge.

Chapter 12

The Concept of Acting Out
in Relation to the
Adolescent Process

In clinical reports on adolescents, the term "acting out" is bound to be prominent. One has in fact come to recognize from experience that acting out during adolescence is as phase-specific as play is for childhood and direct language communication is for adulthood. We have come to consider acting out a typical adolescent phenomenon; indeed, the two have become almost synonymous.

Yet, on closer inspection, we realize that loose generalizations and a careless recourse to the concept of acting out are responsible for the extensive use of the term in relation to adolescence. There is no doubt that normal adolescents in our culture show a proclivity to action which is often of such intense and compelling nature that one is tempted to speak of an adolescent addiction to action. Whether the special condition of adolescence favors acting out or merely gives a predisposition to acting out unbridled reins, this question will occupy us in this chapter.

The theoretical distinction between action and acting out will not be elaborated at this point. The essential differences will gain in clarity through the delineation of act-

First published in *Journal of the American Academy of Child Psychiatry*, 2: 118-136, 1963.

ing out within the total phenomenology of action and through the investigation of the particular function acting out assumes during the adolescent period. In clinical work, we must admit, these delineations are not always as easily established as we might desire. Often we learn from fruitless efforts in dealing with play acting or uninhibited action discharge that what confronts us is an acting-out phenomenon; from the reverse situation, we learn a lesson equally well. What differentiates behavioral manifestations of similar appearance but of different structure will be explored in this chapter. This query will lead to a search for the reasons why the adolescent process tends to promote and favor the mechanism of acting out as a homeostatic device. As a consequence of such explorations, the question will finally be asked whether the concept of acting out in its traditional formulation is too narrow to accommodate relevant adolescent phenomena, and whether it is necessary to expand the standard concept in order to enhance its clinical usefulness.

A Historical Review of the Concept of Acting Out

In the concept of acting out we distinguish three aspects: one is related to the *predisposition* to acting out; another to the *manifestation* of acting out in behavior; and a third to the *function* of the acting-out mechanism. The three aspects are by no means unconditionally interrelated. Acting out, for instance, can occur without an evidently strong predisposition, as is dramatically exemplified during adolescence. Acting-out behavior, then, may be due to a structural characteristic of the ego, or it may be stimulated and precipitated by an acute life circumstance as, for instance, a therapeutic experience or a maturational event such as puberty and adolescence. We can speak of a latent and a manifest aspect of acting out and, furthermore, of a transient and a habitual kind of acting out.

The predisposition to acting out has been formulated by

Fenichel (1945), who speaks of an "alloplastic readiness," which appears as the unique involvement of the acting-out person with the outside world. The adversary in conflict as well as the source of stabilizing powers are experienced as external; this perception, in turn, keeps the individual in perpetual and excessive dependency on the outside world. Fenichel, furthermore, alludes to the oral modality of impetuousness and urgency and to the concomitant intense narcissistic needs and intolerance of tension. Last but not least, he mentions early trauma as a genetic prerequisite for acting out.

Early trauma is no doubt a prerequisite for acting out, but only through the lamination of this factor with other and specific predisposing components does acting out assume its unique quality. One gains the impression that acting out contains little of that special effort to master belatedly a trauma in small dosages by repetition. Acting out by its very nature has forfeited the capacity of mastery and turned it into an act of avoidance. There is a peculiar aspect to acting out which sets it apart from the repetition compulsion of the neurosis. This peculiar aspect lies in defective symbol formation by which normally action becomes replaced or delayed through trial action in thought and fantasy. If memory fails to become firmly and clearly structured through the acquisition of word symbols, then no workable organization of memory exists for an adaptive evaluation of current reality. Under such conditions, the preverbal modalities of problem solving and communication, namely, fantasy and action, remain the only available instrumentalities for coming to terms with a still pressing, i.e., unassimilated, past. In this sense, Fenichel speaks of acting out as a special form of remembering; we might refer to this as the function of acting out.

Greenacre (1950), among others, has investigated more specifically the predisposing factors that render acting out the chosen mechanism for the reduction of tension.

Greenacre refers to three predisposing factors with a specific genetic link to acting out: (1) "a special emphasis on visual sensitization producing a bent for dramatization"; (2) "a largely unconscious belief in the magic of action"; (3) "a distortion in the relation of action to speech and verbalized thought" (p. 227). The latter disturbance occurs in the second year of life and has to be understood in terms of a defective fusion in word usage of the thing denoted and the emotion associated with it. Under such conditions, the function of language has miscarried and the action language of earlier stages continues to operate side by side with it as a form of communication and problem solving. Looking at acting out in these terms we recognize that this form of expression constitutes a highly organized and structured mechanism. This is in contrast to the more primitive discharge process of impulsive behavior about which we shall have more to say in the subsequent discussion.

It follows from the preceding summary that the sense of reality in the acting-out individual is weak and vague; he easily makes transient identifications and plays roles. Such facility in changing the self is often remarkable. Carroll (1954) ascribes this disposition to a rich fantasy life which exists isolated and by itself, and which allows no compromise with reality. Adolescents of this type will tell you that their fantasies are more real than anything in the outer world. Consequently, they accept the outer world only so far as it gives credence to their inner reality; they attack it or they turn away from it as soon as the needed gratification it offers ceases to be in immediate and perfect harmony with the need tension they experience. This condition is typical for the adolescent user of drugs.

Let us make more explicit the distinction between the predisposing factors of acting out and the function of acting out by turning our attention to the function of acting out as a separate topic. Freud (1905a) originally used the term "acting out" in his case report on Dora, the first adolescent to be analyzed. In the Postscript to the Dora case, he referred to her leaving the analysis with these words: "Thus she *acted out* an essential part of her recollections and phantasies instead of reproducing it in the treatment" (p. 119). In other words, Dora took her revenge on the man who had deceived and deserted her. We recognize in this acting out the gratification of a hostile, retaliatory wish. Displacement is the mechanism of defense operative in the acting out that brought the Dora case to its premature termination.

Freud later used the term "acting out" in a paper on technique (1914a). There he applied it to the analytic situation, especially to transference and resistance: "We have learnt that the patient repeats instead of remembering, and repeats under the conditions of resistance." "We soon perceive that the transference is itself only a piece of repetition, and that the repetition is a transference of the forgotten past not only on to the doctor but also on to all the other aspects of the current situation" (p. 151). These concerns and formulations are intended to illuminate the analytic situation and should therefore be treated separately from acting out as a so-called symptom—or rather, a symptom equivalent—which brings many adolescents to our attention.

Acting out within the therapeutic situation requires constant vigilance and scrutiny as to the extent it can and should be permitted to take its course or as to the urgency with which it has to be curbed lest it affect adversely the adolescent's life and defeat therapy. Generally, it can be stated that acting out in the transference or acting out in the service of resistance has to be interpreted or otherwise rendered innocuous. However, other kinds of acting out exist, as we shall see, which do not require the same measures of interference because they serve different functions and pose no threat to the therapeutic alliance.

One further function of acting out has been mentioned by Jacobson (1957). The resistance against remembering effected by acting out constitutes a form of denial. "Acting out," Jacobson says "appears to be regularly linked up with a bent for denial" (p. 91). That this persistent denial goes hand in hand with a distortion of reality is borne out convincingly by patients of this kind. The function of acting out is denial through action; the magic of action and of gesture appears in such cases in great clarity. We touch here on a focal adolescent characteristic. The adolescent has a need to deny his helplessness through action, to affirm by exaggeration his independence from the archaic omnipotent mother, to counteract the regressive pull to passivity by denying his dependence on reality itself. Here, then, we encounter the megalomania of the adolescent who says: "Nobody can tell me," and we witness the adolescent's trust in the magic of action by which he hopes to control his destiny. If we succeed in penetrating the restitutive facade of such defiance, we are bound to discover fantasies barely kept apart from reality since no stable boundary line between them exists. Individuals in whom these conditions prevail "equate reality of thought with external actuality, and wishes with their fulfilment. . . . Hence also the difficulty of distinguishing unconscious phantasies from memories which have become unconscious" (Freud, 1911, p. 225).

The sense of reality is disturbed in all acting-out individuals. However, it is the quality of this disturbance that arouses our attention. We soon discover that outer reality has never been relinquished as the source of direct satisfaction on the level of need fulfillment. The observation that to the acting-out individual the person in relation to whom acting out is effected plays only a small or no role at all, that one is easily exchanged for another, is one more proof of the primitive psychic organization in which acting out is anchored. We recognize in acting out an autoerotic use of the outer world which is always available for momentary and immediate gratification. This condition is contrary to object-oriented gratification. True object relations require the recognition and acceptance of a self-interest in the other person and can develop only within the boundaries of compromise and empathy. The acting-out individual, in contrast, turns to the outer world as a tension-relieving part object. Viewed in these terms, acting out constitutes an autoerotic equivalent. Anna Freud (1949) alluded to this by saying: "The acting-out of fantasies . . . is, therefore, a derivative of phallic masturbation . . . its substitute and representative" (p. 203).

The mechanism of projection plays a prominent role in acting out and easily masks a psychic process such as an incipient paranoid state; this situation is especially true in adolescent cases of acting out. Kanzer (1957b), following a similar line of thought, says: "This regressive need for immediate object possession is probably more primary than the motor activity which serves it—relieving on the one hand castration anxiety and recapturing on a more primitive level the early sense of mastery resulting from the possession of the breast" (p. 667). In this sense, then, acting out has a restitutive function by denying the frustrating limitations of reality, declaring object and self to be intrinsically one and the same, and proving its concreteness by repeated affirmation through action. Consequently, acting out is always ego-syntonic. In fact, whenever acting out yields to a recognition of an ego-alien aspect, then acting out has already passed over into the realm of symptom formation or has become a symptomatic act. This change goes hand in hand with a decline of narcissistic needs and an emergence of differentiated object relations.

One more function of acting out must be mentioned here because it plays a particularly important role in adolescence. I refer to the adolescent's need to establish a temporal continuity within the ego. This continuity can no longer be maintained by proxy, by the simple phrase: "Even if I do not understand or remember or know fully what really happened in the past, my parents do; therefore nothing has been extinguished or lost as long as I continue to re-main a part of them." We know that whenever parents fal-sify by word or action the reality of events to which one of the child's senses was a competent witness, the child exper-iences a disturbance in his sense of reality which may lead to a critical impasse during adolescence. In an attempt to restore the sense of reality we observe acting-out behavior of all kinds, frequently of an asocial or antisocial nature. Such cases often respond extremely well to a rediscovery of the undistorted past. I am inclined to give this fact a weighty significance by saying that acting out in the service of re-establishing temporal ego continuity, or, briefly, in the service of the ego, must be distinguished from acting out in which instinctual demands predominate, in which the re-establishment of a oneness with the object is sought through the magical control of the external world. The lat-ter propensity will finally consolidate in the impulsive or narcissistic personality, while acting out in the service of the ego tends to become stabilized in the compulsive charac-ter. In clinical practice with adolescents, these two types of cases are often difficult to distinguish from each other; only through the systematic use of the therapeutic situation can a differentiation be established in time.

Acting Out As a Phase-Specific Mechanism of Adolescence

The concept of acting out has been discussed in its various aspects: predisposing, manifest, and functional; its complex-ity has been made explicit. I shall now turn to the question: What are the unique characteristics of the adolescent pro-cess that facilitate acting out; in other words, is adolescent acting out determined by predisposing factors alone or can the adolescent process claim acting out as a phase-specific mechanism? Can we speak of an adolescent compliance in the sense of a developmental tendency toward meeting halfway certain predispositions which at other periods of development were dormant or less conspicuous? In any case, experience tells us that the incidence of acting out rises sharply when the child enters puberty. This clinical fact alone clamors for an explanation.

As an avenue toward understanding the adolescent proclivity to acting out, I shall now explore those adolescent developmental characteristics that accompany psychic restructuring and that by previous definition have a special relatedness to acting out. This effort does not require that we retrace the long and intricate pathways of adolescence; I have told this story in great detail elsewhere (1962). Instead, I shall single out certain characteristics of adolescence with a direct bearing on the subject of acting out.

In a broad sense, one may say that the adolescent process is initiated by a decathexis of primary love objects, moves through a phase of increased narcissism and autoerotism, and ultimately reaches the stage of heterosexual object finding. These changes in drive organization are paralleled by shifts in ego interests and attitudes which attain structural stability during the period of consolidation at late adolescence. The detachment of psychic institutions from the parental influence which brought them into being constitutes a major effort of the adolescent ego; conversely, this achievement facilitates the definitive formation of the self.

The disengagement from the internalized love and hate objects is accompanied by a profound sense of loss and isolation, by a severe ego impoverishment which accounts for the adolescent's frantic turn to the outside world, to sensory stimulation and to action. The adolescent turns so frantically toward reality because he is in constant danger of losing it. The protracted process of object displacement opens the door to repeating essential facets of the past in relation to the current situation or the immediate environment. As long as these severance actions last, an astonishing impairment of reality testing—often only selective—is in evidence. The outside world appears to the adolescent, at least in certain aspects, as the mirror image of his internal reality, with its conflicts, threats, and comforts; his inner world is thus summarily experienced as external. Every adolescent is brushed—even if only for brief moments—by paranoid ideation. Reality testing, so flagrantly defective during this process, will be restored after a turn to nonincestuous love objects has evolved and after pregenitality has been afforded its place as forepleasure. This differentiation of drives is accompanied by a hierarchical rearrangement of ego interests and attitudes.

The proclivity of adolescence to action is one of its most impressive characteristics. The confluence of several trends is recognizable in this phenomenon. One is the antithesis of passivity ("being done to") and activity ("doing to others"), which in early adolescence plays a dominant role when the regressive pull to the active phallic (preoedipal) mother and the identification with her give the drive organization of boy and girl a special countenance. Action and motion are valued as such, not necessarily as goal-directed behavior, but rather as means of resisting the regressive pull to the active caretaking mother and of averting the surrender to primal passivity. In this constellation, then, action assumes the quality of a magic gesture: it averts evil (castration), it denies passive wishes, and it affirms a delusional control over reality. This tendency, in conjunction with a narcissistic isolation, compounds the well-known megalomanic trend of the adolescent who uses the external world for his aggrandizement in the same way that the child used the parent for the gratification of his narcissistic needs. In both cases, a supply of inexhaustible riches—even if only imagined, that is, wished for—seems to lie outside; all that remains to be done is to keep these narcissistic supplies steadily flowing toward the self.

The picture of the adolescent process would not be complete without bringing to your attention one more general

trend. The adolescent process, of course, evolves from preceding developmental stages, which are never passed
through without leaving imprints of trauma, arrestments by
fixation, sensitizations as to selective gratificatory modalities, and lacunae in ego continuity. The adolescent process can be accomplished only through synthesizing the past
with the present and the anticipated future. The integration
of ego and drive organizations is the touchstone of this
synthesis. Psychologically, then, the adolescent process is
constantly striving to bring the past into harmony with the
terminal stage of childhood, namely, with adolescence. Is it
surprising to find among the ways of remembering the one
called acting out? In a very real sense, acting out can serve
progressive development. Here we refer to adolescent experimentation which dominates the scene before trial action
in thought and play action in fantasy make it dispensable.

In the selective enumeration of adolescent characteristics, it has been my purpose to emphasize the fact that
the adolescent process contains psychological conditions we
have come to recognize as typical whenever acting out is to
occur. We are not surprised, therefore, to observe acting out
to be a more or less ubiquitous phenomenon of adolescence.
Such typical acting-out behavior is usually transient, benign, and in the service of progressive development. However, any of the component aspects of the adolescent process
which I have enumerated can lead to an impasse, a failure,
an arrestment. In that case, the phase-adequate mechanism
of acting out has turned into a permanent pathological condition. Whether this condition is marked by continued acting out or turns into a neurosis or some other illness will
depend on the predisposing factors. The universal transient
ascendancy of acting out in adolescence can never by itself
develop into lasting acting-out behavior.

It seems to me that adolescence offers an opportune
chance for the treatment of acting-out propensities which to
some extent always represent phase-specific measures in an

effort to cope with the actualities of growing up. These actualities revolve around object losing and object finding, both of which intertwine in the process of establishing mature object relations; they revolve around—not necessarily conscious—remembering and forgetting which intertwine in the process of ego synthesis. The dialectic tension between these opposites is resolved in late adolescence by the definite consolidation of the self. The writer James Baldwin (1956) has put this human condition, epitomized in adolescence, into these words: "Either, or: it takes strength to remember, it takes another kind of strength to forget, it takes a hero to do both. People who remember court madness through pain, the pain of the perpetually recurring death of their innocence; people who forget court another kind of madness, the madness of denial of pain and the hatred of innocence; and the world is mostly divided between madmen who remember and madmen who forget. Heroes are rare" (p. 37).

Clinical Material

The presentation of clinical material on certain acting-out adolescents serves two objectives. On the one hand, the material offers concrete evidence of acting out, while at the same time it demonstrates the intrinsic difficulty of comfortably subordinating the data to the standard concept of acting out. We are confronted with the dilemma of either broadening the concept or assigning some clinical facts to other categories. As a third possibility, we might consider acting out as a typical transient mechanism of the adolescent process which owes its prominence to the temporary weakening of inhibitory and repressive forces and, furthermore, to the ascendancy of regressive libido and ego positions.

Adolescent cases of acting out in the service of instinctual gratification are well known. Typical of this kind of acting out is the pseudo heterosexuality in the girl as either a return to the preoedipal mother via a substitute partner or as a revenge and spiteful action directed against the oedipal mother. I have described in Chapter 11 this kind of acting out which operates in the service of regressive instinctual gratification. We are furthermore well acquainted with those cases in which the adolescent acts out the unconscious wishes of the parent. In contrast, I have selected clinical material which does not belong to any of these categories and which has received only scant attention in the literature. The following cases exemplify adolescent acting out that operates in the service of progressive development or, more specifically, in the service of ego synthesis.

Frank, the Laborer

A late adolescent boy of nineteen had failed in college during his freshman year and found himself at a loss as to what to do with himself after dismissal. Lethargy and aimlessness were prominent, as was a tendency to indulge in sentimental and fairy-story fantasies. He was plagued by indecision and confusion and was unable to make plans for his future.

Frank was an adopted child. Both his adoptive parents had achieved intellectual prominence and outstanding positions. The boy was brought up in the atmosphere of a cultured home; he had fitted well into this milieu. All through school he proved himself able academically; he was socially competent and at ease; he was active in sports and in school life; he was liked by his teachers and peers. Due to this history, his failure in college assumed the dimension of an inexplicable turn of events.

After Frank left college, he started psychotherapy. First he held several jobs as a white-collar worker until he suddenly decided to become a laborer. I felt that his urgency to take a laborer's job was so elemental that I made myself a sympathetic partner of this radical departure from his accustomed life. I decided to wait and see. Frank felt extremely happy in his new job and got along well with his fellow workers. Soon he decided to move away from the comfortable home of his family to live with a fellow worker's family in the grimy section of a large city. He deeply enjoyed the simple pleasures and unsophisticated interests of his new milieu. The acting-out character in this behavior was evident.

During the time Frank resided in the world of his fellow workers, it was possible to penetrate his childhood amnesia and bring crucial memories to consciousness. This step was facilitated by his matter-of-fact familiarity with the new milieu and by associative links relating his present experience to his past. In having changed his milieu, he followed the relentless pull of the infantile object tie to the foster parents of his early childhood: he had lived in a working-class family until he was adopted at the end of his second year. The early reality of his life became revived during late adolescence and was made conscious in therapy after it had been triggered off by remembering in action. Frank became able to recall memories of his early childhood as well as to re-experience the affection he had felt for his foster parents. The acting out as a special form of remembering was translated into verbalized memories of his past. A gradual disengagement from his early love objects followed: he was now able to fall in love and experience the extrafamilial object finding of adolescence proper. As soon as the reliving of the past became dispensable, Frank returned to his adoptive family. Freed from the regressive pull to his original milieu, the abrupt separation from which had been traumatic, Frank returned to college, studied successfully for a doctorate, and became an equal in intellectual pre-eminence to his parents.

Frank's case invites some comments. First, it should be noted that no acting out occurred during the time preceding or during eight years following his late adolescent crisis. While he had talked about his past earlier in therapy and while he knew the facts of his background and remembered some of the circumstances of his early life, the affective component of his memories came to consciousness only through the re-enactment of his early history. It seems that the consolidation process of late adolescence is hampered, delayed, or actually aborted whenever crucially significant, unintegrated memories remain permanently dissociated and resist repression. This situation by itself prevents the formation of a temporal continuity in the ego. Without this psychic achievement of late adolescence, the separation from earliest object relations remains only partial. If the adolescent process, i.e., the second individuation process, is not proceeding normally, it is often frantically simulated by either a restitution in fantasy or a determined return to one's beginnings. These efforts often bear the signs of acting out, as in the case of Frank. This adolescent could not go forward without first making contact with his unassimilated traumatic past in a desperate effort at integrating it. His acting out was in the service of progressive development. We are reminded of the giant Antaeus, the son of Poseidon and Gaea, the Earth. Antaeus proved to be invincible because each time he was thrown in combat, he rose with greater strength due to having touched the earth, his mother. Herakles defeated him by lifting him off the ground and holding him in midair. By thus disrupting the giant's contact with his origin, the source of his strength, he crushed Antaeus to death.

Carl, the Criminal

We are all familiar with adolescent cases in which acting out is related to a family myth. By this I mean a willful distortion of facts concerning the family history. This type of case, in which identity confusion or imposterlike or delinquent behavior often appear as the major symptoms, differs radically in structure from those cases of delinquency in which the outside world becomes distorted through the projection of intrapsychic conflicts. In both instances, an intrapsychic event is experienced as external, but with the crucial difference that in one case the external world is distorted by authority figures in the environment who, as the guardians of reality, must interpret the world of facts and causality to the child, while in the other case the child himself distorts reality for the sake of drive satisfaction or anxiety avoidance. In one instance, adolescent deviancy operates in the service of the rectification of a myth or a lie; in the other, a myth or a lie is created in order to fit reality to needs and fears.

In order to illustrate these remarks, I shall present the case of Carl. This fifteen-year-old boy was brought to me for treatment by a relative who had become worried about Carl's criminal tendencies. Stealing, forgery, truancy, and lying were the presenting symptoms. All four infractions were usually executed in a manner that invited detection. The driving urgency in the boy's behavior, in conjunction with his sense of being fated for a criminal career, gave his delinquency the special countenance of acting out. The onset of puberty marked the onset of Carl's delinquent behavior.

The family myth became known to me through the information provided by the relative. According to this account, Carl and his brother, his senior by three years, had been told by their mother that their father had died. After a divorce, when Carl was three and a half years old, the father was convicted for embezzlement and sent to prison when the child was six. Before this event, the father had lost contact with his children who had not seen him for two years. According to the mother's story, the father had died in prison and she was a widow. The children, aged six and nine respectively, accepted the news about their father's death without any question; they behaved as if it were true. Nobody spoke of the father at home except to compare Carl's "crooked little mind" with that of his dead father. Actually, the father had not died. A psychotic condition which rendered him intractable in prison and which proved to be chronic made his transfer to a hospital for the criminally insane necessary. At the time Carl started treatment, his father was an inmate of this prison hospital.

Upon my questioning it did not appear strange to this boy that he knew no relations on his father's side, that he did not know the date or cause of his father's death or the place where he was buried, that he did not know either the circumstances of his father's crime or the reasons for his parents' divorce. No wonder this boy complained about a strange incapacity to study history because he was unable to remember dates, names, and places. In order to dispose of an impenetrable confusion, Carl himself insisted that his father had died shortly after his birth and that he had never known him. Unconsciously, Carl had obeyed his mother's unspoken command, which was implicit in an incident he later remembered in treatment: "One day an uncle of mine came to the house, cut my father out of every family picture, and removed him from the family album." The correctness of this memory was later confirmed.

Carl's acting out functioned as an attempt to keep the memory of his father alive, as a vindication of the "good father," and as an extension of the temporal continuity of the ego into the dim regions of his early life. The father image was essential as a hold on reality and as a protection against depressive moods. Furthermore, the sense of reality could be sustained only by denying in action the mother's imputation of unrealness to the child's perceptions and their traces embedded in his memory. What Carl remembered about his early childhood were forbidden memories, especially in relation to affectionate and positive feelings toward the father. They had been extinguished as conscious memories by the same stroke of wrath and vindictiveness with which the mother had "murdered" the father. Carl's adolescence was fatally threatened by his submission to the archaic sorceress mother. This submission meant the abandonment of the father image with which he had to come to terms at adolescence, positively and negatively, through identification and counteridentification.

It was obvious that the dead father had to be unearthed and that the past history had to be revived and rectified before the delinquent aspect of acting out would subside. The proclivity to acting out proved only partly reversible; however, the employment of this tendency to bring about the inescapable fate of becoming a criminal was successfully averted by therapy. Carl's visit to his father at the prison hospital was followed by a compassionate concern about him. The boy wanted to send money to his father in order to ease his life and have him more respectably dressed. He conjectured that his father was mute because he was angry that nobody ever visited him or cared. He realized gradually how much he had missed his father, and he became aware of his behaving to older men as if they were fathers who might take an interest in him. At such times, he became demanding and almost expected a restitution from the environment for having been denied the rightful possession of his own father.

A complicating factor in this case must be mentioned because it contributed to the acting out, especially the stealing. Carl had an undescended testicle. This condition, which had been neglected, was corrected by an operation early in treatment. The operation unfortunately served only a cosmetic purpose since the testicle had ceased to function. Carl, who made his own observations on the comparative size and sensation of his testicles, was informed about the true state of affairs. Before the clarification of his genital status, Carl's stealing contained a kleptomanic component; it was a magic attempt to bring about genital intactness.

Through stealing—predominantly men's apparel—he symbolically restored his masculinity and, conversely, defended
himself against feminine strivings, that is, against
homosexuality.

As always in cases where a family myth plays a
pathogenic role, the rectification of the myth hardly comes
as a surprise to the patient. So it was with Carl; the parts
of the puzzle that had always been known to him in dissociated bits and pieces were gradually and laboriously fitted together into a coherent and meaningful whole. Carl recalled the "fancy apartment" he lived in when the family
was once rich and he recognized in his desire for expensive
living a lingering memory of those days. When he toppled
on the verge of stealing again because he needed money in
order to rent a chauffeur-driven Cadillac for an evening
with his girlfriend, he recalled that his father had actually
driven a Cadillac in the company of strange women and
girls. After his parents had separated, his father used to
take him out in a big car. Carl's irrepressible desire to dress
ostentatiously often drove him to stealing either money or
merchandise, until he recognized in his own behavior the
image of his father who was a fastidious dresser. After Carl
had succumbed to another stealing episode, he explained to
the therapist that he was hopelessly compelled to spend
money on his girlfriend. Fragments of memories and overheard conversations pieced themselves together into the
recollection that his father was a lavish spender and enter-
tainer of chorus girls. He began to recognize some expensive
china, glassware, and bric-a-brac at his home as the tangible remembrances of a past come to life and telling its
story.

The acting out in Carl's case was repeatedly followed by
remembering and experiencing particular affective and sensuous states. The cumulative effect of this cyclic process became recognizable in the novel ability to employ trial action
in thought and fantasy, as well as to verbalize thought

whenever the urge to act out arose. This alerting awareness attested to the ascendancy of the self-observing, i.e., introspective, ego which in turn strengthened both secondary-process thinking and reality testing. Acting out as a maladaptive attempt at establishing temporal continuity in the ego gradually lost its genuine character and laid bare the fixation points of drive and ego development. Symptom formation and the defensive nature of action now occupied the center of the clinical picture. Carl's passive tendencies, intensified by his genital defectiveness, were overcompensated by action. Action per se had become identical with an affirmation of masculinity. This second phase in the treatment of this acting-out case lies outside the scope of our special interest.[1]

The acting out and remembering in Carl's case invokes the image of Proust's rediscovering "forgotten years, gardens, people in the taste of a sip of tea in which he found a piece of a madeleine" (from a letter by Proust to Antoine Bibesco, November 1912). Acting out, then, is the establishment of that particular experiential congruence by which present reality provides a link to a traumatic past; in this sense, acting out is an alloplastic, maladaptive, restitutive process. The fact that acting out constitutes an organized psychic operation sets it off sharply from impulsive action, typical of the impulse disorders. Instead of an organized pattern, impulsive action is marked by a primitive mechanism of tension discharge to which J. J. Michaels has referred as "primary acting out" (in Kanzer, 1957a).

---

[1]A follow-up on Carl's case was fortuitously granted. Carl came to see me ten years later when some business and love affair confronted him with "big decisions." I saw him three times. Suffice it to say that (1) I could find no traces of acting-out or delinquent behavior; (2) his vocational activities, after some drifting, had become focused and enterprising, showing ambition and reasonably good judgment; (3) his object relations were shallow, yet caring and responsible; he had formed relationships of some duration, if not of durability, with a few women; (4) he had kept in touch with his hospitalized father through the prison authorities and also personally; he continued to contribute what he thought would make his father's life more comfortable.

Discussion and Conclusion

Let us return once more to the adolescent condition. The adolescent's proclivity to action is obvious. It furthermore becomes apparent in the treatment of some acting-out adolescents that acting out is not an integral component of the personality and, once overcome, shows no further traces in the behavior of the adult. In other cases, it proves to remain a habitual reaction to tension and thus reveals its predispositional component. Acting out per se cannot be considered an insurmountable obstacle to treatment in adolescence since it represents in its genuine adolescent form a phase-specific mechanism of the adolescent process.

As I indicated in the beginning of this chapter, the adolescent's proclivity to action seems to me determined by two factors. First, we have to consider the fact that with the quantitative increase of instinctual pressure due to puberty, earlier drive and concomitant ego positions are regressively revived. The first and oldest antithesis in individual life, the one of active and passive, can be discerned again at adolescence. The early active position which came into existence through an identification with the preoedipal phallic (active) mother serves, especially during the beginning stage of adolescence, as a defensive bulwark against regression to primal passivity. This defensive measure against passivity becomes manifest during adolescence in unrestrained, inappropriate, and self-assertive actions. Second, the delibidinization of infantile love objects during the phase of adolescence proper, and the increase in narcissism during the phase of early adolescence, both result in an impoverishment of the ego. The threat of ego loss which accompanies this process is counteracted by a forceful turn to the outer world. Outer reality offers a restitutive anchorage before stable object relations are again established.

The two sources just described contribute to the dire need for action so typical of the adolescent. Of course, we are equally familiar with the adolescent's inertia, lethargy, and aversion to action, which only highlight the defensive quality of activity in the cyclic sequence of these states. In contrast to the typical adolescent breakthrough of instinctual drives, sexual and aggressive, and their random discharge in action, we come to realize that acting out represents a structured and organized mechanism.

Genuine adolescent acting out implies a fixation on either the phase of preadolescence or early adolescence. Both these phases are characterized by a strong regressive pull, by a revival of pregenitality, by an increase in narcissism, and by the maintenance of a bisexual identity. It goes without saying that these conditions affect adversely the ego's relation to reality. This latent predisposition will assume flagrant proportions under the impact of puberty whenever a defective sense of reality as well as a need for oneness with the object (i.e., with the outer world) existed before adolescence. The fact that both cases of acting out in the service of ego synthesis which I have reported have in common the loss of a significant object in early childhood suggests that similar cases might show a similar etiology.

Whenever acting out is in evidence we assume that an organized mechanism is in operation, not merely a discharge device of instinctual needs. This postulated organization appears in three distinctly different forms which are familiar to us from their clinical manifestations: (1) the repetition of an early object relation and of its gratificatory modality by displacement: (2) the activation of a fantasy and its articulation on the environment, in which case acting out appears as an autoerotic equivalent; (3) the effort at restoring the sense of reality by affirming memories in action which were denied, forbidden, or distorted by the environment during childhood. To the latter, I refer as acting out in the service of ego synthesis.

Acting out as a tension regulator protects the psychic organism against conflictual anxiety: the conflict is exclu-

sively between the ego and the outer world. On the other
hand, acting out in the service of ego synthesis or of temporal ego continuity protects the psychic organism against
anxiety deriving from structural defectiveness or disintegration. Structural anxiety arises as a consequence of ego
lacunae or whenever the sense of reality is in danger of
coming to ruin during adolescence. At this period, the borrowed strength or ego restitution through continued dependency on the parent is no longer desirable nor tolerable,
lest progressive development be abandoned altogether. If
this should occur, we witness the case of an abortive adolescence.

While acting out is generally alloplastic and maladaptive, the distinctions which I suggest seem essential in
terms of a differential treatment approach. In cases of adolescent acting out as an attempt at reviving partly abandoned object relations or drive gratifications by their displacement onto the outer world, treatment initially focuses
on increasing tension tolerance, on internalization, and on a
clearer differentiation between ego and reality, between self
and object. This phase in treatment, then, aims at the establishment of an ego organization which is capable of integrating the second, the interpretive and reconstructive,
phase of treatment. In the case of acting out in the service
of ego synthesis, treatment initially focuses on the reconstruction of the dissociated, traumatic past, and secondarily
assists the ego in the task of mastering anxiety and of integrating the affects that follow in the wake of the confrontation with the historical truth. The various types of acting
out, however, can rarely be categorized as neatly as they
are here, but are usually mixed and require that therapy
maneuver between a changing emphasis on one or the
other.

The problem of adolescent acting out—its genetic,
dynamic, and structural distinctness, clarity, and
differentiation—is obscured by several trends which are

constituent parts of the adolescent process. We have seen that acting out at adolescence is the result of several confluent trends: predispositional, developmental, and functional. The nature of the adolescent process itself tends to blur the clear delineation of the concept within the clinical picture. This difficulty stems mainly from four adolescent characteristics: the alternation between regressive and progressive movements, the role of displacement in the process of disengagement from early love objects, the frantic turn to the outside world in order to compensate for ego impoverishment, and the efforts at synthesis which constitutes the structural achievement of late adolescence. The relation of these adolescent factors to acting out has only partly been elucidated. However, their relevancy to the overall problem has become apparent; furthermore, a reconsideration of the standard concept of acting out has been presented as desirable if the various phenomena of adolescent acting out are to be accommodated within a comprehensive conceptual framework.

Chapter 13

Adolescent Concretization

A Contribution to the Theory of Delinquency

I have chosen a topic for investigation that is remote from
psychoanalysis as a therapeutic technique and yet, at the
same time, is close to the heart and mind of everyone who
practices it. If we look at people of all ages whose emotional
maldevelopment has brought them into disharmony with
themselves or their environment—a disharmony causing a
kind of misery that inexorably works its way down the generational line—and if we then look at our psychoanalytic
expertise, we cannot escape the conclusion that the vast
majority of those afflicted by emotional maldevelopment are
immune to the benefits derived from the standard
psychoanalytic technique, even if such a utopian
availability of analytic treatment were within everybody's
reach. There is no need to let matters rest at this point, because psychoanalysis as a general psychology has flung
open many new gates inviting us to walk on untrodden
ground.

Psychoanalysis has always recognized the limitations of
mutability within the instinctual and adaptive life of man,

Herman Nunberg Lecture, presented at the New York Academy of Medicine,
New York City, 1969. First published in *Currents in Psychoanalysis*, ed. I. M.
Marcus. New York: International Universities Press, 1971, pp. 66-88.

while, at the same time, it has demonstrated the extent of personality transformation that lies within the resourcefulness of man. As analysts we work and exist within the awareness of the unalterable boundaries of human nature; in fact, the exploration of their extent and flexibility is the aim of our science. It is dedicated to the affairs of man and to the facilitation of individual self-realization. Psychoanalysis has always held firmly and passionately to the humanist tradition. Nothing remains more valued and worthy of our endeavor than the harmonizing influence we can exert on the life of man through our science. Contemporary history urges upon us a quest for rational means of intervention that will moderate man's destructiveness and brutality in relation to himself and his fellow man. Any contribution—no matter how slight—if it enlarges our knowledge of these blind forces, of their ontogenetic sources, and of their ways of transformation, answers a communal quest.

I have singled out for psychoanalytic exploration a group of white adolescent delinquent boys who were adjudicated by the juvenile court. The puzzlements these cases present in terms of their assessment and rehabilitation have kept my curiosity at a high pitch for a long time. After decades of concentrating on child and adolescent analysis, I have, as it were, returned to my analytic beginnings. August Aichhorn's example, his work with delinquents and his personal tutorship, which I had the privilege to enjoy, have strongly influenced my choice of profession. I fulfill a legacy of these early years of apprenticeship when I now explore some clinical problems of delinquency.

With the widening of explanatory concepts, extending deeply into the preoedipal stage of development, there has evolved a more complex model of delinquency. That is, we speak of a multitude of delinquencies; they are united by two characteristics—the engagement of the action system in problem solving and the use of the environment as tension regulator. Both these factors work against internalization and against changes within the self. The emotional suffering that moves the neurotic person to implement internal change is an experience totally foreign to the delinquent.

I have come to the conclusion that acting out, the hallmark of this group of asocial adolescents, is a species of behavior with many distinct subspecies. It has been my endeavor to study such identifiable varieties and to distinguish one from the other. My considerations are limited to a particular subspecies of acting-out behavior. Within this narrow context, I shall focus on the processes of internalization and ego differentiation, with special reference to the function of memory and symbolic speech.

The subspecies of acting-out behavior that is the subject of this chapter possesses certain characteristics I shall now describe. In the first place, the action system has assumed to a significant but restricted extent an ego function that belongs, normally, to symbolic speech. The maladaptive behavior impresses the observer as a gestural communication, the content of which is obviously unknown to the gesturer. Bypassing the language channel of expression, it appears that only concrete modalities of expression are found adequate for the externalization of thought, memory, affect, or conflict. The main vehicle of communication is action. It is not simply random action, but neither is it action of volition and intentionality. In analogy to the attention cathexis, as characteristic of thought, one might say that action, as considered here, is selectively cathected in relation to certain affects and ego interests. The idiomatic and restricted absence of symbolic expression via speech in reference to *certain* selective and delineated areas of mental life precludes their integration into higher and more complex mental functioning. Consequently, prelogical mentation survives side by side with age-adequate language usage and learning capacity. We correctly suspect the continuation of magical thought from early childhood into adolescence.

It follows that action, being—in the instances under consideration here—a gestural communication, does not necessarily express an unequivocal statement, consisting of discrete elements such as we can discern in verbalized, logical thought, but such action is a syncretic formation with an implicit irrationality, alien to the communicative use of language. Such syncretism is known to us from dreams in which a person can be several persons at once, without arousing a sense of unreality in the dreamer. Long ago, Greenacre (1950) called our attention to a predisposing factor to acting out that lies in "a distortion in the relation of action to speech and verbalized thought" (p. 227).

We can distinguish two extreme forms resulting from this distortion, either concretism through action or concretism through eidetic imagery; the adolescent can describe both while both remain inaccessible to verbalized interpretation. I have found that imagery, in particular from daydreams, is more prevalent among girls; in contrast, the boy resorts more quickly to action. Both modalities may constitute an equivalent of verbalized thought, in the same manner that we speak of thought as an action equivalent. An adolescent girl I had in analysis told me that she has a picture in her mind for every thought and feeling. She might avoid writing a difficult school assignment, for example, by imagining that she is riding a horse and galloping across the prairie. This imaginary action *is* the school assignment; one might say that it is written through the action fantasy that allows a syncretic imaginary resolution with no action taking place in reality. Interpretations of concretism of action or eidetic imagery remain ineffectual because the implicit primitive, prelogical thought countermands the comprehension of the discrete elements of language governed by the secondary process. Only when the concreteness of eidetic imagery fades into pictorial language and metaphorical speech or, conversely, only if the gesture is replaced by words, do we know that the reality principle has intervened.

The irrationality of thought with which certain delinquents justify, explain, and defend their asocial behavior possesses a fixity and immutability reminiscent of a delusional system. Yet, no thought disorder and no distortion of reality due to psychosis or organicity are in evidence.

On the basis of these characteristic features of this particular subspecies of acting-out behavior, I have called it "concretization." This term has its established place in the theory of psychosis. Here, however, I propose to use the term with a developmental reference. Within this context, concrete and abstract thought describe stages in the ontogenesis of the comprehension of and interaction with the outer world. The concreteness of action and of thing representation, their transition to symbolic speech and concept formation, represents a pivotal developmental point, on which hinges not only the individual mode of communication, but its progressive usefulness for adaptive mastery of the internal and external world.

I am often reminded of dream analysis or parapraxes when I attempt to reconstruct a coherent, latent content from the manifest action, which usually appears disjointed, seemingly irrelevant, extraneous and incidental, with meaningless details that look like fortuitous expressions or accidental occurrences. Seasoned analytic experience is the *sine qua non* for this kind of work. An illustrative action specimen of concretization will help us along at this point.

An adolescent car thief brushed aside all accusations regarding his offense by reiterating, ad nauseam, the fact that the owner of the automobile was, after all, insured and could not possibly care if his car was stolen as long as he got the money. The boy felt that police and court conspired to exonerate the car owner of his money-grabbing greed by branding him, the boy, a thief and a criminal. In defiance he told the police and court to "go to hell" because they did not know what they were talking about. At the assessment interview, the boy repeated his typical indifference to and disinterest in discussing his actions. I realized that his obstinacy was not due to his unwillingness to say anything but to the fact that he had nothing more to say. He had said it all in his action and in his commentary that followed. The *idée fixe* with reference to the car owner convinced me of the concretizing nature of the theft. Indeed, the theft proved to be a condensation of perceptual, cognitive, and affective determinants. The transposition of the manifest into the latent action theme reads as follows: "When I was a little boy of six, my father died; all my mother cared about was the insurance money. She did not mind that he was dead, as long as she got paid for the loss. My mother never loved my father. I hate her for that. She wants to control and baby me now. I do not trust her. She is selfish. She should go to jail. She is a criminal."

It is not necessary to dwell in this connection on the meaning of the stolen car and the symbolic father representation, because these are matters with which we are thoroughly familiar; they are, however, only tangentially useful for the comprehension of the theft and for the choice of the rehabilitative intervention. All I can say at this point is that life history and adolescent conflict coalesced here in a particular form of antisocial behavior. It is obviously not a metaphorical statement when I call concretization a private language; action has usurped a language function which has, however, no communal reference and remains idiomatic in character, comparable to a private dialect. It should follow from this point of view that the theft, as described, is not simply a displacement, but rather a communicative interaction with the environment, a statement of memory, a thought and an affect in juxtaposition to developmental recapitulations and, in this case, abortive resolutions.

Such cases have always impressed me by the absence of conflict and guilt. Yet, we do not deal with a psychopath; furthermore, the superego defect is highly selective and by no means pervasive. Here we might ask ourselves the simple question: How could it be otherwise? The boy, after all, exonerates his dead father and wrests his exalted image of him from the malevolent mother. A hero fighting for a great cause does not feel guilty about any of his actions; quite to the contrary, his actions relieve him from the guilt of passive acquiescence to a crime to which he was and remains a living witness. Should we emphasize in the clinical picture the absence of conflict as well as the absence of guilt, and make these findings the basis of our assessment, then we mistake the appearance for the substance or the manifest for the latent content of the so-called crime.

I have recognized in concretization a nonconflictual ego function. The apparent absence of conflict is due to the fact that concretization can accommodate antithetical strivings and thoughts within its organization. This observation can be expressed in terms of object relations by saying that the perseverance on the level of ambivalence has prevented the fusion of the need-gratifying and the frustrating, tension-inducing object. This perseverance on the archaic object experience never fails to leave its imprint on cognition and on the function of language. Both are rendered unable to rise above the prelogical stage of communication and tend, therefore, to rely heavily on eidetic mentation—"a special emphasis on visual sensitization"—and on gestural communication of various kinds—"a largely unconscious belief in the magic of action" (Greenacre, 1950, p. 227).

The concretizing delinquent attests to a reality of his past and to isolated and forgotten (preconscious) memories. These memories remain excluded from cognitive integration whenever they are openly contradicted or pointedly ignored by the environment. Ego discontinuity is thus inflicted on the child by the ego pathology of his significant caretakers, usually the parents, whose enclaves of denial contradict the child's perception by withholding consensual validation. Here we find an additional cause for the survival of the concrete, due to the fact that sanity hinges on the identity of perception and reality, memory and fact.

The concretizing adolescent uses the environment not only for the gratification of infantile wishes but, simultaneously, he tries to extricate himself, through his actions, from infantile object dependencies; in short, he aims at activating the second individuation process of adolescence. He obviates or corrects through action a piece of historical reality. The denial of reality is of a peculiar kind in the cases I shall present, insofar as what is denied is a piece of unreality which was thrust upon the child by authority figures, through commission or omission, as positive or negative reality.

Concretization implies, by its very nature, a continued and tenacious dependency on the environment. The silent mastery of tension through thought, fantasy, recollection, anticipation—briefly, through processes that are the result of internalization—appears inadequately and electively developed in these cases. We can observe how environmental participation is persistently elicited by provocation. Environmental retaliation and involvement is not something to be avoided but rather something that is sought. The three institutions—family, school, and court—are aroused to counteractions which render "realness" to what the concretizing adolescent gestures with helpless but determined pertinacity.

Before I present further clinical illustrations, one matter needs to be clarified. We are accustomed to speak of thought as trial action. The economy of thought lies in the reduced expenditure of psychic energy. Thought anticipates the outcome of action, weights the pleasure-unpleasure balance, and settles on a course of action that is an adaptive compromise formation. The conscious (often preconscious) process uses awareness and memory via word representations to synthesize a conclusion or a decision. Tensions that arise in this dialectic process are resolved through the mediation of alternatives that lie within the resources of ego and environment. The point I endeavor to make concerns the fact that thought implies potential consciousness and awareness of tension attached to the disequilibrizing strivings or affects in a given situation. The outcome of thought is a deliberate act, positive or negative. In contrast, the concretizing adolescent acts without thinking and without internal resolution of, or accommodation to, tension. He is thus predestined to come into conflict with the environment, to be a delinquent, even if he is never actually confronted by the law. The economy of action lies in the blurring of contradictions in relation to affects, thoughts, and memories.

The reliance on action as tension regulator indicates a state of ego undifferentiation that is noticeable in the vague and fluid boundaries between perception, feeling, and thought. The confusion between the internal and external, namely, the subjective and the objective (Piaget's "adualism"), should have been dispelled by the end of the latency period. Not so in the concretizing adolescent. He seems to be up against a barrier in the path of development which he cannot surmount. He hopes that the environment will surmount it for him. Consequently, the more he struggles against the barrier, the more he falls back into helplessness and rage. This could not be different because "objectification and consciousness are mutually exclusive" (Piaget, quoted by Odier, 1956, p. 113). It follows that the concretizing delinquent is inimical to insight, which is rooted in introspection and contingent on internalization and verbalized thought.

In such cases, the influence of an impersonal authoritative institution, namely, the court, acts as a coercive force, thus lending an effective leverage in an otherwise hopeless situation—provided this power is used judiciously. Toward this end, psychoanalytic psychology illuminates the intricacies of concretization and points the way to a constructive intervention in the vagaries of these recalcitrant and antagonistic subjects.

Rubin

Having described the developmental characteristics of the concretizing adolescent, I shall now speak of a thirteen-year-old delinquent boy. In his case, it was indeed possible to "unhitch a developmental catch," to use Winnicott's felicitous phrase.

Rubin was raised in an orthodox Jewish home. On Yom Kippur he broke into the Yeshiva of his temple where he stole a box of nails and some pencils. This burglary, in conjunction with his chronic truancy, brought Rubin to court. The judge requested an assessment of Rubin for the adjudication of the case. For the reader to appreciate the assessment process and its conclusion, certain facts about Rubin's life have to be told.

The boy and his mother had always lived in the Williamsburg section of Brooklyn. His father, a junk dealer, had died when Rubin was six years old. The child then attended a Yeshiva. At the age of twelve, he refused to continue his religious education and transferred to a public school, where his truancy began. The mother complained about Rubin's antagonism to religious observances and his preference for non-Jewish friends. Through their company he was introduced to petty stealing which resulted in a collection of bicycle parts; the back of his house was thus converted into a junkyard. Rubin's disobedience only intensified the mother's fervor to make her son conform to an orthodox life. These data, which were part of the case history as collected by court, school, and social agencies, hardly sufficed for adequate comprehension of Rubin's behavior.

We are accustomed from our analytic work to gain unexpected insight into a case through minor details, through isolated oddities of thought or behavior, through cir-

cumstantial coincidences, which are viewed against the
major events of a life history and against the developmental
status of the moment. I was curious to know where the boy
had spent the endless hours of his truancy. He told me that
he used to cross the Williamsburg Bridge to Manhattan;
there he would wander aimlessly through the Bowery. His
father's junk shop was once located there, and as a little boy
Rubin had done his first carpentry work there under his
father's tutelage. He still wanted to become a carpenter.
The theft of nails was related to Rubin's early adolescent
struggle to come to terms with the memory of his father
whom he had lost in the midst of the oedipal resolution.
Mourning had to be completed at adolescence.

But why did he steal the box of nails on Yom Kippur
and why from a holy place? Rubin concretized in this action
the parental fights over religious observances by allying
himself with the agnostic father who had never had any use
for orthodox Judaism. The mother's religious coercion of the
son brought the preoedipal fears of the archaic, castrating
mother into prominence around this issue. The mother was,
indeed, unrelenting in her determination to make of Rubin
a better Jew than his father had ever been. Yet, young
Rubin defended his identity through the collection of junk
that he carried home from his exploits in the streets. The
mother tried in vain to rescue her son from the father's influence by eradicating the dead man from his memory or, at
least, by rendering him an unspeakable and unthinkable
person. We cannot fail to detect in the boy's action an effort
to protect his sense of reality, based on a perception that is
contingent on ego continuity and memory cathexis. The de-
ciphered language of Rubin's delinquency spoke eloquently
of his adolescent struggle to rescue the positive father
imago and of the anxiety engendered by the archaic mother.

Rubin had no capacity for verbalization nor any interest
in insight. There was ample reason to expect that he could
make good use of an environment that would offer the

appropriate growth-promoting experiences for a boy of his age and kind. While he would not speak of his father, he was eager to identify with him vocationally. The realization of this ambition might significantly reduce his fear of the archaic mother and his need for delinquent concretization. The thought occurred to me that the desecration of the holy place unified antinomical thoughts: on the one hand, he defended the agnostic father and, on the other hand, he accused him of a crime. Rubin knew right from wrong. The intervention that promised to intercept a delinquent career was the removal of the boy from his mother's fanatical interference with the adolescent psychic restructuring. What was at stake was the completion of mourning, the positive identification with the father, and, generally, the process of adolescent socialization.

The mother rejected the court's remand, refusing to release her son to an unorthodox residential treatment center, even though Rubin wanted to go. Time being of the essence, I resorted to a shortcut in order to implement the rehabilitative strategy of choice. I turned to the rabbi, whose authority the mother respected, and asked him for a dispensation from the dietary laws; this he readily granted. Soon thereafter Rubin left home in haste and hope. In the stern voice of authority that ordered him away from home, Rubin heard, I suppose, a whispered message that told him that it was the mother who had to be taken away from him because the judge condemned her destruction of the oedipal father.

Once established in the residential institution, Rubin never missed a day of school; he elected carpentry as his vocational training. He fit smoothly into the new environment, displayed no deviant behavior, and related well to peers and adults alike. Understandably, he was not eager to make home visits. An autonomous integration of the parental religious antagonism became finally evident when Rubin, voluntarily, began to attend religious services. Two years have passed since his appearance in court; all that can be said today is that Rubin extricated himself from a catastrophic developmental impediment, once the environmental conditions facilitated psychic differentiation, internalization, and vocational identity. Rubin's case is an exceptional one, a simple case I might say, which should not necessarily allow undue optimism toward the treatment of the concretizing adolescent.

Before I proceed to a more complex case, I shall deal with some objections and queries that have, no doubt, been raised by the foregoing material. After all, acting out has been dealt with exhaustively by many analytic writers and it seems uncalled for to split off a unique category from the established concept of acting out. Why do I not simply speak of the externalization of unconscious conflicts, of acting out as an adolescent-specific modality of behavior, as a defense against a depressive core and object loss, as a form of remembering, as a symbolic replication of the past—and let it go at that? I have always adhered to the opinion that acting out within the analytic situation reserves a theoretical position of its own in contradistinction to the extra-analytic acting out observed, for example, in delinquency. Anna Freud (1968) remarked at the 1967 Symposium on "Acting Out" that ". . . reliving in the transference was increasingly taken for granted; and the longer this happened, the more often was the term 'acting out' not applied to the repetition in the transference at all, but reserved for the re-enactment of the past outside the analysis." She continued: "Personally, I regret this change of usage since on the one hand it obscures the initially sharp distinction between remembering and repeating and on the other hand it glosses over the differences between the various forms of 'acting out'" (p. 108). One of these various forms—what I have called a subspecies of acting out—I venture to comprehend in the concept of concretization. Perhaps the one factor that sets this form of acting out apart from the others—in spite of their sharing many similarities—is the effort to uphold a sense of reality and autonomy when both are kept in constant jeopardy by the environment. They are, reactively, stabilized by concretization which is experienced, subjectively, as a lowering of tension and a restoration of self-esteem.

In Rubin's case, the sense of reality and autonomy remained in jeopardy from two sides: from the reality distortions or the denial the mother impressed on the ego of the grieving child, and from the inability of the child's ego to cope, integratively, under these conditions, with selective memories and affects in relation to the father. We have always recognized certain preconditions that are characteristic for all forms of acting out. Could it be that the preponderance of one of the preconditional factors is responsible for the various forms of acting out? The case I am about to report should sharpen the line of demarcation that sets off concretization from other forms of maladaptive behavior generally, and from other forms of acting out, in particular.

Eddy

Eddy was a fifteen-year-old car thief, a chronic truant, a wild boy who was beyond the control of his parents. In desperation they took him to court after he had smashed up a stolen car and nearly killed himself. He had talked about suicide before. In speaking about his accident he presented an amused and detached attitude: he was just playing a game of brinkmanship with death. Some time before, Eddy had, with burglary on his mind, acquired a master key to his apartment house.

Each family member—mother, stepfather, and older sister—contributed a casual strand of information out of which the total fabric of Eddy's history was painstakingly woven. In piecing these random strands together, a picture finally emerged that illuminated the boy's behavior in an unexpected perspective of historical continuity.

Eddy's father had died when the child was two and a half years old. Over the years many versions of his father's death were given to him, none of which the boy could ever fully believe; in other words, the child knew unconsciously that he was never told the truth. Eddy had only one certainty about his father, namely, that he was dead. He did not know his father's vocation or family background, or his paternal relatives, or the location of his father's grave.

The relevant facts of the father's life can be told briefly. He was a professional crook, who specialized in burglary. Working in a hotel he procured a master key and burglarized the rooms. One day when he was carrying stolen goods in his automobile he was, incidentally, followed by a police car. He panicked, tried to escape by speeding, lost control, and smashed into a stone wall where he met his death.

In comparing the father's criminal career and the son's delinquency, we are struck by the replication of crucial details of which the child, supposedly, had no knowledge. Although he was never told the facts, he sensed, no doubt, that the facts were of an unspeakable and unthinkable nature. Here, we must remind ourselves that such denials or repressions are not unusual in the lives of children. Why, then, did they invade Eddy's adolescent action system with a force so compelling that it remained totally unaffected by any outside interference?

It has been my impression that there are two qualitatively different kinds of secrets which parents keep from their children. The essential difference lies in the degree of reality with which the parent himself endows the facts that he keeps from the child. It is easier for the child to deal with prohibitions and taboos than with contradictions, confusion, and inconsistency. Eddy's case demonstrates how the mother's enclaves of denial infiltrated her sense of reality and prevented the child from ever dealing integratively with his father's life and death. The mother could offer the child neither a consensual validation of his perceptions nor a consistent refutation of them. Therefore, no intrapsychic settlement of the catastrophe was feasible; action language remained the only communicative modality by which contact with memory could be maintained. I conceive of this ego effort as the driving force in Eddy's maladaptive behavior and, consequently, I attribute a subordinate role to the identificatory process in this case.

This leads us to a consideration of Eddy's object relations. It became immediately apparent upon meeting this boy that he was passionately involved with the members of his family. He dated the onset of his delinquency as coinciding with his stepfather's leaving the family on one of his mysterious absences, lasting several months. Only the mother knew that he was on a gambling spree. The boy resented the paternal absenteeism and blamed the mother for condoning it. This hardboiled delinquent said with tender feelings: "I thought my [step] father left us because he didn't love us. I wanted so much to have him as my real father." The child had wooed his new father ever since his mother's remarriage when he was four years old; he used the stepfather's last name even though he was not legally adopted. Eddy was a fatherless son in search of a father. It is one of the requirements of adolescence to come to terms with the oedipal father. Preconditional for this task is the establishment of historical ego continuity as independent from parental sanctions and complementations. Here, then, was the point where an early catastrophic developmental impediment became manifest.

Through his actions the boy made it known that he possessed knowledge, albeit unconscious, of all the relevant facts surrounding his father's life and death. This knowledge was confirmed when the father's history was imparted to the boy. How this shared knowledge and the implicit validation of his veiled memories affected his behavior is of particular interest. Concretization, suicidal brinkmanship, and provocative behavior declined markedly. In addition, changes in the boy's affective life were noticeable. As one of them I shall mention the emergence of the boy's tender feelings for his natural father, his grief and compassion for a man who, so he thought, was not loved enough to value life more than death. He rediscovered his father's family on his own initiative, learned about his father's grave, took a job at the store of his paternal uncle, moved to a paternal aunt's family, and fell in love with a girl in this new neighborhood. Through action, rather than through insight, he tried to assimilate his unconsummated past. With adolescent exuberance he turned to the environment for the support of his adaptive efforts.

Concretization, by its very nature, implies an infantile dependency on the environment. Paraphrasing Spitz's (1965) remark, we might call Eddy's actions a permanent dialogue between the self and the surround. Concretization always represents a primitive form of adaptation. Consequently, whether this developmental impasse can be overcome and the arrested internalization process carried forward depends on the responsive cooperation of the environment at the point of crisis. Parents whose need for denial is not unalterably fixed will often contribute decisively to the adolescent's progressive development. But in cases similar to that of Eddy, their participation in a renewed growth process will never occur spontaneously. The mother, who had twice chosen a husband with asocial inclinations, was unable to participate in her son's socialization. The stepfather's sadomasochistic relationship to his stepson entered a crisis when puberty added a homosexual threat to the man's latent perverse inclination of long standing.

The adaptive changes in Eddy's life came to an abrupt halt when his girlfriend left him. He felt he had been wronged and sought restitution. For this he returned to his family where his birthright to unconditional love and acceptance became his battle cry. The inevitable happened: he reverted to asocial behavior, arrogantly calling his parents the true villains and considering himself their victim. The law again intervened when the mother found some "pills" (Methedrine) in his coat pocket. She called the police and Eddy, being just seventeen, was sent to the city penitentiary on Riker's Island. I visited him there after two months of incarceration in order to determine whether it should be recommended to the court that he be remanded to an open residential treatment center in Manhattan.

What struck me in my talk with the boy was the fact that his preoccupation with and idealization of his dead father was now replaced by that of his present parents. He held no grudges against his mother who was directly responsibile for his being in jail; at least she cared, so he felt. He remembered perfectly well his parents' double-talk and selfishness, but he assured me that all this was a matter of the past. He insisted that both of them had changed in heart and mind. This firm belief highlighted the boy's need for all-good parents who would protect him against the revival of his infantile greed and rage that had landed him behind bars. Here his reality testing proved defective due to his primitive ambivalence and to his belief in magic. It is a characteristic of the concretizing adolescent that his need tension creates that imaginary environmental correspondence which will keep such tension in tolerable bounds. A rehabilitative strategy was designed which took its cue from the compelling, maladaptive predilection that he conveyed so convincingly to me when I spoke with him in jail.

I have concluded from my work with concretizing delinquents and family myth cases that, where verbal communication fails to affect behavior and cognition, a carefully chosen concretization, introduced by the therapist, may substitute for symbolic speech. The therapist thus communicates by inducing a specific action. It must be kept in mind that the function of language has miscarried only selectively, as with attention decathexis, and by no means constitutes a comprehensive language abnormality or thought disorder. At any rate, it occurred to me that through induced concretization a bridge might be built to perceptions and affects that had not advanced to word representations or were excluded from them by either ego arrest or dissociation. I shall now discuss a case in which I applied the principle of induced concretization—or if you permit the expression—of "guided acting out."

Mario

Some years ago I was consulted about an eighteen-year-old boy, Mario, who had been in psychotherapy for several years. School failure, uncontrollable behavior, and aimless indifference, coupled with extreme intolerance of frustration, had worn down the endurance of home and school alike. Mario had no capacity for insight, nor could he view his actions or experiences within a time continuum. His only time reference remained the present. Consequently, treatment had deteriorated to a drawn-out stalemate.

Mario had been adopted in Italy by an unmarried American woman. He was almost five years old when he left the orphanage where he had lived since birth. Three findings appeared significant in the consultation: first, Mario's driven and insatiable pleasure-seeking behavior, in conjunction with a resigned acceptance of his weaknesses and failures; second, his incapacity to project himself into the future or into his manhood, except via regressive need-gratifying expectations; and third, his complete amnesia of his life before his adoption. His earliest memory, of his Atlantic crossing, reflected a catastrophic anxiety of annihilation which he described in these words: "Big waves were splashing against the porthole; I was afraid they'd get me and I'd drown." From this time on, Mario's memory proved to be excellent. I attributed particular importance to the fact that nearly five years of his early life were totally unavailable to him for adolescent psychic restructuring and, furthermore, that he was unable to use language for the purpose of reaching, cognitively and affectively, the early formative stages of his development. The particular ego functions that normally facilitate reconstruction were, for all practical purposes, nonexistent. His maladaptive behavior was a groping effort to touch the rock bottom of his life. He could neither move forward nor go backward: he held frantically on to his shaky sense of pretrauma object hunger by meaningless and endless sexual attachments. His life was fraught by a defective sense of identity; in other words, it was marked by an impasse in ego differentiation.

The thought occurred to me that, through sensory contact with his early childhood environment, a continuity in ego might be effected which might lift the primitive, preverbal use of action to a higher level of integration. What I had in mind was his revisitation of the pretrauma locale. How would he respond to the visual exposure to a once familiar scene, to the inner echo of his childhood language, the music of church bells, the intrusion of parochial smells and sights? This romantic composite of sensations attests to my ignorance of what, in particular, might touch Mario upon setting foot on the ground where his orphanage stood. As you will see, I could not have foretold what actually happened.

I recommended that the boy visit his native hill-top village in Umbria. Mario received this suggestion with eager delight and confessed that this had been his secret wish for a long time. He set out to travel to the place of his birth in the company of a college student who spoke the traveler's native tongue. When Mario descended from the bus that delivered him to the village piazza, he was recognized by an elderly woman who shouted his name, rushed over, and threw her arms around him. She was the matron who had

taken care of him during his orphanage years. In a flash he
knew who she was. His first step in his native village carried him right into the depth of his childhood. Next, he investigated his origin. He discovered the circumstances of his
illegitimate birth which followed the seduction of a young
farm girl by an older man. What was more natural now
than to search for his mother? This, I knew, he intended to
do, but I also knew that any advice on this matter would
have remained meaningless to him. He found out who his
mother was and where she lived. But at the moment when
the search of a lifetime seemed to have come to an end,
Mario abruptly turned his back on his past.

What made him shrink back from meeting his mother in
person when she was, finally, in physical reach? In his own
words, it was the realization that his appearance would destroy her marriage and her happiness. The decision reflected an empathy and altruistic protectiveness that I had
never expected to be within his reach. The decisive factor in
terms of progressive development, however, lies, in my opinion, in his volitional move not to see her, thus turning passive abandonment into active separation and leave-taking. I
must confess my amazement upon hearing that this boy,
who never before considered the feelings of others in the
pursuit of his wishes, had practiced forethought and empathy on the threshold of an emotional fulfillment.

The efforts of the induced concretization became slowly
apparent after Mario's return to his adoptive country. Most
noticeable was a growing capacity for introspection and
compromise. He came to recognize limitations within himself, instead of feeling limited by the malevolence of the
surround that had, and would again, abandon him. Not that
he remembered actual childhood events from his Umbrian
voyage, but the view of his future became more organized
and real. What accrued from the experience was a greater
fluidity of thought and emotion, as if the seal that had en-
shrined his past was broken, bringing his total life experi-

ence into the mainstream of the adolescent process. The hypomanic behavior subsided spontaneously. Mario could now experience and tolerate—with the help of psychotherapy—the depressed affect of his early childhood because an emotional as well as a cognitive bridge had established the connection to his preadoption childhood which had been abruptly lost with his traumatic dislocation.

Concurrent with these affective changes, Mario developed a relatively stable and positive relationship with his male therapist. He had now found a model for identification after having used his therapist for years as the target for his helpless demandingness or cynical vindictiveness. When circumstances finally imposed a geographical separation and, hence, a termination of therapy, Mario turned to writing letters. This time, he did not allow circumstances to annihilate the relationship. Consequently, he did not fall back into the monotony of his former pleasure-driven behavior, but developed a more modulated way of life with an active search for an appropriate, if commonplace, work situation that afforded him a sense of satisfaction and achievement. This step did not, however, mean that the total damage that had been inflicted on his personality was repaired; far from it. But, within the irreversible limitations of object relations and ego differentiation, Mario had found an adaptive compromise which was, peculiarly, his own and he was ready to protect it.

A significant characteristic of the concretizing adolescent lies in the participation of ego interests in his maladaptive behavior, in contrast to the purely instinctual gratification in other forms of acting out. It always remains a question of balance or preponderance. Even where a breakthrough of id impulses is unquestionably in evidence, the decisive promoter of the acting out is nonetheless to be found in an ego interest. The next case illustrates what I have in mind.

Steve

A fourteen-year-old boy was brought to court for "assaulting a woman with a dangerous weapon." The boy, Steve, had rung the doorbell of a woman who lived next to his apartment. For the occasion he had pulled a pillowcase over his head and held an open scout knife visible in his hand. The neighbor, terrified by the sight, grabbed the boy's hand and cut herself in the process. Steve, so he claimed, only intended to frighten her. This act proved to be the concretization of an unthinkable fact, which I shall briefly sketch out.

Steve's maternal grandfather, bedridden for some time, lived three flights above the victimized lady's apartment. The sick man was attended by a nurse with whom Steve's father entertained an affair. Steve and his father had always been pals; they both belonged to a Boy Scout troop of which the father was the leader. The knife in question was the father's scout knife. The father's vaguely perceived infidelity and disloyalty hurt Steve beyond endurance. His degradation had lowered the boy's self-esteem to a point where he struck out in desperation. His aim was the rescue of his ego ideal, the father, who was in danger of being destroyed by a predatory woman. Here, an adolescent ego interest asserted itself, to which I assign a top order in the hierarchy of determinants. At any rate, this boy was not a homicidal maniac who had to be isolated from society. He was a little boy who claimed the father whom he loved. After Steve was helped to acknowledge the unthinkable, he bridged, rather rapidly, the gap between concretization and verbalized thought. Due to this fact I recommended that his case be dismissed by the court. Psychotherapy seemed to be the intervention of choice in order to neutralize antisocial concretization. Two years of treatment have borne out this expectation.

Sartre (1952) has given a vivid description of the mak-

ing of a criminal in his biography of Jean Genet, the illegitimate child and ward of the state. Little Jean was declared by his foster parents to be a thief when he was ten
years old because he had stolen some sweets. Sartre writes:

> He [Genet the child] regards the existence of adults as more
> certain than his own and their testimonies as truer than that
> of his consciousness. . . . Therefore, without being clearly
> aware of it, he judges that the appearance (which he is to
> others) is the reality and that the reality (which he is to him-
> self) is only appearance. . . . He refuses to hear the voice of the
> cogito. . . . In short, he learns to think the unthinkable, to
> maintain the unmaintainable, to pose as true what he very
> well knows to be false [pp. 46-47].

It is perhaps the most provocative finding in the cases I
have presented that these adolescents had all suffered a
disastrous loss which they were never able to put to rest or
replace. Yet, none of them showed the clinical signs of depression or withdrawal. Quite to the contrary, they clung to
living and to social participation with an astounding pertinacity. They seemed to want something from the surround
on which their survival depended.

Generally, one internalizes—for better or for worse—the
lost object. Whenever vague and contradictory awareness of
the lost object interferes with this process, the original ambivalence attached to it remains unchanged. The incapacity
to synthesize the good and the bad part of the lost object relegates the loss complex to primitive and prelogical integration. This type of mastery is characterized in my cases by
the magic of action or, in other words, by the concretization
of dissociated memory-traces. The projective mechanism is
invariably at work and blurs the boundary between the self
and the object world. It does not, by any means, operate in
the service of defense, but represents the primitive form of
dealing with the outside world on the level of animism. This
primitivization, however, remains attached to a restricted
psychic content, namely, to unassimilated experiences. Con-

cretization acquires the function of preventing a merger of self and object, of keeping the noxious influence of the surround from spreading through the total personality, and, last but not least, of assimilating a loss by rendering it real, validated by snatches of memory, inferences, and suppositions. We can observe how concretizing behavior tries to avert regressive engulfment while, simultaneously, giving in to it. This see-sawing process reaches a disastrous impasse when the concretizing adolescent is brought to court. Psychoanalytic understanding of this impasse and of its historical determinants is called for at this point to avert, if at all possible, the extreme calamity of developmental stagnation or regression which leads inevitably to so-called recidivism.

In this chapter I have presented theoretical and practical conclusions derived from my study of a special form of acting out which I have called concretization. The analyst, standing today vis-à-vis the vast spectrum of adolescent maladaptive behavior, is expected to offer modalities of intervention that deviate from his customary form of treatment. These modalities have to be invented. It will be no surprise to me if such inventions seem to many a reader nothing more than the result of intuitive, empathic, or identificatory, in essence highly personal, predilections, which are interesting but, strictly speaking, lie outside the psychoanalytic science. It has been my special effort to show that we possess no better guide in the field of adolescent maladaptive behavior than the rigorous application of psychoanalytic psychology. Of course, everyone who has worked with adolescents has taken, at times, recourse to all kinds of so-called unorthodox measures in the face of emergencies. Some of these have proven exceedingly effective and even lasting. What I have proposed is simply to study such seeming effectiveness, because truly restorative processes always lay bare, for our investigation, the nature of developmental and maturational anomalies.

Chapter 14

The Overappreciated Child

It is the essence of conflict to contain, simultaneously, two irreconcilable and contradictory strivings. In early childhood the forces pulling in opposing directions are located, on the one hand, in the child's needs and drives that seek expression and gratification and, on the other, in the restraints and frustrations that issue from the external world. The dynamism of these antagonistic forces, if attuned to the child's integrative capacity at the moment, facilitates development. At this stage, then, the conflict or the yes-no divisiveness lies between the child and his surround. With the growing awareness of self and nonself, as well as with increasing object dependency, the child internalizes the demands and expectations of the caretaking persons around him. This process of internalization brings an internal divisiveness into play. The formation of this new kind of conflict requires an internal and no longer exclusively external management. The transition from one to the other is always slow and both stages overlap to a certain degree, until the maturing ego has attained sufficient resourcefulness for the accommodation (resolution, defense, compromise) of internal conflict. The system of inner control is complete in structure, if not yet in efficiency, when dependency on the object

This chapter is a discussion of E. James Anthony's Biannual Peter Blos Lecture (established in 1971 by the Jewish Board of Guardians), entitled "Between Yes and No" and delivered December 4, 1973. First published in *Psychosocial Process*, 3 (2): 47-54, Fall 1974.

303

is replaced by dependency on the superego; at this stage an impersonal guide gives its "yes," "no," or "maybe" to drive propensities and ego aspirations. This new structure operates with abstract principles rather than within the context of concrete object love. The threat of object loss becomes replaced by the sense of guilt.

This telescoped outline of conflict development was presented in order to provide a conceptual distinction for the assessment of certain adolescent disturbances. Confronted with the painful task of leaving the world of early childhood behind, some adolescents regress to familiar childhood patterns of conduct, affect, defense, and object relations, while others rush wildly ahead and demand that the world consider them as full-fledged adults. Should these trends persist over too extensive a time or be too extreme in their expression, both solutions—flight backward or flight forward—reveal their infantile nature. Here we have to ask ourselves the often puzzling question, whether we deal with internalized conflicts at all, or whether we witness the consequences of a developmental deficit that adolescence has brought to the fore in its inherently catastrophic severity. If the latter is the case, then the mending of a developmental weakness or deficit becomes the therapeutic task.

Developmental deficits are neither helped nor healed by interpretation, but require ego strengthening or, more precisely, the belated completion of those stages in ego development that are accountable for the weakness of the ego structure as a whole. This repair can be achieved, in some cases, only by polarization or "impingement" in the therapeutic situation. The distinction between the two kinds of disturbance (developmental or conflictual) is never as neatly apparent in the clinical situation as in our theoretical formulations nor are they experienced by the adolescent as distinguishable from each other. It is, however, my opinion that these theoretical distinctions help us to bring order into our clinical observations by delineating etiological alternatives.

The clinical picture of adolescent psychopathology is further beclouded by the fact that normative adolescent regression revives infantile positions, apparent in acting-out behavior that either simulates or demonstrates developmental defects. Assessment of this sector of the disturbed personality is never an easy task, yet it is always a critical one. All adolescents seek new models for identification or polarization; some require it for structure repair (developmental defect) while others use it for structure transformation (normative adolescent conflict).

A certain kind of disturbed adolescent boy has come to my attention over the years and during the last decade has, in my view, acquired the configuration of a type, i.e., he can be described in terms of distinct characteristics. He usually comes from a white, middle- or upper-middle-class family. His typicalness becomes more and more apparent, especially through his asocial behavior, between the ages of fifteen and twenty. From experience I have learned that this type of boy requires a long preparatory phase in therapy during which the adolescent conflict with the outer world is drawn into the interaction between the young person and his therapist. What these adolescents have in common is either the absence or the shallowness of inner conflict. Instead, they uphold a deeply felt, righteous sense of unfairness, of injustice done to them, bordering on rage or despair, directed against the world around them. This hostile world is populated by adults and run by public institutions which are—in the vernacular of the young—"all fucked up."

If one becomes familiar with the life of these patients, a common picture emerges of a child who, from the earliest age on, was inordinately praised and admired, while shortcomings and inadequacies were ignored unduly long or excused by the parents. These children developed an uncritical, narcissistic self-admiration which became the preferred or exclusive source of self-esteem and, over time, made them totally dependent on the unrealistic and exaggerated evaluation of their achievements and importance. This high

level of self-esteem can only be maintained if the external
world furnishes a continuous flow of narcissistic supplies.
Should this flow dry up momentarily, a painful sense of
worthlessness and a depressed affect immediately inundate
the self. This dependency, if unchecked, assumes eventually
the characteristics of an addiction.

Another typical aspect in the upbringing of these children should be noted because it lays the foundation for a
specific ego characteristic of an infantilized nature in later
life. Demands on the small child for independent judgment
were made prematurely, forcing the child to become his own
master before having developed the resources for making
the kind of decisions expected. All that the child could do,
was to make choices on the basis of momentary wishes and
desires without taking into account their consequences; developmentally, the child had not yet acquired the capacity
to anticipate the future. Unexpected and disagreeable consequences, therefore, could only be understood as the mean-
ness of the outer world which let them happen.

All through his childhood this child was made to feel
that he was more—in some undefinable way—than he
would or could validate by his performance. He was *hors
concours* from the beginning. This invisible something or
somebody was called the child's potential; it was constantly
talked about, often in rather concrete terms, similar to a de-
tained visitor who is about to arrive any moment. Consequently, there was one Johnnie whom Johnnie knew and
there was another Johnnie, the potential, whom only others
knew. Trusting others (at least in this point) became the secure source of an inflated self-esteem.

In their adolescence these children remember being
lonely and frightened, with periods of ecstatic happiness
and feelings of grandeur. Their years of growing up have
turned into an incessant search for elated states without
which life would become quickly drab, boring, and empty.
These times, when remembered by the patient in later life,

are described as desolate, empty, dark, and frightening. This account portrays the syndrome of the overappreciated child.

When we meet this child at adolescence, the developmental defect becomes apparent in the struggle between the self and the outer world; this struggle is often mistaken as the proverbial and expectable adolescent rebellion of transitory nature and positive valence. These patients only experience internal conflicts of a superficial, meteoric, and vague nature—sharp one moment and gone the next. Early overappreciation, coupled with premature overexpectation, both responsible for the developmental defect, survive in these children like a promise and a sense of certainty that all will go well as soon as they get older. With adolescence the day of fulfillment should have arrived, but the promise remains unfulfilled. The day of fulfillment turns into a day of reckoning. Disbelief, rage, and a sense of betrayal fill their tortured, helpless souls; they hunger for an idealized object world that will restore a shattered inner harmony built on infantile grandeur. They can only say "yes" to what feels good, "no" to whatever lowers their self-esteem; a "maybe" does not exist because they live exclusively for the moment.

I have found adolescents of this type usually intelligent, appealing, and interesting; they can be touchingly tender in their feelings and responsiveness. Many of them possess the untutored, native intelligence, openness, and charm of the three- to six-year-old child, immortalized in the tale of "The Emperor's New Clothes." However, this side of their personality can suddenly and without any apparent cause be swept aside by primitive rage and sadistic fantasies of an infantile, perverse nature. Adolescents of this type will not kill a fly, but in the seclusion of their florid fantasy life they can be cruel, haughty, and vengeful in the style of the Queen of Hearts: "Off with their heads!" Fear of retaliation, horror of their secret evilness haunts their minds, but only for a brief moment. More clever than Orestes, they quickly throw the pursuing Erinyes off the scent and, once again, find happiness in that split-off part of their psyche where goodness and innocence reign supreme. Such respites return often and long enough for the adolescent child to discover the personal and material advantages to be obtained from his utterly convincing purity of purpose, especially when it is afforded credence by the unwitting participation of adults who help to transform the reciprocal play-acting into reality. The social advantageousness of this imposterlike unselfconsciousness is discovered fortuitously in childhood; over time, the discovery is worked into a life style and perfected on an ever grander scale during adolescence.

There is no question that the treatment of this type of adolescent is fraught with pitfalls: unless the therapist declares his stand, makes explicit who he is, and what he can or cannot do, the treatment gets lost in a morass of correct, but useless interpretations. If, however, the therapist misgauges the adolescent's tolerance for polarization, therapy may become a struggle for power. The initial positive emotional contact is decisive for all that follows. To be understanding, patient, and tolerant is not enough; this type of adolescent is stimulus-hungry; it follows that the therapist has to be interesting, stimulating, and engaging. The degree to which the therapist is incorruptible and unseducible (no easy task with such young masters) arouses in the adolescent at first a pugnacious resentment ("I thought a therapist is supposed to *understand*"); this reaction blends slowly into vexation and suspicion ("I'll get you yet—just wait"), mixed with amazement and curiosity ("Does he really mean what he says?"). Gradually, the initial sense of fascination acquires the quality of admiration: the ambivalence balance tips in favor of positive feelings. Within the context of this kind of relationship proceeds the repair of those specific developmental defects I have described, with occasional and abrupt side trips into the regions of defense, fantasy, memory, and affect or, briefly, into the regions of introspection, if not yet of insight.

In order to illustrate these remarks I shall describe briefly the focal feature in the therapy of a late adolescent boy who displayed vividly the syndrome of the "overappreciated child." He himself came to call it the "spoiled brat in me." The case might appear to be an extreme one but, then, most cases of this nature are.

The young man came to see me because nothing of late had worked out to his liking. School failure, lack of interest, aimless drifting through time with depressive moods, sporadic but shallow sexual relations, lasting drug involvement with the fear of getting "hooked" by hard drugs, availability of and disenchantment with the luxuries the profit from "dealing" could offer—all these aspects of his life had compounded a persistent and gnawing sense of unfulfillment. A rapport was easily established because I knew who my competitors were, namely, drugs and fantasies; I also was aware of the intensity of his stimulus hunger. After the opening gambit of establishing rapport I accepted him conditionally as a patient, stating the conditions that, if accepted and then broken by him, would terminate our relationship. I expected him to quit "dealing" (he promised me a higher fee if dealing were permitted) and to keep me informed of his drug use. Even though he accepted these conditions, I delayed for an indefinite time committing myself to treat him because I doubted his trustworthiness. Of course, I told him what caused me to remain reticent and waiting. In taking this stance I reflected the patient's own inner divisiveness and made explicit where I stood in his dealings with me and in mine with him. I gave him no assurance that a fee paid and appointment time kept earned him the privilege to "own me or use me" to his liking. On this basis we pursued a year of rather productive work.

The patient brought this collaboration to a head by confessing to me one day that he had lied to me for a long time by concealing from me his continued (even if reduced) use of drugs, including hard drugs. These he received as gifts from a wealthy friend. I had all reason to believe his assertion that he had given up "dealing" ever since we had made our contract a year ago. Did he now present these assurances (first, not dealing personally but being supported with drugs by his dealer friends and, second, his reduced drug use) as extenuating, even exculpatory, circumstances? At any rate, with this confession he put me to the supreme test: Would I recant my conviction, become a partner of his corrupted superego, and prove, after all, his omnipotence as invincible? I told him that we had reached the point where we had to part. He accepted this verdict almost with relief, but asked if he could return in the future if he had freed himself from drugs and had settled down in work of some kind. (He had made many efforts at jobs and "creative self-employment" during the time he saw me.) I assured him that my door would be open.

The follow-up of this case over a period of two years is of particular interest. Our parting was a turning point in his life. During the following years he reported to me several times. He moved away from his parents to live in another city where he tried himself out on several jobs. He found new friends of both sexes and succeeded, unaided, in giving up the use of hard drugs. He broke off contact with the wealthy friend and the old gang. Finally, he sought admission to the college of his choice. He was admitted on the strength of his creative design work, which he had produced during the second half of the year he was in treatment with me. He embarked on a professional career for which undoubtedly he had talent.

Needless to say, the stabilization of his personality remains an arduous process. The rate of recidivism in cases of this kind is high. True, he has been long enough on a forward and upward road to take a more optimistic view of his future. The decisive turn in the slow repair of this patient's serious developmental deficit occurred, so I believe, when I gave my unequivocal "No." This "No" expressed the thought: "No, you cannot own me, you cannot make me over in your image, you are not God." After the break in therapy a gradual transition, even though tenuous, from omnipotence to object love to identification took its course. On another level, I saw in his forward move the progression from irresponsibility to moral guilt. When he visited me last, he was considering a second installment of therapy in the city where he now lives. No doubt, therapy when resumed again will follow a different path and reach the level of meaningful insight. However, this is speculation.

There are no more appropriate words with which to close my reflections than those of reasoned and seasoned experience:

> Therapeutic life, like life itself, is not as clear-cut or as segmented as it appears in reports. Like life itself, it is essentially nebulous and not an "event system" at all. A system is largely in our heads and abstracted from the stream of consciousness. We chop it all up into categories to make it manageable to think about. If this is true, what value does a report describing the treatment situation have for others? In most instances, it is no more than a new way of looking at very old things [Anthony, 1976, p. 343].

PART FOUR

The Developmental Approach to Psychic Structure Formation

We approach in this section an exclusive preoccupation with theory building. The basic question presents itself: Is adolescence a developmental period during which predominantly or solely a reordering of existing psychic structures occurs, or is adolescence a developmental period in which the formation of new structures occurs? In other words, is adolescence a period that is distinguished by the restructuring or transformation of proto-adolescent psychic organizations or are new structures identifiable as the result of pubertal, adolescent-specific conflicts and their resolutions? Even though we can conclude from clinical observation that both processes are simultaneously at work, I will pursue their respective contributions to adult personality formation separately in order to sort out their dissimilarities, identify their origins, and clarify their interaction. The transition from adolescence to adulthood invites a comparison to the transition from protolatency to the latency period; both have in common the fact that new structures evolve from conflict resolutions that are specific and typical for the respective maturational level. In both instances, the advance in structure formation is reflected in a forward step toward personality consolidation.

I have chosen one particular structure, the ego ideal, to illustrate the assumption that structural innovations make their appearance at adolescence and are, in fact, typical of the adolescent process. From my clinical study of the life history of the ego ideal, in other words, from tracing the genealogy of the ego ideal throughout the total scope of childhood, from early childhood to late adolescence, I have arrived at definite conclusions with respect to adolescent-specific structure formation. These conclusions can be summarized in the proposition that the adult ego ideal emerges from the resolution of the negative Oedipus complex which gains conflictual prominence at adolescence. Compelled by sexual maturation at puberty, the resolution of this oedipal component becomes a matter of developmental urgency at adolescence. The bisexuality of childhood is brought to an end; this radical step is secured by structure formation. Thus, in our study of the adolescent ego ideal we discern new ways of self-esteem regulation, basically different from the ones that served this function during the infantile period.

From my clinical work with adolescents I have gained the impression, indeed conviction, that the Oedipus complex is not only resuscitated at the period of sexual maturation but normally completes the work of resolution during that developmental stage. In other words, the Oedipus complex is suspended rather than resolved—for better or for worse—at the entrance into the latency period; it finds its continuation at adolescence. The new, adolescent, oedipal issue centers on the negative Oedipus complex, the love for the parent of the same sex. The resolution of this issue represents a major segment of the oedipal work of adolescence; adult sexual identity formation is predicated on the resolution of this issue. The adolescent negative oedipal issue is not just a revival of an infantile conflict but an actuality never before encountered with such imperativeness. It cannot be resolved at adolescence by displacement onto a nonincestuous object without homosexual dominances becoming a permanent aspect of object relations.

From my clinical work I have also gained the persuasive, indeed, convincing impression that the resolution of the negative Oedipus complex is accomplished through the elaboration of a new structure to which I refer as the adult ego ideal, in contrast to the earlier, infantile ego ideal. It is perhaps not superfluous to repeat that I speak here of structure and not of content: the saint and the criminal both have an ego ideal as a structure, even if the contents are worlds apart and the developmental levels of the respective ego ideals totally incongruous. What I want to emphasize here is the proposition that the adult ego ideal becomes the heir of the negative Oedipus complex at the termination of adolescence. From an adaptive or psychosocial point of view the adult ego ideal can be viewed as the socialization of narcissism. What I mean precisely by this statement requires a lengthy exposition which is contained in the subsequent chapters.

Of course, revival and displacement of the positive Oedipus complex during the adolescent period remains, normally, a central and conflictual issue in adolescent object relations. In fact, we are well informed about the influence of the positive Oedipus complex on adolescent development through its tumultuous resuscitation during the adolescent period (adolescence proper). However, we must admit that less is known about the fate of the drives attached to the parent of the same sex and how this libidinal tie affects adolescent object relations and the sense of self.

Pondering these propositions we come to wonder how a biphasic—infantile and adolescent—resolution of the Oedipus complex is related to the theory of neurosogenesis. It remains a controversial but consequential inquiry that searches for the respective contribution the biphasic oedipal resolutions make to the formation of the adult neurosis. The developmental dichotomy of which I speak urges us to consider the fact that the organization of the definitive—the adult—neurosis is not completed before the termination of adolescence or, in other words, not before the termination of childhood which is marked by the definitive—normal or pathological—resolution of the Oedipus complex.

Attributing to the adolescent process a limited, even if variable, time span raises the question of how to conceptualize the closure of adolescence. The answer to this question will be formulated in terms of structure formation and developmental tasks. These will be found to be identical with the adolescent process itself. The investigation of this issue represents the final contribution of this section.

Chapter 15

The Genealogy of the Ego Ideal

The adolescent period lends itself particularly well to the study of psychic structures in relation to origin, content, and function. While psychic structures at this advanced stage of development are essentially formed and integrated, it remains a characteristic of adolescence—or of the biphasic development of sexuality in the human species—that a process of psychic restructuring is evoked by pubertal maturation. The course of the ensuing emotional instability is marked by more or less disintegrative processes of a regressive nature, but simultaneously we also observe a vigorous and integrative forward movement in personality formation. Integration and consolidation proceed in a seesaw fashion with violent or mild, extended or brief alternations of regressive and progressive movements. The relative openness and fluidity of the personality during this period of psychic restructuring grant the psychoanalytic observer of personality development the opportunity to gain important insights into structure formation and transformation which no other period in human life offers in any comparable manner. Throughout history, the dramatic reverberations of this process in the life of the adolescent have never failed to be noticed and recorded.

In the course of my psychoanalytic studies I have used this natural laboratory setting of psychic restructuring in

First published in *The Psychoanalytic Study of the Child,* 29: 43-88. New Haven: Yale University Press, 1974.

adolescence for the investigation of those structures that are most decisively affected by the adolescent process. The present study extends this research to the ego ideal. Popular observation and academic psychology have always emphasized the proclivity of youth for high ideals, for idealizations and ideologies. This tendency, usually in conflict with traditional values, taboos, and customs, has given cause either to sanctify or to malign the younger generation. The vagueness of psychological theory in relation to ideal formation in adolescence, in conjunction with the demonstrative, often desperate search for ideals in contemporary youth, makes the study of the ego ideal within the adolescent process a timely issue. My own findings will be viewed in the light of ego-ideal conceptualizations which have been advanced over the years and have become an integral part of psychoanalytic theory.

The Clinical Starting Point

Whatever my contributions to psychoanalytic theory have been, they all have one thing in common—they have issued from clinical observations. The same holds true for my study of the ego ideal. I therefore begin by recounting the course of my observations which originated in the analysis of adolescent boys, especially late adolescent boys.

Several male patients in their late adolescence shared one prominent symptom complex. They had high ambitions, yet they were unable to pursue them; they were aimless and dejected, given to extreme mood swings, to sporadic but short-lived spurts of enterprising action and an unfailing return to monotonous dreams of glory. Nothing ever congealed into purposeful pursuit, novel experimentation, or the visionary excitement of a realistic goal. These typical adolescent characteristics acquired the specificity of a symptom complex only by the fact that they remained static, repetitive, and beyond volitional control; thus, they affected perniciously the common challenges to youth, such as job performance, academic achievement, and the pursuit of gratifying object relations with boys, girls, and adults alike. The irrefutable evidence of failure rendered the present dismal and the future ominous. Flight into rebellion or restitution in fantasy led into the quicksand of helplessness. Negativism, if present, never lasted long; yet, any effort to transcend it could not be sustained. Occupational goals or short-term objectives were easily lost in indecision and doubt; they were often and abruptly abandoned, despite the seemingly strong motivation that brought them into existence.

These and related phenomena have been widely described in the literature, especially in reference to male adolescence. Among the various dynamic and genetic explanations, the male adolescent's rivalry with the oedipal father stands out as the standard model. Defenses against castration anxiety seem to have barricaded the road to progressive development. There can be no question that this theme reverberates through the adolescent struggle of the male. There is always an abundance of direct expressions or associations, ideas, and affects leading in this direction. However, interpretations emphasizing this conflict do not resolve, in my experience, the symptomatology of the pervasive inhibitions and developmental arrests described above.

It occurred to me that in these cases the complementary complex of the male's rivalry with the father—his love of him and his wish to be the recipient of his affection—presents an obstacle to the formation of realistic goals and their active pursuit. In fact, passive aims rise to the surface repeatedly and without fail, even though these aims clash with conscious ambitions and are subject to severe self-criticism. They obviously receive their pertinacity from the secondary gain they secure.

The sexualization of ego and superego functions during adolescence is well known; it applies equally to those ego-ideal formations that precede adolescence. To illustrate, I shall cite a male student whose vocational ambitions were the same as those his father had set for him. Failure had to prevent success because of a four-pronged conflict: as a success he was either offering himself as a love object to the father (castration wish) or he was annihilating him by usurping his position (parricide); on the other hand, as a failure he was renouncing his ambitions and thereby inducing the father to treat him as a contemptible woman; yet, in failure he also established his autonomy, even if a negative one, by repulsing the father's seductiveness, by not becoming his best-loved, his ideal son. The complexity of this constellation is due to the fact that both the positive and the negative Oedipus complex come into play again at the terminal phase of adolescence. The final resolution of both is of course decisively influenced by the fixation points in early object relations and the implicit bisexual orientation of childhood.

Observations of this kind have convinced me that the ego ideal remains an immature, self-idealizing, wish-fulfilling agency, resisting any transformation into a mature, namely, abstracted, goal-intentional, and action-motivating force, as long as the young man's negative Oedipus complex cannot be drawn sufficiently into the analytic work. I am certain that analysts know from experience how impenetrable this aspect of the defensive organization remains in the analysis of the male adolescent. Only after the analysis of the fixation on the negative Oedipus complex has been accomplished, can the formation of an age-adequate, workable ego ideal take its normal course. This has led me to say that the ego ideal, as it emerges at the termination of adolescence, is the heir to the negative Oedipus complex (see Chapter 7). By inference, I assume that adolescent psychic restructuring which progresses unaided by therapeutic help follows a similar course.

Theoretical Formulations

Before pursuing the theoretical implications of what has been said so far, I must say a word about adolescent idealization in general. These comments apply to boy and girl in equal measure, even though their idealizations are different in content and quality. A good reason exists for making a distinction between the idealization of the self and the ego ideal as such. Even though idealizations have their roots in infantile narcissism, we cannot ignore the fact that the advent of sexual maturation draws these early narcissistic formations into the instinctual turmoil of adolescence. Here we encounter them, either in the area of object relations or in a regressive enhancement of narcissism, as seen in self-idealizations. These formations are unstable and subject to rapid fluctuations; they are the primitive regulators of self-esteem. Self-idealization can provide, at least temporarily, a gratification on the order of infantile need gratification. The ego ideal, in contrast, provides only approximations to fulfillment; it involves delay and a state of anticipation; it is a ceaseless journey without arrival, a lifelong striving for perfection. Superego demands can be fulfilled with a subsequent sense of well-being. Ego-ideal strivings can never be fulfilled; in fact, it is the sustained striving for perfection that furnishes a sense of well-being.[1]

The ego ideal has its deepest roots in primary narcissism. Yet, every stage of subsequent development enlarges its scope in terms of content and function. Both ego ideal and superego begin to develop early in life, long before they assume the structure of a psychic agency. They originate in

[1]Hartmann and Loewenstein (1962) have discussed the "change of function" in the evolution of the ego ideal: "the 'striving after perfection' of the ego ideal becomes dynamically a partly independent direction-giving function, which is relatively independent of the objects, and relatively independent also of the instinctual precursors. The aims of the ego ideal are then to a considerable extent no longer identical with the primitive wishes which played a role in its formation" (p. 64).

response to the external world and remain, therefore, prone
to re-externalization. Here, I want to emphasize the fact
that the ego ideal is subject to qualitative changes during
the course of development. That is, the ego ideal easily becomes enmeshed with new drive modalities, as well as with
new ego competencies, as both emerge at different developmental stages. By virtue of this fact, we can expect the ego
ideal to become drawn into the turmoil of the libidinal and
aggressive drives during adolescence. The adolescent
reinstinctualization of those psychic structures that derived
from the internalization of object relations thus encompasses
the ego ideal as well. Its narcissistic core attaches itself to
the narcissistic object libido that finds a renewed outlet
within the resurgence of the negative Oedipus complex. The
oedipal resolution brings the mature ego ideal into existence as the desexualized, i.e., the transmuted, survivor of
the negative Oedipus complex. Even though the early steps,
as well as the final ones, of ego-ideal development are different in male and female, the adolescent structuralization
of the ego ideal determines, for both sexes, the end phase of
the adolescent process; in other words, it marks the termination of psychological childhood.

It is an accepted tenet of psychoanalytic theory that the
Oedipus complex is reactivated during adolescence. In conjunction with regression in the service of development, the
reactivation leads to the loosening of infantile object ties
and initiates the second individuation process of adolescence. Ego dominance as well as the characterological
stabilization of defenses can be observed along the progression of adolescent psychic restructuring. The similarities of
this stage with the transition from the phallic-oedipal to the
latency stage are striking and have attracted the attention
of analytic observers.

It has been my impression that the first decline of the
Oedipus complex at the stage of sexual immaturity forces
the positive component of the complex into repression and

identificatory transformations (superego), and that this is accomplished by more absolute and stringent measures than appears to be the case with the negative component. We have always taken for granted that the triadic oedipal conflict is decisively influenced by the precursory object relations of the dyadic period, carrying forward fixations which pertain to specific drive propensities, patterns of object relations, and preferential affinities to one or the other of the component instincts. The little boy's passive love for the father and his identification with the mother seem to find a bypass, often apparent as a characterological trait or split-off fantasy, during the resolution of the Oedipus complex and the solidification of the superego. The feminine component of the little boy's instinctual life becomes restrained, restricted, or rejected far more forcefully by narcissistic injunctions, manifest in shame and contempt, than by superego interdictions. His mastery of aggression always skirts close to the dilemma of mastery by passive surrender to moral principles (to the father), or by externalization of the conflict through acting out.

It is a well-known fact that the boy's relationship to his father is never better, i.e., less conflicted or more positive, than it is at the dawn of pubescence. The boy enlists the father's assistance in his defense against the regression to the preoedipal—the phallic, castrating—mother. It can be observed how this phase affects the resuscitation of the Oedipus complex, regardless of earlier fixations, and how this phase complicates, in some fashion, the adolescent resolution. It is my contention that not only is the adolescent faced with the revival of the oedipal conflict as it was resolved or abandoned at its first decline, but that the definitive resolution of the complex is the inherent task of adolescence. This task involves the total renunciation of infantile object ties to both parental figures, i.e., to both as sexual objects. An adjunctive resolution pertains in many cases to an incestuous tie to brother or sister.

For the child, the bisexual position is less conflictual, allowing a host of compromises, than is the case for the adolescent who has attained sexual maturity. The resolution of the negative Oedipus complex as an object involvement of a sexual nature confronts the adolescent boy with a relatively novel conflict and task. Displacement to a nonincestuous object can never be a satisfactory solution because this would only extend the complete oedipal constellation, beyond its timing, into bisexual object relations of adulthood. The only road open for the boy lies in the deinstinctualization of the narcissistic, i.e., homosexual, object tie, leading to the formation of the adult ego ideal. In the process, all ego-ideal trends that have accrued over time, from primary narcissism to symbiotic omnipotence, and later, from narcissistic identifications to the stage of homosexual object love, become integrated in the permanent ego ideal that coalesces during the terminal stage of adolescence. From here on, the ego ideal remains an unalterable psychic structure which extends its influence on thought and behavior over a much larger sector of the personality than was the case before adolescence. This shift has to be viewed as collateral to concurrent changes in the adolescent superego. Phenomenologically, these changes are represented by the proverbial adolescent rebellion. Metapsychologically, these changes indicate that ego and ego ideal are taking over some of the superego functions, thereby affecting its scope of influence as well as its dynamic and economic role in mental life (Blos, 1962).

I shall now return briefly to self-idealization and ego ideal in adolescence, because the conceptualization of the adolescent ego-ideal formation permits a more precise differentiation between the two. The acquisition of ideals is not identical with ego-ideal structuralization. One can no less speak of ego ideals than of superegos in the plural. Yet, one frequently encounters the term "ego ideals" in the literature. Both superego and ego ideal denote a cohesive structure or, more correctly, the ego ideal represents an "aspect of the superego system" (Hartmann and Loewenstein, 1962, p. 44).

Self-idealization is a typical aspect of adolescence; it displays, quite unmistakably, its narcissistic origin and function as the regulator of self-esteem. Concurrently, we discern a more or less malignant impairment of reality testing, objectivation, and object relations. At the point where the narcissistic aims of self-idealization are externalized, they are easily confused with the manifestation of the ego ideal. Indeed, the adolescent's uncompromising ideals, expressed in word or action, are often mistaken as evidence of a powerful ego ideal.

My clinical impressions of some of the angry or activist late adolescents, most of them college students, who seek the creation of a perfect society, have convinced me that their belief in a perfect world is rooted in an archaic belief in parental perfection. The "idealized parent imago" (Kohut, 1971), when externalized, lends a fanatic vision to the striving for such a perfect world, while the narcissistic rage, a response to parental disillusionment, finds a belated expression in the irrationality of violence. An imperfect world must either yield to correction or be destroyed. This kind of all-or-nothing principle was demonstrated in the 1960s with particular virulence on American college campuses.[2] The Alma Mater, "the fostering mother," became the target of infantile wrath and recrimination as evidenced in verbal, symbolic, as well as concrete anal defilement. Her refusal to provide need gratification to her foster children was taken literally, in total disregard of the fact that she was fostering (nursing) the mind and therefore was not able to provide instantaneous need gratification. Of course, these comments apply only to a particular segment of campus activists and

[2] A generalization of this thesis on a worldwide scale would only be misleading, because too many heterogeneous factors entered the scene of student uprisings in other countries.

fringe rebels. The so-called faults of the parent appear to them magnified to the size of unforgivable insults of debasement or evil. In some youthful revolutionaries[3] we find the sense of political or historical logic either distorted by "absolutes" or rendered nonexistent by the overriding belief in perfection. Far from being delusional, this kind of behavior and thinking reflects the externalization of the lost parental perfection; furthermore, it demonstrates how extraordinarily painful the effort is to transcend the loss of the idealized self or object.

Psychoanalytic theory has always emphasized the close connection between the ego ideal and the narcissistic losses of infancy. In accordance with its origin, which also influences its function, the ego ideal is basically averse to object-libidinal involvement; as stated above, its roots lie in primary narcissism. It perpetuates, so to speak, an eternal approximation to the narcissistic perfection of infancy. If we follow the course of the ego ideal from infancy to adulthood, we can trace a continuous adaptation of its basic function to the increasingly complex system by which the self measures itself, as it progresses along developmental lines. Thus, the ego ideal becomes further and further removed from those primitive efforts that aim at total narcissistic restitution. In fact, the ego ideal functions as a psychic institution, at least in its mature form, only as long as its goal remains beyond its grasp. Whatever man accomplishes, imperfection remains an everlasting constituent of his endeavors; yet this fact has never held man back from renewing his efforts. While the superego is an agency of prohibition, the ego ideal is an agency of aspiration. "Whereas the ego submits to the superego out of fear of punishment, it submits to the ego ideal out of love" (Nunberg, 1932, p. 146). Many decades

---

[3]We find their prototypical ancestors in the nihilist students Arcady and Bazarov in Turgenev's *Fathers and Sons* (1862). Arcady eventually settles down in marriage and ancestral life, while Bazarov, in a triumph of self-idealization over a thwarted romance, commits suicide.

later we read again: "Our ideals are our internal leaders; we love them and are longing to reach them. . . . We are driven by our ambitions, [but] we do not love them" (Kohut, 1966, p. 251).

During the formative process of the adult ego ideal in adolescence preoedipal and pregenital patterns are reinstated and the strength of fixation points becomes glaringly apparent. The same is true of the component instincts, which once more play a role during the upheaval of the instinctual life at puberty, when the advance to genitality draws a more and more distinct demarcation line between forepleasure and genital arousal. In my work with the male adolescent, I have often been struck by how intensely his self-idealization is cultivated by him as an aim in itself, without being followed up by an act toward realization or achievement. The comparison of this attitude to a fixation on forepleasure is convincing, especially when we observe repeatedly the decline of this mode of functioning with the ascendancy of genitality. This thought, already contained *in nuce* in the clinical starting point, can now be restated: the ego ideal emerges from its infantile state only when, at late adolescence, the narcissistic object attachment, to which the infantile ego ideal has become joined, has lost its homosexual cathexis. This task is accomplished by the adolescent resolution of the negative Oedipus complex.

The Development of the Male and the Female Ego Ideal

Even though we consider the ego ideal to be part of the superego system, they do not evolve from the same conflictual matrix, nor are they overlapping entities at the time of their emergence. Quite to the contrary, their origins are heterogeneous, their starting points are not synchronous, their contents are not identical, and their functions are disparate. What they have in common is their motivational influence on behavior, and their regulatory function of the sense of well-being. In terms of origins, we can "distinguish between the superego, as the later and more reality-syntonic structure, and the ego ideal as the earlier more narcissistic one" (A. Reich, 1954, p. 209). However, the chronology of definitive structure formation is reversed: the superego is established earlier at the decline of the phallic-oedipal phase, while the ego ideal reaches its definitive structure only during the terminal stage of adolescence.

It has often been noted that the narcissistic nature of the ego ideal draws, at an early age, the body image into its realm. It is therefore no surprise that the course of ego-ideal formation is not identical for boy and girl. However, for both sexes, the function of the early ego ideal can be recognized in its aim, which is to repair or wipe out a narcissistic hurt caused by comparison with or slight by others. The narcissistic recourse to a state of an illustory self-perfection induces a sense of well-being, which is, however, acquired at the price of a certain reality distortion. With progressing ego development, such isolated distortions extend an insidious influence on the adaptive resourcefulness of the child.

The Developmental Line of the Ego Ideal in the Girl

In the psychoanalytic literature I have come across only one systematic developmental description of the female ego ideal in a paper by Jacobson (1954). It is her impression that "the little girl develops a nucleus of the true ego ideal even earlier than the little boy and in connection with the early onset of her castration conflict." The girl responds to the discovery of being castrated with a "denial of her supposed deficiency." This conflictual stage leads, over time, to the recognition of her genital anatomy and, in consequence, to an attempt to recover the lost phallus. During this phase her disillusionment in her mother is marked by accusatory, hostile rejection of the mother and depreciatory feelings about herself (body image). This preoedipal conflict finds a resolution in the recovery of the phallus via her turning to the father and "quite commonly . . . a premature relinquishment of genital activities, with withdrawal and shift of narcissistic libido from the genital to the whole body" (p. 118).

My experience confirms this shift, which can be recognized at a later stage in the tomboy when the body-phallus equation is so spectacularly displayed; the same trend can be followed in the older girl, when the body-phallus becomes the exhibitionistic, controlling, and excitatory agent of sexual arousal. A persistent preoccupation with the body-phallus tends to transport the adolescent girl into the quasi-delusional state in which she perceives all males as lusting for her. This perception, in fact, is often quite correct because the phallic-narcissistic "teasing" of her provocative aloofness tends to arouse aggressive and self-assertive sexual behavior in the male.

Jacobson further states:

> My case material left no doubt that these serious conflicts and, in particular, the dangers arising from the little girl's self-deflation and from the devaluation and threatening loss of her mother are mastered by establishment of a maternal ego ideal, though of a very premature and immature one: the ideal of an unaggressive, clean, neat, and physically attractive little girl who is determined to renounce sexual activities.
>
> Frequently we can, indeed, observe that the female ego ideal absorbs and replaces for ever the "illusory penis" fantasy [pp. 118-119].

When the little girl turns to the oedipal father, the recovery of the phallus remains an intrinsic aspect of her sexual wishes. In the pursuit of these wishes we can see a reinstatement of oral incorporative modalities which were the phase-adequate mechanism during the premature formation of her ego ideal. I might add here that these "archaic fantasies of oral and genital incorporation" of the paternal phallus constitute a normal (often pathologically fix-

ated) aspect of the late adolescent girl's strivings for perfection, be this sexually, intellectually, socially, morally, or
otherwise. My observations of this stage confirm Jacobson's
statement that the girl's tendency to regress to the primitive state of her early ego-ideal formation complicates, delays, or aborts the establishment of an independent ego, as
well as an ego ideal of a depersonified, deconcretized, and
abstracted nature. In consequence, the girl conserves a lasting tendency to the "reattachment of her ego ideal to an
outside person" (p. 119). In other words, the female ego
ideal tends to remain enmeshed, or is prone to become re-
enmeshed, in the vicissitudes of object relations.

Within this context, we have to consider the fact that
bisexuality in the female remains, throughout life, less
polarized or conflictual than is true for the male; bisexuality is therefore never subjected to a definitive resolution or
to a repression as rigid and irreversible as is, normally, the
case in the male. We look in vain, during early male puberty, for an unrestrained and ego-syntonic stage equal to
the girl's tomboy stage. Only from the analysis of the young
male adolescent do we have evidence of the boy's deeply repressed feminine wishes and identifications (Blos, 1962; see
also Chapter 7). These findings confirm the fact that both
issues of the Oedipus complex—the first, phallic; the second,
adolescent—follow a different course in boy and girl. At the
critical juncture of late adolescence, when the girl's stabilization of her femininity is to be attained, the regressive incorporation of the paternal phallus as the narcissistic regulator of her sense of completeness and perfection has to be
overcome by an enduring identification with the mother.
The desexualized and deconcretized ego ideal favors the
transformation of infantile penis envy into a striving for
perfection as a woman, removed from envy, competition,
and rapaciousness (sexual "trophy hunting"). This achievement restores a sense of well-being with the attendant assurance that a course of self-realization is indeed possible.

The inexhaustible reservoir of a propelling force toward this goal constitutes the female ego ideal and defines its narcissistic function. Nevertheless, remnants of the "reattachment of the ego ideal to an outside person," to a love object, remain, to some degree, the *sine qua non* of the female ego ideal.

Every analyst who has had adolescent girls in analysis has observed the delicate and painful state of transition from the personalized, dependent, and concretized to the autonomous, impersonal, and abstracted ego ideal. In the course toward this end, the girl often attempts to fit her primitive ego ideal into a love relationship. Her pleasure gain here lies more or less exclusively in the exercise of her power and the narcissistic restoration of the phallus; this is achieved either through vicarious possession during sexual intercourse or via genital (oral) incorporation. These stages on the road toward femininity often appear juxtaposed with eating disturbances, such as compulsive eating or dietary asceticism, which leave no doubt about the oral mechanisms involved. It is a well-known fact that adolescent eating disturbances are prevalent among girls, but a negligible occurrence among boys.

The Developmental Line of the Ego Ideal in the Boy

The first forward step in male ego-ideal development leads from primary narcissism to delusional omnipotence shared with the mother and, beyond that, to narcissistic identifications with idealized objects. These identifications become progressively tempered by the reality principle, which takes a forward leap at the time it is called upon to aid in the resolution of the Oedipus complex. The consolidation of the superego keeps flights into omnipotence and self-aggrandizement in check. The recourse to the state of infantile omnipotence becomes decisively relegated to the world of fantasy.

The creative aspect of fantasy and its expressive modalities (such as play or verbal imagination) reflect, on a
metaphorical plane, the potency and power of the procreative, preoedipal mother who has always, to some degree,
aroused the envy of the male child. This fact may, in contrast to what has been said about the girl, explain the observation that adolescent boys so frequently pine for
creativity, originality, and fame. Girls, indeed, have similar
aspirations, but these have tended to remain more forcefully
attached to the yearnings for a fulfilling relationship. Reverberations of male awe and envy of female procreation
can be detected in the male adolescent's urge to create, be
this a gadget, a fortune, a molecule, a poem, a song, or a
house. Such wishes fall far short of any characteristic we
attribute to the ego ideal; they furnish the repertoire for repetitive daydreams and usually remain shackled to these
nether regions by strong inhibitions. To illustrate, I shall
relate an incident from the analysis of a late adolescent
male patient. He reported one day that he had heard himself say aloud, talking to himself: "Now, Chris, don't be a
woman." At the time, he was languishing in daydreams,
blissfully hoping that all would turn out for the best. He
was startled by his own words, which revealed both his
wish and its refutation—and, more pointedly, his neurotic
conflict.

If the infantile need for oneness with the archaic mother
remains overly strong, the Oedipus complex falls under the
shadow of this fixation. A regressive component in the resolution of the boy's Oedipus complex can be discerned in the
narcissistic identification with the archaic, omnipotent,
phallic mother. Although, to some extent, this compromise
seems to be a rather normal aspect of the male Oedipus
complex, it must not be overlooked that whenever the
preoedipal fixation on the phallic mother weakens the
rivalrous, phallic assertion of the boy, the Oedipus complex
is destined to remain incomplete. This abnormal condition

certainly becomes evident during adolescence, if it has not already become so during the latency period. The time for the outbreak of the neurosis lies, usually, in the period of late adolescence (see Chapter 16), because the physiology of puberty tends to render a feeble masculine component more ascendant during this stage, when "the increase in genital libido produces a welcome decrease in pregenitality" (A. Freud, 1958, p. 266).

One characteristic survival of the regressive component, embedded in the Oedipus complex, is found universally in the young adolescent boy's castration anxiety in relation to the phallic mother, or to women in general (Blos, 1962; see also Chapter 7). This powerful apprehensiveness causes the boy to idealize the father and seek his protective and reassuring peership. Sharing the idealized paternal power and superiority becomes a transient source of narcissistic grandeur that will last until the sexual impulse threatens the arousal of homosexual object libido. At this point, we can observe how the ego ideal again becomes fatefully enmeshed with object-libidinal strivings due to the relatively incomplete resolution of the Oedipus complex. Only the analysis of the preoedipal and pregenital fixations and their ominous integration into the oedipal organization opens the path to mature ego-ideal structuralization. This is to say, or repeat, that the resolution of the negative Oedipus complex plays a decisive role in the forward development toward adult personality formation.

The structuralization of the mature ego ideal reduces excessive self- and object idealizations to the level of more realistic self- and object appraisals. The capacity of objectivation serves as a check against any inopportune aggrandizement of the self. From here on, the ego ideal derives its momentum from the unending flow of neutralized homosexual libido. Thus, it sustains the inexorable "striving for perfection," which is the source of narcissistic sustenance, removed from and remote to the vicissitudes of object relations. The male ego ideal enshrines, so to speak, its history from primary narcissism to the merger with maternal omnipotence and, beyond, to the oedipal love for the father. This last stage is transcended in the ego-ideal structure. Only in terms of this last and decisive step, which integrates the various epochs of the ego-ideal history in its mature structuralization, can we speak of the male ego ideal as the heir to the negative Oedipus complex (see Chapter 7). The confirmation of these conceptualizations will be served best by a consideration of ego-ideal pathology.

Ego-Ideal Pathology

It remains a surprising fact that the normal and often pervasive state of adolescent narcissism has not elicited more extensive investigations of its content, form, and transformation. It is precisely in this psychic territory of fortuitous visibility that my observations are made. I intend to use the period extending from the rise to the decline of adolescent narcissism for the study of the ego ideal. This period demonstrates its primitive as well as its mature forms and, beyond that, the steps in the process of its transformation. The failure in the formation of a mature ego ideal exemplifies, as it were, the conditions of adolescent ego-ideal pathology, highlighting the transitional as well as the final steps that are obligatory for the structuralization of an adult ego ideal.

The customary approach to the problem of adolescent narcissism relates this phenomenon to two major dynamic constellations. One pertains to object libido as it is deflected on the self. The narcissistic state of adolescence is thus regarded as a concomitant of the second individuation process (see Chapter 8), of the emotional disengagement from the internalized love and hate objects of early childhood. It is a well-known fact that these early and earliest object or part-object relations are endowed with extraordinary resources that satisfy—generally speaking—the narcissistic needs of the immature and dependent child. These primitive means of regulating self-esteem and security are easily reinstituted at periods of developmental crisis, such as adolescence. I shall only call the reader's attention to the adolescent propensity to idealize persons, ideas, goals, and endeavors; this characteristic, in conjunction with rebellious self-assertion, tends to give adolescent idealizations per se an exalted, indeed, a revered position. If, however, one views this trend toward idealization as a reliable indicator of progressive development, then its potential deterrent to maturation is ignored. It remains no easy task to discern in these idealizing manifestations the actual extent of adaptive, regressive, and defensive components.

The second dynamic constellation effecting an increase in narcissism pertains to the regressive aspect of adolescence. We observe here the revival of the primitive ego ideal as a phase-specific, but transient, self-esteem regulator. This regressive aspect has received special attention whenever its glaring pathology, especially in adolescent psychosis, dominates the clinical picture. It has received less attention as a concomitant of the regressive movement in the normal development of the ego ideal during the adolescent period. Here I intend to emphasize the temporary enmeshment of the ego ideal in the resolution of the Oedipus complex, especially of its negative component, during late adolescence.

In the past the problem of adolescent ego-ideal structuralization has received only minor attention by authors who have written on this period; only recently has this neglect been corrected. I shall omit, at this point, reference to the many contributions to the concept of the ego ideal, because these will be attended to in a later section. Since my focus is, at the moment, on ego-ideal pathology, I must first pay tribute to the one outstanding clinician and psychoanalyst who has contributed so profoundly to this subject, Annie Reich (1953, 1954, 1960). Her theoretical formulations are invariably embedded in clinical work and I shall draw freely on these findings in order to lay my own, derived from adolescent analysis, beside them for comparative study. Many features of ego-ideal pathology, as described by Annie Reich in her adult patients, can readily be observed either as transient adolescent symptoms or, in their malignant form, as a pivotal component in adolescent psychosis. Between these extremes lies a spectrum of intermediary clinical phenomena which have attracted my attention.

Archaic elements in the superego system, which includes the infantile ego ideal, often lie in dormant enclaves of a pathogenetic valence whose existence becomes apparent only at adolescence. Even though the personality, in many respects, has advanced in structure formation throughout the various phases of development, the narcissistic, more or less ego-syntonic, frequently concrete fantasies of infantile omnipotence and grandeur have never been sufficiently restrained by the reality principle. Consequently, they have failed to harmonize with the older child's perceptions, cognition, and memory; to put it briefly, they have obstructed ego development to a catastrophic extent. In this case, the pathogenetic enclaves continue to serve as the only available and workable regulators of self-esteem (via imaginary wish fulfillment) during the adolescent disillusionment in self and object. These archaic elements stay outside the realm of object love and remain in the realm of primary narcissism.

As indicated, this portentous condition often remains unnoticed during childhood. "Frequently, narcissistic ego ideals become conspicuous only in puberty" (A. Reich, 1954, p. 215). The clinical picture in adolescence, however, frequently leaves a margin of uncertainty as to the pathognomic or transiently regressive nature of these narcissistic states (Blos, 1962). To differentiate between these two pictures or "to come to an understanding of narcissistic nonpsychotic states necessitates the concept of the ego ideal" (A. Reich, 1954, p. 216). The undoing of the separation between self and idealized object always entails some disintegration of reality testing. The child's wish to be like the powerful parent becomes, if not—as normally—mastered by identificatory processes, replaced by the magic and megalomanic conviction of being the same, that is, of being his own ideal object (A. Reich, 1953) or, as it is often incorrectly labeled, his own ego ideal. What is meant here is, rather, the merger of self and idealized object, the primitive state of completeness and well-being.

It is implicit in the nature of adolescence that the primitive state of self-idealization, including the vast spectrum of magic, omnipotence, and grandiosity, becomes challenged as never before. Even with the oedipal realization of physical immaturity, the child could, at that age level, still find a modicum of perfection, if only a borrowed one, in simply living up to parental expectations. Expressions of parental overestimation, derived from their own narcissistic needs, are easily taken by the child as promises or predictions; these never fail to be called into question during adolescence. It is true that postoedipal superego criticism and the attending sense of guilt counterbalance the primitive powers of self-idealization and prevent them from ever dislodging objectivation; however, they never are extinguished. The normal state of a partially integrated and still externally regulated ego ideal of childhood undergoes a radical and lasting change during adolescence. A throwback, in the face of adolescent challenges, to the infantile ego ideal is a rather common occurrence before the more mature appraisal of object and self becomes irreversible. The second individuation process and the consolidation process of adolescence render existing self- and object representations less rigid, but more stable and realistic. If the attendant disappointments, compromises, and losses cannot be tolerated, the adolescent process is doomed to miscarry. "The exclusive production of fantasies that aim at one's own aggrandizement reveals a serious disturbance of the narcissistic balance, particularly when these fantasies persist after puberty" (A. Reich, 1960, p. 296). It is no exaggeration, in this context, to say that adolescence is comparable to the continental divide that determines, once and for all, the direction in which the ego ideal will flow from here on: either it will revert to its familiar source of origin, or it will seek a new course, untested and unknown.

Before the rock bottom of ego-ideal pathology is reached in adolescent analysis, a certain amount of preparatory work in all sectors of the personality must be accomplished. I shall mention only a recurrent theme that bears witness to the complex sources of ego-ideal pathology. What appears as the pathogenetic background is a massive, i.e., cumulative trauma within the narcissistic realm during the preoedipal period. This trauma extends its pernicious influence on the oedipal conflict, rendering it incomplete, i.e., leaving it interlocked with fixations that lie in the dyadic period. When the Oedipus complex in its incomplete state is revived in adolescence, a resolution is attempted in a regressive search for a lost narcissistic completeness through the maternal object of the dyadic period. These early fixations often represent an insurmountable obstacle to progressive development in adolescence and are acted out in an often insatiable need for object possession. This primitive object hunger seeks fulfillment on the level of physical, i.e., sexual maturity. Sexual relations of this nature are devoid of mutual empathy and the perfection of sexual performance is conspicuously pushed into the forefront.[4]

---

[4]This particular pattern of sexual behavior at late adolescence is, to a large extent, derived from the stereotyping of the so-called sexual revolution of youth. Helene Deutsch (1967), in her observations of the American college girl, has described this syndrome as one of sexual "infantilism." The reflection of this condition is always discernible in an immature state of the ego ideal.

In cases of this kind, the positive Oedipus complex takes on a prominent position early in the analysis, screening off the deeper layers of the narcissistic fixations which have been integrated in the defensive organization. The pathological concomitant of this condition is apparent in defective reality testing and in self-aggrandizement; however, if reality testing is fairly intact, we notice that the narcissistic fantasies are relegated to a split-off segment of the self- and object representations, a segment that then displays a florid infantile, sexualized life of its own. These pathological enclaves within the personality are stubbornly preserved by the patient. Any analytic effort to reach them is felt as an aggressive and hostile intrusion or as a narcissistic deprivation. Yet, by this very fact, the analyst is drawn more and more into the realm of the patient's narcissistic needs, both as a provider and as a withholder of gratification. When the patient, finally, experiences these quasi-delusional deprivations as originating and exclusively operating in his own mind, then a decisive step toward a clearer delineation between inside and outside is effected. This step toward introspection and objectivation enhances the analytic work and often carries the adolescent into a period of experimentation, ranging over the whole gamut of human activities. Whatever they may be, they usually lead back to a renewed search for narcissistic perfection in an effort to transcend a pervasive sense of worthlessness, incompleteness, and helplessness.

Sexual relationships of the type described above usually end disastrously. Again, the blame for this failure is put on the analyst, who brought it about by refusing to extend his omnipotence; now, when everything is lost, he is expected to make amends and undo the loss in a magical way. Through shifting mother and father transferences, the incomplete Oedipus complex moves, gradually, forward to its normal triadic constellation. Its negative component evokes, on the level of sexual maturity, the conflicts of bisexuality and draws the narcissistic "striving for perfection" more and more into the analytic work. Fantasies, wishes, and desires of a homosexual kind become apparent in the analytic material; this feature serves as an indicator that the patient is moving toward a resolution of the libidinal attachment to the parent of the same sex. The sex-inappropriate self-representation, inherent in this struggle, is an omnipresent occurrence in the analysis of late adolescents and renders the analytic work, for some time, particularly difficult.

The use of clinical material for the demonstration of the aforementioned propositions is encumbered by two conditions. The first encumbrance relates to the fact that ego-ideal pathology as described in the adult can be observed in late adolescence as a transient phenomenon of seeming likeness. The process of adolescent ego-ideal formation is accompanied by disturbed and disturbing mental states of varied severity. Concomitant regressive, narcissistic, self- and object-idealizing features are apt, at moments, to weaken reality testing to a point where the perception of the self, the body self, and the outer world acquire a quasi-delusional quality. When an arrest at this stage stubbornly precludes progressive development, then many an adolescent seeks psychiatric or analytic treatment. To entertain fantasies about fame, greatness, perfect love is a most common and normal feature of adolescence. It is only the pervasiveness and sameness of these fantasies and their affinity to primitive narcissistic states that render them pathological. To arrive at a differentiation between these narcissistic aspects, normal or pathological, is no easy task for the clinician.

The second encumbrance to the clinical validation of my propositions lies in the fact that integrative and synthesizing processes remain elusive and proceed in silence. The consequences of new formations—whatever they may be—surface only belatedly in observable manifestations, well after the critical point of their structuralization has passed. This is a common enough observation during analysis. Whatever triggers a new thrust of integrative processes is the consequence of antecedent analytic work and surfaces in quite disparate regions of the mind, often not at all in accordance with the analyst's expectations. This phenomenon is particularly characteristic for adolescent analysis, which, at one point or other, always leads back to the anxiety of separateness, loss, and death, followed by narcissistic restitution. The ego ideal, anchored in narcissistic self-containment, becomes, so to speak, the triumphant counter-force to the finitude of life. In its adaptive aspect, it counteracts regression, shapes adult commitments, and gives them continuity and constancy.

The extent to which the demands or expectations of society, in conjunction with adolescent psychic reorganization, are growth-promoting seems contingent on the concurrent formation of the mature ego ideal. Of course, commitments undergo change in time, but, in order to change, they must first have existed. The critical time of life in which they attain mature form and content is late adolescence. But if the adolescent fails in this task and becomes an analytic patient, then one always discovers the presence of a more or less extensive ego-ideal pathology. Assessing a patient's abnormality in functioning from the side of the ego ideal alone restricts the psychological view by the exclusion of other considerations. Nevertheless, to single out the ego ideal for intensive study is particularly suggestive in relation to late adolescence, because we deal here not only with a normative structure formation, but with one that also represents a critical factor within the structure of a given neurosis. Tracing the development of one psychic agency in relative exclusiveness is not an uncommon methodological approach in psychoanalytic research. The ancients have dignified this approach with the phrase: *ex pede Herculem.*

*Tracing the Vicissitudes of the Female Ego Ideal through the
Analysis of a Late Adolescent Girl*

The patient was a girl of eighteen who had to abandon a
successful college career when she suddenly became the victim of severe anxiety attacks. An affectionate, crushlike,
but unfulfilling and unanswered devotion to a female peer
precipitated the sudden breakdown.

Early in the analysis it became evident that, for this
girl, the ideal self and the ego ideal were still undifferentiated; an even more primitive feature was the pervasive
conviction that everything needed for the maintenance of a
stable self had an outside source, indeed an idealized source
in a withholding object. Through ingratiating and supplicat-
ing play-acting, abetted by considerable physical and mental giftedness, she experienced herself as sharing the powers
and excellences others possessed. Object attachment was
always founded on oral greed and incorporation. To be in
perfect harmony with herself, she had to incorporate the object and thereby destroy it. Guilt and panic drove her to
undo the loss and rescue the source of her narcissistic
sustenance by offering herself, again through play-acting, to
the needs, real or imagined, of the idealized object. The infantile state of feeling perfect only when unconditionally
loved remained unaltered, far beyond the symbiotic stage;
in fact, this stage was regressively evoked by any disappointment and played out, first in action and then in fantasy, for long periods of her analysis. The bearer of the excellences she admired was loved; associated fantasies of
sucking on a breast or a penis revealed the primitive nature
of such attachments. Excellences arousing her "voracious
appetite" might lie in the realm of sexual, physical,
academic, artistic, or intellectual perfection. Material pos-
sessions played a rather subordinate role.

This patient's object hunger aimed at oral appropriation
or vicarious enjoyment, through merger, of the envied

riches which others unquestionably possessed. Her pervasive sense of imcompleteness was seemingly dominated by
penis envy. In a primitive cognitive style, she attributed to
all things that mattered to her, positively or negatively, a
male or a female designation. The attainment of perfection
was, accordingly, reserved for the boy; once, when she expressed an intelligent thought in public, she experienced a
quasi-delusional conviction of possessing a penis. If we
speak of an ego ideal in this connection, it would indeed be
an infantile one, because the delusional concreteness of the
idealized body image reflects a distortion of the self-
representation that is alien to the mature ego ideal.

The analysis of penis envy was responded to by a consolidation of vocational direction and intellectual profi-
ciency, indeed, excellence. Yet, the modality of penis envy
lingered on in the exhibitionistic need for intellectual
superiority and the sadistic urge to annihilate, i.e., castrate,
her male peers. Aggressive self-idealization blocked the way
to the emergence of a deinstinctualization of the ego ideal.
The familiar dramatis personae of this emotional configuration were present: the withholding mother who preferred
the younger brother; the seduction trauma inflicted at a
tender age by a beloved, feared, and aggrandized father; the
regressive search for the good and lost nurturing mother;
the restitutive resolution through becoming a boy, albeit a
tomboy. These matters are too well known to require
amplification.

What attracted my attention was the fact that penis
envy was, partially, a secondary and defensive formation. In
other words, phallic intrusiveness and physical completeness not only were an aim in themselves, but represented,
above and beyond, an effort to resist regression to primitive
merger with the mother or, later in life, with any desired
love object. In this sense, the developmental arrest described aimed clearly, in my patient, not only at a maintenance of her separateness (individuation), but also at a pro-

tection of her femininity and at a constant, even if failing,
struggle of disengagement from the archaic mother imago.
With the receding dominance of penis envy, object idealization shifted to women, with an emphasis on oral gratification and depressive or rage reactions to disillusionment or
frustration. Then a sense of hopelessness descended on her;
ego-ideal fragments, which had slowly taken shape within
the self as distinct from the object, were swept away in an
abysmal sense of worthlessness. The withholding object
could be saved from destruction only by blaming the self as
unworthy to be given to; the sense of guilt then moved from
dyadic object destruction and its rescue to triadic jealousy,
competition, and ambivalence.

A decisive forward step in object relations and, consequently, in identificatory stability was facilitated when
the transference neurosis could deal with the splitting of
the object into good and bad, present and absent, giving and
withholding. The whole-object representation began to
emerge as reliable and constant, without requiring idealization for its survival. The reflection of this more mature object representation became apparent in a more tolerant attitude toward the self. The need to obliterate her self-
interests, in order to keep others liking or loving her,
gradually gave way to an assertion of her true self, of her
unadulterated preferences, opinions, likes, and dislikes.
True, such ego-ideal fragments retained, for a long time, a
close affinity to object relations, but the threshold of their
surrender reached a level that gave the maintenance of
self-esteem a larger margin of autonomy. At this stage, fantasy became relegated to the world of play; the reservoir of
her rich imagination opened up, invigorating her giftedness
and intelligence; in turn, both became more productive as
well as gratifying. The same could be said about her relationships and her love life. To conclude: the derivatives of
the rock-bottom yearning for the merger with the idealized
primary object, the mother, could be traced through their
transformations and recognized in the autonomous striving

for perfection, within a constant, self-determined, even if shared, endeavor toward self-realization. At this stage, the flow of narcissistic libido, derived from the exercise of the ego ideal, became the automatized regulator of self-esteem. Now, she could dispense with the use of idealization, of either self or object, and thus protect her hard-won sense of reality.

Tracing the Vicissitudes of the Male Ego Ideal through the Analysis of a Late Adolescent Boy

The patient was an eighteen-year-old college student. Unable to study he was faced with dismissal from college. He was intelligent, seemingly purposeful, personable, well built, and in good health. He had a definite life goal clearly in mind; yet the actions taken in its pursuit were tentative, self-defeating, and erratic.

It became evident early in the analysis that the patient's self-representation was extremely labile, shifting from grandiosity to self-deprecation. His efforts to make himself likeable to men of importance, including the analyst, were easily reversed whenever a critical point in his subservience was reached; he then resorted to negativism, subversion, and procrastination. Emotional withdrawal was noticeable whenever he tried to extricate himself from his passive surrender to idealized objects; he then sought refuge in narcissistic self-idealization. The grandiose self of childhood became regressively revived and temporarily served as the regulator of self-esteem. During such episodes, his sense of time as well as his judgment of others and self were disturbed. Words—on the use of which analysis relies—became masks, shields, or weapons.

It is most common during adolescence, when sexual identity formation moves into its definitive stage, that the polarity implicit in bisexuality contaminates the cognitive and perceptual spheres. What we observe is the tendency, often obsessive in nature, to assign to any opposites the

connotation of male or female. In this patient these bisexual
conflicts presented themselves for analysis via their derivatives in intellectual and behavioral spheres. Successful
academic study carried, unconsciously, a masculine designation, while going through the motions of studying represented the feminine counterpart. Fright and irritation
drew the patient into all kinds of diversions. The fixation on
the negative Oedipus complex forced the patient repeatedly
into failures and, consequently, into a panic of castration
wish and fear. His desire to be loved by the father per-
petuated preoedipal yearnings for and disappointments in
the mother; these had laid down the lasting foundation for
his fear of women and belief in their malevolent intent.
Early sexual explorations of his little sister, especially of
her incomprehensible genital (a study that was interrupted
by the latency period) left the little boy with a confused,
vague, somewhat dizzying image of the "vagina." His earliest explanation of the fact that the girl had no penis was:
"She ate it." It had become invisible. The child expected
from his research to acquire the power of controlling the
castrated, ominous female, or, more accurately, to gain her
imputed power and thus become the master of his impulses,
desires, gratifications, and fears. Here was to be found the
link to his partial identification with the female. When this
early research with its maladaptive resolution was renewed
in late adolescence, it took precedence over any other intellectual or academic curiosity. The incompleteness of the
Oedipus complex became apparent, as did the adolescent
reinstinctualization of those internal directives by which we
identify the superego and the ego ideal.

The oscillations from masculine to feminine positions as
well as the shifts from self- to object idealizations continued
their stubborn repetitiveness under many disguises. In fact,
their circularity gave the impression that they were feeding
on each other. The assault on narcissistic self-idealization
by reality disappointments evoked, in turn, the need for object idealization; through this shift, narcissistic gratification

was restored by sharing the object's perfection and being loved by it. To illustrate: when the patient missed some analytic sessions he entertained the fantasy that his absence would give his analyst the time to work on a book; thus, the analyst would more speedily become a famous man and, in turn, a richer source of narcissistic gratification for the patient, who had been, after all, a silent promoter of the achievement.

When the patient eventually overcame his sexual inhibitions, he reformulated, with a sense of conviction, his vocational goal. However, this progress again came to an impasse through the rather persistent instinctualization of the ego ideal. The analytic work revealed a paradoxical finding. As already mentioned, the preoedipal object tie to the mother was wrought with disappointment, aggression, and fear; these affects, in their full infantile force, sought alleviation by his turning preoedipal object libido onto the father and identifying with the submissive, degraded mother. The father not only became the recipient of the oedipal idealization, but, in addition, he remained the object of the proedipal idealizations of the omnipotent mother. Whatever was bad and evil was split off from the idealized object representation and assigned to the female, especially her genital. The ego ideal, at this stage, reflected, in comparable fashion, divided avenues toward perfect self-realization, namely, those of masculine and feminine strivings.

The analysis of the transference neurosis led to the reconstruction and re-experiencing of infantile ambivalence, which, on the adolescent level, was repeated in homosexual and heterosexual fantasies. Among these, a dream was particularly important because it laid bare the patient's wish for and revulsion of his father's acceptance of him as a girl. It was not until the fixation on the negative Oedipus complex was analyzed that the patient's conscious guiding principles, his ambitions and goals, acquired a constancy that remained unaffected by emotional or circumstantial exigencies. The need for instantaneous self-idealization in the face of tension was replaced by a rather evenly sustained striving toward a goal that would be, at no point in time, attained; yet, at each point in time, appropinquated. The desexualization of the infantile ego ideal at late adolescence made this shift in ego-ideal functioning possible. In the train of this change, one could observe the emergence of a characterological consolidation which tended, in effect, to integrate and automatize the influence of the mature ego ideal on personality functioning. The attainment of sexual identity appears in this process a prerequisite for the formation of the mature ego ideal.

It is of interest to note that only after the resolution of the negative Oedipus complex was accomplished could the patient find his way back to the emotional entanglements with the mother of early childhood. To the astonishment of the analyst and, later to the patient, these had played a most insignificant role in the treatment up to this time. Finally, they appeared in full force, via replications and their attempted corrections, in a love relationship. This attachment was the first one that was not sexually exploitative of the female, but affectionate and caring, despite the imperfections of the partner. These imperfections were recognized with chagrin, but they did not render the woman degraded or unlovable. The mature ego ideal afforded the young man constancy of self-realization and, in the attendant exercise of the striving for perfection, he had found a reasonable independence from the idealized object and the idealized self. The clear distinction between reality and fantasy had gently closed the door on the world of childhood.

Comments on the History of the Ego-Ideal Concept

There is no doubt that the literature on the superego is voluminous, in contrast to ego-ideal investigations. Yet, cursory references to the ego ideal abound, even though the specific meaning of the term can often be inferred only from the context in which it appears. The imprecision of the term plagues us to this day. The distinction between superego and ego ideal has been discussed again and again, and so has the place of the ego ideal in the mental organization. Is the ego ideal a substructure of the ego or the superego? Or is it a separate agency of the mind? Does it acquire an affiliation with both in the course of development and, specifically, during adolescent psychic restructuring? Does its original function change with the maturation of the ego and the adolescent reorganization of the superego? In which way, if at all, is the ego ideal influenced, even determined, by the vicissitudes of object relations? Is shame, rather than guilt, the characteristic response to ego-ideal failures? Furthermore, from where does the ego ideal draw the energy for its maintenance? Should the need to preserve the life line to primary narcissism account for the forceful assertiveness of the ego ideal throughout life? The question then arises: How is ego-ideal content altered with the progressive development of the ego? What are the connections, if any, that become established, over time, between the ego ideal and the three structures of the mind? And, finally, what accounts for the faulty development that leads to ego-ideal pathology?

Many of these questions have been dealt with in the literature only marginally and suggestively, while some have been singled out for detailed discussion. In an attempt to scrutinize anew the problem of the ego ideal I have chosen to view it from the vantage point of the developmental, but normative, crisis of adolescence. In doing so, I take advantage of the disintegration and reorganization of psychic structure during this period. In the literature of the ego-ideal concept, there are many references which have had a suggestive influence on my own observations and conclusions. Therefore, I shall now turn to a historical, if selective, account of the subject under discussion.[5]

[5]I shall not attempt to give a comprehensive historical account of the ego-ideal concept, as this has been done by several authors (Sandler, Holder, and Meers, 1963; Hammerman, 1965; Hunt, 1967; Bressler, 1969; Steingart, 1969).

It is a well-known fact that Freud's (1914b) original use of the term "ego ideal" blended in its definition with that of the superego, as we define it today. Both terms were used synonymously until Freud replaced the term "ego ideal" by the term "superego" in 1923. The original ambiguity of the concept in Freud's writings seems to have been due to the irreconcilable sources and functions of this single psychic agency. The heterogeneity of origin is to be found in primary narcissism and the identificatory processes. In his essay "On Narcissism" (1914b) Freud defined the ego ideal in a way that tries to reconcile its narcissistic origin with the vicissitudes of object libido. The distinction between superego and ego ideal rests progressively on their mode of operation, namely, on the prohibiting and punitive nature of the superego and the nature of wish fulfillment that pertains to the ego ideal (Lampl-de Groot, 1962). This distinction is clearly achieved in "The Ego and the Id" (1923a). Following this clarification, ego ideal, as a technical term, disappears almost completely from Freud's writings (Strachey, 1961).

I return to Freud's intermediary use of the term "ego ideal" in which narcissism and object libido are fused (1914b), because this amalgamation corresponds to my own observations in adolescent analysis. Of course, Freud did not have the adolescent process in mind, but reflected on his clinical observations in adults and, I venture to say, male patients, when he brought the two concepts (narcissism and object libido) together; these later became distinct and separate aspects of the same system, the superego. In the adult patient we often encounter great difficulty in tracing the respective influence of one or the other to the cogent developmental stage. This difficulty is, of course, not surprising because the deviate emotional development that underlies any psychological abnormality implies ipso facto that the adolescent process has been left incomplete in one way or another. The importance I attribute to adolescent psychic restructuring in the final formation of the ego ideal would point to fixations that, strictly speaking, precede those of the superego.

The narcissistic nature of the concept "ego ideal" was implicit in Freud's definition from the very beginning; it was but a small step to tie it together with the narcissistic mode of object choice: "what possesses the excellence which the ego lacks for making it an ideal, is loved" (Freud, 1914b, p. 101). This primitive mode of object choice reappears in adolescence and generally enmeshes ideal formation with object-libidinal aims. In fact, I have observed this enmeshment with regularity in adolescent analysis; it renewed my interest in Freud's early clinical findings, regardless of the incomplete state of his theory building at the time. The pertinent lines I have in mind read as follows: "In this way large amounts of libido of an essentially homosexual kind are drawn into the formation of the narcissistic ego ideal and find outlet and satisfaction in maintaining it" (p. 96). It becomes evident from the succeeding paragraph that Freud drew his observation from the paranoid patient who revolts against the "censoring agency" in the effort to "liberate himself from all these influences" and secures his independence by his "withdrawal of homosexual libido" from the parental domination. This condition is precisely what one frequently observes in male adolescent analysis; I dare assume that this process is a transient and normal state of adolescent development or, more precisely, of the adolescent resolution of the negative Oedipus complex.

It should be mentioned at this point that Freud conceived of the ego-ideal content as "imposed from without" (1914b, p. 100). In so doing, he went beyond the individualistic meaning of the term and related the ego ideal to a social function, i.e., to a dynamic role in group psychology (1921). Due to the fact that group formation "binds homosexual libido," this aspect of social behavior acquires an important function in libido economy: it elevates self-esteem by shared values and aspirations and thus lowers the sense of guilt and social anxiety. A convincing *demonstratio ad oculos* of this phenomenon and the dynamics outlined above can be witnessed in the spontaneous and intense peer group formation of adolescents. These groups are more prominent among boys than girls; the need for this kind of group formation fades away with the advance to adulthood or, as my analytic observations have convinced me, with the formation of the adult ego ideal. Disapproval by the peer group or its value system possesses a most powerful influence on the individual member and induces him to sacrifice, usually transiently, well-established ego and superego norms.

The distinction between superego and ego ideal became less of a theoretical issue for Freud after he had traced the origin of the superego back to the earliest object cathexes and their transformation into identifications, i.e., introjections (1923a). He saw their conflictual involvement in the triadic constellation of the Oedipus complex as being resolved by superego structuralization with ego-ideal components closely built into it. As a consequence of this inclusive conceptualization, the ego-ideal concept became dispensable to Freud's theory building. He did not refer to it again until 1933 when we find a return to the 1914 formulation (Strachey, 1961): an "important function" attributed to the superego is to act as "the vehicle [*Träger*] of the ego ideal by which the ego measures itself, which it emulates, and whose demand for ever greater perfection it strives to fulfil" (Freud, 1933, pp. 64-65). In an editorial footnote, Strachey points out that at this stage of theory building Freud included the upholding of ideals as part of the moral enforcements that constitute the superego.

It is of interest to note that the ego ideal as conceptualized in 1914 represents "the substitute for the lost narcissism of his childhood in which he was his own ideal" (p. 94). In contrast, in 1933 Freud emphasizes that the "ego ideal is the precipitate of the old picture of the parents, the expression of admiration for the perfection which the child then attributed to them" (p. 65). The later formulation pre-supposes a more advanced ego development than does the first one, which refers to the primitive state of primary nar-cissism. Both views have a bearing on the ego ideal as de-velopmentally conceived.

There are good reasons to assume that the postoedipal consolidation of the superego exerts an influence on ego ideal as well. Hartmann and Loewenstein (1962) have put this issue succinctly: "To us it seems reasonable to view the specific character of the ego ideal which is part of the superego in close relation to those other developments which originate in the oedipal conflicts and to distinguish the resulting 'ego ideal' from earlier idealizations. We meet here again an issue which is ubiquitous in psychoanalysis . . . the distinction of genetic continuity and functional characterization" (pp. 59-60). It is, essentially, this kind of approach that has prompted me to view adult ego-ideal formation in the context of adolescence, where the second and final step in the resolution of the Oedipus com-plex is taken.

Returning to my historical theme, it can be observed that 1923 marked the time when the ego ideal had found its secure place, as the narcissistic component of the superego, within the tripartite structure of the mind. The disappear-ance of the term from Freud's writings, with only a cursory reference to it in 1933, and no mention of it at all in the "Outline" (1940), set a trend that is quite noticeable in the psychoanalytic literature. The distinction between the con-cepts of the ego ideal and the ideal ego, of the ideal self and of self- and object idealizations, often became blurred in their usage, but the term "ego ideal" continued to connote a specialized function of the superego.

The relative hiatus in ego-ideal research lasted until about the 1950s. During that decade we notice the upsurge of a renewed interest in the concept of the ego ideal, its place in mental organization, its origin and development, and its specific role in psychopathology. Dating from around that time, an ever-increasing number of papers dealing with the ego-ideal concept in normal and abnormal development attested to the need for an intensive reassessment of the psychic agency called the ego ideal. The widening interest can be attributed, at least partially, to the shift, over time, from symptom neuroses to conditions of ego pathology and a prominence of disturbances rooted in the narcissistic sector of the personality. No doubt, infant studies, child analytic research, and longitudinal studies in child development aided the clarification of the ego ideal. At any rate, from the extensive research accrued a more useful conceptual tool for diagnostic, therapeutic (technical), and prognostic thinking. The continuity of the concept, from its inception to this day, is reflected in the universal agreement that the ego ideal's roots lie in the stage of primary narcissism.

The clinical papers by Annie Reich (1953, 1954, 1960) stand in the forefront of the renewed interest in the ego ideal; she lucidly described ego-ideal pathology within the context of narcissistic disturbances. Her clinical studies led her to the conclusion that the ego-ideal concept was indispensable for the delineation and understanding of the cases she reported. Her major contributions to the ego-ideal concept have been referred to in the preceeding section on pathology and need not be repeated here.

Instead of reviewing individual contributions to the ego-ideal concept, I shall discuss the literature in terms of five lines of thought: (1) the location of the ego ideal within the psychic structures; (2) the developmental point of view as applied to the ego ideal; (3) the reinstinctualization of the ego ideal at adolescence; (4) the differences and similarities between the infantile and the mature ego ideal; (5) the sociocultural determinants of ego-ideal content.

The question of location within the psychic structures

has been tossed about for some time without ever having reached a clear consensus of opinion. Is the ego ideal a substructure of the ego or of the superego? This question of "location" has been poignantly brought to our attention by Piers and Singer (1953), who discern discrete affects, elicited by either superego or ego-ideal failures. They refer to the affect of guilt as characteristic for the tension between superego and ego and that of shame as typically derived from violations of the ego ideal. Intrinsic distinctions between the two agencies are further elaborated by Lampl-de Groot (1962), who states that the superego sets boundaries ("prohibiting agency") while the ego ideal sets goals ("agency of wish fulfillment"). Yet, although Piers and Singer draw a distinction between the two agencies by describing their characteristic nature, they leave aside the question of location. One gains the impression that they view the two agencies as separate structures.

Bing, McLaughlin, and Marburg (1959) have argued that the "ego ideal is 'anatomically' a part of the ego." Viewing the superego and ego ideal along genetic, functional, and structural lines, a separation of the two seems a logical conclusion. Lampl-de Groot (1962), on the basis of genetic and adaptive considerations, concludes that the ego ideal is "an established substructure (or province) within the ego" and can be looked at as "an ego function," but, even in its most highly developed form it "remains essentially an agency of wish fulfillment" (p. 98). Jacobson (1964), expressing her basic agreement with these opinions, states that it would be "more correct to consider the ego ideal an ego formation rather than a part of the superego system" (p. 186). Even though this quote conveys a definite opinion, it should be mentioned that in her further discussion of the subject Jacobson acknowledges the fact that, with progressive ego development, the ego ideal "gradually bridges the two systems and may ultimately be claimed by both" (p. 187). The aforementioned opinions stand, more or less clearly, in opposition to the formulation advanced by Hartmann and Loewenstein (1962), who consider the ego ideal an aspect of the superego system. This controversy of long standing brings me to the second question.

The fact that so many authors have argued the issue of "location" without ever reaching a consensus is very likely an indication of the intrinsic ambiguity of the term. The concept of the ego ideal has suffered all along from conceptual imprecision, inasmuch as, on the one hand, it has been used to suggest a psychic agency, namely, a component of psychic structure, and, on the other, it has been defined by content, as apparent in expressions like "this and that are his ego ideals." The intrinsic ambiguity seems to stem from the fact that the ego ideal's affinity to, or separateness from, the systems ego and superego is a mere reflection of various stages in ego-ideal development, along an ongoing process of structure formation. For this very reason, Steingart (1969) has argued that the ego ideal be viewed in terms of "psychic apparatus development" and within the conceptual framework of self- and object representations. He thus carries forward the ideas of Hartmann and Loewenstein (1962), who took a developmental approach to the concept of the ego ideal; they pointed out that the preoedipal ego ideal reflects drive-gratifying wishes of aggrandizement, in contrast to that of the phallic-oedipal period, when idealization encompasses increasingly new issues. Esman (1971) follows the same path in viewing the ego ideal's changing function in relation to developmental tasks—for example, the support it lends to the sublimatory efforts characteristic of the latency period.

The developmental approach to the ego-ideal concept would imply, then, that the ego ideal takes over functions that for some time had been closely joined to the superego, or that the ego ideal receives accretions of content derived from the ego in terms of inculcated or self-chosen values and goals; such choices can, of course, be made only on the basis of experience, judgment, or generally on the basis of relative ego maturity. The ego ideal, then, becomes an aspect or a reflection of the individual's identity. In other words, the ego ideal ceases, progressively, to be the agency of wish fulfillment through either fantasy or identification. In the course of development, not only ego-ideal content, but also its function undergo changes. One crucial state in the evolution of the ego ideal can best be studied in adolescence when, normally, a reinstinctualization of the ego ideal as well as of the superego occurs. Before we investigate this aspect of the ego ideal, however, it seems imperative that we consider the broader question of developmental progression and the theoretical consequences of such an approach.

The distinction between a primitive and a mature ego ideal is widely accepted. The relation between adolescence and ideal formation has generally been recognized since the time of Aristotle, but the genetic antecedents of this adolescent characteristic have still to be explored in their complexity. We distinguish heterogeneous and discrete aspects in the adolescent-specific proclivity to idealization. These trends range from self-idealization and its externalization to the integrated and subjectively self-evident nature of thought and action. The automatization of the mature ego ideal weaves its function into the context and function of character. The decisive role of the ego ideal in the maintenance of the narcissistic balance, experienced as self-esteem, has too often been stressed to need any elaboration at this point.

It has been said that "the ego ideal can be considered a rescue operation for narcissism" (Hartmann and Loewenstein, 1962, p. 61). This statement, undoubtedly, expresses an opinion of general agreement, but leaves a broader question open, namely, the one of changing content and the specific means—even if the aim remains the same—by which the "rescue operation" is kept in a never-ending state of alertness. The above quote might be paraphrased by say-

ing that the gain of narcissistic supplies is as essential to
personality functioning as object-directed libidinal and aggressive gratifications. When the latter give rise to the
well-known conflicts at adolescence, "object-libidinal strivings are regressively replaced by identifications of the
... early infantile kind" (A. Reich, 1954, p. 215). It is
often only in puberty, as Annie Reich remarks, that the fixation on the infantile ego ideal is revealed. Heightened
castration anxiety leads to the regressive cathexis of compensatory narcissism, or, I would add, to a retreat from the
adolescent resuscitation of the Oedipus complex. Under
these conditions, a mature ego ideal cannot be formed, nor
can mature object relations be attained.

The fact that the ego ideal acquires structuralization
during adolescence renders it qualitatively different from its
antecedent developmental stages, as has been clearly stated
by Jacobson (1964, p. 187): "In fact, the final stages [adoles-
cence] in the development of the ego ideal demonstrate
beautifully the hierarchic reorganization and final integration of different—earlier and later—value concepts, arising
from both systems [ego and superego], into a new coherent
structure and functional unit," namely, the ego ideal. Adolescent psychic restructuring in relation to ego-ideal formation has been affirmed by other authors as well. Murray
(1964) searches out the pathways that lead to the mature
ego ideal; he attributes to the early narcissistic state of the
ego ideal the attitude of "entitlement" (pregenital) and
postulates a sublimation of narcissism and of the affects attached to libidinal objects that are part of the ego-ideal organization. It is of interest to note Murray's clinical observation which he summarizes by saying "that the narcissistic
libido, centered in the ego ideal, returns to the ego to re-
cathect unconscious latent homosexual elements when the
ideal is lost or dimmed" (p. 487). While Murray extends
Freud's (1914b) formulation, he also emphasizes, if I follow
him correctly, the object-libidinal affects that predestine the

ego ideal to become enmeshed in the adolescent conflict of having to forego pregenital entitlements "in favor of the more ideal-oriented relationships with mature libidinal fulfillments, individual and social aims and relations" (p. 500). Murray considers the ego ideal a psychic agency with close ties to the systems ego and superego. The distinctness of the mature ego ideal is defined and preserved by its intersystemic ties, similar to that of a planet whose orderly motion is regulated by the gravitational interaction with other celestial bodies.

A case report which lays bare the determinants—talent being one of them—as well as the dynamics of the ego ideal in the life of a creative scientist is presented by Giovacchini (1965). The analysis of this patient revealed the child's narcissistic dependency on the overpowering preoedipal mother and the young boy's effort to extricate himself from this stifling, yet exhilarating relationship through the re-creation of an idealized father image, embodied in "the canons of science." However, the repressed, object-libidinal components operating within the patient's extraordinary scientific achievements, which represented his ego ideal, not only disrupted his creativity by periods of depression, but, in addition, rendered his object relations to men and women ambivalent and ungratifying. My propositions regarding the formation of the male ego ideal find a convincing clinical demonstration in Giovacchini's case, even though his formulations are not identical with those I have proposed.

A cumulative consensus can be noted in the literature, asserting that a change in content and quality of the ego ideal and of the superego occurs during adolescence, reviving, in its wake, the infantile states of the ego ideal and of the superego as well (Hammerman, 1965). Ritvo (1971), for instance, concludes: "The ego ideal as a structuralized institution of the mind is a development of adolescence" (p. 255). Kohut (1971), in a more general comment, follows a complementary line of thought: "an important firming and buttressing of the psychic apparatus, especially in the area of the establishment of reliable ideals, takes place during latency and puberty, with a *decisive final step in late adolescence"* (p. 43; italics mine). Comparing the primitive and the mature forms of ego ideal and superego, Novey (1955) concludes that the mature ego ideal is acquired later than the oedipal superego. This opinion is widely confirmed; it implies a certain inflexibility of the superego, which is only relatively weakened during the adolescent period by the ascendancy of the ego ideal, as well as by the expansion of the ego. These matters pertain to the topic of personality consolidation and character formation in late adolescence (Blos, 1962; see also Chapter 9). Even though they are more than marginal to my subject, I shall not pursue them further here, but stay within the narrow limits I have set myself.

The condition *sine qua non* for a successful resolution of the adolescent crisis is "predicated," according to Aarons (1970), "upon the preservation of the ego ideal, inculcated but not yet integrated during childhood" (p. 309). Furthermore, he states that the ego ideal is intrinsically correlated with the attainment of object constancy, which I would place between eighteen months and three years. This opinion dates the formation of the infantile ego ideal later than is usually accepted. I conceive of the condition for mature ego-ideal formation in terms of the attainment of post-ambivalent object relations, rather than in terms of object constancy as stated by Aarons (1970): "Adolescence is a test of object constancy and of the integration of the ego ideal. The two are interrelated" (p. 327). Nevertheless, his view that the advance from adolescence to adulthood is intrinsically predicated upon ego-ideal development, from primitive to mature, as well as his opinion that the ego ideal at adolescence becomes enmeshed with regressively revived libidinal-aggressive infantile object relations, are in agreement with my own observations.

Along this line of thought, Alexander's (1970) paper should be mentioned, because it touches on a characteristic of adolescence, namely, the striving toward independence; he assigns to the ego ideal a major role in sustaining this trend. "If the ego ideal contains in a strongly cathected way the ideal of independence, then the ego will expend the drive energies in such a manner as to achieve the skills and masteries which make independence possible, that is, through learning" (p. 55). Of course, what is implied here is the content of the ego ideal rather than the ego ideal as a structural element or psychic agency. Mature emotional independence, so it seems to me, is the byproduct of the successful advancement toward genitality; in other words, not until infantile object dependencies have been transcended, can the mature ego ideal unfold.

Both Murray (1964) and Hunt (1967) assign to libidinal fixations and conflicts a decisive influence in determining the vicissitudes of the ego ideal. Murray's statement, based on Freud's (1914b) essay, reads as follows: "If the relationship between the ego ideal and its appropriate potential for fulfillment fails, the libido returns to a strong intensification of the homosexual impulses, which in turn create guilt and great upsurges of social anxiety" (p. 502). Grete Bibring (1964) emphasizes the fact that "genetically it [the ego] derives its strength mainly from positive libidinal strivings in contrast to the superego, in which aggressive forces prevail" (p. 517). This view is supported by the clinical finding that the ego ideal holds its reins in an unambivalent fashion.

Pursuing the interrelation between the ego ideal and instinctual life, I turn to a paper by Hunt (1967). His case discussion, based on my own formulations (Blos, 1962) and those of Annie Reich (1954), among others, affirms the intrinsic relatedness between ego-ideal pathology and insufficiently attenuated homosexual trends. "The ego ideal as discussed here in regard to homosexuality, involves the persistence of a magical, omnipotent form with aspirations of

creating an ideal state through forming primary identifications with objects" (p. 242). Whenever homosexuality, latent
or manifest, has become the major regulator of the narcissistic equilibrium, the ego ideal remains arrested on an infantile level. The same holds true for the perpetual re-
cidivistic criminal (Murray, 1964) and for the impostor
(Deutsch, 1964), who are examples of what Murray (1964)
has called the "fragmented ego ideal." Ritvo (1971) confirms
these findings when he speaks of the reinstinctualization of
the ego ideal by predominantly homosexual libido as a normative aspect of the adolescent process.

As a last point of this historical review I shall point to
the progressive refinement and sharper delineation of the
ego-ideal concept as it emerges alongside the elaborations of
the concept of the self. Upon closer scrutiny, we often come
to recognize that what appears to constitute an ego ideal is
but a self-aggrandizement, an imitation, as it were, of a
wishful self-image (Jacobson, 1964). What has been described as a false ego ideal might also be referred to as a
primitive, infantile, or archaic one.

In discussing the ontogenesis of the ego ideal, Freud
(1914b) never fails to point to the fact that the content of
the ego ideal is "imposed from without" (p. 100). It includes
not only a personal propensity, but also the ideal of such social formations as family, class, and nation. This is to say
that prevailing value systems as well as social organizations and institutions always stand ready, in every society,
to channel individual narcissistic trends towards goals of a
"common ideal." Whatever the ensuing irrationalities and
distortions, which are due to persistent narcissistic self- and
object idealizations, their form and content are always derived from the social system in which the individual lives.

An exploration of some of these sociocultural factors is
undertaken by Tartakoff (1966), who traces the interpene-
tration of ego-ideal content and social institutions in American culture. Tartakoff concludes that "narcissism may
undergo a special fate in our social structure" (p. 226) or,

more pointedly, "A sociocultural setting which emphasizes the goal of success may perpetuate narcissistic and omnipotent fantasies" (p. 245). This infantile component of the ego ideal, if not relegated to playful fantasy and corrective self-irony, can permeate the analytic situation, turning it into another chance, where "hard work" will bring about an excellence that was once promised and still awaits fulfillment with that pertinacity so characteristic of infantile narcissistic "entitlements." In following ego-ideal content over time, Tartakoff concludes that while narcissistic fantasies do not change, content (values, goals, norms, institutional means) is subject to epochal shifts. To this I would add that the socio-cultural imprint can also be detected in its negative form, e.g., in the adolescent who "opts out."

This consideration bring me to extensions of the ego-ideal concept which, in my opinion, run counter to a developmental conceptualization of the term. Kaplan and Whitman (1965) have proposed the concept of the "negative ego ideal," which they define as "the introjected negative standards of the parents and of the culture" (p. 183). It is suggested that the "devalued parent" forms the core of the negative ego ideal. With this formulation we are forced to abandon the idealizing quality and the genetic history of the ego ideal as it is presently understood. The negative ego ideal is ego-alien, and so is its denigrating content. These conditions, it seems to me, reflect a persistent sadomasochistic tie to the preoedipal parent that is transposed onto the level of values. In accordance with my proposition, this fact alone disqualifies it from the realm of the mature ego ideal and relegates it to an infantile, perverted ideal self. Schafer (1967) also speaks of negative ideals, e.g., "to be a superior con man or a brute" (p. 165), but he does not identify them with the mental structure "ego ideal." The concept of the negative ego ideal can probably best be accommodated within the concept of the self.

In viewing the developmental levels of the ego ideal, we come to recognize a correspondence between the function and content of the ego ideal, on the one hand, and the age-specific level of ego development and physical maturation, on the other. The study of the transitions along this path of ego-ideal formation, its deviancy and arrest, has attracted ever-widening attention. The concept of the ideal self, in contradistinction to the ego ideal, has been elaborated by Sandler, Holder, and Meers (1963); they point to the difficulties, theoretical and clinical, attached to the differentiation between the two, in the indexing of child analytic material at the Hampstead Clinic. This finding only emphasizes the affinity or identity of ideal self and ego ideal as antecedent to their gradual differentiation within the context of developmental progression.

In the field of applied psychoanalysis, the ego-ideal concept has been used in relation to literary figures for an explication of their characteristic features. Murray (1964), for instance, has used this approach to Rostand's *Cyrano de Bergerac* and Oscar Wilde's *Dorian Gray*. But the one personality, studied in depth and portrayed in terms of the ego-ideal consolidation of late adolescence, is Prince Hal. This Shakespearean character displays the enigmatic contradictions of youth—debauchery and high idealism—in flamboyant fashion. Throughout his bewildering actions, Prince Hal never loses touch with his inner struggle. The consolidation of the ego ideal lies at the center of this struggle, in which he first fails, but finally succeeds by reconciling the idealized father imago he loves with the imperfect, if not downright evil, father person he hates. Had his father, the king, not murdered his own cousin, Richard II, whom Hal had followed to Ireland as a boy, whom he idealized, and whose favor he had won?

The son-father conflict of Prince Hal has attracted the attention of several psychoanalysts. Ernst Kris (1948) has interpreted Prince Hal's conduct within the Oedipus complex and the ambivalence conflict that vacillates between obedience, flight, and parricide. The defensive and adaptive role of ideal formation, in the effort to transcend the infantile conflict, is clearly stated. The Lichtenbergs (1969) shift the focus to that "aspect of adolescent development by which a particular adolescent achieves the formation of his ideals" (p. 874). Prince Hal is also the subject of a study by Aarons (1970), who views the son-father conflict in relation to the vicissitudes of the ego ideal. The two components central to this theme are those of object love (the negative Oedipus complex) and object idealization, as I had described them earlier in their intrinsic connection to adolescent ego-ideal formation (Blos, 1962; see also Chapter 7). Prince Hal, indeed, represents a dramatic character of extraordinary plausibility when viewed by Aarons within the ego-ideal concept. The author illuminates Prince Hal's flight from royal dignity at the court to the carousal at the tavern by pointing out that, through peer relationship, the "tie of dependence is broken" and a "recathexis of the ego ideal for which the father stood" is made possible. Aarons calls this the "renewal" of the ego ideal and defines it "as the rescue and reaffirmation of the ego ideal—a sublimation of the love for the father" (p. 333). In surveying the psychoanalytic studies of Prince Hal, from 1948 to 1970, we notice a gradual shift of focus from oedipal strivings to idealization and disillusionment, that is, to the problem of adolescent ego-ideal formation. Falstaff, a split-off father imago, along with the peer world and his drinking companions, reconstitute a proxy family which—by a grand detour—assists the troubled youth in the formation of the mature ego ideal and the assumption of his princely identity. These tumultuous events illustrate the renewed object enmeshment or the reinstinctualization of the idealized object, from which the mature ego ideal emerges.

Epilogue

In using the word "genealogy" in the title of this essay, I had a double reference in mind. One aspect traces the ancestral sources from which the mature ego ideal emerges during late adolescence, and the other traces through the psychoanalytic literature the antecedents of the concept as it stands today. These two explorations, ontogenetic and historical, leave no doubt as to the complexity of both the psychic structure formation and the concept as such. In fact, their complexity defies summary or condensation. I can, however, state what I endeavored to accomplish, namely, to present a developmental view of the ego ideal as it can be reconstructed in its primitive form and as it can be observed *in statu nascendi* in its mature structuralization during the psychic reorganization of adolescence. Clinical observations of contemporary late adolescents give ample evidence of the fact that ego-ideal pathology represents, in the majority of cases, a considerable sector of any disturbance at this age. Erroneously, derivatives of ego-ideal pathology are, in many instances, subsumed under ego and superego deviations. If the concept "ego ideal" can be defined with sufficient specificity to be useful as a theoretical indicator and instrument, then a refinement and deepening of adolescent analysis and psychotherapy may well follow; to delineate the concept toward this end has been the purpose of this investigation.

The study of the ego ideal has impressed upon me ideas of a speculative nature; somehow, no writer on the ego-ideal concept can escape this invitation. The ego ideal spans an orbit that extends from primary narcissism to the "categorical imperative," from the most primitive form of psychic life to the highest level of man's achievements. Whatever these achievements may be, they emerge from the paradox of never attaining the sought-after fulfillment or satiation, on the one hand, and of their never-ceasing pursuit, on the other. This search extends into the limitless future that blends into eternity. Thus, the fright of the finitude of time, of death itself, is rendered nonexistent, as it once was in the state of primary narcissism.

In its mature form, the ego ideal weakens the punitive

power of the superego by taking over some of its function; equally, ego aspects become engaged in its service. The realm of the ego ideal, borrowing Nietzsche's words, lies beyond good and evil. Piers and Singer (1953) speak of the ego ideal as a "magic belief in one's invulnerability or immortality to make for physical courage and to help counteract realistic fears of injury and death" (p. 26). Potentially, the ego ideal transcends castration anxiety, thus propelling man toward the incredible feats of creativity, heroism, sacrifice, and selflessness. One dies for one's ego ideal rather than let it die. "Here I stand, I cannot do otherwise" were Luther's words at the Diet of Worms, when he was urged, under great peril to himself, to recant his belief. The ego ideal is the most uncompromising influence on the conduct of the mature individual: its position always remains unequivocal.

Chapter 16

The Epigenesis of the Adult Neurosis

It is my intent here to delineate the specific contribution of
adolescence to the formation of the adult neurosis. Even
though only one aspect of this issue will be explored here,
its precise conceptualization should sharpen the clinical eye
and lead to the investigation of other, related problems,
such as the shift from a particular childhood neurosis to the
somewhat different neurosis that might emerge during the
postadolescent period. It is not a daring assertion to state
that the psychic restructuring that takes place in adolescence exerts, in some fashion, a decisive influence on the
adult personality, regardless of whether the outcome of this
process is a normal or a pathological one.

I shall begin by discussing the concept of the infantile
neurosis from a developmental point of view. In the course
of that discussion, I shall have to take another look at some
well-known facts pertaining to the distinction between child
and adult neurosis as well as between transference and
transference neurosis. I do this in order to indicate the links
connecting my proposition with the body of psychoanalytic
theory. In tracing the formation of the adult neurosis, I
shall be paying special attention to adolescence, particularly
late adolescence. Finally, I shall support my thesis with

First published in *The Psychoanalytic Study of the Child,* 27:106-135. New
York: Quadrangle, 1972.

clinical material. The way in which my proposition affects both theory and technique will be dealt with throughout this presentation.

A Developmental View of the Infantile Neurosis

The psychoanalytic tenet that an infantile emotional disturbance lies at the core of every adult neurosis has survived many years of discussion. This clinical fact has become so closely linked with the definition of the adult neurosis that the latter has often been construed as the mere repetition or continuation of an illness originating in prelatency. This simplistic formulation, however, has been challenged by child observation, longitudinal studies, and child analysis, which have pointed out the diffuse and transitory nature of most infantile disturbances, as well as the fact that these are, more or less, a ubiquitous part of normal child development. It has been generally accepted, moreover, that prelatency disturbances are unreliable predictive indicators of the nature and severity of an adult illness. No uniquely delineated clinical entity constituting the infantile neurosis has been found by the observer of early childhood, nor, conversely, are neurotic compromise solutions of an internalized conflict ever absent from early childhood; yet, in every analysis of an adult neurosis—every analysis, that is, of the transference-neurosis type—the infantile neurosis never fails to appear.

From longitudinal studies, says Anna Freud (1965), "There emerged first a disappointing discovery concerning a discrepancy between infantile and adult neurotics. . . . there is no certainty that a particular type of infantile neurosis will prove to be the forerunner of the same type of adult neurosis. On the contrary, there is much clinical evidence which points in the opposite direction" (pp. 151-152). Once we acknowledge the prognostic fallibility of the so-called infantile neurosis, we are forced to discard the idea of any direct, monocausal connection between the specific nature of an infantile disturbance and the specific nature of an adult neurosis. For example, a phobic neurosis of childhood may well change, in adulthood, into a compulsive-obsessional neurosis.[1]

A further dissimilarity appears in the degree to which symptoms or personality traits are integrated into the personality structure. In children, these can exist in a rather insular separateness, while in the adult the neurosis has permeated the entire personality structure, so that what we encounter is a highly structured and stable organization. As early as 1935, Waelder-Hall observed, in the classical child analysis of a pavor nocturnus case (Anton, age seven): "What is really missing in this conflict is a picture of genuine compromise formation; instead we still have the conflict itself, instinctual drive and anxiety coexisting directly side by side. . . . The adult neurosis always presents a solution of the conflict, even if it be an unsuccessful, neurotic resolution" (p. 273).

The fact that such analytic observations have failed to be investigated *in extenso* may be attributed to the unqualified acceptance of Freud's belief in the universality of the infantile neurosis,[2] as well as to a literal adherence to Freud's statement that the neurosis of childhood represents "a type and model" of the adult neurosis (1909, p. 147). Genetic connections along these lines are borne out in every adult analysis, despite the fact that an infantile neurosis has not been demonstrable as a clinical entity in early

[1] I am not referring here to Frankie, who was presented by Ritvo (1966) as an example of the change of a neurosis from childhood (phobia) to adulthood (obsessional neurosis). It is my opinion that Frankie's illness belongs to the "borderline" disturbances; therefore it lies outside the scope of the present study, which is restricted to the neurosis proper.

[2] "We know that a human child cannot successfully complete its development to the civilized stage without passing through a phase of neurosis sometimes of greater and sometimes of less distinctness. . . Most of these infantile neuroses are overcome spontaneously in the course of growing up, and this is especially true of the obsessional neuroses of childhood" (Freud, 1927, pp. 42-43).

childhood. No analyst would question that in "every case the later neurotic illness links up with the prelude in childhood" (Freud, 1940, p. 184). It is, however, a by now generally accepted opinion that the neurotic illness of the adult did not pre-exist in an immutable form from the prelatency years up to the time when it irrupts in the form of the adult neurosis. The maturation of the ego during latency and adolescence has effected distinctive psychological alterations, even though the original trauma or nuclear conflict remains preserved under the many layers of cumulative revisions.

We shall now turn from viewing the infantile neurosis retrospectively, and, in contrast, take a forward look at the possible sequels to a childhood disturbance. We stand on the firm ground of clinical observation when we say that certain aspects or components of a childhood disturbance can undergo changes with time, lose their neurotic valence, and arrive at a nonconflictual, adaptive solution. On the other hand, they may become amalgamated with neurotic trends that have acquired a hegemonic position during the course of growing up. In this regard, the impact of accidental factors always remains unpredictable. It is by no means a novel idea that the irruption of a neurotic illness can be averted, despite the existence of a neurotic potential, whenever the growing individual is able to draw on constitutional resources, object relations, and environmental conditions so as to work out a serviceable adaptation to life.[3]

Such a favorable outcome is often helped along by the fact that possession of a special propensity—called gift, talent, "knack," or "bent"—facilitates the resolution of inter-

[3]"There is no yardstick for the pathogenic potential of infantile neurosis except for the long-run developmental consideration. We have to bear in mind that every new phase of maturation creates new potential conflict situations and new ways to deal with these conflicts; but, on principle, it also carries with it, to a certain degree, the possibility of modifying the impact of earlier conflict solutions" (Hartmann, in Kris et al., 1954, p. 35). See also Freud (1927, p. 42f.).

nal disharmonies. The individual's neurotic potential, however, continues to exist throughout his life; indeed, it may
serve as both incentive and activator or, on the other hand,
it may constitute a unique vulnerability. Both conditions,
however, lend direction to the individual's adaptive tendencies and evoke his adaptive inventiveness: the mastery of
early trauma, which is generally cumulative in nature, has
become, under these conditions, a "life task" (Blos, 1962, pp.
132-136). Freud wrote in a letter to Ferenczi: "One should
not try to eradicate one's complexes, but to come to terms
with them; they are legitimate guiding forces of one's behavior in the world" (Jones, 1955, p. 452). Loewald pursues
a related thought when he speaks of "repetition as re-
creation," in contrast to "repetition as reproduction" (1971b,
p. 60).

The foregoing considerations lead to the conclusion that
there is no rigid causal chain linking an infantile trauma to
a later neurotic illness. The causality always remains one of
retrospective determination and verification, both of these
being exemplified in the work of reconstruction. From the
study of creative persons, artists and charismatic personalities, we have come to comprehend, on a grand scale,
the complex vicissitudes of the neurotic potential. Perhaps
on a smaller scale a similar adaptive inventiveness is
operative and, under favorable circumstances, this serves to
keep the neurotic potential from consolidating into a neurotic illness.

Neurosogenesis appears, in this perspective, as an unin-
terrupted process of elaborating the neurosis. This process
starts with an incipient injury to the psychic organism and
then establishes a neurotic potential. This potential is laid
down early in life, yet reaches its terminal stage only later
when, in the form of the adult neurosis, an illness has ir-
rupted that remains unalterable and irreversible by ordinary life circumstances. We have come to view the infantile
neurosis as a specific potential, which may or may not lead

to a neurotic illness in adult life. One could, indeed, question the usefulness and the correctness of postulating the existence of an infantile neurosis, if no adult neurosis, so to speak, ever materializes. Of one fact, however, we are sure: that the infantile neurosis takes on its definitive structure and content only during the formative stage of the adult neurosis, when we acquire full knowledge of its existence through the transference neurosis—that is to say, only during analytic treatment (Tolpin, 1970, p. 277).

The formative stage of the adult neurosis often coincides with the period of adolescence—specifically, with late adolescence. After that point, the adult neurosis can make its appearance as the organized assemblage of selective and crucial experiences, impressions, and affects of an injurious nature, experienced during early childhood; together, these mark the fixation points—the characteristic etiological feature of every neurosis—and they are summarized under the concept of infantile trauma. Greenacre speaks of "fixation to a pattern, rather than only to a phase" (Kris et al., 1954, p. 22). If these earliest interferences with normal development have then been carried forward to the phallic-oedipal level, they thereby come into a position to determine, to a great extent, the particular constellation of the triadic conflict that emerges (p. 18). However, should they fail to have thus been carried forward in sufficient strength, then the neurosis in later life is likely to show features characteristic of the preverbal, the dyadic stage of development, or else the emotional illness will probably belong in the category of borderline disturbances. In order to protect the clarity of my exposition, I have restricted myself to a discussion of the transference neuroses. Excluded from consideration are, therefore, those disturbances of child and adult that are, exclusively or predominantly, due to developmental deficits—i.e., faulty psychic structure—rather than to internal conflict, its neurotic solutions, and their debilitating consequences.

Since the structuralization of the neurosis is the outcome of a disequilibrium or conflict between the psychic agencies, it is necessarily contingent on both the intrinsic and the relative maturational strength of those agencies. This assumption is basic to the understanding of the neurosis, whether child or adult neurosis. If we contemplate for a moment the enormous difference between the prelatency and the late adolescent ego, we should not be surprised to discover different solutions to a basic neurotic conflict at each of these two stages. Whatever the outcome, we shall recognize in the respective conflict solutions, at different developmental levels, the history of the ego, which leaves its distinctive mark on the structuralization of any resolution of a disequilibrizing condition. The adaptive outcome, whether neurotic or healthy, if it is traced along a developmental continuum, cannot remain identical throughout and therefore cannot be regarded as unchanging or unchangeable.

Attempts have been made to distinguish between a child neurosis and an adult neurosis in terms of the nature, in each, of transference, resistance, and working through. The child's emotional dependence, together with the incompleteness of his physical maturation, necessarily sets limits to the analyzability of the pathogenetic potential. The aim of child analysis can be defined as helping the child to regain the developmental momentum commensurate with his age. Such an achievement, however, will not necessarily protect the child from the emotional hazards inherent in the process of growing up. We are never certain, in child analysis, how comprehensively the therapeutic process has eliminated the pathogenetic potential. The well-known fact that a relatively large number of analyzed children take up their analyses once again in later life—during adolescence or young adulthood—may find its explanation in the ideas outlined above.

Late adolescence signals the termination of childhood.

As an integrative process it recapitulates, on a higher level
of psychic functioning, an advance toward independence and
autonomy that I have elsewhere conceptualized as the "second individuation process" (see Chapter 8). Not until biological maturation has been attained, and not until sexual
maturity compels a definitive break with infantile positions,
will the neurotic potential—assuming it still possesses sufficient pathogenetic valence—become reorganized on a higher
level of integration as the adult neurosis. This view of the
adult neurosis gives the term "epigenesis" in the title of
this chapter a special fitness, in that it reminds us of the
Harveian theory, according to which the embryo is built up
gradually by the addition of one part after another in an
orderly sequence of rising complexity. To this should be
added that in the process some parts may atrophy, lose
their function, and become atavistic relics of the past. The
opposing theory is, of course, the one of "preformation" or
"encasement," which is as obsolete to the biologist as its
implication is contrary to the nature of neurosogenesis.

Distinguishing between the latent and the manifest
state of the neurosis is a time-honored aspect of psychoanalytic theory. It is the latent state that has been
conceptualized as the infantile neurosis. Freud (1939) has
related the two in the following passage: "Not until later
[after latency] does the change take place with which the
definitive neurosis becomes manifest as a belated effect of
the trauma. This occurs either at the irruption of puberty or
some while later" (p. 77).[4] There are indeed many references in Freud's writing to the biphasic nature of
neurosogenesis, to which the traumatic neuroses present an
exception. When the neurotic disposition becomes manifest
in adolescence—namely, when the infantile trauma im-

[4]A German-language equivalent of the word "adolescence" was not yet in existence when Freud wrote this passage in 1939. *Adoleszenz* has entered the German language only lately. Until then, the German word for adolescence was "puberty" *(Pubertät);* this one term was used to refer to both the stage of physical
maturation and the concurrent psychological development.

pedes, distorts, or catastrophically disrupts the age-appropriate conduct of life by way of symptom formation—then, that illness constitutes the "definitive neurosis." My implication here is that the "definitive neurosis" is identical with the adult neurosis and, furthermore, that concomitant with the formation of the adult neurosis, the infantile neurosis springs to life, as it were, acquiring delineation and structure. The two are complementary formations: both depend on an advanced stage of ego development for their structuralization, and they are forced into existence simultaneously by the adaptive demands that physical maturation, instinctual development, and social fitting-in exert on the growing personality. The normative regression in the service of development promotes adolescent psychic restructuring (Blos, 1962). Adolescent regression facilitates the overhauling of earlier faulty development at the terminal stage of childhood—namely, at late adolescence—and brings about (if all goes well) a settlement of those early conflictual residues or surviving inner disharmonies that would otherwise obstruct the formation of the postadolescent personality. To this process we have assigned the term "consolidation."[5]

The structuralization of the adult neurosis is inherently linked to the developmental stage of late adolescence. This is the stage of life, as noted above, at which physical growth is completed and sexual maturity attained. In terms of psychosexual development, the major step forward to maturity consists in the relegation of pregenital drive modalities to the realm of forepleasure, thus rendering them subordinate and at the same time establishing a hierarchical drive

[5]Erikson (1968) had something similar in mind when he proposed the concepts of the "psychosocial moratorium" and the "identity crisis." The "Who am I?" query of the late adolescent arises, so it seems to me, out of the confrontations between the almost-adult and the still-child positions during the alternating movements of regression and progression, typical of the late adolescent period. Subjectively, this ebb and flow is felt as a transient diffusion of the self—which can also be said with reference to the process of consolidation.

constellation called genitality. The attainment of genital primacy (not to be confused with heterosexual activity) is gradual and usually remains incomplete. It is a rare instance that does not fall short of the ideal model.

Psychoanalytic theory and practice have left no doubt that the Oedipus complex is reactivated in adolescence and that the individual lives through it once again. Far from this being a replication of its earlier edition, it would be more correct to say that the revived Oedipus complex is this time carried toward its final resolution on a higher level of integration, while the individual moves toward a more definitive mastery of the attendant conflicts. The relatively advanced stage of the ego leads to the first "decline" of the Oedipus complex, inaugurating the latency period; the second "decline," which takes place during adolescence, inaugurates adulthood. The respective resolutions will therefore be dissimilar, regardless of whether they are normal or pathological in nature. When we compare the outcomes of the two stages, one crucial point of difference appears: the coexistence of the positive and negative Oedipus complex can be tolerated in childhood with far greater equanimity than it can in adolescence; at the latter stage, a decisive intolerance has developed because of the social and maturational pressure toward the formation of a definitive and irreversible sexual identity (see Chapter 7). The fact that the valence of the negative Oedipus complex cannot be gauged with certainty during child analysis—especially not in terms of the potentiality of its resurgence at puberty— invites the assumption that, at the threshold of the latency period, the oedipal conflict has been brought only to a partial resolution and a correspondingly relative quietude. Neither the issues nor their forms of settlement are identical at the two stages of oedipal conflict. It was physical immaturity that brought the original Oedipus complex to its first decline, and it is physical maturity that must bring it to its later definitive and irreversible resolution. The phase of late adolescence becomes, then, the Armageddon of the adult neurosis.

The personality changes that mark the termination of adolescence are those of integration and differentiation. On a complex level, this process is demonstrated in character formation (see Chapter 9). In their totality, psychological changes in the late adolescent personality are subsumed under the concept of consolidation. The "definitive neurosis," i.e., the adult neurosis, is the product of the consolidation process, which encompasses the entire preadult personality, and at the close of which an irreversible demarcation line has been drawn between childhood and adulthood. The synthetic function of the ego is relentlessly at work all through this stage, for better or for worse, in that the consolidation process effects normal as well as pathological personality organization.

The late adolescent patient thus confronts the analyst with a paradoxical situation. Developmentally, the patient is involved in the consolidation of the adult neurosis; on the other hand, the fact that this integrative process is still an ongoing one works against his involvement in the analytic process—except, by and large, on the level of acute, here-and-now discomforts and their relief. The attainment of the adult neurosis would, no doubt, facilitate genuine analyzability, a situation that poses a real dilemma for the analyst: he either forestalls the formation of the adult neurosis by interpretive pre-emption, or he hastens its formation so as to get the definitive analytic work under way. In many cases it becomes perfectly clear that the adolescent is not actually resisting analysis; yet, because of his limited involvement, his analyzability is, often unfairly, doubted. The burden of the "impasse" rests heavily on the analyst if he loses sight of the developmental process of late adolescence and attempts to proceed as if the adult neurosis already existed. The resultant ineffectiveness of his interpretations readily mobilizes narcissistic defenses in the analyst himself; these have the effect of beclouding, slowing down, or foreclosing the analysis of the adolescent patient. The difficulties, indeed, the inadvisability of adolescent analysis, have been debated for many years. A good portion of these difficulties, however, stems from a misapprehension of the adolescent process, one reflection of which appears in the technical dilemma I have alluded to.

Clinical Illustration

An eighteen-year-old male college student started analysis following an inexplicable yet total academic failure: his inability to study had, in fact, acquired the nature of a symptom. The onset of the difficulty had been so precipitous, and its severity so massive, that analytic treatment was indicated: a neurotic inhibition of intellectual functioning was threatening to wreck the life of an intelligent young man. Obviously, the presenting symptom only masked the many inroads through which the pathology had been extending its debilitating influence over the total personality. The emotional immaturity had become manifest in the one area that represented to the patient, more than any other, the symbolic attainment of maturity and independence—in short, of oedipal rivalry.

When the patient entered analysis, he was quite well aware of the fact that he could not deal with the problem of academic failure by himself. He realized the utter irrationality of his procrastinations, his continual hoping against hope to succeed, his compulsive disregard of the passage of time until no time was left to make up for time lost. Unwittingly, he had been inviting defeat, in spite of his unshakable intention to study, and in spite of the painful humiliation that his dismissal from college entailed. In brief, when the patient entered analysis, it was with a positive attitude and a genuine desire to resolve an acute problem: he readily acknowledged the irrationality of his behavior, being already aware of his emotional discomfort and loss of direction.

The patient was sophisticated enough to accept and follow the basic rule. He never missed any of his five weekly hours; he talked easily, reporting current events, fantasies, dreams, and childhood memories. In short, he behaved like a good patient. Nevertheless, something was missing that made the analytic work drag and stumble. While it was true that recollections, memories, reports on the day's happenings, fantasies, and life-history data had been piling up voluminously during the course of the first year of analysis, no "grand design" had yet emerged that would lend organization and continuity—in essence, meaning—to the patient's stream of communications.

The area of neurotic conflict, as well as the defensive organization, had already become evident within the first week of treatment. A dream and a transient obsessional thought will serve as illustrations. The patient brought the following dream to the first hour:

> I am in a restaurant with a friend. President Johnson drives up in a black car with his entourage. The car is about fifteen years old. It is a convertible. I was supposed to follow him and I drive a car after him. I didn't know which pedal to push, which one was the brake. Then my father was there. I got afraid and drove away. [Silence.] There was one more thing: there was a girl in the path of my car. I couldn't stop the car. Then the car stopped by itself, just touching her.

After he had finished telling the dream, the patient's mind went "blank." He was obviously blocked when he was "supposed to follow" the analyst's directions—to let his mind "drive along." Instead, he put the brakes on, for fear of "losing control" of his mind. He "got afraid and drove away." Loss of emotional control and fear of the father seemed intrinsically interrelated here; flight was the only escape from both of them. Inhibitions and avoidances had become his "safety measures"; they represented the defensive organization that governed his life.

This historical dating of the President's car, which he was "supposed to follow" in his dream, placed the height, if not the onset of the neurotic anxiety at the age of about three—namely, at the phallic-oedipal phase. The beginning of the dream ("in a restaurant with a friend") and its end ("there was a girl in the path of my car") tied the dream to the actuality of the patient's present life (day residue)—namely, to his fervent wish for friendship with boys and for emotional closeness to a girl. The unattainability of both was painfully felt by him as a strangled spontaneity, which had been impairing and bruising his social relationships for some time, especially since his expulsion from college.

The second indication of a central source of anxiety I found in a transient obsessional thought to which he gave expression during the third and fourth session. After he had assured me that he had to control his mind, since he wished to speak only of "relevant things," he suddenly became fascinated by a minute crack in the ceiling of my office. His mind remained "riveted" to the crack; all he could manage to say was, "It makes me think of nothing." Lewin's (1948, p. 525) comment on the thought of "nothing" led me to guess that both the female genital and a preoccupation with castration lay embedded in the patient's passivity and inhibition. No interpretation was given to him.

It is a common experience in analysis that a patient's first-reported dream or fantasy contains—in a nutshell, as it were—the central conflict of his neurosis. Any conclusion that is drawn from the opening stage of analysis, however, remains nothing more than an educated guess; its verification, modification, or refutation has to come during the course of treatment. Verification did come, indeed—but only after a waiting time of a year and a half.

The first phase of this patient's analysis (eighteen

months) was given over, as has been mentioned, to the obedient reporting of events, past and present; but the associative inconclusiveness prevented any genetic continuity from
emerging. Much of the analytic time was devoted to the ac-
cumulation of a thorough inventory of his life history, including his secret memories and fantasies, as well as those
fears and wishes that had remained part of his conscious
memory. This does not mean that I did not make any use of
the given material to help the patient recognize the
psychological wellsprings of his affects and actions. Such interpretations, however, while accepted by the patient, were
kept by him within the confines of the particular problem
he had defined; as a result, insights could not branch out,
beyond a limited range of actuality, into a deepening analytic collaboration.

The patient's hunger for understanding and insight was
clearly considerable and compelling; my attitude, of course,
complemented the patient's wish. Yet, instead of a genuine
therapeutic alliance, what the patient had contrived was an
illusory empathic liaison: "the two of us both want to understand." The patient was obviously trying to please me;
he had put me into the role of an idealized father who
would "understand," rather than judge by achievement.

This spontaneous transference accounted for the good
rapport, but it also made the patient scan his mind in
search of mental content that would please me and afford
him a favored position in my affection and respect.
Throughout this time, he remained cooperative, rather jo-
vial, and pal-like.

There were many indications that he was imitating admired persons, friends, and family members, by using their
idioms, gestures, and intonations. These imitations he employed as enhancements of his own lovability and unique
worth. Every communication had to be of special meaning-
fulness and extraordinary interest and relevance; otherwise,
it was not worth his talking about it. The transference as-

pect of this selectivity was apparent enough;[6] yet neither transference nor resistance interpretations were of any noticeable consequence. I decided, finally, to refrain from such interpretations, after they had started to become repetitious, even though the material clamored for such comment. My persistence in repeating, driving home the psychologically obvious, was here rendered decisively more moderate by my theoretical propositions and by my engagement in their clinical investigation.

The first eighteen months of analysis were thus taken up with an effort to bring the patient's own affects, moods, and fantasies to his awareness. Most helpful in this process, incidentally, was the patient's verbal expression of his inner stirrings in the presence of an attentive listener and, conversely, his listening to my comments. Spoken words and their responsive echoes rendered the elusive self-perceptions of the patient's inner life more real and observable (conscious) than they had been before, when they existed in the caverns of contemplative silence (preconscious). By this laborious process, data belonging to the conscious layer of the mind were dynamically altered as well. In that way, these same data, having changed their quality through a new cathectic investment, were rendered more useful for the subsequent analytic work.

Dynamic, but not genetic, interpretations were given; yet even these were limited, because they were given outside the orbit of the transference and before the therapeutic alliance—in contradistinction to rapport and cooperation—was established. The analyst as a person was erased by the patient's relating himself instead to an ideal father figure,

[6]The fact that these transference aspects are part of a regressive activation of the "grandiose self" as well as of the "idealized parent imago" (Kohut, 1971) will not occupy us here, because the case under discussion does not belong among the narcissistic disorders described by Kohut. However, it is of interest to note that Kohut's formulations have an additional and special relevance for those patients who are analyzed during the closing stage of childhood—namely, during late adolescence, or, to put it metapsychologically, during the "second individuation process" of adolescence (see Chapter 8).

who would accept lovingly the verbal gifts of an obedient
son. Those longings were gratified whenever I gave proof of
the fact that I remembered some detail of what he had told
me some time before.[7] The belief in the omnipotence of the
loving father and, conversely, the belief in the certainty of a
great reward awaiting the submissive and obedient son—
these were the impenetrable convictions of a child who, by
this very trust, had immobilized himself on the road to
maturity. Such trust is akin to denial; frequently, it appears
in the form of an irrational self-confidence, which stands on
clay feet because it lacks the support of any accomplishments in the real world.

It is the regressive aspect of adolescence—normally, a
regression in the service of development (see Chapter 8)—
that endows adolescent behavior with a childlike countenance. The trend toward idealization is perhaps the characteristic par excellence of youth. It was my impression that
the patient's regression to the idealized father image represented his effort to reach the consolidation stage of late
adolescence. The transference was thus not a regression in
the customary sense—that of the reliving of a pathogenetic
conflict; as a result, nothing in it was akin to a transference
neurosis. The childlike quality was derived from the fixation on his still family-centered emotional life, which the
patient was laboring in vain to transcend by replacement.

Knowing that the transference neurosis—and the patient's illness belonged in this category—is the only means
of reliving, and therefore of coming to terms with, the infantile roots of a neurotic symptom, I waited patiently for
any signs of its appearance. The transference neurosis is,
after all, an emotional involvement from which there is not
a single moment's escape, while transference manifestations

[7]I am reminded here of a little boy who was introduced by his mother to an
outhouse when visiting a farm at the age of twenty months. The child looked with
interest into the hole, and after a while turned his shining eyes up to his mother
and said: "Mommy, so that's where you keep it!"

come and go. The two are of an essentially different order (Loewald, 1971a), even though both play a crucial (albeit different) role in the resolution of a neurotic conflict in the analysis of child and adult. The distinction between the two is in reality not as precise as our terminology would indicate. It is, however, not an artificial one. Transference manifestations bear an ad hoc character, while the transference neurosis reflects a continuous and coherent reliving of the pathogenetic past in relation to the analyst and to the analytic situation; as such, it is a reflection of life par excellence insofar as it selects from among all available stimuli those that will sustain it. In order to avoid the narrow and perhaps stifling concept of the term "transference neurosis," Greenacre (1959) has suggested a less restrictive terminology. She writes: "I have myself been a little questioning of the blanket term 'transference neurosis,' which may be misleading. I would prefer to speak of *active transference neurotic manifestations*" (pp. 652-653). Keeping this proviso in mind, I continue to use the term "transference neurosis" as a useful term, being cognizant of the fact that it is inclusive rather than exclusive.

No signs of a transference neurosis made their appearance in my patient. In deciding to wait, I had also made the implicit decision neither to alleviate unduly his current suffering nor to offer such insights as would only play into the hands of his intellectual defenses and gratify his narcissism, thereby supporting the grandiose fantasies with which he was trying to obliterate his devastating sense of incompetence and helplessness.

I shall now turn to a shift in the analysis. This shift was not wholly attributable—if indeed it was attributable at all—to the analytic work done thus far. It was precisely that aspect of the analysis—namely, the unaccountability of the change—that gave me pause. Before speculating on this point, however, I shall present the clinical material of the second stage of the analysis.

After one and a half years of analysis, the patient began
to verbalize his inhibition against talking freely with me:
his overriding desire had so far been to be a "good patient."
The roving reporting now took on the character of a personalized message. He began, rather suddenly, to complain
about restrictions that the analytic schedule was forcing on
him and about the dependency he had to endure. He felt
that his prior commitment to the analysis had begun to
wane, and that this was due to the coercion implicit in the
analytic contract. These complaints seemed "natural" to
him, and therefore required no further "explanation": it was
self-evident that in a state of coercion and imposition one
cannot "talk freely" or "open up."

One day, this new "theme song" of apparent resistance
and negative transference was played in a different key. I
had noticed that the tirades of provocation and accusing
negativism had begun to give way to spontaneous associations. These were all memories, and what they had in common was the element of danger, fear, and disaster: at the
age of six, a pet animal had died on the living room couch;
one night his bed had collapsed; wild animals in the zoo had
frightened him; he had broken a chair; he was paralyzed by
fear of his father.

When I interpreted these associations by pointing out
his fear of the analyst ("talking freely," "opening up"), the
patient suddenly got excited. Instead of simply rejecting my
comments as irrelevant, or pretending to accept them as he
had previously done, he now responded with genuine affect.
This gentle-voiced young man raised his voice to a shout:
"That's it. I didn't know what I was saying, but *you* knew.
That makes us unequal. *That* I cannot allow to happen."
Nevertheless, he considered my comment and recognized
some truth in my interpretation, which dealt with his fear
of regression, his terror of becoming once again unequal, little and weak, at the mercy of the analyst-father's power. In
short, what I had conveyed to him was the thought that his

fear of being overwhelmed, punished, and subdued was being relived in the analytic situation, where it had become attached to the analytic rule and contract, both imposed on him by the analyst.

This interpretation was followed in the next session by the patient's recollection of a child's story in which a "man who never talks" is hit by his exasperated companion, who has all along been wanting to have a nice conversation with him. The allusion to the analyst was once again not obvious to the patient, and it had to be pointed out to him. Instead of becoming excited and argumentative, however, this time the patient recalled that his father had *never* talked to him—except to encourage him to be good and successful in school. What he had meant to convey by the tale was simply that all his life *he* had never had a "nice conversation" with his father about matters that were of importance to him as a child. How could he dare talk to *me?* He had learned to give the appearance of an obedient child and to live with his rage and his desire for vengeance in a self-enforced solitary confinement.

After these transference experiences and their interpretations, the patient became pensive and introspective. He made the following self-observation: "Memories have taken on a different flavor. Up till now I enjoyed talking about my memories. I enjoyed reminiscing—about anything. It made me feel good. This seems to have changed. My memories have become—sort of threatening. You have become part of them. You see something in them I don't. That makes all the difference, I suppose."

The patient opened one of the succeeding sessions with the remark: "The last few days I have been able to visualize the vagina. This has been totally impossible for me before this." He spoke of it as of a sudden illumination. I was reminded of the persevering thought of "nothing" during the first week of the analysis. This sudden clarity of thought and imagery was sufficient to establish the etiological link between castration anxiety, repressed oedipal aggression, and the inhibition of thinking. Thinking had acquired, especially during adolescence, a defensive function: it had become a cold exercise in sophistry, designed to keep emotions strangulated by thought mastery. Since he had been using the weapons of intelligence, no accusation of hostile intent could be leveled against the victor. Yet the unconscious intent had aborted, more often than not, the effective use of those very weapons.

There was no question that the analytic work had now moved onto a different level. The transference neurosis was in formation, and an effective, object-directed quality had become attached to verbalizations. The emergence of this new affective quality was attributable to the fact that the transference had become an integral part of the patient's mental life. The reliving of the pathogenetic past is the transference neurosis; it gives "all the symptoms of the illness a new transference meaning" and replaces the patient's "ordinary neurosis by a 'transference-neurosis' of which he can be cured by the therapeutic work. The transference thus creates an intermediate region between illness and real life through which the transition from one to the other is made" (Freud, 1914a, p. 154; see also Loewald, 1971a, p. 62). Simultaneously with the emergence of the transference neurosis, the infantile neurosis acquires the structuralization and the clarity it had lacked until then. "The infantile neurosis is the leading pathology in the transference neuroses" (Tolpin, 1970, p. 277), or, in the light of my proposition: the infantile neurosis is the leading pathology in the adult neurosis of the transference-neurosis type; only during psychoanalytic treatment are we enabled to investigate the realm of the infantile neurosis, and only so far as it is reflected in the transference neurosis.

A new dimension had clearly been added to my patient's analytic involvement: what had previously become a waning interest in the analysis was now replaced by an emerging therapeutic alliance. The analytic material, which was for the first time derived from *all* layers of the mind and from *all* periods of his life, acquired psychological cohesion and continuity. This condition rendered interpretations meaningful—that is, they were no longer an end in themselves, but instead the beginning of some new, but related, self-investigative move.

To employ an analogy, I might say that the first phase of the analysis corresponded to the close observation and inspection of the myriad small pieces of colored glass or stone (isolated memories, problems, and conflicts), which were one day to be assembled into a large mosaic picture (adult neurosis). During the second phase (transference neurosis), the grand design of the mosaic was completed (infantile neurosis); now, every observation and every inspection of detail was necessarily carried out in relation to the overall picture, which had acquired a coherent design (the total or the historical personality). In order to correct a misunderstanding I may have created—that it is only with the advent of the transference neurosis that any meaningful analytic work is possible—I must point out that the analytic work of the first period was, in its own way, unquestionably useful. I am inclined to speculate that roaming and wandering through a lifetime of memories—including fantasies, affects, and experiences, in conjunction with the current life of work, moods, relationships, family, etc.—were necessary to facilitate the consolidation of late adolescence, including the neurotic trends. It was the first phase that brought the patient into contact with his inner life; at the same time that it was dealing with acute conflicts as isolated events, it was also throwing light on the pervasiveness of his inhibitions, avoidances, and fears. In their totality, these gave the process of consolidation its scope and immediacy.

This achievement in itself was of no minor import. And yet, if the analytic work had been abandoned at that point, no durable reorganization of the personality would have

been effected. Certain reality achievements, made possible
by the analytic work during the first phase—such as financial independence and responsible, satisfactory performance
on a job—were important in that they gave the patient a
sense of success and of pride and, in general, made him feel
better. Yet, just that sense of accomplishment might well
have served the patient as a reason for wanting to terminate the analysis. In fact, just before the second phase of
the analysis set in, that very step was near realization by
the patient. It was averted by my making a transference interpretation that happened to be the first one to "hit home."

It has been my impression for many years that adolescence cannot remain indefinitely an open-ended process; it
has to come to some closure, even if that be a pathological
one, during late adolescence. By definition, late adolescence,
as a period of personality consolidation, has its biological as
well as its emotional and social timing. Having had a
number of analytic patients who were in the stage of late
adolescence, I have found my theoretical propositions confirmed in other cases as well, cases that also belonged
among the transference neuroses. Naturally, where the
pathology is overburdened by preoedipal ego aberrations
and ego deficiencies, the analytic treatment follows a different course, which lies outside the scope of this investigation.
The diagnostic assessment of these latter cases often remains inconclusive at the start of analysis, but will gain in
clarity during the first phase, the phase of consolidation.

A Comparison of Clinical Observations and Theoretical Propositions

I have been fortunate to find in the psychoanalytic literature several reports on the treatment of late adolescents
and have thus been in a position to compare my own clinical observations and theoretical assumptions with those of
others. Although these other writers used their particular

cases to demonstrate ideas quite different from those set forth here, they were nevertheless cognizant of the specific difficulties this age group of patients presents. There are two writers in particular who have published clinical material to which I now turn my attention.

Hans Loewald opens his paper on "The Transference Neurosis" (1971a) with the case illustration of "an unusually gifted and inhibited young man of 19." There is no need here to go into this late adolescent's psychopathology, aside from pointing out that his clinical picture resembles my patient's to a remarkable degree. Both represent a rather typical maladaptive constellation, which brings a number of such young men of college age to the analyst's office. Loewald made the observation early in treatment "that his [the patient's] relationship to me [the analyst], from the very beginning, tended to be a duplicate of his relationship to his father, which seemed to be a kind of slavish adoration, imitation, and submissive love, with some evidence of rebellion against that position, deep resentment, and of attempts to extricate himself from it." At first sight, says Loewald, the patient seemed to be offering "an example of a very rapidly-developing transference neurosis" (p. 54). He then goes on to pose the question "whether one should speak here of a transference *neurosis,* inasmuch as the transference was so immediate and massive.... [It] clearly had a primitive quality, perhaps not unlike that of children.... while desirable in the interest of maintaining rapport with this isolated patient... [it] worked as a powerful resistance" (pp. 55-56). In view of the massive transference manifestations, the analyst decided that a "resistance analysis... was not called for at this time" (p. 56). Since the character of the transference "would tend in the direction of a mere transference repetition," the analyst's "concern in this case was the danger of an early stalemate or disruption of the analysis" (p. 57).

Loewald then proceeds to ask the pertinent question:

Does the concept of the transference neurosis imply the repetition of the infantile neurosis? If not, then what is it that
distinguishes the massive transference manifestations at
the opening phase of this patient's analysis from a transference neurosis? The analyst, if I may say so, felt "in his
bones" that the two were not the same; I might be so bold
as to assume that it was the unworkable quality of the
transference—or, simply, the patient's unresponsiveness to
transference interpretations—that gave the distinction its
plausibility. In addition, the apparent resistance remained
equally unassailable by interpretations—or, at least, their
repetition had such minor consequences that a possible mis-
comprehension of the pathology had to be considered.
Loewald thus comes to the apodictic conclusion: "No well-
defined symptomatology, no well-defined infantile neurosis,
and thus no transference neurosis" (p. 58). Parenthetically,
I might suggest that the rapidity of the patient's
transference—indeed, his transference hunger or transference compulsion—is a reflection, in and of itself, of a
symptom in formation within the benign context of the
analytic situation.

A further source of clinical material pertaining to the
analytic treatment of the late adolescent is to be found in
two papers by Adatto (1958, 1966), who describes the
analysis of five late adolescent patients. "Following an intensive working through of their conflictual material, there
was a period of psychic equilibrium and absence of analytic
motivation" (1966, p. 485). The analytic treatment was
therefore terminated at this point. But three of these five
patients returned for analysis after they had become young
adults. The striking difference between their first and second analyses lay in "the transference and the emotional investment in me [the analyst], which had been sketchy or incomplete in the first analysis" (1966, p. 486). Analyzable
transference dreams in the second analysis opened the way
to new analytic depth, by moving "towards a situation in

which finally every conflict has to be fought out in the sphere of transference" (Freud, 1912b, p. 104).

I shall now turn to a comparative evaluation of Loewald's and Adatto's cases, in the light of my thesis. There are several aspects in all these cases that permit a comparative view. First, there is the fact that all the patients were in their late adolescence—namely, at that developmental stage in which adolescent psychic restructuring has reached its final stage in the consolidation of the personality. The fact that all cases are male seems, at first sight, coincidental; however, clinical observation might indicate that female adolescent consolidation follows a pattern of its own. Loewald concludes that the absence of a well-defined symptomatology—in other words, the absence of structuralization of the total scope of internal disharmonies in terms of compromise formations—rules out the appearance of a "well-defined infantile neurosis." This conclusion is borne out by my own observation—namely, that the personality consolidation of late adolescence is a precondition for the structuralization of the transference neurosis *and* of the infantile neurosis. If the consolidation process of late adolescence has not yet taken place, we will look in vain for the adult neurosis that constitutes the matrix out of which the transference neurosis and, concomitantly, the infantile neurosis emerge. Loewald makes the same observation that has aroused my own curiosity—that a patient's excellent rapport can easily be taken as betokening the emergence of the transference neurosis and yet that assumption can prove to be erroneous. Furthermore, the same patient's unresponsiveness to transference interpretations may then be given the blanket designation of "resistance." Misjudgments of this kind lead frequently to a disruption of the analysis, or to its incompleteness.

Adatto's cases are extremely instructive here in that they permit one to make a comparative study of the two analytic phases, by focusing on their points of difference. In the first phase, the patients remained rather unresponsive to the analysis of transference and resistance; yet they gained considerable relief from anxiety through the resolution of some of the acute problems that had initially brought them to treatment. This first gain in treatment represents the typical danger point—as we have seen in Loewald's and my own case—threatening a premature termination of the analysis. Adatto (1958) postulates that, in the course of the analysis of the late adolescent, an ego reintegration takes place that does constitute, in and of itself, a progression toward maturity. Concomitantly, however, the patient's need for the analysis wanes and the analysis is terminated. The "ego reintegration" proved, after all, to be less durable than was expected (Adatto, 1966).

By virtue of Adatto's concentrating—perhaps too exclusively—on the amelioration of his patients' acute life problems, these late adolescent patients were sufficiently relieved from anxiety, and thus were able to stabilize their defensive organization. It was this adaptive move that enabled them to go through the consolidation phase well defended, and thereby to gain a temporary postponement of the irruption of the adult neurosis. Here the first, even if incomplete, analysis stood them in good stead. Nevertheless, three of Adatto's patients later recognized the need to complete their prematurely disrupted analysis; this occurred after such accommodations as career, marriage, and children had proved to be of no avail for the attainment of a normal adult life.

Both Adatto and Loewald observe that the analyzability of resistance remains limited at the stage of static transference repetitions. It has been my experience that the developmental forces, which are at this point working against analytic involvement, can be kept within reasonable bounds if the analyst offers insight—even if his insights are limited to, or more or less remain on, the experiential level of comprehending the realities of psychic determinism. Be that as it may, a point of agreement with Loewald and Adatto emerges—namely, that at this preliminary stage of analysis in late adolescence, both the transference neurosis and the infantile neurosis are still to develop. In that regard, they constitute two sides of the same coin. Of course, formation of the transference neurosis takes its time in any adult analysis as well, and there, too, an introductory phase is common enough. The difference has to do, among other things, with the different function of the introductory phase and the different use to which the late adolescent patient generally puts the initial analytic situation. The basic point of difference, however, lies in the fact that the late adolescent patient is fulfilling a developmental requirement that affects the analytic work adversely, by contrast with the adult, whose initial reticence or effusiveness in analysis can be attributed entirely to resistance and defense.

We are now ready to say that the initial phase of late adolescent analysis confronts the analyst with a clinical phenomenon that belongs to the developmental process of personality consolidation. This process occurs in relative silence, outside the analytic work. The achievement of this silent work is the adult neurosis. This process is inherently helped along by the analytic situation, because that situation confronts the patient's ego with an avalanche of experiences on all levels of mental functioning, which the patient is reproducing, either silently or verbally. It is in order to prevent the flooding of the mental apparatus with disorganizing stimuli (thoughts, images, and affects) that the ego erects a "stimulus barrier" in the form of organizing principles; we refer to the implementation of these principles, in their totality, as "the consolidation process of late adolescence."

Contemplating the disruption of the first analysis in retrospect, Adatto reminds us of Freud's (1905a) treatment of the late adolescent patient, Dora, and of his statement in the Postscript to that case history: "I did not succeed in mastering the transference in good time" (p. 118). If we consider Dora's disruption of her analysis in developmental terms, we would say, today, that the consolidation of her neurotic condition had been short-circuited by the fact that her analysis was being conducted as if an adult neurosis already existed. As a consequence, the adolescent ego became overwhelmed by interpretations it was unable to integrate, and it simply took to flight. If there is one thing adolescent analysis has taught us, it is that ill-timed id interpretations are unconsciously experienced by the adolescent as a parental—that is, incestuous—seduction.

Personality Consolidation and the Formation of the Adult Neurosis

From what I have said up to this point, it must have become obvious that I ascribe to the stage of late adolescence a specific and decisive role in the formation of the adult neurosis. The integrative process of consolidation which brings childhood to a close is the outstanding characteristic of late adolescence. This consolidation process entails a progression from partial adaptations and less-than-final conflict resolutions, as well as from reactive, transient, even disjointed emotional and social accommodations, to their unification in terms of a patterned interlacing of psychic functioning, under the aegis of an advanced ego. This step is what we refer to in summary fashion as "personality consolidation." In the realm of character formation, it is reflected in the automatization of reaction patterns (see Chapter 9). The formative process of the adult neurosis draws on these developmental advances toward a definitive, integrated, and autonomous psychic organization.

My formulation stands in contradiction to a widely held opinion—that the existence of a neurotic condition makes it impossible for the personality consolidation of late adolescence to take place; that consolidation *can* take place, so the argument goes, only by way of analysis of the neurosis. This point of view restricts the consolidation process to normal development, regarding its completion as the true sign of maturity attained. It is my opinion, to the contrary, that it is only *after* the consolidation of late adolescence that an analysis can include in its scope the rectification or normalization of the total personality, including those enclaves of the neurotic potential to which child analytic work was often unable to penetrate. Herein lie the limitations placed on the working-through process in the analytic endeavor, prior to the analysis of the adult neurosis (Blos, 1970, pp. 100-109). The consolidation process of late adolescence always proceeds turbulently—whether in a manifest or latent fashion—and even more so whenever a neurotic potential has survived the intervening years of childhood and adolescence.

Regardless of stalemates and retardations in the realms of ego and drive progression—or, what is more frequent, their lack of synchronization and their disharmony—late adolescence will nevertheless bring the process of psychic patterning and organization into a decisive ascendancy. This step forward, I repeat, takes place in relation to pathology as well as to normality. *It is the consolidation process itself that structures the adult neurosis.* The consolidation stage of late adolescence is therefore the incubation time of the adult neurosis, and the patient uses the analytic situation as part of that process. Consequently, patient and analyst often find themselves working at cross-purposes. The analyst's aim is to restructure a faulty *development,* while the patient is occupied with a comprehensive, yet faulty, *structure formation*—that is, with the formation of the adult neurosis.

The consolidation of the adult neurosis takes time, and during that time the patient remains, more or less, unresponsive to the standard technique. There is no lack of cooperation, nor is there any dearth of analytic material;

yet what prevails is an ineffectualness or, rather, a significantly limited usefulness of resistance and transference interpretations. This situation may appear to be the outcome
of either a negative therapeutic reaction or a massive resistance, but in my opinion it is neither; rather, it constitutes
a "holding operation" while the silent work of consolidation
goes on. No doubt, defenses do play their role in this typical
picture, and they can be drawn successfully into the analytic work. The technical problem at this developmental stage
of adult psychic structure formation, however, consists in
the analyst's carefully determining just how much relief
from anxiety he should offer the patient vis-à-vis his current acute distress and tension. Gauging the optimal level
of abstinence thus becomes the delicate task of the analyst.[8]

Dynamic considerations permit one to speculate that too
great relief from anxiety will serve to foster a "consolidation" marked by the defensive conviction that "all is well."
A growing lack of interest in the analytic work will then
emerge and a premature termination of the analysis may
follow. Too little relief from anxiety, on the other hand, can
lead to disappointment in the analytic work, or to disillusionment with the analyst's ability or willingness to help. It
all comes down, then, to "too much" or "too little" responsiveness and stimulation from the side of the analyst.

It must be remembered that the consolidation process,
while developmentally timed, requires sources of tension
and conflict, as well as trust and confidence, in order for its
integrative work to proceed. The aim of analytic work in
late adolescence is, first of all, a successful transition from
the turmoil of the consolidation stage to the analysis of the
adult neurosis. Analytic interventions during the nascent
adult neurosis call for technical inventiveness and tact, both
of them firmly rooted in developmental and theoretical con-

----

[8]The problem of abstinence plays a role, of course, in every analysis, and at any
age. In the present context, it has to do with the analyst's promoting the consolidation of the adult neurosis and thus preventing the disruption of the analysis.

ceptualizations. Adaptation of the analytic technique to the stage of psychic consolidation should be thought of as being a no less appropriate analytic procedure than the one in child analysis, for example, that accepts, rather than rejects, the alternating existence of the analyst as a transference object and a real person. The adaptation of analytic technique to developmental conditions does not, in and of itself, negate the analytic process, but rather enhances it.

The idea that the irruption of the definitive neurosis, or the adult neurosis, coincides with the termination of adolescence becomes plausible once we realize that the Oedipus complex is brought to its definitive decline or definitive resolution only with the attainment of somatic maturity at puberty.[9] What was an emotional reality in the form of a wish, during the phallic-oedipal phase, became thwarted at that time by the reality principle—namely, by physical immaturity; these same wishes, upon being brought to life again during puberty, have since become realizable by physical maturity, but now they are thwarted by emotional conflict. The mythical figure Oedipus, we sometimes forget, was an adult man.

What we refer to, before adolescence, as "childhood neurosis" is attributable to specific conflicts and their maladaptive resolutions, which preclude normal progression along developmental lines.[10] The childhood neurosis lacks the involvement of the total personality; in terms of an all-inclusive and comprehensive organization, this does not exist before adulthood. The term "adulthood" is here used not as identical with emotional maturity, but as relative to physical status and psychic structure. It is this fact that

[9]The origin, latent state, and irruption of the neurosis are summarized by Freud (1940) as follows: "It seems that neuroses are acquired only in early childhood (up to the age of six), even though their symptoms may not make their appearance till much later" (p. 184).

[10]Freud used the terms "infantile neurosis," "childhood neurosis," "neurosis of infancy," etc., as interchangeable designations of the "infantile neurosis," which is the proper term used in the literature today. Childhood neurosis refers to manifest neurotic illness before adolescence.

makes the childhood neurosis different from the adult neurosis. What the two have in common, of course, is the internalization of conflict. With regard to their difference, Hartmann has commented as follows: "many of the very early neuroses are really different from what we are used to calling neurosis in the adult. Many problems in children which we call neurotic are actually limited to a single functional disturbance; and the way from conflict to symptom seems often to be shorter than in adult neurosis" (in Kris et al., 1954, p. 33).

Psychoanalytic theory has always maintained that the infantile neurosis is relived in the form of the transference neurosis. But the fact is that the formation of the infantile neurosis is concomitant with the structuralization of the transference neurosis. The infantile neurosis was never a "clinically manifest entity," but rather "an unconscious configuration" (Tolpin, 1970, p. 278), a neurotic disposition or potential, the existence of which becomes manifest—that is, symptomatic—during adolescence or, certainly, during the terminal stage of adolescence (Freud, 1939, pp. 77-80; 1940, p. 191). I am in agreement with Tolpin's statement that the "term infantile neurosis should be reserved for the metapsychological concept that designates the repressed potentially pathogenic oedipal conflict . . . which is central in the pathology of the transference neuroses" (1970, p. 278).

Conclusion

Starting from analytic observations of late adolescent patients, I have come to the conclusion that the consolidation phase of late adolescence is the formative stage of the adult neurosis. Only after the formation of the adult neurosis can the transference neurosis, as the manifest form of the infantile neurosis, develop within the analytic situation. These considerations attribute a new and special importance to the consolidation stage of late adolescence. Explorations of the terminal stage of childhood—that is, of the formative stage of the adult personality, normal or pathological—have brought to the fore specific questions of analytic technique and theory. I have endeavored to open up to examination this particular area of clinical, developmental, and theoretical investigation by offering a conceptualization of the unique role late adolescence plays in the epigenesis of the adult neurosis.

Chapter 17

When and How Does
Adolescence End?

Structural Criteria for Adolescent Closure

I shall be concerned in this chapter with the question of how to conceptualize the termination of the adolescent process. For too long a time this has been no question at all because it was hardly ever asked. Adolescence seems to be a stage of development one simply outgrows. A widely held opinion tells us that it may linger on indefinitely, in which case people speak of the "eternal adolescent." Such talk is devoid of any biological or psychological reference or meaning. This stricture is a necessary one because normative reference points in relation to developmental stages and to their sequential order represent the requisite and essential data for the assessment of normal or pathological conditions at any level of growth. Therapy, research, and social planning depend in equal measure on normative definitions, because they constitute the only means by which observations or interventions can become comparative, evaluative, predictive, and purposeful.

We are all well acquainted with the milestones of child development formulated somatically, behaviorally, and psychologically. We owe this familiarity to child research

First published in *Adolescent Psychiatry*, vol. V., ed. S. C. Feinstein and P. Giovacchini. New York: Jason Aronson, 1976, pp. 5-17.

and its effort to delineate what is typical or normative of a given stage of development and to define as precisely as possible whatever is characteristic for the beginning or the ending of a developmental stage.

Let us admit at the outset that we are much better informed about the entry into adolescence than about its termination. This fact should not surprise us, because the onset of adolescence is coincidental with measurable somatic landmarks, such as primary and secondary sex characteristics, as well as growth curves and reliable psychological data. We are familiar with somatic sequences and with the chronological and morphological variation of pubertal maturation within the sequential order of somatic maturation. The latitude of these variations within the limits of normality is well documented. The psychological repercussions of these somatic novelties have also been widely studied. Furthermore, we know with certainty when the somatic process of puberty has come to an end. We have, however, no comparable certainty when it comes to psychological changes—their timing, transiency, or stability. The synchronicity between somatic and psychological changes, which is quite apparent during the early stage of adolescence, fades by the time the end phase of adolescence is reached. This disparity should be reason enough to adjust our terminology and speak of puberty only when we refer to the somatic process and reserve the term "adolescence" to denote the psychological changes. These latter changes reflect the psychic and social adaptation or accommodation to puberty. While this statement is, broadly speaking, true, we must not forget that adolescent psychological change not only copes with the ongoing somatic event (puberty), but is equally, perhaps even more urgently, called upon to integrate the individual's immediate social reality with his still active past and his anticipated future.

In summary fashion, I might say that puberty is an act of nature and adolescence is an act of man. This statement

emphasizes the fact that neither the completion of physical
growth, nor the attainment of sexual functioning, nor the
social role of economic self-support are, by and in themselves, reliable indices for the termination of the adolescent
process. In this connection, the history of the word "adolescence" is of interest. Literally, it means "becoming an
adult." According to the *Shorter Oxford English Dictionary*
(1967), this word appeared for the first time in the English
language in 1482. It was used to refer to the period between
childhood and adulthood, extending from fourteen to
twenty-five in the male and from twelve to twenty-one in
the female.

It is obvious from the usage of the word "adolescence"
five centuries ago that a parallelism between psychological,
psychosocial, and physical growth was disclaimed. The
usage of the word implied, at least at that time in history,
that the adolescent personality reaches the state of adulthood in total chronological independence from sexual
maturity. Similar observations, especially with reference to
college students, have suggested to some investigators an
intermediate developmental stage called "youth" (Keniston,
1968) or late and postadolescence (Blos, 1962) between
adolescence and adulthood. Erikson (1956) has suggested
the term "psychosocial moratorium" to denote this period. I
view this stretch of extended preadult life as the terminal
stage of adolescence because the typical psychological development of this period, called consolidation, proceeds in
direct continuation of the adolescent process. Just as any
developmental stage of childhood, if extended beyond its
timing or normative limit, generates a pathological nucleus
or a manifest disturbance, so adolescence too has its time of
closure, be this a normal or a pathological one.

I must stay a moment longer with the issue of the developmental continuum and the adolescent phases that constitute it. As pointed out earlier, puberty follows a clearly
delineated pattern of physical growth. In the realm of emo-

tional development, as well as in personality and character formation during adolescence, however, we have to rely on inferences from clinical data. These, in their totality, make up the theory of adolescence, which borrows its basic assumptions from psychoanalytic psychology. Among these data, we are particularly familiar with the adolescent revival of protolatency or early childhood leanings, predilections, and conflicts which are reworked. These conflicts, with the oedipal conflict as the crucial and prominent one, are resuscitated by the advent of puberty. This formulation is, more often than not, understood as the re-experiencing of a conflict that was settled long ago by the identification, repression, and sublimation that ushered in the latency period. This is, in brief, the psychoanalytic recapitulation theory of adolescence. It postulates that the Oedipus complex was resolved, for better or worse, at the end of early childhood and reappears essentially unchanged at puberty when extrafamilial sexual objects are to be sought, found, and gained.

As I have indicated in the preceding chapters, a more complex picture has emerged. It seems to me that the resolution of the oedipal conflict at the end of the phallic phase is normally a partial one. In other words, there remains a mere suspension of some oedipal issues, a détente if you will, although definitive thresholds of conflictual anxiety, narcissistic vulnerabilities, and idiosyncratic coping styles are established. We might say that the settlement of the Oedipus complex thus achieved was the most effective and growth-protective one that the ego of the child at this tender age could attain. It is my opinion that not only a recapitulation of the oedipal conflict but also a continuation became apparent at adolescence.

What I have found most revealing in observing the fate of this particular childhood conflict at adolescence is the incomplete settlement or the suspended conflict of the reversed or negative Oedipus complex: the child's love for the parent of the same sex (Chapters 15, 19). Psychoanalytic theory has always emphasized the bifold tendency (one being normally dominant) of infantile, object-directed sexuality which culminates in the oedipal constellation. The suspended conflict of this attachment always comes to light in adolescent therapy and presents a formidable obstacle within the context of the oedipal transferences. Pubescence, by its very nature, bestows on this highly ambivalent attachment a sexual quality, discernible in fantasies or in acting out during treatment. Since the resolution of the negative Oedipus complex has to be accomplished during the latter part of adolescence, and since the attainment of sexual identity is predicated on this resolution, it is only to be expected that issues of a homosexual nature constitute an inherent aspect of any adolescent psychotherapy or analysis. The defensive maneuver in relation to the negative Oedipus complex often takes the form of a hostile or aggressive attitude toward the parent of the same sex and an obstinate, even obsessive and intractable clinging to the positive or heterosexual component of the Oedipus complex. In other words, the child's oedipal attachment to the parent of the opposite sex is reactively pushed into the foreground. My observations in adolescent analysis have shown, over and over again, that the boy's oedipal love for his father or the girl's for her mother remains unreachable or well defended for a long time. I have referred to this as the adolescent oedipal defense. It is no easy task for the therapist to tease out such Janus-faced issues and deal with them therapeutically in accordance with their essential references. Normally, the adolescent is eminently assisted in the resolution of these internal conflicts by his maturing ego, by his widened social awareness, and particularly by the psychological support he receives and gives as a member of his peer group.

It is due to the continuation and not merely the repetition of childhood conflicts that I have proposed to extend psychological childhood to the termination of adolescence. Parenthetically, I might add, in supervision I have found that psychiatrists with training and experience in child therapy use this experience to advantage in adolescent therapy by applying child therapeutic techniques and insights whenever appropriate. Usually, it is a quite arbitrary decision by the therapist—a trial-and-error approach—as to where typical child therapy should end and adolescent therapy should begin. Too often, this changeover amounts to nothing more than the pre-emptory introduction of an adultomorphic model of therapy.

It may seem that I have wandered far afield from my topic. I can only assure you that everything I have said so far is essentially related to the thoughts I am going to develop. It must have become apparent that I intend to formulate normative reference points of development or, in other words, psychologically defined criteria that allow us to draw the demarcation line of adolescent closure. Physical status, sexual status, social status, and cognitive level have all proven to be unreliable indices, even though they spell out educated guesses in the pursuit of an answer to our original question. The psychological assessment of an individual's developmental status is a most elusive one, and yet it constitutes the indispensable reference point in the search for a meaningful answer to the question of adolescent closure. The ego, Hartmann once said, is defined by its functions. With reference to the present inquiry, I submit an extension of Hartmann's thought; namely, that—developmentally speaking—it is the degree of coordination and integration of ego functions, old and new, that spell out the completion of any developmental stage. The concept of developmental tasks or challenges has been found most useful in describing and defining developmental stages. In what follows, I take this very approach to answer the question of how the termination of adolescence can be determined.

There are, no doubt, phenomenological criteria that have

been recognized by both laymen and professionals in their efforts to define the end of adolescence. I call your attention to the gradual decline of the typical adolescent mood swings which reach, finally, a point where the state of relative even-temperedness is attained; in other words, the amplitude of the mood swings is lowered. Emotions are now selectively and discriminatively hidden from the public world and become privileged communications between friends and lovers. This capacity to share selectively some aspects of the self with either the private or the public sector of life without feeling divided or wrenched apart is a sign of either adolescence passing or having passed. The attempt to understand oneself renders the need always to be understood (by specific persons or by the larger social order) less urgent, less uncontrollable, and less exalting. This novel characteristic of the consolidation phase, called late adolescence, may also be described by saying that the predictability of behavior and motivation waxes over time in constancy and accuracy until characterological stabilization replaces tentative and arbitrary predictions with an established pattern of individual conduct.

If we conceive of character as the automatization of responses or the patterned behavior that allows no alternative, then we can point to another typical aspect of adolescent closure. Character formation reaches a condition of definitive stability at the end of adolescence when ego autonomy, in alliance with the ego ideal, challenges partially but effectively the dominance of the superego. This agency of the mind, which reigned supreme during childhood and evoked a never-ending struggle between insurrection and submission, attended by feelings of omnipotence or helplessness, guilt or shame, undergoes during adolescence a critical revision within the motivational system. In consonance with the consolidation of the late adolescent personality, the emergence of a life plan, a life style, a purposive striving toward reasonably attainable goals becomes feasible if not, indeed, mandatory. It goes without saying that most adolescents are not offered an abundance of choices and options by the circumstances of their lives; yet, even here a projection of oneself into the future remains indispensable.

To these phenomenological signs of adolescent closure could be added the gradual change in the nature of relationships, personal and communal, in the direction of discriminatory involvements and ultimate commitments within the private and public realms of individual needs and aspirations. Need I add that the vicissitudes of relationships, or their relative lability, remain a lifelong concern, causing indefinite disruptions and corruptions of personal and communal life everywhere and always? Even if the consolidation of late adolescence has done its work in good faith, the framework of any personality structure can only stand up well over time if relatively benign circumstances continue to prevail. With this perhaps pessimistic comment on the human condition, I leave the discussion of the phenomenological criteria that are relevant for the determination of adolescent closure and turn to the psychological criteria, which are the more reliable and also the more crucial ones. This assumption certainly appears convincing in our professional encounters with those adolescents who have failed to reach or failed to traverse the developmental terrain of late adolescence. The impact of maturational, developmental, and social mandates leaves these late adolescents stranded with no other alternative than to terminate adolescence by some kind of psychopathological accommodation. With tongue in cheek I may add: if they are fortunate they become our patients.

Earlier, when I mentioned developmental tasks and challenges, I was aware that such entities are isolated only for the purpose of assessment and discussion. I shall now present four developmental tasks which, collaboratively and in a synergetic way, lead the individual adolescent into adulthood.[1]

The Second Individuation Process

I am not telling you anything new when I say that the adolescent child has to disengage himself from infantile dependencies. Anna Freud (1958) has referred to this as the "loosening of the infantile object ties." Borrowing terminology from Margaret Mahler's research in early childhood, I have spoken of the second individuation process of adolescence (see Chapter 8). Infantile individuation proceeds in relation to the caretaking person, the mother. During the separation-individuation phase the existence of the mother as a discrete object emerges through the process of internalization. In other words, the formation of object and self-representations establishes the boundary between the internal and the external world. The internalized parents and, through them, the internalized culture in the widest sense remain relatively unchallenged until puberty. During adolescence these old and familiar dependencies, as well as infantile love and hate objects, are drawn anew into the emotional life. The object disengagement through individuation at the adolescent level does not proceed in relation to external objects as it did in early childhood; it now proceeds in relation to the internalized objects of early childhood.

A characteristic cathectic shift signaling this disengagement can be seen in the libidinal cathexis of the self, resulting in the proverbial and transient self-centeredness and self-aggrandizement of the adolescent. This narcissistic grandeur rarely fails to elicit its counterpart, namely, the sense of nothingness (the state of helplessness) and despair (the state of object loss). These well-known affective states

[1] These four developmental tasks were also examined in relation to adolescent character formation in Chapter 9.

are akin to mania, depression, and mourning. In other words, the mood swings of adolescence represent the corollary of the second individuation process.

From treatment we know how infantile object attachment appears in many disguises; of these the attachment to fantasies and to quasi-delusional states deserves our special attention. Their stubborn resistance to being left behind as the price of growing up reflects the wish to enshrine for good those infantile object attachments that have acquired an extraordinary importance for psychological survival. It must be remembered that infantile parental imagos perpetuate the belief in perfection. With the advent of adolescence this notion is challenged as never before; a critical deidealization—or humanization, if you will—of the infantile world order is necessary. But this disillusionment has a more or less devastating effect on the adolescent's sense of self. Even if the parents or their societal representatives are perceived by the adolescent as bad or evil, the polarity of the all-good and nurturant infantile object never fails to loom in the background of the adolescent's mind as a realizable alternative. Thus, the adolescent strives to contradict Heraclitus who said you can never step twice into the same river.

The conflictual constellation of the second individuation process can be observed most dramatically in certain forms of acting out. In cases of this kind the internal conflict is experienced as one between the individual and his environment: the conflict is externalized. The developmental reel, so to speak, is played backwards. Much of what we see as adolescent rebellion is a turn to the surround as the object of love and hate. The imperfections of social institutions become the wholesale target of aggression; they become the projected, inanimate reifications of rejecting, noncaring, engulfing, indifferent, or selfish internal objects. As such they are endowed with intentionalities perpetrating frustration and humiliation on the adolescent when his need for support in the pursuit of self-realization reaches a critical peak. Speaking in the broadest terms, we might say that the imperfections of the wider world to which the adolescent turns upon leaving the dependencies of his childhood are bound to upset his narcissistic balance. In the narcissistic rage that follows he either succumbs to defeatist, sullen resignation (called "passive aggression"), to psychotic regression, or he sets out to shape a perfect world by force. Incapable of resolving the internal state of dependency, he resorts to the mechanism of externalization with the aim of creating a new and perfect, i.e., need-gratifying world; the imperfections of the old have to be eradicated by whatever means will serve this purpose. Such rescue operations of infantile narcissism ward off—at least temporarily—the disillusionment in self and object by the projection of evil onto social institutions and the concrete as well as the symbolic mandates of society. The student rebellion of recent times has brought these developmental dynamics to my attention through radical students who were my patients. The same dynamics are applicable to other epochs and other social arenas in which the second individuation process is enacted in one form or another.

In order not to be misunderstood I must add here a word of caution. So-called adolescent maladaptation always points to serious defects, inconsistencies, archaisms, and corruptions in the social order. It takes historical and political astuteness to bring about needed changes; no doubt, some late adolescent rebels acquire these faculties. To consider all adolescent radical or reformist activism, be it political or social, as mere projection, externalization, or displacement is simplistic nonsense. I do not conceive of the revolutionary or activist personality per se as developmentally regressed or arrested, as taking recourse to the externalization of his emotional disharmonies. I can only repeat: behavior alone never renders a reliable assessment of any individual's developmental status, nor does it reveal the workings of his motivational system. In fact, a valid case could be made for the contributory role the nonconformist adolescent plays in the reform of societal patterns.

Ego Continuity

I come now to the second task or challenge the late adolescent has to meet in order to bring the adolescent process to a close. "Ego continuity" is the term I have chosen and I shall describe what I mean by it. For the child to survive in the world into which he is born, he needs for many years the support, guidance, and orientation provided by caretaking persons. In this extended psychological ecosystem the parents function as extensions of the child's ego; adolescence alters this state radically. During normal adolescence the growing child uses his advanced cognitive faculty and somatic maturity to gain emotional, moral, and physical independence. This is the time when he forms his own view of his past, present, and future. The past is retrospectively subjected to a kind of historical reality testing. Here we witness the ascent of self-conscious man who, as never before, has become aware of his unique, yet ordinary, life that lies between birth and death. So-called existential anxiety cannot be experienced before adolescence; the same is true for the sense of the tragic.

Disturbances in the formation of ego continuity or its clinical pathology are most clearly reflected in cases of a special kind of reality distortion. In these cases a reality misrepresentation was willfully inflicted on the child's mind. As a result the child accepted as real what he was told was real, thus sacrificing the veracity of his own perception and cognition. This kind of reality distortion is to be distinguished from psychotic delusion or the contamination by a psychotic parent or primal-scene traumatization. The pathogenetic factor lies rather in the unavailability on the conscious level of circumstances the child once shared with others but was afterwards (by gesture and innuendo) forbidden to acknowledge as real. Disturbances in reality testing are always, in such cases, a part of the clinical picture. A brief reference to a patient of mine will make this clear.[2]

A seventeen-year-old delinquent boy was brought to me by his maternal uncle because incidents of truancy, shoplifting, forgery of checks, and lying had reached a point of most serious legal consequences. The culprit's attitude was one of resignation to the fact that he was "fated to become a criminal." He showed none of the aggressive and defensive indifference or downright oppositionalism we are used to observe whenever acting out is, at least partially, based on simple impulse discharge. The boy told me that he had no memory of his father because he had lost him when still an infant. He had never known him; his mother had told him about his death. From the uncle who had taken a fatherly interest in his nephew I knew a piece of family history that contradicted these facts. In brief: the father had been sent to prison for embezzlement when the child was six years old. Preceding this event, father and child had lost contact for a few years after the parents' divorce when the child was three. According to what the mother had told me, the father had died in prison and she was a widow. The child accepted this fact and never again asked a question about his father. In his own mind the child had predated the father's death to a time when he was an infant, thus eliminating all possible memory of image and affect. These were both replaced by the sense of being fated to become a criminal—thus resurrecting and rescuing the father image by identification. In fact, the father was alive in a prison hospital for the criminally insane. Space does not permit me to go into the labyrinthine search for the lost past. But I must mention that treatment was initiated by my telling the boy the facts about his father's life or, conversely, his

[2]This case was also reported in Chapter 12 in the context of adolescent acting out and its conceptualization.

mother's lie. As always in such cases, the patient reacted to this information as if he were told what he had always known—even if not consciously. With the gradual restoration of his personal history—what I have referred to as ego continuity—the delinquent behavior lost its compulsive character.

It became clear that delinquent acting out in this case was an abortive maladaptive effort to rescue the integrity of his perception and cognition, even though it was contradicted and declared illusory by the strictures of his environment. A follow-up after ten years presented the following picture: criminal behavior had long since become a matter of the past; besides having built his own personal life and a satisfying career, he had sent regularly to his father the material comforts which—so the son felt—would make his hopeless existence more endurable. From his mother, on the other hand, he had become estranged, even though he kept up a perfunctory family tie. I may add that my telling the boy his factual history was based on the assumption that a reality distortion which is willfully imposed from the outside on the child has to be rectified by a rational or truth-loving environment of which the therapist is the representative and guardian. Only then can treatment begin and proceed to the child's *self*-initiated distortions of reality and their dynamic as well as genetic implications.

Residual Trauma

The third challenge or task is related to the concept of trauma. I consider it as axiomatic that trauma—usually of a cumulative kind—is an inevitably injurious experience in the infantile period. Whatever the accommodation to or neutralization of these noxious jolts to psychological growth may have been, there remains, nevertheless, at the end of adolescence a residue that challenges the adaptive resourcefulness of the late adolescent. Idiosyncratic vulnerabilities due to residual trauma are part of the human condition. Even heroes and demigods have to live with them: Achilles had his vulnerable heel by which Thetis held him when she dipped the infant into the river Styx to fortify him against mortal injury. Another demigod, Sigurd, better known as Siegfried, had a vulnerable spot on his shoulder where a leaf had fallen when he bathed in the blood of the slain dragon, Fafnir. Mythology tells us that such extraordinary protection against "the slings and arrows of outrageous fortune" is acquired only during babyhood and youth and never without a minor, accidental miscarriage of the intended absolute invulnerability.

This brings me back to the concept of residual trauma, namely, that aspect of trauma that is never resolved and, in fact, can never be resolved. Far from being a lamentable impediment, this universal predicament gives a driving impetus to its mastery. This persistent impetus propels the late adolescent into a more or less definitive set of commitments of a personal as well as an impersonal nature. The mastery of traumatic residues proceeds within the scope of those opportunities which societal institutions and social alliances offer, such as training facilities, work associations, ideological affiliations, and intimate relations of various kinds. In this sense, we might speak of a socialization of the residual trauma during late adolescence. This process coincides with the waning intrusion on the motivational system of infantile fantasies and their transposition or relegation to the world of daydream, playfulness, and restorative communal associations—from bullfighting to reciting poetry. In essence, the residual trauma serves as an organizer that promotes the consolidation of the adult personality and accounts for its uniqueness. The socialization of residual trauma is heralded in therapy whenever the young patient takes over the responsibility for his own life, tolerating a modicum of tension and ceasing to mourn the death of his infantile fantasies and expectancies. The complexity of this process is of such magnitude that I must refrain from giving a case illustration; instead, I encourage you to search your own case material for relevant links to the thesis I have submitted.

Sexual Identity

I come now to the fourth and last challenge in my schema of developmental criteria in relation to adolescent closure, namely, sexual identity. This concept is distinct from gender identity which is established early in life. Sexual activity per se is no indication of normal adolescent closure and offers no assurance that gender-specific sexual identity has been attained. Sexual-identity formation is predicated on the transmutation of the gender-inadequate component of the sexual drive into a new psychic structure, the ego ideal. What I have in mind is the transmutation of the infantile, narcissistic ego ideal into the adult, desexualized, abstract ego ideal (see Chapter 15). It is a common experience in adolescent therapy that this forward step is an extraordinarily difficult and slow process; it requires the relinquishment of infantile self- and object idealizations. An unabated persistence of infantile aggrandizement precludes the formation of stable, adult human relations.

The typical adolescent regression, which I have termed regression in the service of development, stirs up in its wake the infantile dichotomy between the all-good and the all-bad object. This state reflects a primitive, preambivalent object tie. Not until the state of mature ambivalence becomes structurally stabilized in late adolescence can an enduring adult relationship take its course. It is no exaggeration to say that the most harrowing and most painful subjective experience within adolescent psychic restructuring is related to the process of deidealization. What this transformation of the self reflects is, indeed, a purgatory through which winds the path from childhood dependency to adult humanization.

I have elsewhere (Chapter 5) discussed this complex sub-

ject in greater detail. At this time I want to stress one
point, namely, the intrinsic interconnectedness between
sexual identity formation and deidealization of self and object. I am convinced that a review of your own experiences
with adolescent patients will give my proposition an almost
self-evident ring.

Conclusion

The four structural criteria I have outlined were lifted
from my work with adolescents because they had served me
well over time to bring order to my clinical observations. It
should, however, be understood that the four developmental
challenges or tasks I have defined represent integral components of a *total* process. All four act synergically and in
unison; their developmental resolutions are global; one
without the other can never bring about a normal termination of adolescence. Due to this interconnectedness of the
four challenges, it is possible to gauge from the assessment
of a component aspect the relative progress toward adolescent closure as a whole. Ultimately, however, it is the integration of the four challenges, or the nodal intersection of
the four coordinates—if you will—that assures us with
reasonable certainty that the developmental stage of adolescence has reached its termination. I know very well that
this formulation of mine is an ideal one, rarely or never encountered in real life. It should be looked at as a schema.
Experience tells us that unresolved psychological issues are
always bound to remain; it is, however, their stable integration into the adult personality—the work of the consolidation stage—that gives these persistent issues a patterned
and rather irreversible structure. The characterological stability, thus attained, signals that adolescence has passed.

PART FIVE

The Body Image:
Its Relation to Normal and
Pathological Functioning

The fortunate coincidence of having three cases of cryptorchism, each referred for a different psychological disturbance, made it possible for me to make a comparative study as to the particular influence of the anatomical anomaly on the development of each boy. Despite the individual differences in the presenting psychopathology, certain trends emerged regarding symptomatic behavior, symbolism, fantasies, and restitutive mechanisms which, in their totality, permitted me to make generalizations about the mental representation of a physical defect and its relation to deviant development. Furthermore, the study made clear that some ominous disturbances in behavior and thinking were directly linked to body-image disturbances. This link proved in some cases to be conditional to such an extent that the correction of the physical anomaly, either surgically or spontaneously, resulted, if not in the disappearance, then decidedly in the treatability of the psychological disturbance. As the case material shows, therapeutic help was of the essence in this process. Treatment, however, proved to be effective with far less therapeutic work than was anticipated in light of the presenting disturbance. What struck the clinician as bizarre behavior, and was looked at by the boy's environment as "crazy," took on an entirely different pathognomic valence once the symptoms were related to the distorted body image.

It must be made clear that each body anomaly has to be looked at and studied as a unique entity. My clinical research on cryptorchism offers an example of how a particular physical anomaly affects mental functioning and by which psychic processes this was effected. For any other anomaly a reference system of its own particularity has to be worked out.

An anecdote will illustrate some of the above remarks. A child therapist told me about some bizarre behavior in an eleven-year-old boy with an undescended testicle. This boy's behavior had puzzled the doctor until we discussed the case

423

in the light of my research. What had appeared as a quasi-psychotic, compulsive symptom, took on the character of a symptomatic act with far less serious diagnostic implications when looked at within the reference system of cryptorchism. The boy's behavior was as follows.

For a considerable length of time he had engaged in a repetitive "game." Whenever he met a man (never a woman) whom he knew and who was familiar with the rules of the game, he would, with quick action, pinch the man's cheek and hold on to it until the victim would say the "right word." If the boy had grabbed one cheek, the word was "cheek"; if he had grabbed both cheeks, as he usually did, the word was "cheeks." Only when he was given the right answer would he let go. The metaphor of the game lay in the either-or, plural or singular, and in the displacement from below to above. The boy was saying: "Tell me, do I have one or two testicles?" The similarity of cheeks and skin-bags lent to the displacement the typical literalness we generally observe. The same boy appeared for his medical examination with his right arm contortedly retracted in the sleeve of his jacket, with the empty end floppily dangling at his side. This incident occurred at a time when his right testicle was in the process of descending.

A historical note of interest should be added here. The writer of the World War II British marching song (quoted in Chapter 18) alludes to Hitler having only "one big ball." Only later did Hitler's autopsy by the Russians reveal that he did indeed have only one testis. "One could infer that it must have been larger than normal due to compensatory hypertrophy, since the Russians said nothing about a second testis being found intra-abdominally."[1]

The peculiar transposition of a limerick by an unknown expurgist might be mentioned in connection with "organ equivalents" as discussed in relation to cryptorchism. The limerick goes like this:

[1]Personal communication (1971), John K. Lattimer, M.D., Chairman, Department of Urology, College of Physicians and Surgeons, Columbia University.

> A peculiar chap from Devizes
> Had balls of various sizes;
>   One was so small
>   It was nothing at all,
> But the other took several prizes.

This limerick reads in Louis Untermeyer's (1961) *Lots of Limericks:*

> An odd looking girl from Devizes
> Had eyes of two different sizes. . .

Obviously, the two limericks are related and it is not difficult to guess which the original one was. In the variation we encounter the displacement from boy to girl and testes to eyes. The same displacement from testis to eye appears in the subsequent case material; it is also known from the Oedipus myth.

Chapter 18

Comments on the Psychological Consequences of Cryptorchism

A Clinical Study

The psychoanalytic literature contains only scant references to the testicles and their role in the mental life of the male child. This fact alone invites a report on cases with undescended testicles in which these body parts, due to their abnormal state, assumed a role of specific psychological import. There is no doubt that the male child concentrates almost exclusively on one part of his genitals, the penis, while the other parts (scrotum, testes) are but peripherally and transiently acknowledged. With reference to this fact Freud (1923b) has commented: "It is, incidentally, remarkable what a small degree of attention the other part of the male genitals, the little sac with its contents, attracts in children. From all one hears in analyses, one would not guess that the male genitals consisted of anything more than the penis" (p. 142n.). The male child is not totally unaware of the scrotal region, however, and possesses tactile as well as visual knowledge of it. This fact is exemplified by the self-observation of a two-and-a-half-year-old boy who noticed that an undescended testicle had come down into the scrotal sac and was perturbed by this change. The father, a pedia-

First published in *The Psychoanalytic Study of the Child,* 15: 395-429. New York: International Universities Press, 1960.

427

trician, had paid no special attention to the previous condition and was surprised at the child's self-observation and negative reaction. The little boy wanted it changed back to the way it had been; he "didn't like" two testicles. The change and newness of this body part were initially disturbing to the child but were assimilated within a short time.

Analytic experience with male patients, both children and adults, bears out the fact that the penis as a pleasure-giving organ is more highly cathected with libido and aggressive energy than the other parts of the male genital. Under the abnormal condition of an undescended testicle, however, the genitals assume a special role. It is not my contention to infer that, in the deviate condition of an undescended testicle, a primary cathexis of the testicle appears in magnified dimension. Quite to the contrary, I consider the dominant role of the testicle apparent in the following cases to be of a secondary order, determined by environmental influences. I do not consider cryptorchism in itself as pathogenic. Only secondarily, within the matrix of a disturbed parent-child relationship, does this condition acquire a profoundly detrimental influence on the mental development of the child. The anxious (aggressive) preoccupation of the environment with the child's genital defectiveness eventually designates the testicle as the focal genital part in relation to which the formation of the body image and psychosexual development in general become specifically distorted. The genital defect, then, serves as the "organizing experience" (Greenacre, 1956) in the mental life of the child and results in ego deformations of a rather typical pattern.

Fantasy life, restitutive acts, ego functions and defensive operations, self- and body image, sexual identification were all studied in a number of cases of cryptorchism, three of which are reported here in detail. It must be borne in mind that the usual body-damage anxiety of the male child is in these boys associated with a missing testicle, i.e., with an already accomplished fact over which they have no control.

The body-part loss is no longer a threat because it is palpably verifiable. On the other hand, a restitution of the loss is always kept within the realm of possibility as attested by the frequent medical checkups and interventions. Napoleon's famous dictum, which Freud (1912a) paraphrased into "Anatomy is destiny," assumes in these cases a special meaning, because here anatomy remains alterable—at least, that is the promise the environment never ceases to impute. Consequently, anatomical uncertainty is destiny.

It became apparent in the cases presented how the body image is shaped by sensory perception in conjunction with environmental responses to the body and its defect. In this connection it was particularly striking to see that the body change, as in spontaneous descent (case of Larry) or successful operative corrections (cases of Steven and Joe), resulted in a rapid shift of behavior, attitudes, interests, and skills. This change cannot be credited to the resolution of endopsychic conflicts alone. The clinical observation of cathetic shifts brought about by the restoration of body intactness has theoretical and therapeutic implications which shall be discussed after the case material has been presented.

In all three cases a mysterious exclusion of the physical condition of unilateral cryptorchism from the presentation of the case history occurred. In two cases the fact of undescended testicles had to be surmised through symptomatic acts of the child. The parents did not mention the child's condition initially, nor did the boy himself ever refer to it. Symbolic representation of the genital defect was abundant in the play material and behavior. In all cases a medical clarification of the genital status was attained. Therapy always came to an impasse whenever the medical planning for restorative intervention (injection or operation) was indefinitely postponed. The therapist had hoped against hope that the child, after having worked through his fantasies, would in due time disclose spontaneously his genital condition. Only under the pressure of medical intervention did such fantasies become available in therapy, and thus serve as a vehicle to interpret distortions and defenses. Anatomical as well as sexual enlightenment was given in great detail, especially in cases where the child had to be prepared for an impending operation.

The three boys studied were of prepubertal age. The orchidopexy on Steven was performed at the age of ten years, three months, and on Joe at the age of twelve years, ten months; spontaneous descent was confirmed in the case of Larry at the age of ten years, eleven months. This presentation is in no way a report on the therapy of the three boys. Their respective diagnostic categories had little in common; however, their symptom pictures showed significant similarities which were due to the identical genital defect they shared. The presence of this physical factor indeed blurred the diagnostic and prognostic assessment of the cases to a considerable extent.

Where the maldescent was corrected spontaneously there was far more doubt about and distrust in the permanency of the restoration than in the operative cases. In the latter cases the action was accepted as final; more faith was lent to the surgeon's knife than was given to an act of nature. This difference we can attribute to the masochistic and the castrative wishes which, contrary to all expectations, turned the defective boy into an intact man. He who entered the lion's den had come out alive. Besides the assurance of body intactness, the operation also demonstrated that the body had not been permanently injured by masturbation. Of course, we can detect behind the masculine euphoria following the operation an overcompensation of persistent feminine strivings.

The mere condition of an undescended testicle certainly does not lead to similar diagnostic entities, because cryptorchism cannot be considered as pathogenic in itself. It does, however, lend different conditions some points of similarity since the genital defect assumes in these cases an influence of dominant importance. Whatever the diagnostic category, the "organizing experience," namely, cryptorchism, was the same for all of them. The existence of identical symptoms in my cases became apparent: motility disturbances (hyperactivity), learning difficulties, and accident proneness in the form of a compulsive toying with physical danger. To this triad must be added a state of social inadequacy and chronic indecision, as well as a tendency to exaggerate, to lie, and to fantasy. Most striking was the disappearance or drastic diminution of these symptoms once the intactness of the genital organ was established, either spontaneously or operatively. The clinical material suggests that cryptorchism influences symptom choice, regardless of the nosological designation of the case. It seems that the different disorders represented in the case material found in the genital defect a palpable and visible reality around which the respective pathology of each case was articulated.

Clinical Material

The Case of Steven

Steven, a slender, friendly boy of eight, was brought to treatment by his mother on the recommendation of the school: in the third grade, he was still practically a nonreader. He gave the impression of an atypical (borderline) child, with poor motor coordination (clumsy gait, "like a drunkard," inept in games, illegible handwriting) and infantile behavior (does not feed, bathe, dress himself; chews on his clothes; messy child; drops ink, flour, food on the floor; spills soil from flowerpots in his room and on his bed). He showed an intense preoccupation with death and time and seemed anxious and worried.

Steven was born with the left testis undescended. A tumor on the scrotum was removed at five months. The mother felt that she had caused the tumor, "by poking

around these parts so much." At seven Steven had a tonsillectomy with subsequent hemorrhaging which necessitated
his return to the hospital. In the same year he received
eight hormone injections which were not followed by a descent of the testis but increased the size of the penis and
stimulated the growth of pubic hair. Numerous doctors were
consulted. Finally, the source of all of Steven's troubles was
thought by the mother to be located in a weak muscle of the
left eye, but the ophthalmologist did not confirm this.

The mother was of the opinion that Steven was oblivious
to his testicular condition and did not know why so many
doctors had examined him. She believed that her show of
pseudo confidence and unconcern had protected him from all
doubts about his bodily intactness. This defensive attitude
on her part was due to her narcissistic involvement with
the child: having been disappointed in her own career, in
her husband, and in her first son, she had made Steven the
center of her emotional life and wanted him to be the
genius who would fulfill her wildest ambitions. Steven's
father was a passive and withdrawn man who, according to
the boy, "does not know what goes on at home." Five years
before Steven's birth the father had suffered and recovered
from a psychotic episode with paranoid delusions. He never
showed any interest in Steven's therapy.

During the first interview Steven questioned the
therapist as to why he was visiting a doctor again. His guidance teacher had wanted him to go to the eye clinic, but he
had been told by the doctor that there was nothing wrong
with his eye. In the second interview he stated that he had
kissed a girl and got two sores on his mouth from it. At
least, that is what his mother had said; he himself was not
sure: he thought his lips were chapped before.

After this introduction he became involved in dramatic
play in which he was the doctor taking care of dolls suffering from a polio condition, which was due to the fact that
they had been born with a knife which made them stiff.
Identifying with the aggressor, he became now the surgeon

who could be trusted to have a sure hand. But at other times his anxiety came through. Steven's grandfather had died after an operation. Steven professed ignorance of the nature of this operation (actually a prostate operation), but he was sure "it was not in the leg system; it might have been bleeding ulcers." At such times of blatant denial he did not want the dolls to be operated on.

Later in the treatment the boy's play shifted to aggressive themes of shooting and killing; he and his therapist were the two best gunmen in the world. Dynamite (clay) had to be hidden from the outlaws, for it could easily blow up the world. Over and over he kneaded the clay without ever shaping anything; he always wanted the clay he had been kneading to be saved for the next session.

The mother still maintained that the child had no knowledge of his condition. But when the doctor decided to perform an operation, Steven had to be told of it. This the mother did gingerly, only to be interrupted by the boy, who told her that he was not stupid and had known all along why people had been poking around there. In his treatment he now openly revealed his anxiety which was so intense that he was unable to comprehend an anatomical sketch his therapist drew for him. His play during these sessions became very infantile.

Steven made a last effort to dispense with the operation. He wanted to sit in the therapist's chair: "I like to be you and you to be me." Could "hes" be made into "shes?" He was completely ignorant of the origin of babies and the function of the testes: the growing testis "in the stomach" was confused with the fetus. Soon after the boy admitted that he had always "felt himself" (masturbated) he could listen to the details of the operation. He was then also able to recapitulate his long history of medical interventions. Several months after a successful operation, Steven described the sensation in his testes: he knew what he felt, he no longer was confused.

His play now consisted in building a Stevensville

Museum: two marbles of special stone were on exhibit. He soon lost interest in this kind of play and became more oriented toward schoolwork, the Boy Scouts, friends, chess play, piano lessons, etc. His active interest in the environment reflected the appearance of a belated latency period. Peer relations and organized physical activities began to play an important part in his life. His clumsiness improved noticeably. Near the end of therapy, one year after the operation, he had advanced to his grade level in reading. His critical judgment about himself and others had increased; there was less need to ingratiate himself by being charming and cute; he had made striking gains in the realm of social effectiveness. Still, in times of stress, he reverted to infantile and disorganized reactions. The separation from his mother, which he now aggressively enforced, was laden with guilt and anxiety. The simple comfort found in dependency was no longer available to him. As to the mother, she had been helped to refrain from involving the boy in her own fantasy life; her need to deny his imperfections had significantly lessened. The growing adequacy of the child was recognized by the father, who became progressively more interested in his son.

The Case of Larry

When Larry was referred to the clinic at the age of nine years, ten months, he presented such a variety of symptoms that it was feared that the neurotic manifestations in conjunction with conduct and habit disorders might mask a more malignant pathology. The major complaints were: soiling, nocturnal enuresis, psychogenic headaches, accident proneness; he fought with other children, refused to do his homework, could not concentrate in school; he had fright reactions to the dentist, to blood, and to monsters which appeared in his fantasies and nightmares; he had difficulty in falling asleep and refused to be covered up or held down.

The mother was vague and contradictory in her description of the child: she appeared on the one hand to be indulgent when the child was "nice," but on the other hand she beat him with a strap for misbehaving; she was full of angry contempt for the weak males of her family, her husband and three sons. Larry had two brothers, one two years older and the other four years younger. The father, when he was finally seen, presented himself as a withdrawn man, afraid of his wife's criticism, and obediently carrying out her orders. Actually he had genuine and warm feelings for Larry, and much sympathetic understanding of him.

Larry had been a healthy infant. At two and a half years he was noted to have a hernia and a hydrocele, referred to by the mother as a "skin tumor on the left testicle." The conditions were corrected at a hospital where the child stayed for ten days. During this period he was frightened, depressed, or uncontrollably wild. The hyperactivity, accompanied by many accidents, had been part of his behavior pattern since that time. The most tragic mishap occurred while he played in the park soon after he had started treatment at the clinic. A stick thrown at him hit his eye as he stood paralyzed in the course of the approaching missile. This accident resulted in the loss of his left eye. The child expressed to his therapist great rage at his mother who had not told him after the operation that his eyeball had been removed: he had noticed it on the doctor's chart while still wearing his bandage. This irreparable, self-induced injury was subsequently linked to the physical restraint imposed on him during the operation on the genital and to the mother's demand for passivity. A circuitous process had been established: the motoric rage had become turned against the self, bringing about actively what he feared suffering at the hands of the "monsters."

A ritual accompanying his headaches was soon revealed: they were always due to a "strong light" hitting his eyes. He then had to lie down in the dark with his face covered and he would fall asleep. The headaches always followed an arousal of anger and hostility; they seemed to have started at the time of the operation on the genital. This ritual enabled us to understand the sadomasochistic conflict in Larry.

Ever since the loss of the eye, Larry complained of "bellyaches." A dynamic link seemed probable: the suspicion arose that the boy had an undescended testicle. The mother was questioned, and the assumption proved to be correct. Larry, however, was supposed to ignore this fact. His confusion about operations, needles, hernia contained a tacit accusation against his parents for never having told him the truth about his physical problems. The question arose whether the sacrifice of the eyeball was a substitute bodypart relinquishment in order to salvage the more precious ball buried in his belly. Or was the self-castrating act a masochistic surrender of his masculinity which brought temporary relief from an intolerable state of panic and terror of being attacked by a castrating monster-woman? Soiling ceased soon after his fear of going to the toilet was understood as a fear of losing his undescended testicle with his feces.

Finally, the boy's fear of "another operation" came to the fore. He had overheard his father speak of this possibility in case "the testicle does not stay down." This prospect made the child anxious, which in turn aroused in him aggressive feelings toward his parents and resulted in a bicycle accident. He became panicky about an infection of his good eye (which was in perfect condition) and feared going blind; he requested that a night light be kept on in his room so he could see whenever he woke up during the night. This assured him that his eyesight was intact and that his good eye was still there. He dreamed of getting pieces of glass into his good eye and losing it. He dreamed of an "eye bank" where new eyes could be gotten.

Treatment had progressively become the boy's refuge. He used the therapist's name at home to restrain the mother from undue interference. In his sessions he turned tables by playing the role of the teacher, who for so long had been a phobic object, and asking the therapist to be the pupil. At home he was steadily gaining in independence; he bathed and dressed himself. At school he became more attentive and interested in his work. By the same token he had become more compulsive and worried about his homework, etc. When the boy urged his therapist to see his father, this facilitated a discussion of the boy's undescended testicle, and the father arranged for a medical examination to determine whether an operation was indicated. The examination ascertained the fact that the left testis had descended, was permanently located in the scrotum but was somewhat smaller than the right one. Larry, of course, knew this.

Constructive self-assertion and compulsive cautiousness gradually replaced the alternating bursts of destructive rages (such as "to blow up the whole family" with his chemistry set) and self-damaging activities which once threatened to make an invalid of him. Larry's realistic interest in science had grown steadily; he had set up his own chemical laboratory at home. He no longer threw himself headlong into new experiences but interposed judgment before he embarked on a new course of action. He now played with boys of his own age instead of with younger children. In his daily tasks he took initiative and was no longer a pawn in the hands of terrifying monsters. His aggressive drive had found sublimated expression in his activities: at school he became captain of the safety squad. At home he defended himself against his mother's influence with stubborn determination; it was now only she who found Larry unreasonably difficult to manage or to get along with.

The Case of Joe

Joe, a tall, heavy, light-skinned Black with pubescence already manifest, was nine years old when he was referred

to the clinic by his school because of his restlessness, excessive boasting, daydreaming, and learning difficulties. He
was found to be a lonely and fearful child whose history revealed that his activities had been restricted until the age
of six because of a congenital heart murmur. His urge for
activity had then broken through and asserted itself in uncontrollable hypermotility.

The mother, who wanted her boy to be gentle and
mild-mannered, was doing her utmost to suppress in him all
upsurges of male self-assertion. The child's two older sisters
had been taught to baby the little "invalid." The father was
disappointed in Joe's lack of boyish behavior and interests,
and although a good provider, he spent little time in the
home and did not share in the life of the family.

Joe had been in treatment for three years before his
undescended testicle was inadvertently mentioned by the
mother. His petty stealing, his tall tales, his constant references to secrets, the compulsive chair balancing which led
to his falling, all became intelligible when related to the
genital defect. It was decided to concentrate on two areas:
the ego dysfunction, i.e., his inability to read, and the anxiety attached to the genital defectiveness. It was also decided
to try and enlist the father's cooperation in spite of Joe's
strenuous attempts to leave his father out of his treatment.

The interviews the therapist had with the father resulted in his taking Joe to the doctor: the course of treatment was explained to the child. The ensuing period of injections was one of anxiety for the boy. The fact that "nothing happened" after the injections opened up the frightening possibility of an operation. Joe refused to discuss this,
insisting that he had talked to his sisters about it and that
there was nothing more to say. His behavior became quite
mischievous, almost delinquent, and he was full of complaints about the tutor who, he said, was unable to help
him.

The now impending operation was linked by Joe with

his tonsillectomy. The doctor might find that the testis was no good, cut it out, and throw it away. His fear of sterility, should he be left with only one good testicle, was talked over with the therapist. Joe now felt free to ask questions about it; at the same time he was making progress in reading. His tutor also noticed an increased ability to learn and a longer concentration span. Joe at this time introduced a new topic in his treatment—his girlfriends. A sudden wave of interest had swept him into the realm of early adolescent emotions. With bravado he told the therapist that he knew everything about sex.

The father's distrust of doctors and the mother's helplessness in planning for the operation ("I only know how to take care of girls") forced the therapist to assume the main responsibility for making all arrangements with the surgeon and hospital. Joe was appreciative of this help. Yet, for the first time, as soon as the operation was planned, the boy's aggression against his mother came to the fore: she was not helping him, she was trying to make a girl out of him, he was not going to tolerate being treated in this way. He considered it an insult to his masculinity to have a woman doctor examine him at the hospital. At the same time his fear of castration was expressed: he often referred to his tonsillectomy, when "the knife had slipped and cut a hole in his throat."

As the time for the operation approached, a flood of interest in sexual information burst forth. The rising competition with his father, combined with his usual attempt to submit to his mother, precipitated an acute struggle in sexual identification which became intensified by the impending operation.

After the operation was performed successfully, it was the healing process in conjunction with the imposed restriction of activity that made the boy anxious and angry. He oscillated between his passive-submissive and his aggressive-masculine trends. The doctor's opinion served during this time as a yardstick for the realistic evaluation of his condition. Joe now desired to learn to swim, to play ball and fight. He expressed the wish to improve himself generally. An itch in the genital area, which he located in his testes, opened up a discussion about masturbation and nocturnal emissions. It was essential now for the therapist, a woman, gradually to transfer the discussion of sexual enlightenment to the father because the excitement relating to such interchange promoted too intense an erotic attraction. The father, in the meantime, had become more accepting of his now "complete" son.

Learning, which had taken a leap since the operation, continued to progress. Joe could do his homework; he went to the library; he asked his father for help and opinion on such topics as elections and strikes. The struggle for his masculinity now dominated his life; therapy entered a drawn-out period of "working through" in which the liberated affects had to be guided into the phase-adequate conflicts of adolescence, thus preventing the extremes of a surrender to submissiveness or a blind thrust into frantic self-assertion and rebellion.

Discussion

Cryptorchism and Family Interaction

The pre-eminent role the genital defect played in the mental life of the three boys appears to be of a secondary order. The three boys had mothers who promoted feminine tendencies either by rejecting the maleness in the boy who was afflicted with a genital imperfection (Steven, Larry) or by showing a strong preference for a female child and holding out a love premium for passive, submissive behavior (Joe). All three boys were dependent on their mothers in terms of her narcissistic needs. These needs became manifest in the mothers' extraordinary ambitions which had to be realized by her male offspring (Steven, Larry), or in the mother's contempt of male sexuality which she considered destructive and undesirable, leading to her total acceptance of the genital defect in her son (Joe). In the latter case, the genital defect represented for the mother an asset rather than a calamity. Whether the mother concentrated on this imperfection because of her own unrealized ambitions and hopes (overcompensatory expectations), or whether she welcomed the defective state of the son, in either case the mother's attitude had to be considered as the pathogenic factor of primary order: it had a castrating impact.

This effect was further elaborated by the father's remoteness in the lives of all three boys. All concern and initiative had been delegated to the wife. The genital defectiveness of the child engendered in each father a sense of disappointment and dissatisfaction which deepened with the boy's fearful and "unboyish" behavior. The three fathers tried to disengage themselves from the difficulties their sons encountered and it was necessary in each case firmly to request the father's visit to the clinic. The fact that the father subsequently became a partner and supporter of the son's therapy proved to constitute an essential dynamic configuration for treatment: it represented to the boy the paternal approbation of his male strivings and consequently facilitated masculine identification. As long as the boy was exposed to the mother's belittling attitude toward the father, he felt that his own masculinity was acceptable only on his mother's terms.

The fathers responded to an earnest appeal by the therapist with cooperation and active interest. It goes without saying that their own precarious marital position had made them eager sympathizers with their son's plight, and we gained the impression that the fathers had secretly waited for a cue to speak up and be heard. Forrer (1959) in a report on the mother of a defective child makes the same observation: the belittled and excluded father turned out to be the child's respected and loved parent. As in our study, the mother described her husband as "A dull, uncommunicative and unreasonable man" (Forrer, 1959); on closer inspection this man turned out to be an intimidated, shy, but quite capable and loving father.

The emotional distance the fathers maintained in the marriage extended to their sons, who felt deserted by them and left to the controlling (castrating) influence of their mothers. A typical rescue maneuver employed by two of the boys in this dilemma consisted in the idealization of the father, or rather in a summary denial of the negative and depreciatory feelings he extended toward his son. An illusory father image, unshakable by reality, served as an anchor in the masculine position of the Oedipus complex and could be upheld only by a scotomatized view of the father's role in family interaction. Joe, emotionally deserted by his father and pressed by his mother into feminine tasks, exclaimed with desperate insistence: "My mind is my dad." Larry's mother actually entered into a conspiracy with her son and allowed him to swim in unsafe waters in spite of the father's explicit disapproval. Consequently, he and mother shared a "secret" which aroused oedipal guilt and made itself felt as resistance in treatment.

While the genital defect occupied all the mothers either actively ("poking around," examining, going from doctor to doctor, etc.) or negatively (ignoring it, postponing examination, not following or forgetting medical advice, hoping naïvely for a spontaneous descent "because the sac is there to receive it," etc.), it was striking to notice how they either had managed to conceal the genital condition at intake or had sidetracked it in some fashion to forestall any definitive clarification. The insignificant role the mothers tried to attribute to the genital condition was further demonstrated by their stubborn emphasis on other issues, such as the child's learning difficulty or his lack of friends. The referral was usually made by the school because only under duress could the mother be mobilized to take a step that would publicly demonstrate her own defectiveness and expose her inability in modeling the child according to her wishes. The mother's ambition for the child to be a genius, or to excel academically, or to be perfect and well behaved, reflected her own insufficiency feelings, forcefully denied by displacement of the child's genital defectiveness to areas of intellectual achievement and exemplary behavior. These three boys disappointed their mothers' ambitions; the school had to impress on the parents that their sons had failed. The mothers maintained an illusory image of their sons in order to ward off a narcissistic defeat. They maintained the fantasy that their own concentration and determination would succeed in changing the child (Forrer, 1959). They had a tendency toward depressive reactions in which their aggressive, retaliatory, and castrating wishes toward the male constituted an essential part.

The mothers' suppressed sadism became apparent in the unreasonable delays over medical intervention such as injection or operation. Their fear of a disaster (e.g., hemorrhaging in Steven's case) deterred them from an objective appraisal of a medical recommendation. Their impaired judgment appears throughout in relation to the child, especially in matters of health: Steven's mother, for example, told her son that he got two sores on his mouth from kissing a girl, and Larry's mother attributed his headaches to not eating properly. In this connection, of course, the devious and deceptive treatment of the genital condition deserves mention; in order not to arouse the child's self-consciousness or suspicion the mother would examine the boy without explanation or would give an irrelevant reason. The deception appeared also in the falsification of facts; Larry, for instance, was told that he needed injections for a hernia which, the boy knew, had been corrected at age two and a half. Such parental opinions are expressed with a single-mindedness of conviction that leaves the boy uncertain as to the validity of his own observation, thinking, and experience.

The particular way in which the genital defect is perceived and experienced by the parents, particularly the mother, accounts for the child's preoccupation with the testes. The perpetrator of the body damage is in the child's mind identified with the mother. Her castrating possessiveness and the father's passive aloofness both constitute a matrix of family interaction in which cryptorchism gives rise to a typical symptom picture. The parents' attitude in conjunction with the child's own observation of his anatomical abnormality combine into a body schema, or body image, around which any existing psychological impairment is elaborated. The defective body image itself was found to be responsible for specific aspects of the pathology in each case.

The Prototypical Experience (Trauma)

An operation trauma had occurred in the lives of all three boys. This trauma became subsequently linked to the genital defect and to any medical intervention which might occur sooner or later. Fantasies and drive propensities that had rendered the first operation, such as hernioplasty or tonsillectomy, a traumatic event attached themselves by a process of direct substitution to the genital actuality.

In Steven's case we can recognize in the testicle complex an aggregate of experiences dating from various periods of his life. Their accrued effect appeared in condensed form in his play productions. The first operation (hydrocele) involved the scrotum. The mother's guilt and conviction that she had caused the "tumor" had made her particularly attentive to her son's genital region and to the clumsy gait presumably associated with it. This gait persisted up to the time of his orchidopexy. Another body-damage anxiety (castration fear) attached itself to the genital defect and found expression in the doctor play when Steven announced that his doll patients had to have an operation on account of their "stiffness." Steven, the doctor, postponed the operation several times; when it was finally performed several of his patients died.

In this connection the consequence of hormone injections at the age of seven should not be overlooked or minimized. The sudden rise of sexual stimulation caused a flooding of the ego by instinctual pressures and became manifest in genital sensations (erections) and erotic feelings (kissing of women). At this very time of increased sexual pressures, a tonsillectomy was performed. This operation made a lasting and terrifying impression on the child due to two hemorrhages which followed the operation and required rehospitalization. Fear of doctors and operations and fear of death remained with Steven from then on; all three fears found eloquent expression in his doctor play. Furthermore, he ascribed the death of his grandfather either to the surgeon's clumsiness ("the knife had slipped") or to an uncontrollable bleeding, to a hemorrhage, to "bleeding ulcers." His fear of castration was affirmed by his negation, expressed in the statement that his grandfather's operation (prostatectomy) had "certainly not been in the leg system." It is interesting to note that Steven attached the blame for the death of his doll patients to the nurse who was clumsy. He voiced in this accusation what I have already alluded to, namely, that the archaic mother is held responsible for the "genital death" (castration).

In Joe's case tonsillectomy at four years of age left an indelible impression; the memory of it, with the typical infantile distortions, offered itself as a model for the impending orchidopexy. The testicle would be excised as the tonsils had been and thrown away if found to be no good. Joe was still convinced that the doctor had "cut a hole in his throat"; this "castration wish" phantom organ he expected to become real by the orchidopexy, i.e., he fantasied that the operation would make him into a girl.

In Larry's case the hernioplasty at the age of two and a half years served as the prototypical experience in which the attack on his eyes (bright light) became linked to body-damage anxiety as a retaliation for his uncontrollable rages against the mother. His headache ritual preserved this trauma, which he attempted to master by repetition, until it finally yielded to the combined effects of insight into his aggressive urges on the one hand and the attainment of genital intactness on the other.

A twelve-year-old boy who had a long history of medical examinations in connection with "one testicle being smaller than the other" might be mentioned here. Psychotherapy had been at a standstill for an alarmingly long time due to the parents' persistent plea that the testicle condition not be discussed with the boy since this would only make him "self-conscious" and add insult to injury. The boy's symptomatic behavior, such as walking around "blind" (with his eyes shut) in order to test whether he would hurt himself, pointed clearly to the "testicle syndrome" described here. This behavior made it mandatory to have the physical condition moved into the focus of awareness through medical evaluation. The medical examination, requested and arranged by the clinic, established that one testicle was atrophied. When the therapist discussed the examination and its findings with the boy, he insisted that the doctor could not find anything wrong with him. Confronted with the fact, he admitted his knowledge of the testicle condition which he had rendered vague and unreal by "not having touched" (investigated) himself "for quite a number of years." Then he changed the subject, significantly, to a discussion of his tonsillectomy. Soon it became apparent that his knowledge of the male and female genitals was contained in a bisexual, distorted imagery. Only after the body had attained, by medical dictum, a state of definitive structure—in this case one of permanent genital defectiveness—was it possible to cope in treatment with the psychological implications of the body reality.

The various focal apprehensions outlined above represented a fusion of the early operation trauma with subsequent drive organizations. Every threat to the body integrity revived the original trauma in a phase-specific modality. By reprojection the child experienced the current danger in terms of the past traumatic event. This might be paraphrased by saying: "What I thought happened to me then will certainly be repeated now." This reasoning is exemplified by Joe's equating tonsils and testicles, by his belief that the testicle would be thrown away as the tonsils were, and last but not least, by his experiencing the early operation as a castration. These connotations of childhood operations are well known and have been described by Anna Freud (1952b), Jessner, Blom, and Waldfogel, (1952), and others.

In all three cases it became clear that the genital defect served as the "organizing experience" which subordinated early trauma as well as all subsequent phase-specific anxieties about body damage to the persistent genital defectiveness. How this condition affected the formation of the body image will be discussed later. The facts that the genital incompleteness had existed as far as memory extends and had at the same time remained uncertain as to its ultimate outcome, and furthermore, that operative correction remained for years a whispered prospect, necessarily kept the early operation trauma alive in terms of specific, primitive misconceptions and distortions. Body-damage anxiety became a chronic affect, the mastery of which was attempted by various means. Obviously an early operation trauma is not an obligatory experience in cases of cryptorchism in order to produce disturbances similar to those described here. Nevertheless, we shall find that traumatic body-damage anxiety (related to body-part loss as in bowel training or castration fantasies), which under normal circumstances is gradually mastered, remains in an unbound state due to the continuance of the physical defect to which it is attached. The concreteness of the defect in conjunction with the uncertainty of its correction does not allow any definitive settlement of the issue—indeed, of any issue. It is therefore characteristic of cryptorchism that by its very nature it precludes the definite psychic integration of the defect and instead favors fluid defenses. These defenses were found to yield rather easily under the impact of a definitive physical repair and were then replaced by more stable defenses and adaptive behavior.

Body Image and Ego Impairment

We are well acquainted with the fact that clarity and stability of the body image exerts an essential influence on the development and structure of the secondary autonomy of the ego. Any serious distortion of the body image will become manifest in some specific ego impairment. Experience tell us that some component functions of the ego possess greater resistivity to impairment than others.

In cases of body defect the choice of defensive measures as well as restitutive fantasy elaborations is influenced by the nature of the defect and by its physical location. The distinction of inside and outside of the body does not apply clearly to cryptorchism. The defect is palpable and observable but not exposed to the public eye; at the same time it is not definitive but reparable. These factors determine to a large extent the concept of genital defectiveness the child evolves. The physical condition, due to its undecided and unpredictable nature, lends itself to the absorption of the specific emotional conflicts and body-damage anxieties that play a more or less transient role in the development of every male child.

The genital defectiveness had played a prominent role in the lives of the three boys from an early age on. Later it became the focus of comparison with and likeness to other boys, affecting the sense of identity and resulting in social incompatibility and maladjustment. Having no friends and not knowing how to make friends were equally evident in all three cases. Steven turned to little girls, Larry to a younger immature boy, and Joe to semidelinquents in order to gratify their social hunger. The emergence of more adequate social relations became evident in all three cases at the end of treatment.

The ego impairments most marked in these three cases appeared as disturbances in learning, memory, thinking, and time-space perception; they could be linked to the mother's inconsistent attitude by which she tacitly forbade the child to recognize his physical defect clearly or to think rationally about it. Furthermore, these impairments were due to a defective body image which had remained undeveloped by having retained primitive qualities of vagueness, indefiniteness, and incompleteness; in some way, it had never been fully assembled. Peto's remarks (1959) are relevant here: "Symbolism in dreams and folk-lore indicates that finding and evaluating external reality is to a great extent determined by refinding one's own body in the environment. Thus the body image is of decisive importance in grasping the world around us. Peculiarities of one's body image may then cause to be conceived as a world which is different from that visualized by the average human being" (p. 413).

The concept of time played a particular role in these cases because only "time will tell" which form the body, namely, the genital, will finally assume. The close connection between spatial perception, spatial conceptualization, and the experience of the body needs no lengthy elaboration. Whenever the body-image formation is impeded, a primitive spatial concept, analogous to the body form, continues to persist despite the fact that other ego functions have progressed normally. Werner (1940), in discussing spatial concept formation, comments as follows: "Primitive terms for spatial relations suggest that the body itelf with its 'personal dimensions' [Stern] of above-below, before-behind, and right-left is the source of a psychophysical system of coordinates. Therefore it may be inferred that objective space has gradually evolved from this primitive orientation" (pp. 167-168).

The massive influence of body-image diffusion was well summed up in Steven's statement: "They [his doll patients] cannot see, hear, or think until the operation is over." We might paraphrase his words by saying that the reliability of the distance perceptors and their usefulness for cognitive processes can be achieved only after the body has attained its complete and definitive form. The consequences of this state of affairs for reality testing and for the sense of reality is self-evident. For the time being then, Steven, as well as the other boys, took refuge in illusory accomplishments, in aggrandizement, in bragging, and in fantasies of magic powers. These defenses permitted continuous narcissistic replenishment. I shall later elaborate on how ego impairments were rapidly surmounted after the genital intactness was established once and for all.

Steven, who was easily insulted by criticism, made use of all the aforementioned defenses in order to ward off a narcissistic injury. He considered himself a "magical person" who could make everybody smile at him by smiling at them. He thus robbed everybody of their aggressive, i.e., dangerous, potential. Consequently, Steven had a poor grasp of social situations and was completely unable to recognize the correct motives in other children for their respective actions. Here we see the influence of the mother who maintained a distorted, idealized concept of her child and easily falsified reality in order to protect him. The mother, in denying Steven's physical defectiveness, devoted all her life's energies to its correction by magic. She gave up work and devoted herself totally to the child's care. The mother's denial became the child's erroneous self-image.

We notice that Steven, despite his "smiling disposition," was preoccupied with time and death. In these fears we recognize the tantalizing waiting time until genital certainty would be attained, as well as a "genital death" fear rooted in the still uncertain state of castratedness. In his earlier figure drawings, Steven gave the girl and the mother figure five fingers on each hand, while he drew a boy with no fingers at all. The boy, he said, was holding on to his parent's hand. Thus, his body deficit was undone by making himself part of a complete and powerful person.

Both Larry and Joe presented learning disturbances which were seriously aggravated in Joe's case by a stubborn reading disability. Again, illusory achievements and lies about school grades appeared as disclaimers of academic deficiencies. Forgetting, i.e., memory disturbances, presented serious obstacles to a tutorial approach in remedial reading. A decisive turn for the better became noticeable when medical as well as psychotherapeutic attention focused on the physical condition, its correction, and on body-damage anxiety generally.

The restoration and maturation of ego functions as well as their clinical evidence will be discussed later. Changes in the body image became indirectly observable through psychological tests. Steven's male figure in the second, postoperational test was large, compact, and had five fingers. Larry's "tree," which had first had a hole in the center of the trunk, showed later a clear and simple outline without any aberrant features. Examples could be multiplied from the test material. Suffice it to say that the second test gave enough evidence of a changed body image (self-concept) to allow the conclusion that the distorted, vague, and incomplete body image exerted a pathogenic influence on ego development. The ego impairments were erroneously treated for some time as if they were the result of endopsychic conflicts only. When the ego impairments were approached via the body image, its correction and completion—that is, when the physical (genital) reality was given a definitive structure—then a desirable change in ego functions was finally brought about. The clinical material illustrates the close relationship between body experience, body percept, body image, and ego functions.

Accident Proneness: The Masochistic Surrender

In the three boys hypermotility was conspicuously present. Its relatedness to physical self-damage was constantly demonstrated inside and outside the treatment room. Hypermotility in these cases constituted a complex form of behavior in which the pressure of instinctual drives, anxiety, and defensive operations were tightly organized. Hyperactive, aimless, and erratic moving about had a frantic, searching, anxious quality which at times invited danger and resulted in accidents. The tendency to self-damage, called accident proneness, revealed the child's concept of the genital defect as the result of an act of aggression, of a destructive attack on his body (castration). The identification with the aggressor, namely, the mother, prompted a feminine identification and turned passive submission into active execution. The child thus made himself the victim of his own aggression.

It is difficult to say to what extent accident proneness or the compulsive toying with physical danger was linked either to passive masochistic castration wishes, or to the avoidance of narcissistic mortification. This avoidance can be paraphrased by saying that it is better not to be a boy at all than to be half a boy. We shall later see how the anatomical condition was unconsciously identified with femaleness. The masochistic yielding to female identity found expression in the many castrative actions of more or less serious consequences. The sense of incompleteness and castratedness was visibly, palpably, and permanently linked to a bodily condition; moreover, the idea of an operation had attached itself intimately to it. Both these factors contributed to the striking concreteness with which body-damage fear and wishes were represented and executed.

The body-damage complex was kept alive by the unde-cided fate of the testicle, a condition that fostered ambiva-lent relationships, worked against the establishment of sta-ble identifications, and resulted in a fluid self-representation, particularly in relation to aspects of sexual identity, i.e., phallic versus castrated. The ambivalence of drive propensities in conjunction with defensive maneuvers seemed to move along a circular path with the nodal sta-tions labeled as follows: (conscious) Nothing can happen to me—I am in control of everybody—I know everything; (un-conscious) I am not a boy—I will never be a boy—I shall make myself into a girl—I deserve castration—I shall at-tack others—surrendering of a body part is relief, is pleasure—I want castration.

Accident proneness as observed in these cases illustrates the substitution of the genital organ, more particularly, the testicle, by the whole body. This *totum pro parte* principle or the body-phallus equation was well expressed in Steven's play in which the patients had to undergo an operation for their "stiffness." The *totum pro parte* principle received massive support from the mother, who customarily used the "total child" as a representation of his defective organ and concentrated her efforts at rectification of the genital defect in terms of substitutive perfections, such as academic excel-lence. Displacement from below to above was also apparent. In this connection the role of the eyeball as a substitutive organ for the testicle is noteworthy. This substitution is known from mythology and analysis. A blinking tic of an eleven-year-old boy reported by Fraiberg (1960) was trace-able to the fear of damage to his testicles. In mythology, King Oedipus gouged out his eyes in symbolic emasculation to atone for his incestuous crime. An eye involvement ap-peared in all three cases, most prominently in the case of Larry with his self-induced eye loss.

I am inclined to attribute the accident in Larry's case to

a compromise formation, consisting in the sacrifice of a body part, the eye, in order to rescue the missing testicle and, furthermore, to bring about the sought-after injury by his active submission, rather than by waiting for the expected attack from the "monster woman." The boy's description of the accident clearly reveals the motoric paralysis of a masochistic excitement at the very moment the stick came flying at his eye. The fear for his "good eye" repeated the original fear for his "good testicle." Both fears subsided with the correction of the genital defect. Larry was the one boy who most vigorously fought against a masochistic surrender, who, it is true, most damagingly victimized himself but nevertheless showed the most striking recovery.

Accident proneness is closely linked to the vicissitudes of the aggressive drive, to the erotization of injury, and to the need for physical punishment as a relief from feelings of guilt. The defective genital became almost automatically associated with sexual guilt since all three boys had progressed to a more or less firm foothold on the oedipal level. The aggressive-drive discharge was restricted to hyperactivity, counterphobic manifestations, and self-damage. In the course of therapy the intensity and primitiveness of the aggression became apparent. Quite naturally, the seat of the explosive, destructive, and vengeful energy was to be located in the testicle. We recognize this in the hidden dynamite of Steven's play, or in Larry's chemical experiments which were designed to blow up the house. Such expressions of unbridled aggressive fantasies eventually gave way to alloplastic adaptations when neutralized energy became available. Larry, for example, overcame his accident proneness successfully by making it his job to protect others from dangers: he became captain of the safety squad at his school. The other boys showed no signs of compulsive toying with physical dangers after the genital defect was corrected. The repetition compulsion was short-circuited by an anatomical change which facilitated ego alterations of a

more complex kind. These ego alterations became recognizable in characterological modifications and in the development of special realistic interests and inclinations.

Symptomatic Acts and Organ Symbols

The anatomical defect of an undescended testicle favors
expression of the condition through substitutive behavior or
through symbolic objects in an effort to master anxiety. The
concrete, direct, and symbolic nature of both play and behavior is strikingly demonstrated in the case material. The
primitiveness of thought implicit in this form of mastery
leaves no doubt that the inferred, vaguely conscious tem-
porariness of the defect foreclosed an integration by more
complex psychic processes of which the three boys unquestionably were capable.

Werner (1940) remarks, "The structure of primitive
thought is concretely determined in so far as it has a tendency to configurate pictorially, and it is emotionally determined in so far as it unites that which is affectively related" (p. 302). The case material indicates that aspects of
"quantity" and "size" were definitely equated with power,
potency, and masculinity. As another boy expressed it: "If I
have two testicles I can have twice as many children." The
frequent accidents represented symptomatic acts, explained
by each boy circumstantially, but they obviously constituted
reassurance actions by reaffirming repeatedly that no fatal
damage had been done.

The testicle as the seat of aggressive and destructive
forces has been mentioned earlier. We can recognize this
idea, furthermore, in the defensive belittling of the testicles,
the bearers of which are fear-provoking men. This attempt
to attenuate castration anxiety is well expressed in the
marching song of the British soldiers imprisoned during
World War II by the Japanese in the Burma jungle: "Hitler
has only one big ball/Goering has two but they are small/

Himmler has something similar/But little Goebbels has no balls at all."[1]

Joe's insatiable interest in the contents of drawers, his running through the corridors of the clinic in order to see if anybody could stop him; Steven's curiosity about secrets and his use of the number three (male genital) in aggressive play—these incidents illustrate in displaced form the nature of their common concern.

The concrete representation of the testicle by objects is noteworthy inasmuch as it is somewhat out of keeping with the age and intelligence of the three boys. The directness of symbolic representation that we notice in Joe's stealing a ball from the treatment room, only to return it after he had undergone a successful operation, is almost ludicrous in its simplicity. The same is true for Steven's museum in which he exhibited two precious marbles for everybody to see after a successful operation had brought his testicle into a position where it finally became visible to the world. Steven also rolled two small clay balls during the session following the operation; he remarked that he would make two more balls every week and he wanted the therapist to keep them for him. Here one is reminded of Larry's "eye [ball] bank."

By displacement the testicle is, furthermore, identified with other organs. These other organs assume attributes and meanings that render them fitting substitutes for the testicles. In this connection we can speak of organ symbols. The most outstanding substitute organs for the testicles are the eye, tonsils, breast, and fetus. (Their relatedness to bisexuality is discussed below.) It is partly the symmetric location, partly the operative history, partly the relatedness to component instincts that is responsible for the fitness of these body parts to serve as organ symbols for the testicles.

One gains the impression that the genital defectiveness

[1]While the melody of this song echoes through the sound track of the movie *The Bridge over the River Kwai,* the words of the song have, of course, been changed for the public presentation of the historical scene.

lends itself to direct, concrete, symbolic (substitutive) expression by objects in the outer world and, furthermore, to the use of the whole body or body parts for the mastery of the anxiety the anatomical defect engenders.

The Bisexual Identity

The defective genital condition was perceived by the three boys as castratedness, i.e., femaleness. In these cases of cryptorchism we do not observe a genuine feminine identification but rather recognize in the self-image the compliance of passive, feminine tendencies to a physical genital reality. The passive tendencies received a powerful recourse from the operation trauma and a ceaseless stimulation from the physical condition of cryptorchism itself. In this connection the following remarks by Anna Freud (1952b) are relevant: "When studying the aftereffects of childhood operations in the analysis of adult patients we find that it is not the castration fear but the feminine castration wish in a male child which is most frequently responsible for serious postoperative breakdowns or permanent postoperative character changes" (p. 75). To this we might add the finding that in the case of cryptorchism, by the very fact of a defective genital, the feminine castration wish did not advance to the state of an integrated self-representation but stayed attached to the genital organ in its physical reality. Feminine tendencies became, therefore, organized around this organ defect and remained in a state of unsettledness due to the implicit reversibility of the condition. The resultant bisexual identity was apparent in play productions, fantasies, transference behavior, and projective tests.

The confusion of sexual identity prevented any clear concept of the male and female genital from developing. An egomorphic image of a hermaphroditic nature became the universal body schema. Joe expressed this confusion in asking: "Does it mean that I have something other boys don't have, or don't I have something other boys have?"

Having one testicle was found to be identical with being half a man and half a woman, with sterility, or with femaleness in general. Steven showed his doll patients to the therapist with these words: "Look at them, they look like nothing." This statement better than anything else expresses the sense of self Steven had to contend with. In such a dilemma an operation was wanted and feared: in order to retrieve the lost treasure, the testicle, another organ, namely, the penis, might have to be sacrificed. In the overvaluation of the missing body part, we recognize an overflow of cathexis from the penis to the testicle.

Operation anxiety was warded off by identification, by assuming the active role vis-à-vis the therapist. Larry asked his male therapist to be his pupil while he himself was the teacher. We notice the same reversal of roles in Steven, who was the surgeon while the therapist became his nurse. When the operation was imminent, he seated himself in the woman therapist's chair and said: "I like to be you and you to be me." If it is not possible that "hes" can be made into "shes," Steven argued, why not have only "hes"? Then, we might add, castration would be eliminated once and for all. In his logical way, Steven concluded that in that case the "hes" had to get the babies in order to keep the world going. There was, after all, no way out of having two sexes.

This comment brings us to the equation of the deliverance of the testicle (orchidopexy) and giving birth. The testicle in the abdomen was equated with the fetus. Steven thought that it took twenty-one days for a baby to grow in the mother, a span of time that represented the exact number of days he had to wait for his operation. Joe's figure drawing of a woman showed two balls in the abdominal region; when this drawing was repeatedly traced, as the examiner suggested, the balls moved up in each consecutive figure tracing until they had reached the exact location of the breasts. The association of the absent testicle with the female organ of the breast only serves to emphasize once more the bisexual identity we have found characteristic for cases of cryptorchism.

It was no surprise then to discover that the orchidopexy evoked a state of dual expectancy: either to achieve masculinity or to meet with final castration. Partly, indeed, a confusion existed as to the simultaneous accomplishment of both. This confusion is apparent, for instance, in Steven's idea that the testicle would be pushed from the "stomach" into the penis; the state of having obtained two external testicles would thus cancel out the use of the penis for urination and necessitate another body orifice for this function. Such disturbing admissions were quickly extinguished by aggrandizing fantasies until a recourse to castratedness gained once more the upper hand. These shifts resulted in a chronic state of indecision and of fluctuating sexual identity. Fineman (1959) has reported similar observations on a boy, aged five and a half, with a congenital genitourinary defect: "The first attempt to present his actual condition [extrophy of the bladder] to him, although softened by the additional statement that he could do everything else that boys could do, was met by him with considerable anxiety which he spontaneously brought under control by playing at being mother and cooking meals" (p. 116). The acceptance of being a boy took first the form of exaggeration, namely, "fantasies of being a powerful hunter who killed lions and tigers with his father's or grandfather's gun" (p. 116).

The bisexual sense of identity observed in the three cases poses some theoretical problems as to identification and instinctual fixation. None of the boys behaved in a, strictly speaking, effeminate or "girlish" way. However, they lacked in boyish assertiveness, in active pursuits, and definitely shrank away from competition within their male peer group. They all responded positively to the father's changed attitude when he took a more active interest in their lives and acknowledged his own importance and influence in helping his son toward a more masculine orientation. After the father had rescued the son from the castrating mother, after he had shown pride in his son's masculine strivings, a competitive oedipal upsurge became manifest which soon was resolved by an identification with the father. None of the boys offered himself as the passive love object, as might have been expected from the prevailing emotional trends. The flight into a feminine position, namely, castratedness, was not anchored in either an instinctual fixation or a stable feminine identification. No doubt, these tendencies existed, as they do in the young male generally, but they never progressed to a passive homosexual orientation.

The defense of castratedness is akin to denial insofar as the child denies the genital defect by a radical removal of the last vestiges of maleness which gave rise to anxiety and upset his narcissistic balance. "Being a girl" was never sufficiently supported by a pregenital drive or ego fixation to prevent a forward movement of the libido; however, the intolerable genital condition in conjunction with the dependency on a castrating mother provided feminine propensities with a ceaseless updrift. The perseverance of the female body image and the defense of castratedness (body-part surrender) were directly related to a body reality rather than to a psychologically integrated drive and ego organization. The bisexual identity reflected a physical reality; consequently, a change of the physical reality brought the provisional state of pseudo bisexuality to an end. The restoration of genital intactness gave masculine sexuality a decisive push. The overbearing quality of this newly acquired and unequivocal masculinity invited, however, doubts as to a completely victorious outcome. We shall return to this question later.

The Positioning of the Testis in the Scrotum: Its Influence on Integrative Processes

The effects of the newly acquired genital completeness were followed by us with interest and surprise. First of all, the rapidity and the scope of ego maturation accompanying the new body reality called our attention to the fact that the anatomical change itself must account for a specific impetus for ego change. The influence of the new body reality was so massive and immediate that the question arose as to the respective psychological processes initiated by therapy on the one hand and by the anatomical transformation on the other. While it is no doubt true that psychotherapy had, so to say, prepared the mental ground for the genital intactness to take roots or to effect a changed sense of reality, the physical change itself must be credited with an equally important contribution toward the improvement of mental functioning. The most striking changes occurred in the areas of learning, cognitive processes, elaboration of age-adequate interests, social adaptation, and masculine identity formation. The ego impairments affecting all these areas have been described earlier.

Let us first recall that a tacit parental prohibition existed, in all three cases, regarding recognition and thinking about the genital condition. In Steven's case the mother's unconcern, her denial, was projected onto the child ("He does not worry, he knows nothing") and impeded his ego development, especially the faculty of reality testing. The child, consequently, lived in a state of confusion, not knowing what was real; he was at a loss to say whether what he perceived was real or what his mother wanted him to know. This global perceptual confusion was counteracted in treatment when the "veil of twilight vision" was lifted and a sense of reality restored. In the psychological test this change appeared as a "differentiated view of the world."

Steven had already predicted in his play that after the operation, if successful, his patients would "be their own self again; everything depends on this operation."

It is interesting to note that he as well as the other boys expected a return to a genital state that must have once existed, so to speak, in prehistory. They expected to receive what had always been theirs. Steven eagerly investigated his newly acquired testicle and described clearly his physical sensations related to the positioning of the testicle in the scrotum. Before the operation, Steven said he always felt confused. With finality an interim state had come to an end: "Once the operation was over, it was over." After the physical restoration, Steven's emotional and intellectual maturation took a remarkable leap. The infantile, self-absorbed child became more and more oriented toward schoolwork, reading, the Boy Scouts, friends, chess playing, piano lessons, etc. Taking into account all the psychotherapeutic endeavors, the rapid consolidation of psychological gains derived a unique recourse from the bodily change itself. Before that change nothing was final or complete.

Larry and Joe were both retarded in reading and consequently seriously handicapped in school. In all cases a reading disability existed (e.g., Steven was almost a nonreader when he started treatment); this disability was strikingly ameliorated soon after the genital restoration or even shortly before the operation. In Larry an improvement in his spatial perception was also noticeable. The aimless wandering of his mind through horror movies and the destructive use of chemistry gave way to a genuine interest in science. Larry's accident-seeking turned into accident prevention. His second psychological testing showed startling changes: the serious ego impairment, which had raised the suspicion of borderline functioning, was no longer in evidence. His body image had changed radically: the male figure, drawn earlier with fuzzy strokes and vague forms, was now set down with firm outlines and precise shapes. Passive submission had given way to active mastery of the environment. The higher level of integrative processes stands out as the most remarkable finding in his second test series.

Joe showed many of the same features of change described in relation to the other boys. The spurt in ego maturation in his case also was remarkable: learning capacity and handwriting improved, an interest in factual knowledge appeared, his concentration span lengthened; moreover, he could for the first time think of the future in terms of a vocation, of being a man when he would be grown-up.

All three boys appeared much more alert mentally and capable of more complex psychic processes after body intactness was established. A higher level of differentiation and integration appeared in their second test series. On the behavioral level this advance was manifest in the delay of action and the interposition of thought between stimulus and motor discharge. Along with this came a decline in hypermotility, which had been characteristic for the three boys. It is assumed that the anatomical change affected the body image in terms of a definitive masculine identity. The influence of the anatomical reality on the ego via the body image resulted in a firmer sense of reality and, consequently, in greater clarity of thought and the establishment of more effective, namely, adaptive, defenses.

In spite of these gains we should not overlook the fact that genital intactness was initially seized upon as the savior who would keep feminine strivings at bay. Efforts at repression or characterological absorption of these still powerful strivings were preceded by an overbearing show of masculinity directly following the physical changes.[2] The thrust into assertiveness following body intactness had two

---

[2]The positioning of the testicle into the scrotum does not affect—that is to say, does not increase—the hormonal activity of this organ. The suddenness of change in behavior is therefore a purely psychological phenomenon.

phases. The first was characterized by an upsurge of masculine sexuality and an exaggerated display of forcefulness
and cocksureness. An almost euphoric sense of power became noticeable which can be paraphrased: "Now that I am
a real boy, the sky is the limit to what I can do."
Heterosexual excitement (e.g., Joe's pictures of nude
women) became—perhaps too soon and too completely—
repressed, and a tendency to compulsivity and affective con-
striction took over. No material on the boys' masturbation
was forthcoming, which left an unfortunate lacuna in the
understanding of their sexual development.[3] There is no
doubt that the display of phallic masculinity had a defensive quality. Its ultimate effect on character synthesis, however, cannot be assessed with certainty before late adolescence.

For the time being, treatment in conjunction with genital restoration had made psychic functioning on a higher
level possible. Thus it facilitated adaptive processes and the
use of stable defenses less damaging and debilitating than
the ones originally employed. One might say that Joe was
prevented from entering a delinquent career; Steven was
saved from an infantile, autistic state; and Larry was rescued from physical self-destruction. Due to the fact that the
defective ego development was firmly attached to a physical
condition, the pathological retardations and distortions
were, so to speak, prevented from inundating the psychic
life of the child and from causing irreversible ego alterations. The thought occurred to me that these boys might
have been more seriously affected by their environment,
especially the mother, if they had not been afflicted by a

[3] I am indebted to Dr. Mary O'Neil Hawkins for the idea that continued examination of the scrotal sac may sensitize, so to speak, accidentally, this genital area
which thus becomes the seat of erotic feelings. The manual investigation by the
child of his body defect consequently may turn into a masturbatory activity with
the focus of sensation in the scrotal region. Castration anxiety, on the other hand,
may lead to a complete desensitization of the genital. Our clinical material is inconclusive as to the particular masturbatory practices in cases of cryptorchism;
here further analytic investigation is needed.

genital, reparable defect. The concreteness of body-damage fear had not been totally internalized and welded to instinctual and conflictual anxiety. This fact might explain the reversibility of symptoms that would ordinarily have indicated a most serious disturbance. Much that appeared at first in diagnostic evaluation as ominous pathology changed radically under the impact of the genital restoration. Psychotherapy alone can hardly be credited with the massive improvements. The idea forces itself on the observer that the physical condition itself represented a reality according to which the ego became modeled and remodeled; furthermore, that which appeared initially as an endopsychic conflict represented in fact a body-reality confusion aggravated by reality fear. As far as the body reality was internalized, psychotherapy was the proper helper; as far as the body reality could be corrected, namely, made definitive, the surgeon was called upon to help. Both specialists have to synchronize their contributions in order to discharge their respective functions in a coordinated approach. The cases of Steven and Joe have illustrated this point.

Summary

Three prepubertal cases of cryptorchism were presented. The complementary effects of psychotherapy, physical correction of the genital defect (two operative, one spontaneous), and treatment of the parents, especially the mother, were explored. On the basis of the clinical data the following conclusions were reached.

1. Cryptorchism is not a primary pathogenic factor. The particular way in which the genital defect is experienced by the parents, particularly the mother, accounts for the child's preoccupation with the testes. The perpetrator of the body damage is in the child's mind identified with the mother. Her castrating possessiveness and the passive aloofness of the father both constitute a matrix of family interaction in

which cryptorchism gives rise to typical symptoms despite the fact that the three cases belong to heterogeneous nosological categories.

2. In all three cases an early operation trauma had occurred, and served as the prototypical model for body-damage (castration) fear. The genital defect (cryptorchism) served as the organizing experience which subordinated early trauma as well as all subsequent phase-specific anxieties about body damage to the persistent genital incompleteness. An operation trauma per se is not considered an obligatory experience.

3. A distorted, vague, and incomplete body image exerted a pathogenic influence on ego development. Resultant ego impairments were manifest in defective functioning relative to learning, memory, thinking, time-space orientation, and motility. These impairments could furthermore be linked to the mother's inconsistent attitude by which she tacitly forbade the child to recognize his physical defect clearly, or to think rationally about it.

4. The tendency to self-damage (accident proneness) present in the cases was understood as the child's idea that the genital defect was the result of an act of aggression (castration). Through identification with the aggressor the child turned passive submission into active execution and made himself the victim of his own aggression. Castrative wishes were clearly in evidence.

5. Cryptorchism favors direct, concrete, symbolic (substitutive) expressions by objects in the outer world, the use of the whole body or body parts for the mastery of the anxiety the anatomical defect engenders. Substitutive organs (organ symbols) for the testicle were found to be: eye, tonsils, breast, and fetus.

6. A bisexual sense of identity reflected the physical reality of anatomical indecision. The perseverance of the female body image and the defense of castratedness (body-part surrender) were directly related to a body reality

rather than to a psychologically integrated drive and ego organization. This relation became evident through the reversibility of the body-image confusion once genital intactness was established.

7. Coordinated efforts of surgeon and therapist resulted in a striking amelioration of ego impairment. The changed body image exerted an immediate and direct influence on ego functions. What appeared initially as an endopsychic conflict represented in fact a body-reality confusion, aggravated by reality fear. In light of the influence of the anatomical correction on differentiative and integrative psychic processes, the conclusion was reached that the concreteness of body-damage fear prevented total internalization of the body reality and its amalgamation with conflictual anxiety. The delay of internalization was maintained by the reparable genital defect and the undying expectation of a changed body reality. This particular state of affairs in the presence of a bodily defect may explain the reversibility of an emotional condition with severe ego impairments, which in children would generally indicate an ominous pathology.

The findings in this paper are restricted to cryptorchism. It seems that the particular survival value, the interference with perception, with the physical grasp of objects, with phase-specific gratifications, as well as other factors related to a defective body part, introduce elements absent in cryptorchism per se. The sifting of similarities and differences in cases with other bodily defects lies outside the scope of this presentation. The clinical study of three cases of cryptorchism aimed at an investigation of the mutual influence of body reality, body image, ego development, and internalization within the matrix of a specific pattern of family interaction.

PART SIX

Summary: Contributions to the Psychoanalytic Theory of Adolescence

My contributions to the psychoanalytic theory of adolescence are dispersed throughout this volume. Each chapter explores a particular theoretical or technical issue. What they have in common is a developmental approach to the study of the adolescent process. This characteristic gives the totality of my research coherence and unity. Within this unity, however, one can distinguish two categories of contributions to adolescent psychology. One represents new ways of looking at old and well-known problems, leading to the suggestion of treatment approaches different from the customary ones; for examples I might refer to the chapters on acting out and delinquency. Under the other category I subsume conceptual formulations, based on inferences from clinical observations, which affect basic psychoanalytic developmental theory; for examples I might refer to the chapters on the genealogy of the ego ideal, the second individuation process, and the epigenesis of the adult neurosis.

I have often been asked to put together the contingent propositions I have elaborated over time in discrete studies and published here and there in scattered places. In order to convincingly portray the persistent developmental point of view and the internal coherence of theory throughout my work and, furthermore, demonstrate their firm embeddedness in the history of psychoanalytic thought—I needed to present my basic ideas in a comprehensive exposition. The subsequent chapter is designed to accomplish this task.

Chapter 19

Modifications in the Classical Psychoanalytic Model of Adolescence

The decades I have spent in clinical research of adolescence have resulted in the harvest of many findings: they encompass a body of knowledge—theoretical and practical—which I shall outline here in a systematic and comprehensive form. In doing so, I intend to clarify especially those of my findings that diverge from the familiar or widely accepted view of the adolescent process. My psychoanalytic investigations have always issued from clinical observations that presented me with intriguing problems of theory and technique due to their particularly perplexing nature. Whatever my clinical observations were at the time, they continued to sustain my attentiveness to comparative considerations along similar lines in other cases. An investigative approach of this nature leads either to a verification, a revision, or a rejection of whatever the theoretical inference may have been. In some instances, clinical observations have led to theoretical constructs and finally to propositions which, tested over time, have become part of my psychoanalytic thinking about adolescence. I am fully aware that much of what I shall lay before you in this presentation remains controversial and debatable for many of my colleagues. This fact is no deterrent, but rather an incentive

Sophia Merviss Memorial Lecture, delivered in San Francisco, California, April 24, 1978.

to report my findings, because I consider controversy a desirable and productive enterprise as long as it is rooted in the unique methodology of psychoanalytic observation.

Before I proceed, a word of caution is in order; I fear I may convey the impression of not appreciating sufficiently the vast psychoanalytic research that has so immensely enriched our knowledge of the adolescent process. It is in many instances quite beyond my faculty to sort out authorship and origins and accord credit to the many suggestive and seminal ideas which, as by a quantum leap, coalesce in a new theorem. I owe more to what I have read and heard over time than I can possibly acknowledge by searching most diligently my memory. I have therefore omitted references altogether. In a presentation of this kind, in which I summarize my own thoughts, I must leave much of the referential associations to the reader. What gives me the courage to present an exclusively theoretical essay derives from my conviction that therapeutic advances in the field of psychological, emotional and developmental, disturbances have always been predicated on vigorous and often daring theory building. The history of psychoanalysis offers the most convincing evidence of this fact.

My presentation has one other shortcoming which I shall announce before you discover it yourself with a sense of disappointment. This so-called shortcoming lies in the nature of my subject. Due to the broad theoretical scope which forms the framework of this essay, I had to forego the customary inclusion of illustrative case material. This material can be found in the other chapters in this volume, the essence of which I reformulate here in order to weave them into the fabric of the current theory of adolescence. I suggest that you review in your mind's eye your own cases alongside my exposition.

The issue I shall discuss first concerns the psychoanalytic recapitulation theory of adolescence. According to this view, the revival of infantile sexuality and of the vicissitudes of early object relations is initiated by the biological event of puberty. In accordance with the classical recapitulation theory, the revival and renewed resolution or transformation of the Oedipus complex represents one, if not *the* essential aspect of the adolescent process. It is beyond doubt that oedipal issues emerge at adolescence with regularity. However, we must acknowledge the fact that a decisive expansion of the ego has accrued from middle childhood, i.e., latency, which has altered, qualitatively and quantitatively, the re-experiencing of the oedipal conflict on the adolescent level. The resourcefulness of the adolescent ego allows it to cope with the revival of infantile object relations in consonance with bodily maturation, thus bringing the state of infantile dependencies to a close. This achievement usually, if not always, contains rectifications or resolutions of conflicts or immaturities carried forward from the infantile period to the adolescent level. In this sense we speak of adolescence as a "second chance." This normative developmental advance is forfeited whenever the child fails to acquire the appropriate ego differentiation or ego supremacy during the latency period.

What I have foremost in mind when I speak of an impeded ego development during latency are drive fixations on the level of infantile narcissism. As a consequence, oedipal passions remain weak, their conflict resolution is incomplete, and the superego never gains the autonomous sway over infantile self-idealization that is preconditional for the entry into the latency period. Looking at this constellation from the side of the ego, one would refer to the fact that no clear or stable line of demarcation between fantasy and reality has become part of the latency ego structure; thus the ego's capacity to critically assess self and object is stunted. "I am what I do" becomes facilely replaced by "I am what I wish to be" or "I am what others think I am." Under these conditions it is only natural that the voice of the self-observing ego remains weak, contradictory, or silent. The repercussion of this state on reality testing, especially in the world of object relations, never fails to alert the clinical observer to a developmental anomaly. However, one cannot ignore the fact that, regardless of drive fixation and ego immaturity, some latency children are capable of the most remarkable cognitive and creative achievements, the defensive nature of which does not reveal itself until adolescence.

What follows from such a developmental lag is an abortive adolescence or a failure in the autonomous mastery of internal, disequilibrizing tensions and in the capacity to use selectively the social surround in terms of sublimatory and identificatory adaptations. Under these circumstances, the social field fails to acquire an age-relevant presence on which to articulate the emerging needs for new object relations beyond the family matrix; consequently, new object relations within the peer group show the characteristics of simple object substitutions rather than those of elaborated replacements. In other words, adolescent development takes its normative course only if the latency ego has progressed along age-adequate developmental lines. Considering adolescent therapy, it follows that latency ego deficits often demand our attention above all else, even though sexual and dependency conflicts occupy the forefront of the behavioral and mental stage. While such conflicts are real enough, they have to be scrutinized as to their defensive aims which push these conflictual, typically adolescent themes into the forefront of the patient's awareness.

I shall now pursue another strand of the recapitulation theory of adolescence. I refer to the implication that the resolution of the Oedipus complex has brought about the closure of the phallic phase, thereby structuring the superego and ushering in the latency period. With the advent of adolescence the conflicts of the phallic phase are resuscitated due to the biological condition of physical maturation and the human-specific incest taboo. From my work with adolescents—male and female—I have gained the impression that the decline of the Oedipus complex at the end of the phallic phase represents a suspension of a conflictual constellation rather than a definitive resolution, because we can ascertain its continuation on the adolescent level. In other words, the resolution of the Oedipus complex is completed—not just repeated—during adolescence. It should be made explicit at this point that I refer to both the positive and the negative component when I speak of the Oedipus complex in general. For clarification let me say that the negative Oedipus complex refers to the child's love relationship with the parent of the same sex. The word "negative" does not imply any negative connotation of the complex itself.

My attention was directed to the above considerations by clinical observations, by the fact that the negative Oedipus complex presents a most difficult therapeutic problem in the treatment of the adolescent. I have not observed a similar severity, marked by stubborn repression and denial, in the analysis of most children. The love for the parent of the opposite sex is always intensified during adolescence. However, a distinction, even if obvious, needs to be made at this point. The term "oedipal love" implicitly refers to the sexual component of infantile object relations, in contrast to feelings of affection, admiration, and loyalty which never cease to flow—ambivalently and reciprocally—between the child and both parents. My clinical observations concerning the negative Oedipus complex have led me to the conclusion that oedipal love, directed toward both mother and father, does not burden the young child with intrinsic contradictions or mutual exclusiveness as is the case in adolescence when the polarities of masculinity and femininity reign supreme. Their coexistence cannot be tolerated by the sexually maturing individual. In other words, the state of bisexuality is tolerated in the prelatency child without the catastrophic disharmony at puberty. It is the positive Oedipus complex that falls under repression or finds its resolution through identification and the regulatory influence of the superego at the termination of the pallic phase. It remains the task of adolescent oedipal resolution to transmute the negative Oedipus complex, the sexual love for the parent of the same sex.

Clinically, this aspect of the oedipal constellation appears at adolescence in a paradoxical disguise that is in evidence whenever a drive fixation on the negative oedipal position is interwoven with symptom formation or characterological defenses. Such pathological development is often not recognizable on first sight, especially when the adolescent pushes heterosexual behavior and fantasies into the center of his therapy sessions or his life in general. The urgency of and the preoccupation with sexual affects and desires during adolescence are familiar to us. In fact, their attendant conflicts, anxieties, and defenses play a large part in our interpretative work. It has been my experience that, alongside the adolescent effort to reach a heterosexual identity, we also have to reckon with an intrinsically defensive element that aims at keeping the conflict of the negative oedipal love in repression. I have called this adolescent maneuver the oedipal defense.

If you contemplate for a moment your therapeutic work with the male adolescent (of middle and late adolescence), I think you will agree with me when I say that it is, relatively speaking, less laborious to deal with the defenses against sexual and erotic fantasies and feelings in relation to mother or sister than to father and brother. The affects directed toward the female remain in the realm of a gender-appropriate position and are ego-syntonic. In contrast, the uncovering of the negative oedipal fixation leads inescapably into the realm of homosexuality, latent or manifest, and into the center of sexual identity problems. Should these remain unaltered by the adolescent process, we may speak of a secondary adolescent fixation. In that case, the adolescent choice of defense will determine the adult character consolidation and, due to the unaltered infantile libidinal position, this fixation will engender disharmonious affects and moods in the adult love life. The dread, horror, and ego-dystonic nature of homosexuality or perversion is often voiced quite directly by the adolescent girl or boy and constitutes in many cases the first productive approach to the problem of sexual identity.

It might now be stated: since the resolution of the negative Oedipus complex is the task of adolescence, the coming to terms with the homosexual component of pubertal sexuality is an implicit developmental task of adolescence. In fact, we might say that sexual identity formation is predicated on the completion of this process. Our adolescent patients always display the twofold oedipal strivings because the incompatability of their heterogeneous objects and aims has brought the maturing individual up against an either-or of decisive finality.

I would like to remind you of a common adolescent complaint, namely, the sense of vocational indecision or noncommitment, of floundering or academic failure in college. These problems are frequently adjuncts of a symptom complex we are called on to unravel. On first sight, defeats of this nature look like oedipal inhibitions, especially whenever a boy sets out to follow in the vocational footsteps of his father or, generally, when the young person feels called upon to fulfill the ambitions one or both parents harbor for their offspring. The oedipal factor plays, no doubt, a decisive role. But juxtaposed to it—as we see in so many cases of gifted boys—is the infantile trend of renouncing oedipal competition and envy in exchange for the regressive contentment derived from standing in the glow of shining grandeur that radiates from the imago of the oedipal father. In this way, the small boy once experienced the pleasures—pervasive but hardly acknowledged—of the submissive passive position. In this connection we must remember that every boy once—fleetingly or more last-

ingly—identified with the role of the envied and admired procreative woman: the mother. I have observed how
these trends in the small boy become pathologically aggravated when the father, disillusioned in his conjugal life,
shifts his need for emotional fulfillment from his wife to his
son. Whenever I hear a father say in the consultation preceding treatment: "The only one I love in this world is my
son," I feel alerted to the central complex of the patient. In
following such cases in treatment, I have been repeatedly
impressed by the emergence of the Janus-faced oedipal
passions and of the alternating conflicts they inexorably
contain. Should the conflicts attached to the incest taboo
and bisexuality remain beyond resolution, the adolescent
patient protects himself by a stubborn denial of any self-
limitation, that grave affront to narcissism. We see here
once again how ego maturation takes its cue from drive
maturation. That intrinsically social facilitations are part of
this process should be self-evident. However, it needs emphasizing in this context that the use the individual is able
to make of such facilitations remains predicated on drive
and ego maturation or, in other words, on the unimpeded
forward movement of the adolescent process.

We have reached the point where it behooves us to contemplate some inherent puzzlements that issue from the
foregoing propositions. Let me give you an account of the
question I have asked myself. Psychoanalytic theory has
shown us in great clarity the course the positive oedipal attachment follows from early childhood through adolescence
to adulthood. All along this course, there remains one unaltered characteristic, namely, its implicit gender appro-
priateness; the object remains one of the opposite sex. We
have come to consider gender polarity along the shift from
infantile to adult sexuality as a developmental axiom. Some
amendments, however, become plausible and exigent when
we follow the developmental course of the negative oedipal
constituent. Its sex-inappropriate nature is bound to reach

an impasse at puberty when sexual maturation can no longer accommodate infantile negative oedipal strivings. Obviously, there is no displacement of these object-directed drive components available within the sexual identity whose definitive structure is acquired during adolescence. One might relegate the transformation of the drive component under consideration entirely to neutralized, i.e., desexualized, emotional attitudes, to character traits, and to sublimatory endeavors. This would be the logic by which the classical psychoanalytic theory explicates the resolution of the negative Oedipus complex; the implicit dynamics of these transformations are by now taken as self-evident in the light of clinical experience.

The schema just outlined has only partially been borne out in my analytic work with adolescents. I have found it necessary to postulate an intermediate step in the process. Freud's (1914b) ideas concerning narcissism and ego ideal are here brought to bear on the adolescent process. I shall present a condensed version of the proposition my clinical observations have suggested and confirmed over the years. The negative oedipal attachment is a narcissistic object tie ("I love what I wish to be"); at adolescence, the libido invested in this tie becomes desexualized and thus initiates the narcissistic structure of the adult ego ideal. From an adaptational or psychosocial point of view one might speak of this process as the socialization of oedipal narcissism. At the adolescent juncture I speak of, the infantile ego ideal of self-aggrandizement, as an always attainable gratification and self-esteem regulator, becomes transformed into the adult ego ideal, which constitutes a drive toward perfection. The infantile belief in the realizability of perfection becomes replaced during late adolescence by the drive toward its approximation. It thus becomes a journey without arrival. Its intention and direction are ego-syntonic and always unequivocal; by implication, there is no place for doubt or thought. Whatever the edict that emanates from the adult ego ideal, it is self-evident to the rational mind as well as to the emotional being. Should this not be the case, we very likely deal with superego issues, which resemble so often those of the ego ideal. This dubious accountability is one more reason for outlining differentiating criteria that lie beyond the well-known reactions of guilt or shame as indicative of superego or ego-ideal neglect.

The above thoughts are derived from clinical observations which have demonstrated to me that the resolution of the negative oedipal conflict in adolescent analysis effects a personality change of a particular nature; we recognize these changes in an emerging self-determination, in a projection of the self into a realistic adult life, and, last but not least, in the tolerance of self-limitations. The intrinsic precondition for this developmental advance to adulthood lies in the deidealization of self and object or, in more general terms, in the acceptance of life's existential imperfections. These budding characteristics, which stand in such marked contrast to the patient's preanalytic life, have become to me trustworthy indicators of the adult ego ideal *in statu nascendi*. I have credited the decline and paling influence of the infantile ego ideal or, conversely, the emergence and structuralization of the adult ego ideal to the analytic work which has brought about the resolution of the negative Oedipus complex. The dynamics of this structural innovation of adolescence lead me to say that the adult ego ideal is the heir to the negative Oedipus complex.

An adolescent issue of overriding importance centers around the alternation of regressive and progressive movements which last over a considerable time of adolescent growth. We are accustomed to recognize in regressive phenomena a normative adolescent characteristic. A shift in emphasis, however, has been noticeable ever since infant research has so vastly extended our knowledge of the preoedipal child. The reflection of earliest structure formation in the adolescent process has become an integral aspect of adolescent psychology. The vicissitudes of preoedipal object relations and the varied traumatizations of normal childhood are, to a great extent, offset as to their noxious potential by subsequent ego development and structural stabilizations. However, they can never be discounted in their effect on the oedipal stage, its formation, conflict, and resolution. There is no doubt that preoedipal components have increasingly attracted our attention in the treatment of the adolescent child.

Viewing this development from the vantage point of adolescence, I have referred to it as the second individuation process. One crucial developmental advance to be accomplished at adolescence deals with the self-divestiture of infantile dependencies; obviously they are, at this advanced stage, of an internalized nature; we refer to them as object representations or imagos. Should they be persistently externalized or projected onto the outer world during adolescence, the disengagement from infantile dependency objects is thwarted or precluded. This kind of adolescent pathology is well known to us. In the first—the infantile—stage of individuation the young child gains relative independence from the physical presence of the mother through internalization. Once the small child has acquired a representational imagery of his physical and emotional surround, his maturational potential—motoric, sensory, and cognitive—dashes forward into an outburst of new faculties and masteries.

I have paid explicit attention to the individuation process of infancy because of its relevancy for an understanding of adolescent individuation. The first step in infancy accomplishes a relative independence from external objects, while the second, the adolescent step of individuation, aims at the independence from internalized infantile objects. Only when this last process is completed can childhood be transcended and adulthood attained. This internal change comes about through the normative adolescent regression,

which is nondefensive; due to this fact I have called it regression in the service of development. At no other developmental stage except, perhaps, at Mahler's rapprochement subphase is regression an obligatory condition of
growth (Mahler, Pine, and Bergman, 1975, pp. 76-108). It is
by way of nondefensive regression that the adolescent comes
in contact with lingering infantile dependencies, anxieties,
and needs. These are now revisited with an ego equipment
infinitely more resourceful, stable, and versatile than the
one the small child had at his disposal. Furthermore, the
ego of this advanced stage is, as a rule, sufficiently reality-
bound to forestall a regressive engulfment within the undifferentiated stage, namely, in a state of ego loss or psychosis.
It is a well-known fact that the adolescent process and
psychotic illness are related by a developmental risk which,
in my opinion, lies in in the individual's capacity to keep
the nondefensive regression of this age within bounds, i.e.,
staying on the advanced side beyond the unindifferentiated
stage. It is only through a delimited regression that infantile object dependencies can be overcome. It remains a constant query for the therapist to differentiate between what
in the clinical picture is defensive regression, causing developmental arrest and symptom formation, and what is regression in the service of development, which we have come
to identify as a prerequisite for progressive development to
take its course and sustain its momentum. I know that the
chaotic and inconsistent behavior of the adolescent often defies our wish for clear-cut differentiations, but I also know
that relevant clues are forthcoming if the clinician's pa-
tience and attentiveness do not grow weary.

These deliberations of preoedipality in relation to adolescent psychic restructuring permit me to say that the
preoedipal stage of object relations rivals the oedipal stage
in its respective contributions to adolescent personality formation. However, there are good reasons to designate the
oedipal stage as the *primum inter pares,* because—at that

particular juncture—a forward step in psychic organization has been reached which reflects an entirely new—namely triadic—complexity of conflictual object relations. Their resolution is memorialized in the definitive structure of the superego. Within this developmental context we speak of the phase-specific infantile neurosis which is self-liquidating in the normal course of development. Whenever neurotic psychopathology prevails in childhood or adolescence, we can be certain that preoedipal traumatic remnants have been carried forward and have worked their way into oedipal formations.

As a common example I mention the "abandonment malaise" of the adolescent who tells us in endless variations of his conviction that "nothing will ever work out" in his love relationship, or that he "will never accomplish anything great the world needs, admires, and loves." Encouraging beginnings always fall apart. The roots of such dysphoric moods are of preoedipal origin, even though we usually encounter them amalgamated with oedipal anxiety, guilt, and inhibitions. Excessive indulgences, such as the overeating of the adolescent girl or drug use in both sexes, point to preoedipal fixations, even though a pseudo-oedipal stance is often forcefully and frantically displayed.

From clinical work we have learned that the persistent, irrepressible psychic irritants of a preoedipal nature make their appearance in treatment, demanding therapeutic interventions able to reach the primitive emotions and infantile needs which appear in all kinds of sophisticated disguises. In practice, the treatment strategy veers constantly between preoedipal and oedipal realms, while the therapist attempts to relate to the adolescent's present life situation or the other way round. The respective vehicles of these efforts are—in ascending levels of abstraction—advice, judgment, explanation, interpretation, and reconstruction. Preoedipal components in adolescent therapy often lie concealed behind the patient's guarded, critical, and suspicious

attitude or behind his unshakably trusting expectancy of
the good life the therapist will deliver. A precious sense of
security and safety derives from being part of an idealized
object, the preoedipal mother, reified in the person of the
therapist. Parenthetically I might mention that fathers as
idealized maternal imagos appear more frequently in contemporary adolescent patients than in those of the past, because many more parents have shared of late the caretaking of their small children. Be this as it may, the revival of
the idealized parent imago in the person of the therapist,
man or woman, demands a most delicate work of actuating
object deidealization. What, at best, is the outcome of this
process, we refer to as trust, the bedrock of the therapeutic
alliance.

The adolescent patient needs to be exposed—gradually
and repeatedly—to a disillusionment in self and object.
Over time, this leads to a tolerance of imperfection, first in
the object and finally extending to the self. How difficult
and painful the process of deidealization of object and self is
for the adolescent never ceases to impress me. Indeed, I feel
inclined to say that the process of deidealization of object
and self represents the most distressful and tormenting single aspect of growing up—if any such generalization can be
made at all. The magnitude of this step at adolescence is
comparable to the Copernican revolution, which deprived
man of his place in the center of the universe—a truly sobering, existential awareness. Having made this cosmic
analogy, I might mention in passing that not until adolescence does a true sense for the tragic emerge, as is implicit
in the acceptance of the human condition. In contrast, the
young child tends to fix blame on caretaking people and
thus experiences feelings of sadness, fright, anger, or abandonment. Mourning follows a different pathway before and
after the second individuation and the deidealization of self
and object, both of which are completed during adolescence.
For the work of mourning to take its course, the attainment

of what I shall call "mature ambivalence" is essential; otherwise, a split in the ego of the postadolescent personality occurs. This state will preserve a split between the acceptance and the nonexistence of the finality of death. The irreconcilability of these positions threatens the cohesiveness of the psychic organism and disables the ego's integrative function in all aspects of life.

We have arrived at a fitting moment to relate a pertinent piece of psychoanalytic history. Freud's (1905a) "Fragment of an Analysis of a Case of Hysteria" is a time-honored specimen of oedipal pathology in a late adolescent girl by the name of Dora. The very diagnosis of hysteria epitomizes a sexual conflict characteristic of this neurotic illness. The patient's symptoms—in this case conversion symptoms—reflect the pathological elaborations of an unresolved, virulent Oedipus complex at adolescence. The case history portrays in greatest clarity how the affective and sexual conflicts of Dora's love for her father became fatefully interwoven with the life of a married couple, Herr and Frau K., who were friends of her family. Dora's father had started an affair with Frau K., whose husband Herr K. was enamored with Dora, then an adolescent girl of sixteen. At eighteen Dora started treatment with Freud. How ingeniously Freud pieced together the details of fact and fantasy, conscious and unconscious, in the course of the treatment is too well known to require any comment here.

When Dora suddenly disrupted the analysis after three months, Freud searched for the emotional currents that had caused this impetuous action. What, furthermore, puzzled Freud was the unsatisfactory relief from symptoms, despite the clarifications and interpretations he had offered the patient which, undoubtedly, were correct. What was amiss in the work that left it incomplete on two accounts? As to the disruption, Freud concluded that "I did not succeed in mastering the transference in good time" (p. 118). Dora—a hysteric of eighteen—might well have responded to the objective detailed discussions of sexual matters of the greatest delicacy as she had done once before to the seductive intimacy of Herr K., from whom she had fled in panic and vengefulness.

Be this as it may, it is quite another aspect of the case history I want to bring to your attention. This aspect concerns the preoedipal fixation on the dyadic relationship which, on the oedipal level, leads to a revival and the subsequent repression of the negative oedipal tie. A fixation on this preoedipal attachment, when resuscitated at adolescence, is frequently silenced—in life as well as in treatment—by the diversionary display of heterosexual wishes, actions, conflicts, and agitations. I have alluded to both these issues in my antecedent discussion of the normative homosexual conflict in relation to adolescent sexual identity formation and, furthermore, a specific adolescent reaction I have termed the oedipal defense. By quoting from the Dora case I wish to demonstrate that Freud was fully aware of both these issues, but kept them confined to his commentary on the case. He never alluded to them in the treatment, where he pursued with single-minded pertinacity the positive oedipal theme, namely, the acting out of Dora's wish for and rejection of Herr K.'s attempted seduction (p. 25). In fact the case has been—and still is—read without attributing to preoedipal issues the general developmental validity they deserve in adolescent psychopathology.

While working on the Dora paper, Freud wrote to Fliess (letter of Oct. 14, 1900) that in the case at hand "the chief issue in the conflicting mental processes is the opposition between an inclination towards men and towards women" (1887-1902, p. 327) in an adolescent girl. Dora declared, after her conflict was thoroughly analyzed, that she couldn't "forgive him [father] for it [affair with Frau K.]" (1905a, p. 54). She complained, " 'I can think of nothing else' " (p. 54). Freud postulated that *"this excessively intense train of thought must owe its reinforcement to the unconscious"* (pp. 54-55). This comment he clarified by saying: "For behind Dora's supervalent train of thought which was concerned with her father's relations with Frau K. there lay concealed a feeling of jealousy which had that lady as its *object*—a feeling, that is, which could only be based upon an affection on Dora's part for one of her own sex" (p. 60). Freud concluded that the girl was jealous of her father and not of his mistress; in other words, she wished to be the object of the woman's love.

Freud viewed this attachment in the context of adolescent boys and girls who "show clear signs, even in normal cases, of the existence of an affection for people of their own sex" (p. 60). Once more, in the Postscript, Freud returned to this crucial and central complex in Dora's pathology; here we read: "I failed to discover in time and to inform the patient that her homosexual (gynaecophilic) love for Frau K. was the strongest unconscious current in her mental life" (p. 120n.). Thus Dora's two dreams, especially the second, in which the Sistine Madonna figures prominently as an association (p. 96), might be understood differently in terms of that "strongest unconscious current in her mental life."

The two women Dora had loved finally betrayed her. The girl discovered that "she was being admired and fondly treated [by her governess] not for her own sake but for her father's" (p. 61). As a repetition of this, Frau K., with whom "the scarcely grown girl had lived for years on a footing of the closest intimacy" (p. 61), "had not loved her for her own sake but on account of her father" (p. 62). We can confidently assume that at the bottom of Dora's sense of betrayal lay a sense of emotional abandonment by the mother, even though the case history tells us nothing factual or reconstructed about it.

Dora's thwarted love for the two women became forcefully removed from her conscious affective life, while the heterosexual drive was histrionically pushed into the forefront of her mind. Freud referred to this as "noisy demon-

strations to show that she grudged her [Frau K.] the possession of her father; and in this way she concealed from herself the contrary fact, which was that she grudged her
father Frau K.'s love" (p. 63). With scientific objectivity
Freud explained that he would not "go any further in to
this important subject . . . because Dora's analysis came to
an end before it could throw any light on this side of her
mental life" (p. 60).

In a final opinion of this case which, for a long time, has
typified the psychopathology of repressed heterosexual
libido, Freud stated that the mortification in the betrayal of
the two women whose maternal love Dora craved "touched
her, perhaps, more nearly and had a greater pathogenic effect than the other [case], which she tried to use as a screen
for it,—the fact that she had been sacrificed by her father"
(p. 62). These realizations came too late or were postponed
too long to have benefited the patient.

I must confess that I myself did not read the Dora paper
in the present light until I became aware through my own
clinical work of the concepts presented earlier in this chapter. Even though in the Dora case Freud stated such contingent observations and conclusions as I have endeavored
to highlight, these were never systematically incorporated
in the classical psychoanalytic theory of adolescence. While
I present here my own conceptualizations about adolescent
development, I also want to show that some of them were
contained *in nuce* in the Dora paper. To do homage to
Freud's genius I have presented a neglected aspect of the
Dora case, in the hope of stimulating its re-reading with an
altered and broadened focus of attention.

The revisitation of the Dora case lends itself to the introduction of a topic I have explored for many years. I refer
to my efforts to trace the divergent developmental lines in
male and female adolescence, sorting out, as it were, their
inherent similarities and intrinsic differences. I shall not
dwell on the male and female oedipal constellation because

it is a topic so well known and so firmly established that it needs no comment here. However, some words about the preoedipal period of both sexes are in order, because the reverberations of these early object relations determine, to such a large extent, the adolescent-specific relations to male and female, to people generally, as well as to the world at large, to abstract thought, and to the self.

From therapeutic work with adolescent girls and young women we know of the powerful regressive pull to the preoedipal mother, leading to symptom formation and acting out. Overeating and nibbling are common-enough habits of the female adolescent. When the girl goes through the preadolescent phase, we recognize in her object relations the regressively revived imagos of the good and the bad mother. The reflections of this phase appear in merger fantasies and violent distancing behavior. Their enmeshment with oedipal issues is always part of the clinical picture. The infantile tie to the mother, however, remains for the girl a lasting source of ambivalence and ambiguity, because it contains by its very nature homosexual components; these are bound to be reinforced by puberty. We always discover in the heterosexual acting out of the adolescent girl—especially the young adolescent girl—a twofold aim; one leads to the gratification of infantile, tactile contact hunger, while the other seeks to strengthen the girl's still infirm sexual identity. Both these aims are entangled in the young adolescent girl's—initially defensive—attachment to the opposite sex. Her advance to adult genitality occurs only gradually and often remains incomplete without, however, necessarily endangering the healthy personality integration of the woman. The future capacity and pleasure in mothering is, to a large extent, facilitated by the mature female's unconflicted and open access to the integrated good-bad mother imagos. Adolescent emotional development determines in a decisive way the outcome toward this end. In my opinion, there is no treatment of the adolescent girl in which the features of the regressive pull and the ambivalence struggle with the early mother are not issues of central importance. We can always detect in the woman the remnants of that premordial love in her relations to members of her own sex. The fact that the girl, but not the boy, has to change in later life the gender of the first love and hate object, the mother, renders the psychological development of the girl more complex than that of the boy.

In contrast, the boy's infantile tie to the early mother remains throughout the phase of adolescent regression sexually polarized and, consequently, a source of conflict essentially different from that of the adolescent girl. The girl tends to extricate herself from the regressive pull toward merger by a forward rush onto the oedipal stage. The small boy, on the other hand, normally goes through a stage in which the fear of the archaic castrating mother—the original caretaker and organizer of all infantile body functions—forms the nucleus of the male's apprehensiveness vis-à-vis the woman. This formation is most convincingly demonstrated during male preadolescence when we observe this apprehensiveness in either the avoidance of the opposite sex and hostility toward women in general, or in the sexual bravado of juvenile machismo. These conflicts of early childhood and adolescence, universal as they are, never cease to affect the relations between the sexes throughout life. As an aside, I call your attention to the statistically well-known facts about adolescent incest. Besides oedipal components, incest for the adolescent girl is a defense against maternal merger, while incest for the adolescent boy represents merger and ego dissolution within the undifferentiated stage, i.e., psychosis. Here lies one reason for the fact that for the adolescent girl incest is a more frequent occurrence than for the adolescent boy. For the girl incest is not necessarily linked to personality disintegration, while for the adolescent boy incest remains a most rare occurrence, and the boy proves invariably to be psychotic.

The preoedipal elements in the Dora case, which I have lifted from the larger context of Freud's reconstructions, have by now gathered enough clinical evidence to be looked at in the light of a typical adolescent regressive paradigm. We must attribute, therefore, a normative character to the reworking at adolescence of both preoedipal and oedipal stages of development. With the growing recognition that analytic work legitimately encompasses preverbal mental content, the intrinsic role of preoedipality in adolescent therapy or in the normative adolescent process has to be reconsidered as well. This is to say that in every oedipal pathology we will discover precursors from the preoedipal stage of development; these have to be identified and dealt with in therapy. This work is usually done in conjunction with oedipal issues and ego problems because they have all become enmeshed with each other in a comprehensive pathological formation by the time adolescence is reached. If we take for granted that preoedipal regression is normative for adolescence, this fact presents a particular problem for the clinician who treats adolescents.

Preoedipal fixations have become identified with borderline conditions, a diagnostic category of established validity. However, in the assessment of adolescent preoedipal regression, so it seems to me, an essential differentiation must be established. Within the framework of adolescent regression we may recognize a belated developmental forward thrust toward the triadic or oedipal level or, in contrast, regression may reveal a retrograde pathogenic pull to the dyadic stage of early infancy. The testing ground for these relativities, which are of such critical consequence for the outcome of the adolescent process or for adolescent therapy generally, lies in the realm of the transference. Broadly speaking, the dependent preoedipal needfulness of some adolescents can be of such an elemental nature that only a limited developmental progression can be attained in treatment, and that mainly through identification. Such a benign alteration of an archaic introject is no minor achievement. In contrast, the adolescent who has become able, through trust and insight, to tolerate the frustrations and thwarted expectations in the therapeutic situation, with all their attendant affects of aggression and guilt, tells us by this very fact that he has reached the level of oedipal conflict. The differentiation between developmental arrest and developmental conflict remains only too often not as clearly distinguishable at first sight during assessment and initial therapy as we might wish. This ambiguity defines an area into which adolescent research might profitably move.

Earlier in this presentation I developed a clinical rationale for stating that the Oedipus complex, in its positive aspect, undergoes a resolution, normal or abnormal, before the latency period can set in, but that the negative Oedipus complex does not reach a conflictual crisis and undergo a resolution, normal or abnormal, until adolescence. Thus we might speak of a two-timed or biphasic oedipal resolution, one in early childhood and one at adolescence. Of course, the influences of both on the ensuing nature of adult object relations are always interwoven and cannot be neatly isolated; the best one can do is to speak of preponderances, dominances, and idiosyncratic urgencies in relation to the respective residues from preoedipal and oedipal resolutions. Since the normality of adult object relations hinges fatefully on these resolutions and since such basic elements of the personality as, for example, the adult sense of self, sexual identity, and the adult ego ideal are determined by the totality, i.e., positive *and* negative oedipal resolutions, this issue deserves our most thoughtful attention.

The proposition that the totality of the oedipal crisis has not passed until the adolescent process is completed leads to the conclusion that the termination of childhood coincides with the closure of adolescence. It is not just a matter of speech to declare adolescence to be the terminal stage of childhood, after which the stage of adulthood asserts itself. Let me pursue just one line of reasoning that rests on the above proposition and has a bearing on our clinical work.

If—as I have postulated—the resolution of the Oedipus complex in its totality is biphasic, then we must conclude that the infantile neurosis represents a psychic formation that obviously excludes the adolescent-specific oedipal conflict with the parent of the same sex, as well as its resolution. These considerations lead me to conclude that the "definitive neurosis"—using Freud's (1939) words—is a psychic formation that can only reach its final and lasting structure during the terminal stage of childhood, namely, during the consolidation stage of late adolescence. At this stage, then, the adult neurosis, "the definitive neurosis," consolidates as an integral aspect of psychic structuralization, heralding the closure of adolescence.

These theoretical conclusions derive from clinical observations of late adolescent patients whose symptoms were due to internalized conflicts, therefore constituting, by definition, a neurosis. In the analysis of these older adolescents I have encountered stubborn resistances that failed to yield to any kind of intervention, until they vanished without any cause for which I could claim credit. Having observed this phenomenon for some time, I have come to the conclusion that the patient's apparent disinterest in or retreat from the therapeutic engagement reveals a particular kind of psychodynamics, which diverges from the standard definition of resistance. If this kind of psychological distancing or uncommunicative self-absorption is treated as a resistance, the effect is nil. In other words, if repeated interpretations referring to so-called "inner dangers," of which the transference reaction is one, remain ineffectual, we might well look for other determinants. The distraction, so it seems to me, is attributable to internal organizing processes structuring or consolidating the definitive neurosis. It appears at such times unavoidable that patient and

therapist are at cross-purposes, because the patient is engaged in the structuralization of his neurotic complexes,
while the therapist is eager to cure the disturbance that
brought the patient to his office. Paradoxically, analytic
cure can be accomplished best if neurotic formations exist;
however, their incubation time removes the therapist—in
various degrees to be true—from keeping up his good work.
Resorting to resistance interpretations is a common attempt
to overcome such stalemate situations. Of course, dynamic
or genuine resistances never fail to appear alongside those I
have set apart as typical for the consolidation period of late
adolescence. I am far from suggesting that these developmental occurrences are a counterindication for adolescent
analysis; regardless of the silent work of neurosogenesis at
late adolescence, therapy proceeds, working its way from
the surface to the depth as usual. What I introduce here is a
modification in the understanding of the resistance
dynamics in the analytic treatment especially at late
adolescence.

The therapeutic issues outlined above are typical for
adolescence; they are quite familiar to us from child
therapy. Due to the adolescent's physical status, desires,
ambitions, and social roles, we tend to align the adolescent,
especially the older adolescent, with the adult and see him
as an adult manqué. I can report from decades of supervision that the therapist who is at home in the treatment of
children usually orients himself with greater ease in the
world of the adolescent than the therapist whose therapeutic work has been preponderantly with adults.

One further thought, implicit in the foregoing developmental considerations, should be made explicit at this point.
Speaking of the consolidation stage of late adolescence, it
should be understood that at this stage psychic structures
acquire a high degree of irreversibility. They lose, so to
speak, the unique fluidity or elasticity of childhood that
facilitates, as late as adolescence, adaptive corrections of the

past. The structural stabilization at the closure of adolescence is epitomized by the finality of character formation. This acquisition of the late adolescent personality marks the passing of childhood or, in common parlance, of adolescence. I assume, therefore, on the basis of all that has been said, that adolescence cannot remain an open-ended developmental stage. Adolescent closure follows the epigenetic law of development; like all other stages of childhood, adolescence also loses its developmental momentum, regardless of whether the tasks or challenges of this period have been fulfilled or not. Adolescent closure occurs at a biologically and culturally determined time, be this in a normal or abnormal manner. It seems to be a law of development that fixation points at any stage are carried forward into the next developmental stage, thus keeping alive an ongoing effort of the ego at the harmonization of sensitivities, vulnerabilities, and idealizations that make up the essence of each individual self. In this sense we can say, quoting Wordsworth, "The child is father of the man."

References

Aarons, Z. A. (1970), Normality and abnormality in adolescence: With a digression on Prince Hal—"The Sowing of Wild Oats." *The Psychoanalytic Study of the Child*, 25:309-339. New York: International Universities Press.

Abraham, K. (1921), Contributions to the theory of the anal character. In: *Selected Papers on Psycho-Analysis*. New York: Basic Books, 1953, pp. 370-392.

———— (1924a), The influence of oral erotism on character formation. In : *Selected Papers on Psycho-Analysis*. New York: Basic Books, 1953, pp. 393-406.

———— (1924b), Character formation on the genital level of libido-development. In: *Selected Papers on Psycho-Analysis*. New York: Basic Books, 1953, pp. 407-417.

Adatto, C. P. (1958), Ego reintegration observed in analysis of late adolescents. *Internat. J. Psycho-Anal.*, 39:172-177.

———— (1966), On the metamorphosis from adolescence into adulthood. *J. Amer. Psychoanal. Assn.*, 14:485-509.

Aichhorn, A. (1925), *Wayward Youth*. New York: Viking Press, 1935.

———— (1949), Some remarks on the psychic structure and social care of a certain type of female juvenile delinquent. *The Psychoanalytic Study of the Child*, 3/4:439-448. New York: International Universities Press.

Alexander, J. (1970), On dependence and independence. *Bull. Phila. Assn. Psychoanal.*, 20:49-57.

Anthony, E. J. (1976), Between yes and no: The potentially neutral area where the adolescent and his therapist can meet. In: *Adolescent Psychiatry*, vol. 4, ed. S. Feinstein & P. Giovacchini. New York: Jason Aronson, pp. 323-344.

Aristotle, *Selections*, ed. W. D. Ross. New York: Charles Scribner's Sons, 1927.

Baldwin, J. (1956), *Giovanni's Room*. New York: Dial Press.

Balint, M. (1955), Friendly expanses—horrid empty spaces. *Internat. J. Psycho-Anal.*, 36:225-241.

Benedek, T. (1956), Toward the biology of the depressive constellation. *J. Amer. Psychoanal. Assn.*, 4:389-427.

Bernard, C. (1865), *An Introduction to the Study of Experimental Medicine*. New York: Dover, 1957.

Bernfeld, S. (1923), Uber eine typische Form der männlichen Pubertät [A typical form of male puberty.] *Imago*, 9:169-188.

Bibring, G. L. (1964), Some considerations regarding the ego ideal in the psychoanalytic process. *J. Amer. Psychoanal. Assn.*, 12:517-521.

Bing, J. F., McLaughlin, F., & Marburg, R. (1959), The metapsychology of narcissism. *The Psychoanalytic Study of the Child*, 14:9-28. New York: International Universities Press.

Blos, P. (1962), *On Adolescence: A Psychoanalytic Interpretation*. New York: Free Press.

——— (1970), *The Young Adolescent: Clinical Studies*. New York: Free Press.

Bressler, B. (1969), The ego ideal. *Israel Ann. Psychiat.*, 7:158-174.

Brunswick, R. M. (1940), The preoedipal phase of libido development. In: *The Psycho-Analytic Reader*, ed. R. Fliess. New York: International Universities Press, 1948, pp. 231-253.

Carroll, E. J. (1954), Acting out and ego development. *Psychoanal. Quart.*, 23:521-528.

Carson, R. (1962), *Silent Spring*. Boston: Houghton-Mifflin.

Cassirer, E. (1944), *An Essay on Man*. Garden City, N.Y.: Doubleday, 1953.

Deutsch, H. (1944), *The Psychology of Women*, Vol. I. New York: Grune & Stratton.

——— (1964), Some clinical considerations of the ego ideal. *J. Amer. Psychoanal. Assn.*, 12:512-516.

——— (1967), *Selected Problems of Adolescence*. New York: International Universities Press.

Durrell, L. (1961), Interview. *Réalités* (April).

Erikson, E. H. (1946), Ego development and historical change. *The Psychoanalytic Study of the Child*, 2:359-396. New York: International Universities Press.

——— (1956), The problem of ego identity. *J. Amer. Psychoanal. Assn.*, 4: 56-121.

——— (1968), *Identity: Youth and Crisis*. New York: Norton.

Esman, A. H. (1971), Consolidation of the ego ideal in contemporary adolescence. In: *The Psychology of Adolescence*. New York: International Universities Press, 1975, pp. 211-218.

Fenichel, O. (1945), *The Psychoanalytical Theory of Neurosis*. New York: Norton.

Fineman, A. D. (1959), Preliminary observations on ego development in children with congenital defects of the genitourinary system. *Amer. J. Orthopsychiat.*, 29:110-120.

Forrer, G. R. (1959), The mother of a defective child. *Psychoanal. Quart.*, 28:59-63.

Fraiberg, S. H. (1960), Observations on the homosexual conflicts of adolescence. In: *Adolescence: Psychoanalytic Approaches to Clinical*

Problems and Therapy, ed. S. Lorand. New York: Hoeber, pp. 78-112.

Freud, A. (1936), *The Ego and the Mechanisms of Defense. The Writings of Anna Freud,* 2. New York: International Universities Press, rev. ed. 1966.

—— (1949), Certain types and stages of social maladjustment. In: *Searlights on Delinquency,* ed. K. R. Eissler. New York: International Universities Press, pp. 193-204.

—— (1952a), The mutual influences in the development of ego and id: Introduction to the discussion. *The Psychoanalytic Study of the Child,* 7:42-50. New York: International Universities Press.

—— (1952b), The role of bodily illness in the mental life of children. *The Psychoanalytic Study of the Child,* 7:69-81. New York: International Universities Press.

—— (1958), Adolescence. *The Psychoanalytic Study of the Child,* 13:255-278. New York: International Universities Press.

—— (1965), *Normality and Pathology in Childhood. The Writings of Anna Freud,* 6. New York: International Universities Press.

—— (1968), Acting out. *The Writings of Anna Freud,* 7:94-109. New York: International Universities Press, 1971.

—— (1974), A psychoanalytic view of developmental psychopathology. *J. Phila. Assn. Psychoanal.,* 1:7-17.

Freud, S. (1887-1902), *The Origins of Psychoanalysis: Letters to Wilhelm Fliess, Drafts and Notes,* ed. M. Bonaparte, A. Freud, & E. Kris. New York: Basic Books, 1954.

—— (1905a), Fragment of an analysis of a case of hysteria. *Standard Edition,* 7:7-122. London: Hogarth Press, 1953.

—— (1905b), Three essays on the theory of sexuality, *Standard Edition,* 7:135-243. London: Hogarth Press, 1953.

—— (1908), Character and anal erotism. *Standard Edition,* 9:169-175. London: Hogarth Press, 1959.

—— (1909), Analysis of a phobia in a five-year-old boy. *Standard Edition,* 10:5-149. London: Hogarth Press, 1955.

—— (1911), Formulations on the two principles of mental functioning. *Standard Edition,* 12: 218-226. London: Hogarth Press, 1958.

—— (1912a), On the universal tendency to debasement in the sphere of love (Contributions to the psychology of love, II). *Standard Edition,* 11:179-190. London: Hogarth Press, 1957.

—— (1912b), The dynamics of transference. *Standard Edition,* 12:99-108. London: Hogarth Press, 1958.

—— (1913a), The disposition to obsessional neurosis. *Standard Edition,* 12:317-326. London: Hogarth Press, 1958.

—— (1913b), Totem and taboo. *Standard Edition,* 13:1-161. London: Hogarth Press, 1955.

—— (1914a), Remembering, repeating and working-through (Further recommendations on the technique of psycho-analysis, II). *Standard Edition,* 12:147-156. London: Hogarth Press, 1958.

——— (1914b), On narcissism: An introduction. *Standard Edition*, 14:73-102. London: Hogarth Press, 1957.

——— (1921), Group psychology and the analysis of the ego. *Standard Edition*, 18:69-143. London: Hogarth Press, 1955.

——— (1923a), The ego and the id. *Standard Edition*, 19:12-66. London: Hogarth Press, 1961.

——— (1923b), The infantile genital organization: An interpolation into the theory of sexuality. *Standard Edition*, 19:141-145. London: Hogarth Press, 1961.

——— (1924), Neurosis and psychosis. *Standard Edition*, 19:149-153. London: Hogarth Press, 1961.

——— (1927), The future of an illusion. *Standard Edition*, 21:5-56. London: Hogarth Press, 1961.

——— (1931), Libidinal types. *Standard Edition*, 21:217-220. London: Hogarth Press, 1961.

——— (1933), New introductory lectures on psycho-analysis. *Standard Edition*, 22:5-182. London: Hogarth Press, 1964.

——— (1939), Moses and monotheism. *Standard Edition*, 23:7-137. London: Hogarth Press, 1964.

——— (1940), An outline of psycho-analysis. *Standard Edition*, 23:144-207. London: Hogarth Press, 1964.

Friedlander, K. (1947), *The Psychoanalytical Approach to Juvenile Delinquency*. New York: International Universities Press.

Geleerd, E. R. (1961), Some aspects of ego vicissitudes in adolescence. *J. Amer. Psychoanal. Assn.*, 9:394-405.

——— (1964), Adolescence and adaptive regression. *Bull. Menninger Clinic*, 28:302-308.

Giovacchini, P. L. (1965), Some aspects of the development of the ego ideal of a creative scientist. *Psychoanal. Quart.*, 34:79-101.

Gitelson, M. (1948), Character synthesis: The psychotherapeutic problem of adolescence. *Amer. J. Orthopsychiat.*, 18:422-431.

Glover, E. (1924), Notes on oral character formation. In: *On the Early Development of Mind*. New York: International Universities Press, 1956, pp. 25-46.

——— (1956), Psychoanalysis and criminology: A political survey. In: *The Roots of Crime*. New York: International Universities Press, 1960, pp. 311-324.

Greenacre, P. (1950), General problems of acting out. In: *Trauma, Growth, and Personality*. New York: International Universities Press, 1969, pp. 224-236.

——— (1956), Re-evaluation of the process of working through. In: *Emotional Growth*. New York: International Universities Press, 1971, pp. 641-650.

——— (1958), Early physical determinants in the development of the sense of identity. *J. Amer. Psychoanal. Assn.*, 6:612-627.

——— (1959), Certain technical problems in the transference relationship. In: *Emotional Growth*. New York: International Universities Press, 1971, pp. 651-669.

—— (1967), The influence of infantile trauma on genetic patterns. In: *Emotional Growth*. New York: International Universities Press, 1971, pp. 260-299.

Hammerman, S. (1965), Conceptions of superego development. *J. Amer. Psychoanal. Assn.*, 13:320-355.

Hartmann, H. (1939), *Ego Psychology and the Problem of Adaptation*. New York: International Universities Press, 1958.

—— (1944), Psychoanalysis and sociology. In: *Essays on Ego Psychology*. New York: International Universities Press, 1964, pp. 19-36.

—— (1950), Psychoanalysis and developmental psychology. *The Psychoanalytic Study of the Child*, 5:7-17. New York: International Universities Press.

—— (1952), The mutual influences in the development of ego and id. *The Psychoanalytic Study of the Child*, 7:9-30. New York: International Universities Press.

—— & Loewenstein, R. M. (1962), Notes on the superego. *The Psychoanalytic Study of the Child*, 17:42-81. New York: International Universities Press.

Hunt, R. L. (1967), The ego ideal and male homosexuality. *Bull. Phila. Assn. Psychoanal.*, 17:217-244.

Inhelder, B. & Piaget, J. (1958), *The Growth of Logical Thinking from Childhood to Adolescence*. New York: Basic Books.

Jacobson, E. (1954), The self and the object world: Vicissitudes of their infantile cathexes and their influence on ideational and affective development. *The Psychoanalytic Study of the Child*, 9:75-127. New York: International Universities Press.

—— (1957), Denial and repression. *J. Amer. Psychoanal. Assn.*, 5:61-92.

—— (1964), *The Self and the Object World*. New York: International Universities Press.

James, M. (1970), Review of Erikson, E. H., *Identity* (1968). *Internat. J. Psycho-Anal.*, 51:79-83.

Jessner, L., Blom, G. E., & Waldfogel, S. (1952), Emotional implications of tonsillectomy and adenoidectomy on children. *The Psychoanalytic Study of the Child*, 7:126-169. New York: International Universities Press.

Johnson, A. M. & Szurek, S. A. (1952), The genesis of antisocial acting out in children and adults. *Psychoanal. Quart.*, 21:323-343.

Jones, E. (1918), Anal-erotic character traits. In: *Papers on Psycho-Analysis*. Baltimore: Williams & Wilkins, 5th ed., 1948, pp. 413-437.

—— (1955), *The Life and Work of Sigmund Freud*, Vol. 2. New York: Basic Books.

Kanzer, M. (1957a), Panel report on acting out and its relation to impulse disorders. *J. Amer. Psychoanal. Assn.*, 5:136-145.

———— (1957b), Acting out, sublimation and reality testing. *J. Amer. Psychoanal. Assn.*, 5:663-684.

Kaplan, S. M. & Whitman, R. M. (1965), The negative ego-ideal. *Internat. J. Psycho-Anal.*, 46: 183-187.

Katan, A. (1951), The role of "displacement" in agoraphobia. *Internat. J. Psycho-Anal.*, 32:41-50.

Kaufman, I. & Makkay, E. A. (1956), Treatment of the adolescent delinquent. In: *Case Studies in Childhood Emotional Disabilities,* Vol. 2, ed. G. E. Gardner. New York: American Orthopsychiatric Association, pp. 316-352.

Keiser, S. (1944), Severe reactive states and schizophrenia in adolescent girls. *The Nervous Child*, 4:17-25.

Keniston, K. (1968), *Young Radicals.* New York: Harcourt, Brace & World.

Kohut, H. (1966), Forms and transformations of narcissism. *J. Amer. Psychoanal. Assn.*, 14:243-272.

———— (1971), *The Analysis of the Self.* New York: International Universities Press.

Kris, E. (1948), Prince Hal's conflict. In: *Psychoanalytic Exploration in Art.* New York: International Universities Press, 1952, pp. 273-288.

———— et al. (1954), Problems of infantile neurosis: A discussion. *The Psychoanalytic Study of the Child*, 9:16-71. New York: International Universities Press.

Lampl-de Groot, J. (1962), Ego ideal and superego. *The Psychoanalytic Study of the Child,* 17:94-106. New York: International Universities Press.

———— (1963), Symptom formation and character formation. *Internat. J. Psycho-Anal.*, 44:1-11.

Laplanche, J. & Pontalis, J-B. (1973), *The Language of Psycho-Analysis.* New York: Norton.

Le Bon, G. (1895), *The Crowd.* London: Benn, 1947.

Lewin, B. D. (1948), The nature of reality, the meaning of nothing, with an addendum on concentration. *Psychoanal. Quart.*, 17:524-526.

Lichtenberg, J. D. & Lichtenberg, C. (1969), Prince Hal's conflict, adolescent idealism, and buffoonery. *J. Amer. Psychoanal. Assn.*, 17: 873-887.

Lichtenstein, H. (1965), Towards a metapsychological definition of the concept of self. *Internat. J. Psycho-Anal.*, 46:117-128.

Loewald, H. W. (1971a), The transference neurosis: Comments on the concept and the phenomenon. *J. Amer. Psychoanal. Assn.*, 19:54-66.

———— (1971b), Some considerations on repetition and repetition compulsion. *Internat. J. Psycho-Anal.*, 52:59-66.

Mahler, M. S. (1963), Thoughts about development and individuation. *The Psychoanalytic Study of the Child,* 18:307-324. New York: International Universities Press.

———— Pine, F., & Bergman, A. (1975), *The Psychological Birth of the Human Infant.* New York: Basic Books.

McDougall, W. (1920), *The Group Mind.* London: Cambridge University Press, 1927.

Mead, G. H. (1932), Time. In: *On Social Psychology,* ed. A. Strauss. Chicago: University of Chicago Press, 1956, pp. 328-341.

Murray, J. M. (1964), Narcissism and the ego ideal. *J. Amer. Psychoanal. Assn.,* 12:477-511.

Neavles, J. S. & Winokur, G. (1957), The hot-rod driver. *Bull. Menninger Clinic,* 21:28-35.

Novey, S. (1955), The role of the superego and ego-ideal in character formation. *Internat. J. Psycho-Anal.,* 36:254-259.

Nunberg, H. (1932), *Principles of Psychoanalysis.* New York: International Universities Press, 1955.

Odier, C. (1956), *Anxiety and Magic Thinking.* New York: International Universities Press.

Piaget, J. (1954), *Les relations entre l'affectivité et l'intelligence dans le developpement mental de l'enfant.* Paris: Centre de Documentation Universitaire.

Piers, G. & Singer, M. B. (1953), *Shame and Guilt.* New York: Norton, 1971.

Polanyi, M. (1974), *Scientific Thought and Social Reality [Psychological Issues,* Monogr. 32], ed. F. Schwartz. New York: International Universities Press.

Peto, A. (1959), Body image and archaic thinking. *Internat. J. Psycho-Anal.,* 40:223-236.

Redl, F. (1942), Group emotion and leadership. In: *When We Deal with Children.* New York: Free Press, 1966, pp. 155-196.

———— (1956), The phenomenon of contagion and "shock effect." In: *When We Deal with Children.* New York: Free Press, 1966, pp. 197-213.

Reich, A. (1953), Narcissistic object choice in women. In: *Psychoanalytic Contributions.* New York: International Universities Press, 1973, pp. 179-208.

———— (1954), Early identifications as archaic elements in the superego. In: *Psychoanalytic Contributions.* New York: International Universities Press, 1973, pp. 209-235.

———— (1958), A character formation representing the integration of unusual conflict solutions into the ego structure. In: *Psychoanalytic Contributions.* New York: International Universities Press, 1973, pp. 250-270.

———— (1960), Pathologic forms of self-esteem regulation. In: *Psychoanalytic Contributions.* New York: International Universities Press, 1973, pp. 288-311.

Reich, W. (1928), On character analysis. In: *The Psycho-Analytic Reader,* ed. R. Fliess. New York: International Universities Press, 1948, pp. 106-123.

———— (1929), The genital character and the neurotic character. In: *The Psycho-Analytic Reader,* ed. R. Fliess. New York: International Universities Press, 1948, pp. 124-144.

———— (1930), Character formation and the phobias of childhood. In: *The Psycho-Analytic Reader,* ed. R. Fliess. New York: International Universities Press, 1948, pp. 145-156.

Ritvo, S. (1966), Correlation of a childhood and adult neurosis: Based on the adult analysis of a childhood case. *Internat. J. Psycho-Anal.,* 47:130-131.

———— (1971), Late adolescence: Developmental and clinical considerations. *The Psychoanalytic Study of the Child,* 26:241-263. New York: Quadrangle.

Sander, L. W., Stechler, G., Julia, H., & Burns, P. (1975), Primary prevention and some aspects of temporal organization in early infant-caretaker interaction. In: *Infant Psychiatry,* ed. E. N. Rexford, L. W. Sander, & T. Shapiro. New Haven: Yale University Press, pp. 187-204.

Sandler, J., Holder, A., & Meers, D. (1963), The ego ideal and the ideal self. *The Psychoanalytic Study of the Child,* 18:139-158. New York: International Universities Press.

Sartre, J.-P. (1952), *Saint Genet.* New York: Braziller, 1963.

Schafer, R. (1967), Ideals, the ego ideal, and the ideal self. In: *Motives and Thought* [*Psychological Issues,* Monogr. 18/19], ed. R. R. Holt. New York: International Universities Press, pp. 131-174.

Schmideberg, M. (1956), Delinquent acts as perversions and fetishes. *Internat. J. Psycho-Anal.,* 37:422-424.

Spitz, R. A. (1957), *No and Yes—On the Genesis of Human Communication.* New York: International Universities Press.

———— (1965), *The First Year of Life.* New York: International Universities Press.

Steffens, L. (1931), *Autobiography.* New York: Harcourt, Brace & World.

Steingart, I. (1969), On self, character, and the development of a psychic apparatus. *The Psychoanalytic Study of the Child,* 24:271-303. New York: International Universities Press.

Strachey, J. (1961), Editor's introduction to S. Freud: The ego and the id (1923). *Standard Edition,* 19:3-11. London: Hogarth Press.

Szurek, S. A. (1954), Concerning the sexual disorders of parents and their children. *J. Nerv. & Ment. Dis.,* 120:369-378.

Tartakoff, H. H. (1966), The normal personality in our culture and the Nobel Prize complex. In: *Psychoanalysis—A General Psychology,* ed. R. M. Loewenstein, L. M. Newman, M. Schur, & A. J. Solnit. New York: International Universities Press, pp. 222-252.

Thompson, C. (1945), Transference as a therapeutic instrument. *Psychiatry,* 8:273-278.

Tolpin, M. (1970), The infantile neurosis: A metapsychological concept and a paradigmatic case history. *The Psychoanalytic Study of the Child,* 25:273-305. New York: International Universities Press.

Turgenev, I. (1862), *Fathers and Sons*. New York: Farrar, Straus & Giroux.

Untermeyer, L. (1961), *Lots of Limericks*. Garden City, N.Y.: Doubleday.

Waelder, R. (1930), The principle of multiple function: Observations on over-determination. *Psychoanal. Quart.*, 5:45-62, 1936.

—— (1958), Neurotic ego distortions: Opening remarks to the panel discussion. *Internat. J. Psycho-Anal.*, 39:243-244.

Waelder-Hall, J. (1935), Structure of a case of pavor nocturnus. *Bull. Phila. Assn. Psychoanal.*, 20:267-274.

Werner, H. (1940), *Comparative Psychology of Mental Development*. New York: International Universities Press, rev. ed. 1957.

Winnicott, D. W. (1965), *The Maturational Processes and the Facilitating Environment*. New York: International Universities Press.

Zetzel, E. R. (1964), Symptom formation and character formation. *Internat. J. Psycho-Anal.*, 45:151-154.

Name Index

Subject Index